Native Hoops

Native Hoops

The Rise of American Indian Basketball, 1895–1970

Wade Davies

University Press of Kansas

Published by the University Press of Kansas
(Lawrence, Kansas 66045), which was organized
by the Kansas Board of Regents and is operated and
funded by Emporia State University, Fort Hays State
University, Kansas State University, Pittsburg State
University, the University of Kansas, and Wichita
State University.

Library of Congress Cataloging-in-Publication Data

Names: Davies, Wade, 1969– author.
Title: Native hoops : the rise of American Indian basketball,
1895–1970 /Wade Davies.
Description: Lawrence : University Press of Kansas, [2019] | Includes
bibliographical references and index.
Identifiers: LCCN 2019025463
ISBN 9780700629084 (cloth)
ISBN 9780700629091 (paperback)
ISBN 9780700629107 (epub)
Subjects: LCSH: Indians of North America—Sports—History—
20th century. | Basketball—History—20th century.
Classification: LCC E98.G2 D18 2019 | DDC 796.323089/97—dc23
LC record available at https://lccn.loc.gov/2019025463.

British Library Cataloguing-in-Publication Data
is available.

Printed in the United States of America

10 9 8 7 6 5 4 3 2 1

The paper used in this publication is recycled and
contains 30 percent postconsumer waste. It is acid
free and meets the minimum requirements of the
American National Standard for Permanence of
Paper for Printed Library Materials Z39.48–1992.

For Madoc and Maren

Contents

Acknowledgments

I became interested in writing a comprehensive history of American Indian basketball two decades ago, soon after completing my dissertation research on the history of health care on the Navajo Nation. During long drives through Navajo country, headed to one hospital or another, I saw an endless parade of basketball hoops outside virtually every home and gathering place. Every type of rim and backboard imaginable was on display—store bought and homemade, pristine specimens and timeworn relics. As an icebreaker, I began my conversations with Navajo (Diné) health professionals by saying how fascinating it was to discover that people there were as crazy for basketball as people in my home state, Indiana—maybe more so, if such a thing were possible. Inevitably they smiled at this and we exchanged a few stories. Basketball's mention lightened the mood and evoked happy thoughts even in a serious hospital environment. Clearly the sport mattered to them, not just as entertainment but as a greater force for good in their communities. Those conversations made an impression on me, as did subsequent observations of Native teams competing before a sea of die-hard supporters at the 1999 Arizona high school basketball tournament. I found myself committed to finding out how and why Indian country's obsession with this sport began.

The main challenge I faced when I started my research was that other than scattered newspaper reports, little had been published on the topic of American Indian basketball to serve as a foundation. There were thankfully a few intriguing academic articles explaining how contemporary Navajo players fit basketball to their cultural values and norms. Another by Peter Donahue discussed basketball's influence on Native novelists who, through works of fiction, claimed basketball as an "authentically Indian game" that reinforced communal bonds and traditions.[1] The only related book-length work at the time was Larry Colton's *Counting Coup: A True Story of Basketball and Honor on the Little Bighorn* (2000). That engaging, and somewhat controversial, volume documented the contemporary experiences of a Crow high school player, her teammates, and her family. These varied works portrayed the Native basketball experience as something both intensely passionate and triumphant and at times tragic for players and communities who expected too much from it. All these authors inspired and informed me, but none supplied the historical context I was searching for.[2]

As life intervened, I moved in and out of my research on the topic and, in the meantime, two groundbreaking books came out that provided me a strong historical foundation from which to work. First came Tim Brayboy and Bruce Barton's *Playing Before an Overflow Crowd* (2003), which told the history of American Indian basketball in Robeson County, North Carolina, primarily involving the Lumbee people. It was an extraordinarily well detailed and refreshingly positive account that later led me to Tim Brayboy himself, who graciously agreed to share more of his stories with me and helped inspire me to see my project through to completion. Then came Linda Peavy and Ursula Smith's *Full-Court Quest* in 2008, which was the first work of scholarship to focus on the early years of American Indian basketball, specifically telling the story of the Fort Shaw Indian School girls' team that rose to national fame in the early 1900s. The book was a popular success, especially in Montana, where Fort Shaw is located, and has since been a source of pride for many Native people. Both works were invaluable to me, not only for their content but also as examples of how old stories about Indian basketball could bring joy to a modern generation.[3]

Besides the limited scholarship specifically dealing with American Indian basketball, I also benefited from a small but growing body of work focusing on the history of other Native American sports—both indigenous and introduced. In addition to several good biographies of Jim Thorpe, Charles Bender, and other American Indian sports legends, some books of broader scope stood out. Stewart Culin's *Games of the North American Indians* (1905), Kendall Blanchard's *The Mississippi Choctaws at Play* (1981), Peter Nabokov's *Indian Running* (1981), Joseph Oxendine's *American Indian Sports Heritage* (1988), Thomas Vennum, Jr.'s *American Indian Lacrosse* (1994), Gregory Cajete's *Spirit of the Game* (2005), and Matthew Sakiestewa Gilbert's *Hopi Runners* (2018) were essential reads, allowing me to understand the richness of Native peoples' sporting heritage and where basketball fit within.[4] Collectively, these authors emphasized sports' positive influence on Native communities in ways physical, social, and spiritual. With the exception of Culin, they also detailed how Native peoples maintained indigenous sporting traditions through changing times and, in many cases, stayed true to those traditions while transitioning to competition against non-Natives.

I also benefited from exceptional works by a small group of authors who focused specifically on Native athletes playing introduced sports besides basketball that allowed them to take part in a broader sports culture while still expressing indigenous identities. Among these books were Peter

Iverson's *Riders of the West: Portraits from Indian Rodeo* (1999), Jeffrey Powers-Beck's *The American Indian Integration of Baseball* (2004), Lars Anderson's *Carlisle vs. Army* (2007), and Sally Jenkins's *The Real All Americans* (2007)—the latter two focusing on Carlisle Indian school's illustrious football program. Anthologies by C. Richard King (2005) and Frank A. Salamone (2013) introduced me to article-length works by Ann Cummins, Cecilia Anderson, Georgia Briggs, Stacy Sewell, Ellen J. Staurowsky, and Sean Sullivan; all of whom helped me understand the depth and breadth of basketball's impact on Indian country over many generations. I was also thankful to have King's two-volume encyclopedia, *Native Americans in Sports* (2004), which directed me to many of the all-time great players featured in the following pages.[5]

Regarding the development of sports within the Indian boarding schools, and student responses to them, David Wallace Adams's *Education for Extinction* (1995), John Bloom's *To Show What an Indian Can Do* (2000), and Oxendine's *American Indian Sports Heritage* were all foundational to my work. Adams provided me the context to understand where basketball fit into the larger Indian school experience, and his discussion of football's public relations significance to those schools influenced my understanding of basketball in that regard. I also owe a special debt of gratitude to Oxendine for laying the foundation upon which I could work, as he was the first historian to discuss in detail the role sports played in these institutions. John Bloom expanded on that story, thankfully, and his focus on Native students who used sports meant to assimilate them to instead express their indigenous identities has influenced my work, to be sure.[6]

I also benefited from access to a handful of fine histories of American basketball that were not focused on the Native experience, such as Robert W. Peterson's *Cages to Jump Shots* (1990). Peterson's book enabled me to assess the development of Native playing styles relative to changing rules, styles, and tactics in the broader sport. His work, together with Kathleen S. Yep's *Outside the Paint: When Basketball Ruled at the Chinese Playground* (2009), also provided context about barnstorming that helped me tell the stories of some great Native professional teams. Yep also offered parallel accounts of Chinese American athletes who, like many American Indians, used basketball as a source of empowerment amid the injustices and indignities they were often subjected to in their twentieth-century lives. Through this game, they asserted ethnic pride and maintained a sense of community. Ignacio M. Garcia has told a similar story about some remarkable high school players and teams from Sidney Lanier High School in *When Mexicans Could Play Ball: Basketball, Race, and Identity in San Antonio, 1928–1945* (2013).[7]

The above-mentioned authors and dozens more cited in the following pages provided the contextual and thematic foundation I needed to pursue this project, but the task was nevertheless daunting. I decided early on not to focus on a single team, community, level of play (e.g., boarding school, high school), era, or region, but rather to tell as complete a story as possible. This breadth was needed, I believed, to fully appreciate how basketball, or any sport, could proliferate so rapidly and widely to peoples so diverse, as well as to provide proper context within which Native peoples' stories could be told. The only constraint I placed on the project was to limit it to Alaska Natives and American Indians in the continental United States rather than consider indigenous peoples elsewhere in the Americas or in Hawaii.

Opting for a wide geographical and chronological scope seemed ideal until it came time to do the primary research. Completing that work in a timely manner while teaching full loads was not easy. This was especially so given that the only research method that made sense to me was to search for everything I could find about American Indian basketball, and Native sports more generally, wherever I could find it. Among other things, this meant visiting more than a dozen archives in places stretching from Washington, DC, to southern California, from Helena, Montana, to Fort Worth, Texas, and researching more than thirty collections held at those repositories. It meant locating thousands of relevant articles in 235 municipal, tribal, and Indian school newspapers, which was possible only thanks to online newspaper databases that became available in recent years. The newspaper research proved vital to the project because most of the players and teams discussed in this book were otherwise lost to history. And it meant talking to as many people as were willing to share their experiences as players, coaches, and fans. Thankfully, my employer, the University of Montana, awarded me a small grant to help me complete the final stage of this project. I am grateful for that.

I did this research in starts and stops, with the stops sometimes stretching many months. Although the work produced a few journal articles and book chapters along the way, it seemed like the end of the project was always years away. It would probably still seem that way now had acquisitions editor Kim Hogeland at the University Press of Kansas not contacted me a few years ago inquiring about my work. In acknowledging all the people who helped me along my way, she is at the top of the list, not only for prompting me to finish what I started but also for providing valuable guidance. Thanks also to managing editor Kelly Chrisman Jacques and copy editor Penelope Cray for skillfully shepherding this book through to completion. I also owe a special debt of gratitude to Peter Iverson, my mentor, teacher, dissertation advisor, past coauthor, and friend. A big part of what made me interested in this subject were the conversations I had with him about my observations on the Navajo Nation. He also told me stories of his own days playing pickup basketball there and shared with me, through his writings, other people's basketball stories—especially Peterson Zah's. Iverson's scholarship, detailing how rodeo became an American Indian tradition, has also greatly informed my own.

There have been so many archivists and archives staff members who have assisted me in this project over the years that listing them all would take at least two pages, and I would fear accidentally omitting deserving names in the process. Suffice it here to thank Lori Cox-Paul for assisting me on numerous occasions over a span of years, as I returned more than once to conduct research at the National Archives regional branch in Kansas City, Missouri. Special thanks also to Brita Merkel and Wade Popp for assisting with the many National Archives images that appear in this book.

I also have friends, colleagues, and fellow historians Tim Brayboy, Dave Beck, Rich Clow, and Dave Kemp to thank for encouraging me in my work and reading drafts of the manuscript. I also appreciate Rich for agreeing, along the way, to coauthor an article with me about the illustrious Lakota teams from St. Francis Mission. Thanks as well to David Adams, Rich King, and Matthew Sakiestewa Gilbert, who generously gave their time to read either my research proposal or the final draft manuscript, or both. Their encouraging words and guidance are greatly appreciated. The suggestions and detailed corrections all these people provided made this a better book than it would otherwise have been.

If I have misspelled any names, misstated any player statistics, or misidentified anybody's tribal affiliations or family relations, I apologize and would welcome hearing corrections. When people first appear in this book, I have listed their tribal affiliation (if any is known to me) next to their name unless it is made obvious in the discussion. In doing so, I have given the names of tribes as they are most commonly used in scholarship, and as they are most recognizable to a majority of readers, unless I am aware of strong preferences for using tribal names as spoken in their own languages. As do other historians, I also use the terms Native, Native American, American Indian, Indian, and indigenous interchangeably throughout the text to vary the prose, although I employ Native most often as the commonly favored term in recent years. I apologize for any offense any of my choices on these matters may cause.

My favorite parts of this book are those based on interviews I have done over the years with people intimately involved with the subject. I am grateful to four people in particular not only for sharing their stories and perspectives with me but also for introducing me to other people. Dave Kemp of the Mariah Press was an endless font of knowledge on everything to do with South Dakota basketball; he put me in touch with some wonderful individuals. This was possible because Dave knows a lot of sports lovers in South Dakota, and a lot of sports lovers in South Dakota know Dave. The same is true of Tim Brayboy when it comes to basketball fans in North Carolina. All the generous and knowledgeable Lumbee people I spoke to over the telephone were introduced to me by Tim. Kevin Kickingwoman did the same for me regarding my adopted state of Montana and Michelle Guzman for neighboring Idaho, referring me to the great Native players produced by these states over the years. I also thank Paula A. Baker, chair and manager of the University of Montana's Institutional Review Board, and Lola Wippert, chairperson of the Blackfeet Nation Institutional Review Board, for their generous assistance.

In addition to those already mentioned, numerous people took the time to tell me what Indian basketball is all about. When this was done as a formal interview, I have used and cited this information and occasionally quoted people directly. In other cases, these were brief or informal conversations that were no less inspiring even if the information they provided and their names are not included in the text or citations. No matter the case, they all encouraged me and pointed me in the right direction. I am grateful to all of them and thank them for their generosity and friendship. They are Sydney Beane, Jr., Stephan Chase, Mike Chavez, Ronnie Chavis, Iva Croff, Jesse DesRosier, Kash Donaldson, Paul Fasthorse, Anne des Rosier Grant, Rose Hill, Sterling Holywhitemountain, Peter Iverson, Cheewa James, Melissa Johnson, Agnes Picotte, Norbert Picotte, Joseph Oxendine, Ray Oxendine, George Price, Nancy Redhouse, Max Sage, Mike Sakelaris, Richard Sattler, Simon Tapaha, Ervin Trujillo, Zachary Wagner, and Ryan Wetzel.

As is the tradition for many authors, I acknowledge and thank my family last but not least. I realize what a personal sacrifice, and terrible bore, it is to have a spouse or parent writing a book. Even when I have been in their physical presence the past few years, rather than secluded in my office, my mind has too often been on the book. And so I thank my mother, Norma, for her love and encouragement and, most of all, my wife, Colleen, and kids, Madoc (ten years old) and Maren (four), for their love, patience, and support.

Native Hoops

Introduction

People in Indian country love their basketball. No sport draws bigger crowds there or stirs more emotions than the one they affectionately call "hoops." Its intense appeal was apparent in March 2014, when hundreds of Native fans flocked to Kentucky to see two Umatilla sisters play for the University of Louisville. They came from across the continent, some traveling more than a thousand miles, to support these talents from Oregon named Shoni and Jude Schimmel.[1] It did not matter whether they were from another tribe; to cheer for the pair was to celebrate everything basketball had meant to generations of Native athletes and all they had achieved. Many of these enthusiastic travelers were young girls from the reservations and cities who dreamed of following in the Schimmels' footsteps. These girls would be overjoyed a few weeks later to hear the Atlanta Dream select Shoni in the first-round of the Women's National Basketball Association draft. "She *made it*!" they would exclaim and feel a part of it all.[2]

Indian country's outpouring of support meant a great deal to the Schimmels. Like most Native athletes, they understood playing basketball was less about individual accomplishment than it was about competing for your family, your tribe, and Natives everywhere. They understood that this sport was about expressing the value of community in all its local and multitribal forms. Like all who achieved basketball fame before them, Shoni and Jude knew they had the weight of their people and their collective history on their shoulders. This had been too heavy a burden for some to bear, but it drove the Schimmels and countless other Native players to achieve on the court. "We've had a lot of things taken from us, so you kind of remember it deep down inside that you're out there playing for your Native American people," Shoni once said while in high school. "We'll never stop running. We'll never stop shooting. We'll never stop stealing. We just keep going. That's what we do."[3]

This same perseverance and dedication to community showed through years later in the conduct of some high school boys from Montana's Flathead Reservation—home to the Bitterroot Salish, Upper Pend d'Oreille, and Kootenai peoples. Under Coach Zanen Pitts, the Arlee Warriors electrified their town and reservation by winning back-to-back Class C state championships in 2017 and 2018.[4] Like the Schimmels, these boys knew what it meant to their people to bring trophies home to them, but they were determined to do more. And so just prior to the 2018 tournament, they drew on their newfound celebrity to start the Warrior Movement. Its purpose was to combat suicide, a killer that was taking lives at an appalling rate on the reservation. It had taken too many of their dear friends and relatives, and so they felt compelled to act. They released two suicide-prevention videos. In the second, they bounced basketballs in unison on the court while proclaiming "We are the Arlee Warriors, we are dedicating this state tournament to fight against suicide." Each of them, in turn, looked into the camera and delivered portions of a message that charged viewers to "fight for each other and ourselves" to defeat "hopelessness." The post received more than a million views and led to the Movement's formalization as a nonprofit organization. With that, kids on the Flathead had champion players to look up to who had honored their warrior name by fighting for their people.[5]

Basketball's utility for expressing community values was also on display in eastern Montana during the 2010s, among the Assiniboine and Sioux tribes of the Fort Peck Reservation. People there kept up a decades-long tradition of honoring high school basketball players by giving away star quilts at tournament time. This practice was said to have begun in 1947 during a time out in a game between teams from Poplar and Brockton. Tessie Four Times came from the stands into the huddle of Brockton players to wipe the sweat from her grandson Dennis Blount's back with a shawl. She then threw it to the floor, where Phoebe Jones came forward to pick it up, shook Dennis's hand, and carried the shawl back into the stands. In orchestrating the exchange, Four Times honored her grandson for his dedication and athleticism as women in her community had honored generations of male warriors returning from battle. For years, this act was discussed at Fort Peck, eventually inspiring Virginia Spotted Bear and other women to make star quilts to give away at halftime during a 1964 Class C District Tournament game in Sidney.[6]

Thereafter, families on Fort Peck maintained this tradition by offering star quilts each year to honor their player relatives. Those players then selected the ultimate recipients of the quilts, who were often coaches or opposing team members worthy of recognition based on their athleticism and sportsmanship.[7] In 2014, Dennis Blount's younger brother Dean observed players from Fort Peck continuing this tradition of giving "from the heart" to people they respected. By that time, the ritual had taken on further meaning as an instrument for improved race relations. Assiniboine and Yanktonai Sioux players sometimes gave quilts to their non-Native opponents, and some of their non-Native teammates gave away quilts as well.[8]

In addition to exemplifying all the ways Native peoples have expressed community values through basketball, the star quilt giveaways on Fort Peck are symbolic of the larger story told here about basketball's rise to significance in Indian country. Native peoples adopted both the craft of quilting and the sport of basketball at a difficult time in their collective history. Both ways enabled them to perpetuate community traditions, artistic and athletic, that were under assault and appeared in danger of vanishing. It is thus fitting that these two traditions eventually merged as they did in the basketball giveaways.

The giveaway is a timeless practice for most tribes, but the star quilts were late arrivals. Native women on Fort Peck, and elsewhere, first learned the craft and the signature star pattern through interacting with white quilters in the late nineteenth century. This was at a time when the decimation of the bison herds and rise of the reservation system was diminishing their access to the hides they used in their material and artistic traditions; and so they adopted the cloth quilt as a new medium for perpetuating aspects of these traditions. Quilting became a part of life, and quilts with the star pattern at their center grew especially popular. Over time, they were incorporated into the giveaway ceremonies that honored military veterans, high school graduates, and, beginning in 1964, basketball players.[9]

In taking up quilting and basketball, Native people adopted ways from a non-Native culture that was threatening their existence. They nonetheless saw in these ways opportunities to keep celebrating life in difficult times and tailored them to suit their needs and fit their values. And so, just as Native peoples carried over their artistic traditions from hide to cloth, they carried over their athletic traditions from grass fields to hardwood courts. This book tells the story of how this came to pass, concentrating on the period from 1895, when basketball was first adopted, to 1970, by which time it had become Indian country's most popular team sport.

Indian basketball was born of hard times, as the star quilts were, and it was born of hard places. Its evolution is largely traceable back to the boarding schools—or "Indian schools" as they were known—which are remembered traumatically by many American Indians as places that took their children and tried to take their languages and cultures. But these were also places where, around the turn of the twentieth century, American Indian boys and girls discovered basketball and made it a force for good in their lives. This was the beginning of it all. This is where the passion that today's communities have for the game, and their athletes, originated, excepting in the minority of Indian communities that never sent their children to boarding schools (some of their basketball histories are also told in the pages to follow).

That basketball grew to be so popular in Native communities might seem peculiar given its association with those old Indian schools and their assimilationist mission.[10] To be sure, this association was more than incidental. The non-Native administrators who oversaw the schools often plied basketball as a tool for social control, culture change, and racial integration, but its effects on students in many ways diverged from these intentions. Young Native athletes related positively to basketball despite the traumas many of them experienced in these boarded environments, and many relied on it to lessen the severity of those traumas. They could do this because the schools inconsistently managed and monitored athletics—students and Indian employees asserted a surprising degree of control over basketball's institutional and stylistic development within the schools—and because Indian people were resilient and innovative enough to adopt this new way without forfeiting their indigenous identities.

This theme of resilience and adaptation in the context of Indian school athletics has limitations of course. Native athletes were not totally immune to efforts to influence their personal behavior and cultural values through sports participation. Nor did all students who played basketball have the same beliefs about what it meant either to be indigenous or to be American. They responded to basketball and the competing cultural influences swirling about it in myriad ways, but most held on to their peoples' core values and identities.

Because the Indian schools were so important to the rise of Indian basketball, the bulk of this book (chapters 2 through 7) focuses on students playing it in and for these institutions, but that is only the beginning of a much larger, more complicated story. As the later chapters document, basketball evolved into a tribal community sport, and so became a tradition, because these Indian school students carried basketball home and spread word of its joys. This process of dissemination started while the first generation of student players were still in the Indian schools and accelerated as they began departing these places. Some left basketball behind, but others kept playing wherever life took them. They used it to find solace, joy, and companionship as they faced new challenges and dealt with difficult circumstances. From 1900 through the 1960s, Indian school alumni played hoops in American military service in times of war and in urban areas while struggling to make new homes for themselves. A few of the most talented took up professional basketball careers for a time or were among a small number of graduates who overcame great odds to compete in college. Most eventually returned home after these experiences. There they joined former schoolmates who had already begun teaching their tribespeople to play and love basketball, and they helped further that process.

Indian school students and alumni also received some help spreading basketball to their communities. Chapter 10 details the ways church groups and federal officials also promoted basketball's development on the reservations, as well as in nonreservation Native communities, through missions, day schools, and government New Deal programs. By the 1930s, public schools were also promoting basketball's popularity across Indian country. In some parts of Native North America, like Robeson County, North Carolina, where boarding schools and reservations were never parts of peoples' experiences, public schools were basketball's primary disseminators from the start. The game kept increasing in popularity both on- and off-reservation in the postwar era, reaching new heights during the 1960s, when Native-operated tournaments and independent teams became commonplace and basketball achieved its status as the most popular team sport in both rural and urban Indian communities.

The fervor over the Schimmels in Louisville, Arlee's Warrior Movement, and the star quilt giveaways on Fort Peck are just a few examples of ways that today's generation has benefited from the sport handed down to them by their predecessors. For more than a century now, basketball has drawn Indian people from their homes to common spaces where they have nurtured old relationships and forged new ones.[11] It has improved their health and provided youths with opportunities to learn to work and play together and overcome adversity. It has been a way to express family, tribal, and pan-tribal identities. It has been an inspiration to Native novelists, filmmakers, and quilters, some of whom, quite fittingly, stitch two-dimensional basketballs into their work. In all these ways, an Indian school game has become an engrained part of community life. It has become an American Indian tradition.[12]

This is more, though, than a history of basketball's social and cultural influence on Indian country. It is also a sports history, telling the stories of some of the great Native players and teams who helped make basketball one of the most popular, expressive, and ethnically diverse games the world has ever known. Even in the early decades of the century, when rules and styles of play were much different from those of today, Native athletes took possession of basketball and changed its very form. The up-tempo style of play that they collectively developed in the Indian schools and that later evolved into what is referred to as "Indian ball" or "Rez ball" enabled them to stand out within, and at times apart from, the non-Native basketball world but also to make inroads into that world. It made their play thrilling to watch and won them the admiration of Native and non-Native peoples alike. In many cases, it made them champions—state champions, national champions, and even world champions.

This book focuses primarily on the theme of unity and common purpose through sports, but it also tells of some diverse individuals and communities who followed their own paths. Of course, not all Indian peoples have had the same historical experiences with basketball, have played it in an identical style or equally as well, or have all agreed it has been a wholly, or even largely positive influence on their communities. Although I believe that it is necessary to give voice to the diversity of perspectives found in Indian country when it comes to basketball's triumphs and defeats, benefits and costs, and have endeavored to do so in the pages that follow, I nevertheless take to heart what Iva Croff, a Blackfeet tribal member, told me. "I don't know *anybody* in Indian country who isn't a basketball fan," she said.[13] This story is therefore told mainly for the majority of Native Americans who are passionate about this game. It is told without apology as a story of hope, achievement, and celebration.

I should note before continuing that saying basketball has become an American Indian tradition is not to say it has or could easily replace the indigenous games Native peoples have played for millennia, many of which are central to their oral traditions and ceremonial lives. These timeless athletic traditions, however, have always allowed for diversity and adaptation. Long before they came into contact with Europeans, different tribes played a diversity of sports and games that each had their own functions, meanings, pedigrees, and protocols. Many times, tribal cultures adopted each other's sports and games and gave them their own meanings when they did. The argument here is that they did the same with basketball, as indeed they did with baseball, rodeo, and other introduced sports, even though this post-contact exchange occurred during times of intercultural conflict. Basketball may not be traditional in all respects, but it *is* traditional in that it binds communities more tightly together, maintains a millennia-old emphasis on athleticism, and has been developed by Natives to serve their own needs over the course of many generations, from the Indian school years to today.

It is also the case, as the first chapter explains, that early Indian school students and their tribespeople gravitated to basketball, in part, because they never regarded it as entirely foreign to begin with. Its basic design elements paralleled those of many of their indigenous sports in certain respects, which students could clearly perceive. And so for them, adopting basketball was not about turning away from their culture but rather about embracing something that appeared both new and exciting and familiar and comforting. In basketball, they saw a reminder of the past and hope for the future. They saw in it a way to be who they already were as Native people, to be proud, have a good time together, and keep scoring victories in hard times.

1

Origins

In Sherman Alexie's fictional work *The Lone Ranger and Tonto Fistfight in Heaven*, the narrator speaks of Aristotle Polatkin, a reservation basketball legend "who was shooting jumpshots exactly one year before James Naismith supposedly invented basketball." When the Spokane-Coeur d'Alene author was later asked about basketball's prevalence in his writing and whether Native people invented that sport, Alexie said it was "just me fooling around" but added that indigenous peoples of the Americas had at least played a *form* of it centuries ago. "We may not have invented it," he said, "but it's been in the air for a long time."[1]

Alexie is not the only intellect who has suggested that indigenous Americans played basketball, or a form thereof, centuries ago or who has otherwise questioned whether Dr. Naismith invented it late in 1891, in the city of Springfield, Massachusetts. In addition to arguments citing indigenous antecedents, several alternative theories over the years have ascribed basketball to other non-Native inventors, including Lambert Will of Herkimer, New York. Most of these theories are easily refuted, but less so those pointing to indigenous inspirations.[2] Although there is little reason to doubt the veracity of Naismith's own account or deny him credit for his achievement, Alexie is correct in saying that, among Native peoples, basketball has "been in the air for a long time." Naismith did in fact draw partial inspiration from a Native American sport: lacrosse. His game was also, by coincidence, structurally similar to a variety of other Native sports. It is also the case, though, that Naismith drew on non-Native athletic traditions and designs in crafting his game, and, in its exact combination of elements, basketball had no antecedent. This sport therefore would have appeared as something both familiar and novel to Indian school students who encountered it for the first time in the 1890s.

Native Sporting Traditions

Native Americans played their own sports for millennia before encountering those non-Natives created. Since ancient times, indigenous peoples of the Americas had participated in a panoply of team sports, individual sports, dice games, and guessing games—each community developing their own distinct traditions. These communities thoroughly weaved these sports and games into the fabric of their lives, relying on them to perform a wide variety of functions. Some of these competitive activities endure today and continue performing their same functions, but to understand how the earliest Native players might have judged basketball's worth relative to these ways, it is useful to consider them from the vantage point of the 1890s, when Naismith's game appeared.

Those early basketball players understood their indigenous sports had always provided their people with entertainment and promoted their physical well-being. They had bonded community members together, facilitated the trading and wagering of goods, and been used to establish and maintain intertribal alliances.[3] Sports had also been integral to Native forms of artistic expression, material and musical. Playing implements, like the colorfully beaded hoops targeted in accuracy throwing games, the bison hair-stuffed balls batted about in the field-hockey-like sport of shinny, and the intricately carved sticks wielded on lacrosse fields, had been shaped, stitched, and fashioned by the same craftspeople who made other things of beauty. Field sports and sit-down dice and guessing games had also been venues for drumming and singing that emboldened athletes and gamers locked in fierce competition.[4]

Those first Indian basketball players also understood there was a spiritual significance to athletic competition that went beyond what most non-Natives recognized. As lacrosse was for the Iroquois, or *pok-ta-pok* for the Maya, certain indigenous sports were linked directly to the stories cultures told about the creation of the world and peoples' place within it. Sports were means to interact with immortal culture heroes who were athletes before the dawn of time. Native people learned from these stories that athletic competitions were not mere diversions for their immortal predecessors but ways to resolve disputes between cosmic forces, thereby establishing a universal order, making the world inhabitable for humans, and laying down ethical laws. Peter Nabokov explains, for example, that running, a root athletic form in Native America, enabled tribal cultures to "create a bridge between themselves and the forces of the universe." Such a thing occurred, for instance, when Jicarilla athletes ran their relays in New Mexico as the sun and moon once raced along the Milky Way. Doing so connected them to that creation story and helped maintain their vital relationships with powerful nonhumans.[5]

Although their cosmologies were diverse and distinct, most tribes shared a view of a universe where human fates are interconnected with those of immortals who can access transformative powers to help them thrive. Indigenous sports were means to facilitate this reciprocal process. It was thus possible for generations of Oneidas and Choctaws to play lacrosse or stickball to heal the sick, influence the weather, or fulfill powerful visions.[6] Not only were some competitions essentially ceremonial in nature, but spiritual action could also accentuate their benefits or influence the flow of play. Athletes prepared for competition through pregame ceremonies, feasting and fasting, prayer and self-sacrifice, drumming and dancing. Whether playing physically dangerous field sports or seated across from opponents playing hand game, people employed those universal spiritual powers they could ethically access (used *medicine* some might say) to supplement their mental and physical abilities.[7] Unconnected to peoples' creation stories as it was, basketball could never fully replicate all the cultural functions that sports like lacrosse performed, but this did not preclude Native people from seeing value in it or adopting it as a component of their richly diverse athletic traditions.

Those first Indian basketball players would also have known that their home communities had used sports as instructive and training tools catered to their needs. They were still doing so in the late nineteenth century despite all the changes and disruptions reservation policy had wrought. In 1902, Dakota physician Charles A. Eastman—also known as Ohiyesa—described sports and games he had played as a boy that "were molded by the life and customs of our people; indeed, we practiced only what we expected to do when grown."[8] The accuracy throwing and running games once common throughout Native America improved the manual dexterity and endurance skills required of hunters. Team ball games taught the social, mental, and physical skills required of tribal leaders and warriors. Competitions like the cross-country kick ball race, lacrosse, and the stick counting games kids once played allowed youths to mentally map their landscape, recall their creation stories, and hone their math skills, thus equipping them for successful lives.[9] That basketball would initially be associated with schools might therefore seem appropriate, but this represented a departure from the world Eastman once knew, because these white-run, brick-and-mortar institutions tried to sever athletics and education from their tribal community contexts.

Native athletes in the late nineteenth century also knew sports and warfare were often intertwined pursuits for their ancestors. They understood basketball's potential to serve somewhat similar functions as indigenous sports in this regard, but in ways more metaphorical than physical. Before the late nineteenth century, indigenous field sports were means to train warriors for combat and occasionally served as direct surrogates for full-on battle between contesting tribes. The level of violence involved in sports played for such purposes was elevated to the point where serious injury or death could result, but it was not so extreme that the cost in lives and limbs matched that incurred when battling with edged weapons. Whether games of stickball played by southeastern tribes—in which two sticks were used to carry or propel a ball toward a goal—or indigenous forms of soccer played long ago in California and Florida, indigenous field sports were punishing affairs as scores of players wrestled, slashed, and body checked each other to gain possession of a single ball.[10] It was no coincidence that some Native groups referred to stickball as "little brother of war" and used lacrosse sticks that closely resembled war clubs. Much further south, in more ancient times, the sport frequently referred to as the Mesoamerican ballgame also required a warrior's courage to play, even on those occasions when winners or losers were *not* ritually sacrificed at their conclusion, as they sometimes were.[11]

As a so-called non-contact sport, basketball could not replicate the imminent danger of some of these sports, but Native athletes would find that it could be much rougher than advertised and that a warrior's skills and determination could translate to a hardwood court. Even with the prospect of mortal injury removed, many of them would come to view their basketball contests against non-Native and tribal opponents as akin to the athletic battles their ancestors had waged on ancient playing fields.

This was not just true for the men. Traditional athletic contests that resembled warfare had been primarily male-oriented, but in the many cultures where women were heads of household, key political decision-makers, and sometimes warriors themselves, female sports had been deemed just as significant and been just as strenuous as male sports. Depending on the community, there were certain traditional sports that men and women shared and occasionally played together. Other sports were the domain of one gender. Although they became less prevalent during the late nineteenth century, the indigenous sports that young women had long played paralleled in some ways the men's. One of the most vigorous was double ball, a game in which teams advanced two balls attached by a leather thong toward a goal, throwing and carrying it with a single stick. Women and sometimes men also played shinny, in which they advanced a single ball along the ground with curved sticks.[12] Both double ball and shinny were contact sports played without protective pads, meaning women were more likely to suffer cuts, bruises, and broken bones in these games than in basketball or other sports introduced later. For Native women as much as for Native men, sports fundamentally mattered and were worth playing hard. Any new game that allowed them to vigorously express this athletic spirit was to be welcomed.

Structural Parallels

American Indians were more likely to embrace basketball when they first encountered it if they perceived structural parallels between it and their indigenous sports. Such parallels would both suit their tastes and allow them to carry over skill sets they already possessed. Anybody, of course, more enjoys doing something they have a knack for. If it was familiar in this regard, while also new and uniquely challenging, one would expect it to attract interest. Basketball did indeed possess these combined qualities, making it especially appealing to Native youths in the 1890s and in following decades.

As Indian school students would discover, all the major team sports that non-Natives introduced structurally paralleled indigenous sports to a high degree in that they emphasized running, physical endurance, dexterity, quick thought, and team work.[13] With the exceptions of baseball and volleyball, non-Native team sports also shared with many of their indigenous counterparts the objective of collectively advancing a ball toward a goal against a direct defense. Basketball would not have been judged as novel in this regard and, at least initially, would appeal less to some Native youths than football because it was comparatively less vigorous. But it also had unique elements that made it stand out in their minds. What most distinguished basketball from other team games, Native and non-Native, was the horizontally oriented elevated goal requiring a ball to be thrown in an arcing trajectory. There were dozens of Native sports that required accuracy throwing, running, and team play, and even a few that had horizontally oriented goals, but none combined these elements quite like basketball. Therein lay much of its appeal.

Most early Indian basketball players who were experienced at their indigenous sports were already accustomed to throwing objects through hoops, although they had thrown sticks rather than balls and their hoops had been rolling across grass fields on their rims. For centuries before basketball's invention, Native cultures throughout North America had played a variety of accuracy throwing games that historians refer to collectively as "hoop and pole," in which players stop rolling hoops by spearing them with hand-thrown poles, arrows, or darts. In the late nineteenth century, many tribes still played these games, including one that Geronimo's band of Chiricahua Apache played during the 1880s while in captivity in Florida in which pairs of men threw long reeds at 12-inch diameter rolling targets. Variables in these games included different sized hoops that players either ran alongside or threw at as they rolled past.[14] There were also lesser known accuracy games that more closely resembled the motions used in basketball because the targets were horizontally oriented, but they lacked running, passing, and guarding. Involving a wide variety of thrown objects, from sticks to stones, such games were still played at the turn of the twentieth century in a few places as far apart as Nova Scotia and Arizona. The Akimel O'odham (Pima) for example played Haeyo, in which groups of men stood in holes set fifty feet apart, throwing large rocks from one hole into the other.[15]

Other indigenous team sports, though lacking a horizontally oriented goal, nonetheless combined more elements later found in basketball. One of the oldest of these stands apart from the rest in that the goal was elevated. The original name of this sport is unknown, but an image of it may have been captured by Theodor de Bry in a 1591 engraving he based on prior descriptions by French explorer Jacques le Moyne de Morgues. The image depicts Timucua men in Florida throwing balls about the size of baseballs at a vertical grid atop a tall post. Scholars have questioned the historical accuracy of de Bry's engraving, but the sport it depicts strongly resembles one played by southeastern tribes in later centuries, including groups who incorporated descendants of the Timucua.[16] A version of this game is still played today by multiple tribes that were removed from the American Southeast to Oklahoma in the 1830s, including Seminoles. Known as the one-pole version of stickball, this is one of the few indigenous Native sports where men and women competed together. It allowed the women to throw the ball by hand at an elevated vertically oriented target, while also adding running, passing, and guarding elements. Meanwhile, male competitors used stickball racquets to aim for the same target. It was either a cow skull or a carved wooden fish on a pivot that, if struck, earned more points than if the throw scored a hit within the marked zone just below this icon. The game was played in 360 degrees around the pole without any out-of-bounds, and the women could body check the men with impunity.[17] Lacking two horizontal goals stationed on opposite ends of a playing surface, the one-pole game was not basketball, but it may have been its closest indigenous parallel.

No sport, however, has received more attention as a possible indigenous precursor to basketball than the Mesoamerican ballgame, one of the oldest team sports in the world and the first to be played using a rubber bouncing ball. Numerous historians, archeologists, Native basketball fans, and

Figure 1. Timucua men playing sports in Florida, engraving by Theodor de Bry. *Brevis Narratio Eorum Quae in Florida*, Plate 36.

others have noted its similarity to basketball. Some have even argued that the ball game likely inspired Naismith to incorporate his essential hoop. J. C. McCaskill, a boys' advisor at Haskell Institute—one of the largest Indian schools—noted the parallels in a 1936 school newspaper article, in which he reported that "archaeologists excavating recently in the ruins of Xochicalco, a buried city in Mexico, found evidence that the former inhabitants of this city played the game of basket ball. They unearthed the court with its baskets, and later found the ball. Thus long before Dr. Naismith and Springfield College were ever heard of, the Indians of Mexico were playing basket ball." Stephan F. de Borhegyi went a step further in an article for *Natural History* in 1960, suggesting that "Dr. Naismith, understandably interested in any new type of sport, may well have read about the ancient ball games of Mexico and incorporated the idea of putting the ball through a hoop."[18]

I will consider whether Naismith knowingly borrowed elements from the Mesoamerican ball game below, but suffice to say here that while there are striking parallels between this game and basketball, there are also fundamental differences. In the Mayan and Aztec versions known respectively as *pok-ta-pok* and *ullamaliztli*, a victory could be achieved by propelling the ball through a stone ring that was roughly equivalent in diameter to a basketball hoop, but it was oriented vertically, meaning that scoring on it more resembled scoring on a miniature soccer goal. Elaborate versions were played on permanent masonry courts, which were close to the size of a modern-day basketball floor, but players were confined to their own side, as in volleyball. The many variations most likely involved players hitting a bouncing, airborne, or rolling rubber ball, perhaps five times heavier than a basketball, primarily using their hips. This was a dangerous proposition because it was more equivalent to playing with a bouncing cannon ball than with a basketball. Players never, or rarely, used their hands, and if they did, they used a punching rather than a throwing motion, contacting it with a stone object held in their hand as one would hold brass knuckles. The possible variants where players punched the ball or struck it with a sort of bat may have come closer to basketball (or baseball for that matter), but the flow of play was dissimilar.[19] There may have been other variations of this sport, or unrelated sports played in Mesoamerica where players used their hands, but ulama, a likely descendent of the ball game played by indigenous people to this day, is less like basketball than was the ancient game. Players sometimes use their forearms in this modern equivalent, as well as their hips, but the masonry court and the scoring rings are gone.[20]

So to say that none of these games *were* basketball is not to say that Native people had never played games *like* basketball. When composited, as they were by Native individuals who traditionally played many of their sports rather than specializing in just one, these games provided an array of experiences that could be reproduced in basketball. None of these structural parallels would have mattered though, unless Indian school students who played basketball in the 1890s had personally played their indigenous sports. So had they?

Indigenous versus Introduced Sports

Basketball entered Native peoples' lives at a time when their athletic traditions were at a crossroads. Although many Indian school students during the 1890s indeed had firsthand experience playing indigenous sports, at least to a degree, this was becoming less the case with each passing year. We know this, in part, thanks to Stewart Culin. Just as Naismith was inventing his game, Culin, a curator of ethnology from the Brooklyn Institute of Arts and Sciences, was documenting the past and present existence of indigenous North American sports for an exhibit at the 1893 World's

Columbian Exhibition in Chicago. From this project research, he published in 1905 *Games of the North American Indians*, which remains the most expansive written account of Native sporting traditions. Relying primarily on museum collections and non-Native informants, Culin uncovered information about so many types and variants of sports and non-aerobic games in his research that he filled more than eight hundred pages with brief descriptions.[21] His sources indicated that as many as two-thirds of these activities were still being played at the time basketball was introduced to the Indian schools.[22]

This glass-half-full finding, however, could not obscure a larger story of loss. In addition to the one-third of documented sports and games that had already been lost, how long the others would survive was an open question. It was apparent to tribal elders in Culin's day that their sports had suffered significant deterioration over time and that this process was accelerating. Culin also perceived this, arguing that the remaining activities were showing signs of "decay." This negative trend was the product of historical forces that had been in motion for centuries. Over the years, Native people had willingly discarded some sports and games that no longer interested them, as all people do, but others had been traumatically surrendered. In some places, like the Caribbean in the 1500s or in the California gold fields during the 1850s, the loss of Native sporting traditions had reached totality as European-introduced disease and colonial violence took a devastating human toll. Some sports had also disappeared elsewhere because of the less deadly effects of colonization, including the general erosion of traditional knowledge and disruptions caused by shifting economic practices. Such may have been the case with the throwing game chunkey, which disappeared among the Choctaws in the nineteenth century after craftsmen failed to pass on skills for manufacturing the required target stones.[23] Most Native sports that had disappeared by the late nineteenth century were likely lost in one of these ways.

Other indigenous sports had gone extinct by Culin's time as well, or were in the process of fading, because non-Natives had deliberately targeted them as uncivilized and frivolous. The Mesoamerican ball game, which had been many cultures' most significant sport for centuries, drew both the Spanish conquistadores' curiosity and repression and faded in their wake.[24] Spanish priests in seventeenth-century Florida also stamped out a traditional kick ball sport they referred to as "that demonic game," which they said facilitated sorcery, idleness, and rebellious behavior.[25] Native sports drew similar scrutiny from moralizing non-Natives in the mid-to-late-nineteenth-century United States. Few federal agents and Christian missionaries on the reservations made note of the indigenous sports, but those who did often condemned them for encouraging gambling and hindering the civilization process. They claimed these activities were wasteful distractions that encouraged immoral and physically brutish behavior.[26] Using this logic, federal agents in North Carolina urged Eastern Band Cherokee men to give up stickball during the 1840s. The State of Mississippi took things further in 1898, outlawing traditional wagering on that sport and causing its steep decline in Choctaw communities.[27]

Europeans had not always been dismissive of indigenous sports, sometimes going so far as to adopt them, but this also had some negative effects.[28] French and British colonists were particularly intrigued by lacrosse, the widely played indigenous sport in which teams advanced a ball to a goal by carrying and throwing it with a netted stick. This cross-cultural interest, which could have led to the mutual enrichment of both Native and European athletic traditions, was instead a motive for cultural theft. In 1860, a Montreal dentist named William George Beers began formulating new rules for the sport, eventually creating a modern version that, as he wrote in 1869, was "much superior to the original as civilization is to barbarism, base ball to its old English parent of rounders, or a pretty Canadian girl to any uncultivated squaw." Beers's version had set sidelines and regulations and came with his rule 9, section 6, mandating that "no Indian must play in a match for a white club, unless previously agreed upon." Natives who played the sport in the late nineteenth century under these new rules often had to hide their heritage or accept dramatized roles as "savage" novelties to entertain white spectators.[29]

Nothing did more to accelerate the erosion of the old sporting ways in the late nineteenth and early twentieth centuries, however, than the proliferation of Indian boarding schools. Officials who oversaw these schools did not launch sustained initiatives to wipe out indigenous games even though they did target Native traditions more generally. The schools nevertheless took a toll on the indigenous sports because they were not taught to the thousands of Native youths who attended these institutions generation after generation. They instead learned sports and games that non-Natives played, and so, for students who enrolled at young ages, sports like football, baseball, and basketball were often the only ones they knew intimately. Lacrosse was the only exception to this rule. The two largest Indian schools fielded Native teams in the sport—Haskell Institute beginning in 1908 and Carlisle in 1911. There was, however, some bitter irony to this because, while school publications freely noted that lacrosse was a Native-invented sport, they failed to point out that their students were compelled to play it by Beers's rules. Nor did lacrosse ever rise to the level of being a premier sport in either of these institutions, both of which were renowned for their football prowess.[30]

As more traditional sports declined in the late nineteenth and early twentieth centuries, Natives began turning toward non-Native sports. Most of them encountered these activities for the first time in the boarding schools, but some entered the white-dominated sports world by other routes. Distance runners were some of the first to compete against non-Natives in public events. John Steeprock (Seneca) ran competitively against whites in New Jersey during the 1840s and Tom Longboat (Onondaga) won the 1907 Boston marathon in record time.[31] Western reservation communities that had taken up cattle ranching as a form of economic development also began producing Native cowboys, some of whom became professional rodeo competitors in the first two decades of the twentieth century. Although many Natives got into baseball via the boarding schools, some did by other means as well. On- and off-reservation, Native communities learned the game from missionaries, soldiers, and neighboring white and African American teams. By the 1880s, some Native men were trying out for professional baseball clubs, and in the early 1900s, amateur teams appeared in tribal towns throughout the West and parts of the South.[32]

The growing influence of these new sports in Native communities contributed to the decline of some indigenous sports and exposed athletes to different value systems, but they were not in all ways corrosive to Native traditions. The new sports were vehicles through which Native athletes expressed timeless passions, and many retained their emphasis on community values. Not everyone agrees on this latter point. Some scholars contend that Native athletes playing non-Native sports began to value a brand of individual competitiveness that conflicted with communal values.[33] More than a few Native Americans in the twenty-first century still share this concern, but many, past and present, have also honored athletes' individual achievements and competitive spirit so long as they have conducted themselves respectfully. Historian Peter Iverson has argued that the competitiveness that Native people began to display through early-twentieth-century rodeo, and still display today, is a perpetuation of timeless ways rather than a departure from them. These competitors have belonged to communities whose creation stories speak of immortal heroes who, not unlike human athletes, had to "undergo some kind of journey, confront risks and dangers, overcome such adversity through self-assertion and self-discipline, and return in hard-earned triumph." These stories "tell of races to be run and games to be won," explains Iverson. "They reflect the importance of doing something well—of being somebody."[34]

Some of the earliest and most ardent proponents of the new sports in the Indian schools were Native employees who believed that youths benefited from participating in these activities and could do so without surrendering their indigenous identities or values. At least one of them, however, publicly advocated retaining the old ways alongside the new. Although George W. Bent, Jr. (Southern Cheyenne-Kiowa) promoted the new sports in his position as an Indian school athletic director, he paused in 1915 to remind readers of Haskell's *Indian Leader* that Native people had a rich athletic heritage of their own. "We realize that we must be up to the times and be modern sportsmen," he wrote, "but what about our own Indian games, the games that we used to love to play by the full moon before the time for the ghosts to begin their wandering? What has become of the old Indian ball games, one of the pastimes of our people?" Although he offered no solutions, Bent insisted that "something should be done to revive some of these Indian games. Soon the only way we will know that the Indians had any games at all will be what we can find in some early history."[35]

Fortunately for those who shared Bent's concerns, enough people in the home communities honored and enjoyed their indigenous sports to maintain them through the Indian school years. Not all the old ways survived, to be sure, but many did. The new sports nevertheless continued gaining popularity in Native communities through the course of the twentieth century and would eventually outpace the indigenous sports in terms of participatory and spectator interest. What George Bent did not realize in 1915, though, was that one of these new sports was directly linked to one of the "old Indian ball games" he feared would disappear.

Naismith's Game

Dr. Naismith never said he had Native peoples or their sports in mind when he wrote the original rules for basketball, but neither did he explicitly exclude a possible influence. He never said he created basketball from scratch but rather that he blended rationally selected elements from existing games to meet a perceived need. In describing this inventive process, he later wrote that "basket ball, unlike the majority of our games, is not the result of evolution but is a modern synthetic product of the office." The key phrase was "synthetic product," by which he meant synthesizing preexisting forms to create something unique. His mentor and teacher, Luther Halsey Gulick, Jr., had inspired him in this by saying "there is nothing new under the sun. All so-called new things are simply recombinations of the factors of things that are now in existence."[36]

Naismith began inventing his new sport in the fall of 1891, the year after his enrollment at the International Young Men's Christian Association (YMCA) Training School in Springfield, Massachusetts. A Canadian from a small town in Ontario, Naismith was an enthusiastic athlete and had taken an interest in studying for the ministry, making him an ideal convert to the gospel of "muscular Christianity." This reform philosophy emphasized the value of clean and robust sports in nurturing the mind, body, and spirit. It had been adopted by the YMCA through Gulick's influence and served as the foundation for Naismith's belief in the personal and societal benefits of people playing well-crafted sports.[37]

In this spirit, Naismith accepted Gulick's assignment to develop an indoor winter sport as an alternative to uninspiring calisthenic exercises. It had to be compelling, inexpensive, and easy to play, thought Naismith, so it could inspire anyone and everyone to pursue team sports through the winter. The sport needed to be vigorous and flexible to challenge the body and mind but sufficiently ordered to discourage physically rough play and to minimize injuries. He first attempted to modify existing outdoor games for indoors, hoping to benefit from their established popularity. He had always loved American football and soccer, but after experimenting with teams of young men in the school gymnasium, he decided these sports were too intense for indoors.[38]

He turned next to what he called "the best of all games," lacrosse. Gulick may have inspired Naismith when he said earlier in 1891 that "football or lacrosse" were the sort of competitive sports to which a new indoor game should aspire; but Naismith would likely have come around to lacrosse on his own. As an athletically minded Canadian, he admired this sport and had played it in college and briefly for a professional team called the Montreal Shamrocks. His experiments with an indoor version were nonetheless disheartening. "In the group there were seven Canadians," he later recalled, "and when these men put into practice some of the tricks they had been taught in the outdoor game, football and soccer appeared tame in comparison. No bones were broken in the game, but faces were scarred and hands were hacked."[39]

Undeterred by these failures, Naismith abandoned the idea of modifying an existing sport—abandoning indoor lacrosse for the time being—and chose instead to scientifically engineer a new one made of composite parts. He decided that the game should use a ball like most popular sports but that the ball should be a large round one that could be advanced by hand. He had a soccer ball on hand to complete this piece of his puzzle. By prohibiting running with the ball and encouraging passing, he accented the team element and removed the need for tackling. That players might one day dribble the ball did not occur to him.[40] Considering all the ways teams scored in other sports, his thoughts returned to lacrosse. He envisioned "a goal like the one used in lacrosse at each end of the floor" but needed a way to prevent players from charging through each other or hurling the ball at high velocity to score. His solution gave basketball its unique character.

Naismith claimed that at this point he recalled his favorite childhood game called "Duck on a Rock" (or duck on *the* rock). It involved players throwing rocks, known as ducks, at another player's duck sitting on a boulder. When one of them managed to dislodge the duck, a player known as the guard tried to tag the throwers as they scrambled to retrieve their own and return home. The boys who threw their ducks in a more arcing motion, landing it nearer to the boulder, had an advantage in retrieving them without being tagged. This finessed throwing, thought Naismith, is what his game needed. "With this game in mind," he explained, "I thought that if the goal were horizontal instead of vertical, the players would be compelled to throw the ball in an arc; and force, which made for roughness, would be of no value."[41]

Everything then fell into place. He elevated the target to prevent players from accessing it by hand, borrowing two peach baskets from the custodian and affixing them to the lower rail of the gym's balcony. Sitting in his office, he handwrote thirteen rules for what he called "basket ball." In its early form, this was a lower scoring and less physical game than it would later be. It required a center jump after each score, used a game clock that ran incessantly but no shot clock, placed up to nine players on the floor per team, involved no dribbling, jump shots, or free throws, and required a ladder for an official to retrieve the ball from the closed basket.[42]

This was *Naismith's* game in that no prior sport combined these elements in this manner, but it nonetheless had an indigenous North American root in lacrosse. This root influence, however, was indirect—the sport Naismith borrowed being William George Beers's modified version. Naismith was always explicit about lacrosse's part-influence on basketball, telling a reporter in 1935, "I helped myself to soccer, lacrosse, and duck-on-a-rock."[43] Lacrosse did not just inspire Naismith to opt for a target goal; he also claimed in 1936 that the sport had "suggested the placing of [basketball] players as forwards and guards." Naismith never made note of the fact that he had in effect taken a sport whites appropriated from Natives, lifted elements from it, and then watched as the Indian schools introduced it back to Natives as part of basketball's DNA. Whether he realized that lacrosse was originally an Indian sport he did not say, but as an educated Canadian player, he likely knew. He nevertheless disregarded this fact because he was no ethnologist. It made no difference to him which cultures had invented which sports. His only interest was in lacrosse's attractive components that could be repurposed to create a new sport with universal appeal. He worked under the muscular Christian ideal, which was premised on the notion that what was good for white, middle-class, Protestant gentlemen was good for the world. But throughout his life Naismith never spoke of matters of racial or cultural superiority, believing that good sports should be accessible to all of humanity.

Whether other Native sports also influenced Naismith is hard to say, but he never claimed to know about the Mesoamerican ball game or its elevated vertical hoop. There is no way to prove that Naismith did not forget or lie about having such knowledge, nor that someone else who did—Gulick perhaps—had not passed on to him the idea of using a hooped goal. Any of these scenarios are possible, but none are likely. Naismith never tried to patent basketball or gain riches from the sport. If he tried to hide something about its origins, it could only have been motivated by ego or, perhaps, a racist refusal to deny non-white influences, but neither of these personal traits are ascribed to him by his biographers and neither meshes with the fact that he spoke so openly of lacrosse's influence, which was widely known to have Native origins.[44]

Regardless of whether it had indigenous roots beyond its connection to lacrosse, Naismith's game diverged from Native sports in ways that reflected his ethics and beliefs about what an ideal sport should be. It was decidedly nonindigenous in that it was played by written rules to a ticking clock and discouraged physical contact and overexertion. At the same time, because his ideas about what made for a good game were not always different from those of Native peoples, it included parallel elements: the hoop, the ball, running, teamwork, the need for quick reflexes, and even the initial rule giving a ball out-of-bounds to the first player to touch it, similar to most indigenous games that lacked sidelines. Naismith's talent lay in his ability to combine varied athletic elements to create a sport that appealed to diverse populations. He had no idea at the time of basketball's invention that Native Americans would be prominent among them.

Basketball's Early Popularity

American Indians who gravitated to Naismith's game early in its history were in good company. The sport caught on remarkably quickly in diverse environments around the globe. Basketball's early spread across the United States and overseas was fueled by the YMCA, which had nearly a quarter of a million members and 348 gymnasiums by 1892.[45] An account describing basketball and including the original thirteen rules first appeared in the Y newspaper, *The Triangle*, in mid-January 1892. Word was also carried forth by some of the young men who had first played the sport with Naismith in Springfield who went on to be Y directors in the United States, Canada, France, and India. The YMCA played a central role in promoting the sport in China and the Philippines as well. American Y members had become so enthusiastic about basketball by the mid-1890s that some Y directors began to worry about too much of a good thing. They were concerned that a single sport was monopolizing access to their gymnasiums and that the formation of intensely competitive Y teams distracted from the Christianizing mission. Believing that the sport's growth had outpaced its ability to develop and enforce rules governing the hundreds of teams then playing it, the YMCA opted in 1896 to hand over regulatory responsibility to the Amateur Athletic Union (AAU).[46]

Other organizations outside of the YMCA were also taking an interest in basketball, appreciating the fact that it was easily learned, was adaptable to both outdoor and indoor spaces, and did not require much equipment or player gear. US military branches introduced basketball to their recruits and fielded scores of competitive teams in the early 1900s. The YMCA furthered basketball's popularity within the military during World War I by hosting athletic activities for troops stationed in Europe. Military teams playing in France at the war's conclusion and returning servicemen then helped increase the sport's popularity on both continents. Settlement houses, including Hull House in Chicago, also employed the sport in their efforts to acculturate urban youths and promote their moral and physical well-being. Protestant church leagues sprang up in urban areas as well, as did Catholic and Jewish leagues sponsored by the Knights of Columbus and the Young Men's Hebrew Association.[47]

Basketball had also become a public school sport by the turn of the twentieth century, significantly expanding its reach beyond eastern cities. These institutions used basketball for some of the same reasons that the Indian schools would: to improve physical health, increase morale, and maintain discipline. American educators in the early twentieth century drew on new educational and athletic theories to argue for well-supervised athletics geared to children based on juvenile stages of development. Basketball fit well within this scheme and came at a reasonable monetary cost. In 1915, social reformer and playgrounds promoter Henry S. Curtis referred to basketball as "the game most commonly played at present in school yards by older children," and he deemed it suitable for all students thirteen years and up. Professional educators, however, faced the same dilemma the YMCA did, as they came to realize they could not bend public desire for basketball to fit a reformist agenda. As basketball gained popularity in American high schools, local communities became more invested in hometown teams, prompting school boards to promote varsity play at the expense of the larger student body's athletic needs.[48]

Although it would take decades for basketball to become a major college sport, Yale, the University of Minnesota, and the University of Chicago had all fielded teams by 1895. Independent amateur and professional teams also began appearing around the turn of the century, some of them spin-offs from local YMCAs that could no longer contain them. A team from Trenton, New Jersey, may have been the first independent team to play for pay in 1896, as well as the first to adopt the wire mesh cage enclosing the court to prevent players from chasing errant balls into the crowd—leading to the term "cagers" to describe players. The professional game would not become prominent for many years, but it exerted an early influence on the sport's development, injecting a profit motive and a physically rougher style of play, neither of which Naismith or Gulick condoned.[49]

While professionals were taking basketball in one direction, women were taking it in another. Even though men played basketball first and YMCA members hoped the game would encourage a virtuous masculinity, just a few months after its invention, interested women in Springfield, Massachusetts, began playing it too. Senda Berenson, the physical education director at Smith College, a few miles north of Springfield, took particular interest in Naismith's game because it had been deliberately designed to limit rough play. It thus offered women a more acceptable way to be athletic in a society that deemed them too emotionally and physically frail for rigorous sports. Berenson nevertheless understood that their involvement in even this sport would be controversial, and so she modified it. In the early 1900s, it became increasingly common for women to play by her rules, further minimizing contact between players by confining the guards, centers, and forwards to three separate zones of the court. Concerns about feminine modesty also forced most women's teams to wear bulky dresses or bloomers rather than more functional uniforms. Even though some women's teams retained the more vigorous men's rules until after 1910, they had to be prepared to use women's rules against certain competitors. Regardless of which rules they employed, many early-twentieth-century women loved basketball. In some western locations, including at many Indian schools, basketball appeared as a women's game first, making for a curious dynamic whereby it was originally perceived to be a feminine sport in some parts of the country and a masculine sport in others.[50]

Basketball's mix of athleticism and practicability also attracted African

Americans, Chinese Americans, Jewish Americans, Mexican Americans, immigrant Catholics, and other non-white or non-Protestant groups during the early to mid-twentieth century. Quite often, members of these groups were first exposed to basketball in urban YMCAs, settlement houses, community centers, and recreation programs that employed it as an acculturative tool, but they gravitated to it because of the excitement of competition and the opportunity basketball afforded them to gather as communities. As they navigated a multicultural and often times prejudiced athletic world, these diverse groups contributed to basketball's stylistic evolution and used the game to reinforce cultural identities, much the way American Indians would.[51]

Big Stone Lake

It has been thought that the first Natives to play basketball were young Dakota men at a YMCA summer conference on the shores of Big Stone Lake, in northeastern South Dakota. Naismith had not been there, but he claimed that his friend Henry F. Kallenberg organized this basketball game. An instructor at Springfield who left in 1891 to become a YMCA physical director in Iowa City, Kallenberg had first learned about basketball in a letter from Naismith. According to Naismith, Kallenberg later told him:

> In the summer of 1892 I attended, with [Charles] K. Ober, conferences of Sioux Indians held at Big Stone Lake, South Dakota. The following summer I attended the same conference which was held at Pierre. At both of these conferences I introduced basketball, and it was played for the first time by the Indians. We cut small saplings for uprights and in place of baskets we used a rim made of willows and fastened to the uprights. The Indians took to the game like ducks do to water, and soon basketball became their chosen form of recreation.[52]

Other sources confirm this account, except that either Kallenberg or Naismith seem to have given the wrong year for the conference.[53] The first conference at Big Stone Lake took place in 1896, not 1892, meaning a handful of Native people (mostly young women) had already played basketball in some of the Indian schools by this time, although not for long. It is possible, however, that Kallenberg had taught the sport to multiple Native groups before this. In a 1932 radio interview, Naismith told a reporter that sometime after arriving in Iowa, Kallenberg had "visited a number of the Indian reservations, in each of which they set up a pair of goals made of wooden hoops and the Indians played the game with a great deal of enthusiasm and became quite proficient."[54]

The 1896 conference had been Charles Eastman's idea. Eastman revered his Dakota heritage but believed Native peoples' best way forward was to learn to succeed within the dominant culture. He had been raised in the traditions of his people before being prompted by his father to pursue an English-language education—a path that ultimately led him to Dartmouth and to the Boston University School of Medicine. He would later help found the Society of American Indians, a contentious but influential organization dedicated to advancing Native interests. In 1894, he accepted Ober's invitation to serve as the Indian secretary of the YMCA International Committee. A Christian and a believer in the mental and physical benefits of modern sports, Eastman became a strong supporter of the Y mission and helped organize more than forty Indian Y associations across the West. To further these efforts, Eastman proposed annual summer conferences, beginning with Big Stone Lake.[55]

This first conference took place over ten days in late June and early July 1896, with Eastman, Ober, and Kallenberg helping train Dakota YMCA members for missionary work in their home communities. Their encampment surrounded a large central meeting tent, and these young men spent their days attending lectures and devotional meetings and engaging in organized recreation. Future commissioner of Indian Affairs Francis Leupp reported on the same outdoor basketball game that Naismith later described. "Here some hours were consumed in 'putting the stone,' basket ball, and other games and feats of strength. The Indians entered into these amusements with the keenest zest, and showed wonderful cleverness in learning the new points," said Leupp. "After the fun had lasted long enough the whole party, hot and jolly, rushed for the lakeside, where, in a bay with a fine sandy bottom, they swam and splashed and frolicked for an hour longer before separating for supper." Leupp regarded the overall conference as "a very interesting spectacle, and a noteworthy sign of the times in the field of Indian civilization."[56]

That these young men were already YMCA members does not necessarily mean they perceived this new game of basketball as an extension of that organization's acculturative and Christianizing mission. What they may have appreciated most was the chance it gave them to break from the seriousness of the lectures and sermons and do what young men had always done to have a good time. Leupp noted that some of them were not English speakers and, like Eastman, it is highly likely that more than a few of them had grown up playing their indigenous games. The willows Kallenberg used to fashion the rims not only proved the practical adaptability of Naismith's game but may have spoken to the young Dakotas in an unintended way. The distinct smell of willow and the sight of its long twigs shaped into hoops would have been familiar to them. Dakota people had used willow to make the wooden "snakes" for their sliding games, just as Native peoples elsewhere used it to make their double ball sticks, their rolling hoops, the darts and poles used to spear them, and the counting sticks used to determine victors.[57]

The young Dakota men at Big Stone Lake, and other Native athletes, learned that this well-planned game was even more flexible than Naismith had intended. As a "synthetic product of the office," it had built-in structural and stylistic parameters, but Natives would push these outward. They discovered that basketball could be liberating and had practical advantages and attractive features that could be tailored. The process through which Native players took Naismith's game and crafted their own began for some at Big Stone Lake, but for most, it would take place amid their struggles to cope with life in the Indian schools.

2

Emergence

The boarding schools seemed to be unlikely seedbeds for basketball to begin its development as Indian country's favored sport. These government- and church-operated boarding facilities rose to prominence in the late nineteenth and early twentieth centuries as promoters of Indian assimilation policy. They were designed as total institutions, meant to keep Native youths away from their homes for extended periods to prevent them from learning their peoples' ways. Students were instead raised by employees whose job it was to impart American values by emphasizing English-only education and employing a daily curriculum composed of academic classroom instruction and work-based vocational training. The schools also sponsored team sports, believing participation in them would improve student health, morale, and discipline while imparting the life skills and values necessary for Native youths to become productive American citizens.

The Indian schools' large enrollments afforded them significant power to reshape how Native peoples related to sports. In 1900, a majority of American Indians who were enrolled in a school—about eighteen thousand pupils in all—attended boarding institutions. About one thousand of them went to church-operated boarding schools where they were as likely to play organized team sports as in the government schools. The only students not exposed to organized sports in some fashion were the nearly four thousand in small reservation day schools.[1]

Basketball and other sports, however, were never the tools for directed social change that some policy makers and school administrators hoped they would be, in part because of how sports were managed. In the Indian schools, national policies did not always dictate local realities when it came to athletics. Federal officials often encourage schools to offer team sports, but they largely left the management of athletic affairs to the local superintendents. Acting on their own initiative, these superintendents were the primary architects of Indian school athletic programs, but they too deferred their management to employees of lesser authority and, to a degree, to the students themselves. This diffused management afforded Native employees and students the leeway to influence basketball's early development in these institutions. Native people gravitated to the game, as they did to other Indian school sports, not only because it allowed them to express their indigenous athleticism but also because they could exert some personal and collective control over this activity in otherwise authoritarian environments.

Indian School Athletics

Basketball was a latecomer to the Indian schools, which had begun developing competitive athletic programs years before. Few superintendents considered it anything special when it first arrived on their campuses in the mid-to-late 1890s, and only occasionally were they the ones who introduced it. To most, it seemed a minor diversion compared to football, a sport that had been all the rage in the schools since its introduction to Carlisle Indian Industrial School in Pennsylvania. Founded in 1879, Carlisle was the largest and most influential government Indian school. It was also the first to establish a physical health program that combined calisthenics and military drills with voluntary team sports. Under Superintendent Richard Henry Pratt, Carlisle ushered in the era of Indian school competitive sports, fielding both football and baseball teams by the early 1890s. Pratt's hiring of Glenn S. "Pop" Warner as the athletic coach in 1899 and his enrollment of exceptional players, most notably Jim Thorpe (Sac and Fox), made Carlisle a football powerhouse, and the school's teams soon gained national fame by defeating some of the country's best college teams.[2]

Pratt was a man of his age who combined a social reformer's belief in sports' physical, mental, and moral benefits with a propagandists' knack for playing on their symbolic value. He emphasized interracial football contests, in particular, because they allowed Carlisle to advertise a boarding school's ability to transform "uncivilized" Indian boys and men into well-disciplined models of American masculinity. Nothing could rival this most martial of games in its ability to entertain the American public while demonstrating how Pratt and Warner had taught Native pupils to control and channel their aggressions. Football victories, Pratt believed, also proved to his players and white spectators alike that Natives could compete on an even playing field with non-Natives, in this literal sense, symbolizing their acquired ability to do so socially and economically once thrust into the American melting pot.[3]

Carlisle's nationally renowned athletic programs greatly influenced the development of Indian school athletics elsewhere, which not everyone overseeing or working in these schools appreciated. In its efforts to maintain winning teams, Carlisle inspired other Indian schools to create their own highly competitive football and baseball programs, which often attracted peer and public criticism for creating inequities within their student populations. It appeared to some critics that the schools cared more about athletic glory than about using sports to promote their academic and assimilationist missions. In this, the Indian schools dealt with the same internal struggles over the meaning of athletics and faced the same outside criticisms as did YMCAs, public schools, and colleges of that era. Controversies regarding the advisability and ethical application of varsity athletics within Indian school curricula would continue to hound their athletic programs through the early decades of the twentieth century.[4]

Though they were aware of the associated criticisms, the superintendent and employees at the Haskell Institute in Lawrence, Kansas—one of the largest Indian schools—were envious of Carlisle's athletic accomplishments. Superintendent Hervey B. Peairs so admired Pratt's program that he became a strong sports promoter himself and was fielding varsity football and baseball teams by 1897. After Carlisle was converted to an Army hospital in 1918, Haskell assumed its status as the most influential athletic program in the Indian school network, its employees touting the school's nickname as the "New Carlisle of the West."[5] Haskell was as football-centric as Carlisle, but it established a stronger basketball program than Carlisle ever did and exerted a profound and sustained influence on the development of that sport in its sister institutions. In this respect, Haskell became the cradle of *Indian* basketball, just as its host Lawrence, for reasons I will explain later, is considered by some the "cradle of basketball."

It was natural for government Indian schools to take cues from each other when developing their athletic programs. School employees kept apprised of sports news from sister institutions by reading Indian school journals and newspapers, as well as newspapers published in neighboring towns.[6] The tendency for employees and Native students to transfer between schools also played a role. A cross-pollination dynamic developed where school superintendents, athletic staff, and student athletes transmitted their knowledge of sports programs from one institution to another—the bigger off-reservation boarding schools, like Carlisle, Phoenix Indian School, Chemawa in Oregon, and, above all, Haskell, serving as hubs in this informal network. Whenever the Indian schools produced a great basketball coach or player, odds were he or she had passed through Carlisle's or Haskell's doors (or both) at some point in their athletic careers. Consistencies in the ways that different Indian schools ran their athletic programs resulted more from this cross-pollination dynamic than from centralized policy initiatives.

During the first decade of the twentieth century, the United States

Office of Indian Affairs officials who oversaw the Indian schools at the national level were slow to develop standard athletic policies. They did not consistently disavow, emphasize, or regulate team sports but instead issued broad policy statements prioritizing the performance of daily calisthenics. Some policy makers in the Progressive Era no longer shared Pratt's belief that Native people would achieve complete cultural and social assimilation and focused instead on preparing them for quick economic absorption. They therefore emphasized physical exercises to strengthen a laborer's body.[7] Such was one focus of the Indian Office's 1901 *Course of Study for the Indian Schools of the United States*, which directed teachers to provide pupils with basic forms of physical training to "counteract the influences of unfortunate heredity and strengthen the physique, in order that they may be able to bear the strain that competition in business and earning a living will impose."[8]

Federal officials more actively promoted and regulated Indian school athletics after 1910. The Indian Office issued its most extensive athletic guidelines to date in 1915 as part of an updated course of study. Hervey Peairs' influence as chair of the drafting committee partially explains the guideline's increased emphasis on team sports, given the personal emphasis he had placed on them at Haskell. This policy shift was also a delayed response to trends in public education. Soon after the turn of the century, American public schools nationwide began promoting and asserting control over team sports they had previously allowed students to manage informally. They did so in recognition of the character-building value of sports and to eliminate the perceived improprieties of student-controlled activities.[9]

Echoing recent trends in physical education, the Indian Office's 1915 guidelines emphasized the need to involve all Native students in team sports as part of their physical training. These sports could be taught as full-on competitive activities or at rudimentary levels according to defined stages of juvenile development. In the category of desirable activities for students aged ten and older, "basket ball" was listed along with other team sports. Special emphasis was placed on this and other "group competitive games" for older students because they required "planning, managing, and effort to overcome obstacles," and thus taught leadership skills. Basketball was classified along with these "games of real worth," all of which afforded "an opportunity to use the mind as well as the muscles."[10] These detailed national-level guidelines were years behind local developments, however, having been issued many years after football, baseball, and basketball had become established components of most Indian school athletic programs. And as carefully crafted as these guidelines were, the Indian Office still did little to monitor and regulate athletics in the schools beyond asking local superintendents to submit annual reports and conducting occasional performance audits.[11]

Enter Basketball

Thus it was that the Indian schools did not all adopt basketball at the same time as part of a coherent policy initiative. It emerged locally and spread organically. Lower-ranking employees, outside volunteers, and students introduced it as often as the superintendents did. These diverse parties had learned about Naismith's game through involvement with the YMCA, their past experiences at other Indian schools, or reading about it in Indian school newspapers. Only after they introduced it to their home institutions did most superintendents, and later still the Indian Office, take special note of the sport and begin promoting it.

The YMCA played its part in introducing basketball to the Indian schools but only indirectly, rather than as part of a planned initiative. Many superintendents and staff members were Y members, and Indian schools often had their own Y student associations. The organization's presence in these forms increased the likelihood that at least a few employees and students had played, seen, heard, or read about the sport by the mid-1890s. The Y also asserted an external and sustained influence through its local basketball teams, which were the most readily available opponents in neighboring towns for the early Indian school teams.[12]

Carlisle was almost certainly the first Indian school to take up basketball—students began playing the game sometime between 1894 and early 1895—though how the sport originated there is unknown.[13] There had been a YMCA at Carlisle since 1884, and Y teams had also been established in towns throughout Pennsylvania by late 1892, so anyone on campus could have seen the game played and might have inspired employees or students to give it a try.[14] However it arrived, its development at Carlisle was quick and even surprised Naismith, who cited the Indian school as one of the first institutions of any kind to play basketball "outside of the YMCA."[15]

Initially, basketball figured most prominently as a female activity at Carlisle. It was featured this way in the 1895 spring commencement exercises. According to a syndicated newspaper report, the program included a demonstration in the gymnasium of "a game of basket ball, played by young Indian girls, in uniforms of blue flannel, made in Turkish divided skirt fashion, fastened at the knee, displaying extremely small feet in low soft shoes and black stockings. One team wore bright red sashes under their loose

Figure 2. The Carlisle women's basketball team (class of 1903) wearing the same style of uniform the original Carlisle players wore in 1895. *Left to right*: Amy Dolphus, Maude Snyder, Amy Hill, Minnie Johnson, Lillian Cornelius, Sophia A. Horse, Elizabeth Williams, Nannie Sturm, Mollie Welch, Mabel Greeley, Emma Skye, and Alice Doxtator. Richard Henry Pratt Papers, Yale Collection of Western Americana, WA MSS S-1174. Courtesy of Beinecke Rare Book & Manuscript Library.

blouse waists, and others dark blue, to match the suits." The article disregarded details about the actual game in its fascination with the team's student-made attire. After all, the point of the piece was to prove that Carlisle had made great progress in teaching female students "womanly accomplishments, such as sewing, washing, ironing, darning, mending, baking, etc." Although their names remain a mystery, the young women who competed that day were likely the first Natives to ever play basketball in front of spectators and maybe the first to play it, period, depending on what date one accepts for the game at Big Stone Lake.[16]

Basketball soon became Carlisle's primary female sport.[17] In the winter of 1895–96, its school newspaper the *Indian Helper* reported that "basket ball [was] the amusement of the hour among the girls" and spoke of it as the only game they played two evenings a week as an alternative to drills with dumbbells and the bowling-pin-shaped wooden bats called "Indian clubs."[18] Male students had a greater variety of athletic activities available to them, but they too began playing basketball as a form of physical training. Carlisle had begun to play basketball as a male interscholastic sport as well by the spring of 1896, and the newly formed team defeated neighboring Dickinson College 5–4 in one of its first games.[19] Both genders learned Naismith's original nine-player configuration and shot at an iron hoop with no backboard, even though the five-player game and backboards were then becoming standard fare in America.[20]

As basketball gained influence at Carlisle, its school publications began disseminating news of the sport to other Indian schools, and at least one government boarding school far to the west likely received the game through a personal connection with the flagship school's fledgling program. Fort Shaw Indian School, located west of Great Falls, Montana, did not have a YMCA during the 1890s. The smaller off-reservation school had fewer than three hundred students—a quarter of Carlisle's enrollment—but it soon produced a basketball powerhouse.[21]

Historians Linda Peavy and Ursula Smith say basketball was likely introduced to Fort Shaw sometime in 1896 by Josephine Langley, a Pikuni Blackfeet employee and aspiring teacher. Before returning to Fort Shaw in 1896, the nineteen-year-old spent a year studying at Carlisle. Langley had arrived in Pennsylvania in early 1895, not long before the commencement game between the teams in "bright red" and "dark blue." She probably watched this contest and may have played in it. Peavy and Smith suggest that "Josie" recognized something familiar about basketball, connecting it in her mind to the stories her grandmother had told her about double ball, the once dominant but then dormant game her female ancestors had played for centuries. In speculating about Langley's first impressions, Peavy and Smith write that like "double ball, this new game, 'basket ball,' required teams of girls to protect their own goal while trying to get the ball to the opponent's goal."[22]

Langley must have liked what she saw because she returned to Fort Shaw a basketball disciple. The probability that she introduced the sport to the school (and in effect to the state of Montana) is supported by the timing of her return and the game's initial appearance and by her captaining the first team the school assembled.[23]

Langley was not, however, the only Native employee at Fort Shaw who had an interest in sports. Two other employees, Louis Goings (Shoshone), a shoemaker, and Chauncey Yellow Robe (Lakota), a relative of famed Chief Sitting Bull, a Carlisle alum, and the school's disciplinarian, also embraced sports.[24] As a baseball enthusiast, Goings likely encouraged Superintendent William Winslow to develop an athletic program at the school.[25] Yellow Robe, however, probably had more to do with making basketball a formalized part of it, along with Langley. He likely shared her firsthand knowledge of the game, as he had graduated from Carlisle in the class of 1895 and thus been with her at the time of the commencement game. Yellow Robe, A former YMCA member and later Indian rights advocate, at least gave basketball an added boost at Fort Shaw.[26] As part of the school's commencement on June 30, 1897, he coordinated a literary, music, and sports program including a basketball game that bore resemblance to the one previously staged at Carlisle. "The field sports closed with a lively and interesting game of basket ball by the girls," the Choteau *Montanian* reported. "The contestants in the game were distinguished by red and white uniforms, the whites winning by a score of 7 to 6."[27]

From this humble beginning, Fort Shaw's girls' basketball team was destined for great success, in large part because of Fred C. Campbell's appointment as superintendent in August 1898. At a time when his peers at other Indian schools had little involvement with basketball, Campbell became a dedicated supporter of the girls' game. Having observed Carlisle's success using sports to attract positive attention, Campbell decided to do the same at Fort Shaw, believing a strongly competitive girls' interscholastic basketball team could do wonders for the school's reputation. Campbell played an active role in building a dominant team—scheduling games within and well-beyond Montana's borders, personally accompanying them on road trips, and stepping in as the coach in 1902—a rare move for a superintendent.[28]

As Native girls were first learning to play basketball at Fort Shaw, both boys and girls were doing the same six hundred miles west at Chemawa Indian School (also known as the Salem Indian Industrial School) in Salem, Oregon. Word of the new sport had reached the northwest coast soon after its invention, with a local newspaper reporting in January 1893 that basketball had become "all the rage" at the Salem YMCA.[29] Students belonging to Chemawa's Y association attended a YMCA convention in town in late October 1895. As part of the convention program, Chemawa student delegates Elijah Brown, John Ely, Henry Lewis, and George Moore attended a basketball game between the Salem and Portland YMCAs. Following this experience, the boys likely shared their interest in the sport with schoolmates who then began playing it as a pickup game at Chemawa.[30] It became very popular over the next couple of years. "Basket ball, in the gymnasium, is the favorite game of both boys and girls at present," reported the *Capital Journal* in March 1897. "They have no organized teams but we hope they will effect an organization in the near future, as it will then enable them to play with the teams of the surrounding country."[31]

Ten days after that article appeared, Chemawa received a visit from Frank E. Brown, the gymnasium director at nearby Willamette University.

He volunteered to organize and coach a girls' varsity team at the Indian school to serve as an opponent for the squad he had assembled at the university. Chemawa's boys were not initially included, but by December a school "YMCA team" had also been formed to compete against Willamette's men.[32] A week after Brown's visit, the two female teams played in Willamette's gym using nine-player formations of three "backs," three centers, and three forwards. Chemawa won two to zero, with the game remaining scoreless until the close of the second half when a Native player finally placed "the ball in the basket" (in 1897, the nets were still closed on the bottom). The lackluster score notwithstanding, the era of interscholastic basketball had arrived at Chemawa.[33]

At century's end, both the Indian school and the American collegiate basketball worlds converged on Lawrence, Kansas. Basketball arrived curiously late to Haskell Institute. Even though there had been a Y association at the Indian school since 1891, none of its members had started a basketball program through the mid-1890s. It took an association member from the outside, named U. S. G. Plank, to introduce the sport in later years.[34] We know this from James Naismith's own recollections after he accepted a faculty position at the University of Kansas in 1898. The inventor's years there spent with legendary coach Phog Allen later gave rise to Lawrence's "cradle of basketball" claim to fame. As Dr. Naismith recalled, Plank introduced basketball to Haskell around the same time that Naismith introduced it to the university, in the fall of 1898.[35] The two men had no prior association, and so it appears that Plank already knew the rules of basketball before arriving in Lawrence. Plank, originally from Wooster, Ohio, had served as a day school teacher on the Grand Portage Reservation in northern Minnesota before transferring to Haskell as boys' disciplinarian.[36] After arriving in the summer of 1898, he took on added duties as Haskell's athletic director and physical director at the city YMCA. He met Naismith in the latter capacity and the two became friends. In letters to his wife, Maude, Naismith teased that Plank acted "like a child" whenever he was ill but said he was a "splendid fellow and a genuine good man." Naismith also told Maude he heard students gossip that Plank was part-Indian, but Plank never identified as such.[37]

Within weeks of his new posting, Plank began organizing men's basketball teams at both the city YMCA and Haskell. He loved song as much as sport and so recruited a glee club at Haskell first before carrying over two of its student members, Edward Valley and Theodore Perry, to help found a basketball team.[38] After giving his teams from the YMCA and Haskell some time to practice, Plank scheduled a game between them on January 24,

Figure 3. Female players pose in Chemawa's gymnasium in 1900. They stand beneath an early-era basket that is closed at the bottom. Photograph by Trover Studio. Courtesy of the Oregon State Library.

1899, which the Native players won 18–6. Plank orchestrated this contest not only to nurture his students' love of basketball but also to advance the YMCA's mission of preparing young men of all races for lives as cultured Christian gentlemen. Before and after the game, the YMCA treated the Haskell team and a crowd of townspeople to a social hour complete with refreshments, musical selections by a male quartette, and a literary program. A local reporter judged the whole affair a "very enjoyable evening" despite the fact that the featured game had been "rather rougher than it should have been" due to both teams being "comparatively new." A few days before this, Plank had organized a similar social for student members of the Haskell YMCA. During the event, he sang a duet with one of the teachers and passed out handwritten slips to spark "progressive conversation" on such topics as "The Spanish-American War," "The New Auditorium," and, of course, "Basket Ball."[39]

Plank was assisted in developing Haskell's first basketball team by Frank O. Jones, a young Sac and Fox man from Oklahoma who served as team manager. Jones, in his early twenties, had taken a fifth grade teaching position at Haskell after graduating from its normal program in 1898.[40] Before attending Haskell, he had studied at Carlisle from the fall of 1895 to the spring of 1897, meaning he likely had prior knowledge of basketball before Plank's arrival. In addition to continuing to manage the student team, Jones was an enthusiastic player on informal employee teams he organized at the school in the spring of 1900.[41]

The sport soon became an integral part of Haskell's athletic activities, even though the school still did not own a basketball as late as January 1900 (they had been purchasable from Spalding's since 1894). This is made clear by the *Indian Leader*'s account of a game that month between Haskell's varsity men and the "Junior team" from the University of Kansas. "The work of the Haskell boys was fine," it reported, "but the KU players were more expert in putting the ball in the basket as they were using their own ball, while the Haskell boys have been playing with a football."[42] At this time, Naismith served as both the KU coach and the game referee, while Plank and a mixed group of university and Haskell students served as umpires. Haskell fared less well against the Jayhawks' varsity team later that January, losing twelve to five, again with Naismith and Plank serving as officials.[43] A Haskell "juniors" team was in place later that year playing regional teams like the Topeka YMCA, while a squad of "middle weights" and at least two other teams drawn from the student Y played exclusively on campus. A women's team was added in March 1901 to compete against high schools in Kansas and Missouri. All of these teams, including the women, played the five-player version of the game.[44]

If there was any doubt that basketball had become a sensation at Haskell by 1900, one simply had to read the March 9 issue of the *Indian Leader*. Next to a detailed account of the varsity men's disappointing 26–16 loss to the Topeka YMCA were reprinted student letters home describing their interest in the new sport, like one sent by an unidentified female student. "Basket ball is all we know now," she said. "In the girl's building we play in the halls sometimes, with a bucket for a goal." The issue also included a report on a recent basketball-themed dinner party attended by two teams of female employees. "At each plate was a neat card on which was a ball just entering the goal and an appropriate inscription in basket ball language," it said.[45]

This basketball fever endured through the following March 1901, when Haskell students and employees filled the school gym to see the varsity men take on the Lincoln, Nebraska, YMCA. The game "was a regular whirlwind on both sides," reported the *Indian Leader.* Forward James Oliver (Chippewa) "was able to keep out of the vortex, and close to the Lincoln goal. Then the ball would sail over the heads of the other players into his hands and then into the basket." Oliver led his team to victory, accounting for twenty of the team's fifty-two points and whipping the crowd "up to football heat." If this zest for the game kept growing, the *Indian Leader* speculated, "basket ball will prove a formidable rival to football."[46]

As basketball was taking Haskell by storm, it was also continuing to spread throughout the government boarding school system. By the end of 1901, the sport was being played in most of the larger off-reservation government schools and a few smaller ones as well. Genoa Indian School in Nebraska reported that boys were having "lots of fun" learning to play the game for the first time in late March or early April 1901, but from most schools that year, one heard of girls picking up the game first.[47] At Chilocco in Oklahoma, girls' teams were organized that spring by former Haskell students Anna May, Laura Secondyne, and Emma Whitecloud, who had transferred or taken staff positions at this off-reservation institution to the south.[48] Meanwhile, girls at Phoenix Indian School were reading in their school newspaper of the great times Haskell students were having with basketball and impatiently awaiting their own chance to play. They were already practicing when school employees began to lay out an outdoor dirt court for them in May, and the *Native American* reported that they were "eager to learn and enter highly into the spirit of the game." Within a month of this, in defiance of the desert heat, outdoor basketball had "become a very popular amusement with the girls. They play on the South lawn after supper and the office veranda makes a fine gallery for spectators, which the boys were not slow in finding out. Now each evening there is a fringe of legs and feet hung over the veranda floor, and the waving arms and lusty lungs above them attest to the interest taken in the play."[49] The year 1901 also brought news from a smaller reservation school in Sacaton, Arizona, where Akimel O'odham (Pima) boys were busily throwing baseballs while girls were picking up their first basketballs. By the fall, the game had also caught on among girls attending Albuquerque Indian School in neighboring New Mexico.[50] In the years that followed, extending through the 1910s, basketball spread to the remaining government institutions one by one, as well as to many Protestant and Catholic Indian schools.[51]

These stories of basketball's proliferation throughout the Indian school system together compose an image of environments that, while

Figure 4. Female students playing at Phoenix Indian School in 1903. Barry Goldwater Historic Photographs, FP FPC 1. Courtesy of Greater Arizona Collection, Arizona State University Library.

authoritarian in many respects, nevertheless allowed eager employees, outside volunteers, and students to play their parts in introducing and promoting this game.[52] Basketball was not forced on Native people in the schools but rather was welcomed and in some cases pursued by them. Native people would continue doing their parts to promote the game as the decades passed, in their capacities both as students and, quite often, as employees. This grassroots activity was more feasible in the athletic realm than in the administration of other school affairs. This was in part the product of the late-nineteenth-century tendency for American educators everywhere to allow students considerable control over the organization and management of team sports. Indian school administrators generally conformed to this decentralized model of athletics management at the time that basketball emerged.[53]

The Indian schools' general administrative structures also proved conducive to Native employee agency in athletic matters. The superintendents had a wide variety of responsibilities that bumped athletics down on their list of daily priorities, prompting them to delegate such matters to lower-level employees, many of whom were recently graduated students beginning their Indian Service careers. The Indian Office, which oversaw the Indian Service, provided the superintendents no formal athletic staff lines, so these men hand-selected employees they preferred to handle these duties as supplemental responsibilities. Annual employee turnover rates were also high at most Indian schools. All of this meant there were ample opportunities for Native employees like Langley and Yellow Robe to assume athletic staff positions and, in those capacities, promote basketball or other sports of their choosing, pending the superintendents' approvals.[54]

Although outside volunteers, employees, and students had often been basketball's first advocates in the schools, its long-term institutional survival depended on the superintendents lending sustained support. This initially seemed unlikely to occur as, with the exception of Fred Campbell at Fort Shaw, Indian school superintendents between 1895 and 1900 devoted little attention to the game. Things began changing in the early twentieth century, however, as superintendents everywhere learned that this particular sport offered distinct institutional advantages and as they acknowledged the sustained enthusiasm students had for an activity that was no longer a mere novelty.

3

An Indian School Sport

Soon after its introduction, basketball became a permanent fixture of Indian school life. By the early 1900s, most superintendents had realized the practical potential of this novel game and granted it official status as a component of their athletic programs, complementing existing team sports like football, baseball, and track. They were won over by two distinct advantages that basketball offered in contrast to the other activities. Most of all, it was the winter game Naismith had designed it to be, and that they needed: playable indoors in cold weather and just as easily transportable outdoors in warmer months and temperate climates. Many superintendents also deemed it safe and appropriate for female students, allowing them to extend the benefits of interscholastic team sports to a previously underserved population. In addition to recognizing these primary advantages, the superintendents appreciated that basketball was an easily learned and appealing sport they could sponsor on tight budgets.

Positive student responses and self-initiatives over sustained periods were just as important to basketball's institutional rise as the support it received from administrators. Many became enthusiastic basketball players and promoters within the schools. They tried out for varsity teams in large numbers and played basketball informally whenever and wherever they could, sometimes setting up their own makeshift courts. They organized and joined a variety of intramural teams representing the trade, academic, and social-subgroupings to which they were relegated or chose to belong. As basketball grew in popularity, superintendents also called upon students, as well as Native employees, to help feed, equip, and transport the varsity teams. Students even helped build the larger gymnasiums needed to house the sport and were among the throngs of spectators filling the seats and breathing life into the schools during the depths of winter. Although basketball never displaced football as the primary student spectator sport and main money maker, it had become the schools' leading winter sport by the end of the first decade of the 1900s and the most played team sport of all by the 1920s. Basketball thus became a quintessential Indian school game, embraced by the administrators, employees, and students.

The "Great Indoor Game"

Basketball provided the schools with a way to maintain their athletic programs year-round while offering students a welcome release on cold days. Soon after the turn of the century, this "great indoor game"—as journalists called it—became the primary winter sport in the Indian schools.[1] Superintendents began to recognize the special value of a team game that was playable indoors during inclement weather. As had YMCA directors across the country, Indian school superintendents were looking for a sport to keep their students physically and mentally engaged, and their varsity athletes fit, during the void between the football and baseball seasons. The need was especially pronounced in these institutions, populated as they were by Native students who were often disgruntled and demoralized. Well aware of these morale problems, superintendents feared the consequence of prolonged periods of physical inactivity not only on their students' bodies but also their hearts and minds. They therefore perceived basketball as a godsend. There was nothing else quite like it. There were other indoor sports available to Native students, including wrestling, volleyball, the softball-like game known as "indoor baseball," and the occasional indoor track meet, but with the exception of boxing at some Indian schools later on in the 1930s, none were major spectator sports or appealed to their students as much as basketball.[2] Nor would any outdoor winter sports come to the fore as the twentieth century progressed. Students occasionally skated frozen ponds, but ice hockey never developed south of the Canadian border as an Indian school sport to rival basketball's winter reign.[3]

Moving a team sport inside nevertheless posed challenges for institutions previously unfamiliar with the concept. Naismith had promised a game that could be played "on any ordinary gymnasium floor," but few Indian schools had "ordinary" gymnasiums.[4] As modest as basketball's spatial requirements were, most reservation boarding and day schools at the turn of the century lacked inside room to accommodate it, which either delayed its adoption, required the repurposing of existing indoor spaces, or pushed the game outdoors.[5] The larger off-reservation Indian schools normally had gymnasiums by the early 1900s, but only Carlisle had a spacious one.[6] The others were generally oddball facilities, ill-suited for basketball as Naismith envisioned it being played. Fort Shaw's first "gymnasium" was a low-ceilinged, dirt floored dance hall, and Haskell's a poorly lit, albeit relatively large basement beneath the school auditorium. Neither had been constructed with team sports in mind. Both had floors hemmed in by dangerously unpadded support columns, Haskell's metal variety encroaching a few feet onto the playing surface to clobber distracted players.[7]

Most of the early Indian school courts made a sport Native students would come to regard as liberating first appear confining and prison-like. Besides the tight quarters, there were the unattractive mesh screens. The full-court cages found in the professional game were never used in the Indian schools, but Haskell had a chicken wire cage encircling portions of its court during the early 1900s.[8] The other Indian school courts had numerous small wire screens protecting light fixtures and windows from errant balls. These grids set against the panes were not only unattractive but also posed egress hazards for students at schools where shoddy construction made building fires common threats.[9] At least three of the early Indian school gyms—at Albuquerque, Chilocco, and Fort Totten in North Dakota—burned down during the early 1920s, all thankfully with nobody inside. As time wore on, other aged Indian school gymnasiums posed increased risks. In 1937, Crow Superintendent Robert Yellowtail referred to his school gym as a run-down "dangerous fire trap," reporting that it had partially burned once and that it "leaks whenever a rain or snow storm is in progress."[10]

Some students were less than impressed with the notion of playing sports in these confining spaces, especially since their ancestors had played their sports on fields of grass lacking boundaries. William Sutton (Arapaho), for one, said he opted not to play basketball at Chilocco because it was "too much indoors." He was far more interested in the open-air games of football and baseball. So was the anonymous author of a student letter sent from Haskell in April 1905. "The baseball season has just begun," the pupil exclaimed. "I like to play baseball two times better than basketball." Other students, however, looked past the less than ideal accommodations. They came to appreciate basketball's enclosed spaces for what they were; discovered that they could express themselves athletically indoors as well as out; and learned that freedom could be tasted within the confines of the gymnasiums.[11]

Native students and their coaches made do with their makeshift accommodations and, over time, grew to appreciate them. They became accustomed to their courts' unique dimensions and structural quirks and sometimes turned them to their advantage. Haskell's players, for example, often outwitted their opponents by banking shots off the sweet spots on the chicken wire cage and grabbing the support columns on the fly to swing their bodies away from defenders.[12]

Indian school players also softened in their opinions of their own courts when they discovered that many of their non-Native opponents had it worse. This was especially so in the 1890s and early 1900s when many YMCA, college, and professional courts in the United States were quite small and so haphazardly shaped as to be narrower on one end than the other; the perfectly rectangular variety became standard only after 1900. Many were studded with support columns, had hot steam pipes along their perimeters, or had lit potbellied stoves intruding onto the playing surface, making basketball a particularly hazardous game in its early years. If a player was fortunate enough not to be knocked out cold by a steel pole, they might suffer sundry burns and bruises from the stove, in addition to wounds inflicted by opponents.[13] Carlisle's gymnasium was cavernous compared to many of these places. Haskell's court, with all its warts, was also superior to most in its region, including its smaller crosstown counterpart at the University of Kansas.[14] One of the Kansas City gymnasiums where Haskell's varsity men played an away game in 1901 was downright laughable. It was, the *Indian Leader* reported, "nearly square and so small that it was not difficult to stand in any part of it and reach the basket."[15]

It was not just basketball's ability to move indoors that made it a practical fit for the Indian schools, but also its transportability outside. This indoor-outdoor flexibility allowed it to be practiced year-round nearly anywhere on campus and made it suitable for boarding schools of any size or location. In warmer climes, basketball could leave its indoor confines entirely and be accommodated easily outdoors in small areas without the need for sodded fields. In contrast to their counterparts on the Northern Plains and Midwest, students at Indian schools in places like Fort Wingate, New Mexico; Greenville, California; and on the Tulalip Reservation in Washington, first knew basketball as an outdoor sport, played on undulating ground under open sky.[16] The same was true at Phoenix Indian School, where the school newspaper attributed basketball's popularity among female students to the opportunity it afforded them to be outside, reporting that "as it is all in the open air and every day is suitable for outdoor playing their appetites do not need coaxing."[17] Some schools in less temperate regions also took advantage of the sport's indoor-outdoor flexibility to offer the benefits of fresh air when weather permitted, as did Fort Shaw and Haskell in the mid-1900s when they added supplemental outdoor courts.[18] Defying the elements, Indian school students also played outside at some places lacking any indoor space, as pupils did at a government school on Montana's Blackfeet Reservation, utilizing a frigid plot known as the "basketball grounds."[19]

A Sport for Female Students

Basketball's availability to both male and female students at the interscholastic level also gave it a breadth of appeal no other sport could match.

Although originally introduced to some Indian schools as a girls' activity, the number of male students playing basketball system-wide had surpassed the number of females by 1910. This shift occurred because male athletes, who were more numerous in general, increased their interest in the game, not because female interest waned. In fact, female pupils were generally crazy for basketball from the time it was introduced onward. If they played any sports at all, this was typically their favorite. Basketball held special significance for them because of the rare opportunity it provided them to compete interscholastically. For the boys, it was the premier winter sport, whereas for girls it was the premier sport, period.

In Native traditions, women's team sports were usually played hard and played to win, but when girls arrived at the Indian schools, they were told they were too delicate for vigorous sports. They heard for the first time that being competitive was primarily a male trait and that physical overexertion could harm them mentally and physically—even endangering their reproductive capacity.[20] Based on these sexist myths, many Indian school superintendents deemphasized female team sports, preferring controlled physical exercises and ballroom dancing routines designed, as John Bloom says, to better develop their "physical appearance, posture, and body control."[21] Some superintendents nonetheless afforded females limited opportunities to be athletic, believing they could benefit from team sports so long as gender-appropriate restrictions were in place to ensure their physical safety and maintain their womanly virtues. And so, depending on which superintendent was in charge, the girls' athletic prospects ebbed and flowed, school to school, year to year, never matching those of the boys.[22]

There were a few sports female students were permitted to play at most Indian schools besides basketball, but none were as much a fixture of school life. Rarely if ever interscholastic activities, they were played mainly during physical education classes, as light recreation, or less often in organized intramurals. The schools commonly offered archery, croquet, soccer (beginning in the 1930s), tennis, and volleyball on these limited levels. They also made available bat and ball sports, including indoor baseball, softball, and sometimes hardball, all of which were generally well received. Young women at Carlisle, for example, were particularly enthusiastic about baseball and eagerly organized their own intramural teams starting in the late 1880s. Most girls' bat and ball activities were restricted to home campuses, although teenage girls at Concho, in Oklahoma, did play a few interschool softball games later in the 1930s.[23] Track and field, too, was generally a boys-only interscholastic sport, but girls participated in the occasional meet at Chilocco, Phoenix, and some schools in Montana and the Dakotas.[24]

Indian school superintendents who condoned females playing interscholastic team sports of any kind tended to favor basketball over other options. They felt more comfortable with it, perhaps in part because it was initially a girls-only activity, and so were less likely to view its players as invading a masculine domain.[25] Administrators may also have been swayed by physical educators like Senda Berenson, who argued that basketball, when played according to appropriate rules and monitored properly, promoted physical and moral fortitude without overstressing the female body or encouraging immodest behavior.[26]

Indian school basketball thus proved a blessing for female pupils over the years who longed to be athletic, but it never became a gender equalizer. Female players perpetually confronted restrictions, sexist slights, and disappointments unknown to their male counterparts. Basketball was advertised as a safe and ladylike game for Native girls, and Indian school administrators maintained a watchful eye to make sure it stayed that way. The superintendents set stricter safety restrictions for female athletes than for male, and they were less likely to entrust the enforcement of restrictions solely to their athletic staff when it came to female teams. This was one area where they remained vigilant. The superintendents worried mainly about the effects of overexertion on the female constitution, particularly on the heart, and insisted that appropriate protective measures be applied.[27] Examples abound. At Haskell in 1903, the *Indian Leader*, speaking on behalf of the school administration, applauded the women's varsity team for their 25–5 win over Topeka High School while cautioning them and the managerial staff against their tendency toward "over strenuous work" on the court. At Chemawa in 1927, Superintendent James McGregor ordered the varsity girls to the doctor's office for physical exams "on account of the energy" they put into one of their court contests that was harder fought than usual. And at Santa Fe Indian School during the 1930s, the administration allowed the girls to play basketball but required them to take a two-hour nap every Sunday.[28]

Native girls and young women pushed back as they could against this cautious paranoia. Many viewed themselves as the hardy athletes their female ancestors had been on double ball and shinny fields and gave their all on the court. One Santa Clara woman who attended Santa Fe Indian School in the 1920s, for example, later said she had looked forward to basketball and exceled in it more than she did at track because of her fierceness. "I was better playing basketball," she said, "because I was mean and

agency

rough!"[29] But there were limits to how rough female players could get without losing access to the sport. Another Santa Fe Indian School student recalled that the administration, sometime during the 1920s, suspended girls' basketball for the remainder of a season simply "because one of the girls broke her arm."[30]

In contrast, Native schoolboys never worried about losing basketball for a season owing to a single injury. Administrators were far more lax in monitoring their safety, because basketball and other sports were meant to encourage masculinity. Physical aggressiveness and the ability to play through pain were deemed admirable qualities for male athletes so long as they stayed within the rules. Students attending Haskell got this message by reading the *Indian Leader*. In 1919, for example, they read about varsity basketball captain Emmett McLemore (Cherokee) playing out a game in a "dazed condition" after being injured and lying on the floor "unconscious for several minutes." Later that year, Benny Murdock (Chippewa) finished out a game as the sole remaining starter. The other four had been allowed to start in spite of preexisting injuries suffered in practice and to a man were knocked from the game. Two years later, Murdock himself was praised for playing an entire game on a sprained knee. The *Indian Leader* had no qualms about reporting any of these details, seeming to suggest that the injured students were true men for playing hurt.[31]

Haskell was not the only Indian school that maintained a double safety standard for male and female basketball players. In South Dakota, for example, boys attending the Pierre and Pine Ridge Indian schools in the 1920s were permitted to play through injuries as serious as those their ancestors had suffered in their indigenous field sports. A sports reporter illustrated this through his coverage of a hard-fought contest between the two schools in February 1925. "The game was so terrific," he wrote, "that three of the Pierre boys were knocked out," *literally*. At least one was taken to the hospital on a stretcher. So was one of the Pine Ridge guards who "played a whale of a game" before collapsing unconscious to the floor near the end. Pierre won 18–17. The next day, the school's athletic staff and superintendent permitted the team to return to action against Rapid City Indian School. Although some of Pierre's players were recently concussed and all were exhausted, they fought hard and kept things close, losing narrowly 26–22.[32]

While boys attending Indian schools were allowed to compete past the point of injury, the girls often competed under Berenson's tedious women's rules that virtually chained them in place. This was not initially the case. Before 1910, many American schools, including Indian schools, opted to forgo these rules. Superintendent Campbell's decision to do without them helped Fort Shaw play a more open style of basketball that dazzled spectators in the early 1900s.[33] The Phoenix girls at that time also used men's rules under coach Winfield Warder, who was reported to be unfamiliar with Berenson's rules. U. S. G. Plank was slightly more conservative at Haskell in 1903, using "men's non-interference" rules that allowed full-court play but prohibited defenders from stealing the ball if an opponent had two hands on it.[34]

By the 1910s, most Indian schools had adopted women's rules, but they did not all use the same version of them.[35] In 1916, basketball's ever-evolving official rules allowed three women's options depending on the dimensions of the court, including six-player versions played with either one or two court division lines and a two-division nine-player version. In all of these iterations, girls played shorter halves than boys (fifteen as opposed to twenty minutes) and were allowed to dribble only one bounce before passing. The center's roles shifted depending on which version was played, because only she could range the entire court in the two-division game. She was not, however, always permitted to shoot.[36]

Given that some of the Indian schools' opponents in the West still used men's rules, this made for a baffling array of options. No girls' teams could know just one version of the game if they wanted to compete with outsiders. In interscholastic play, superintendents and coaches negotiated which to employ and had to be prepared to switch things up. In arranging a game with Pipestone in 1931, Bismarck's superintendent Sharon Roscoe Mote proved just how adaptable his team could be. "Coach Doyle informs me that our girls prefer to play boys' rules," he told Pipestone's superintendent, James W. Balmer, "but will play girls' rules or modified girls rules, 2 or 3 division court, 5, 6, or 7 on a team, whichever you prefer."[37]

Indian school girls made do with whichever rules they had to use, but they knew the boys had the better deal. So did Elsie Blue George back East. Unlike the young women attending off-reservation Indian schools, she and other Catawba girls in South Carolina learned to play basketball at a mission school from their Mormon teacher in the early 1920s. They nevertheless had the same distaste for women's rules. "After he taught us to play by the boys' rule, then he taught us the girls' rule," Blue George remembered many decades later. "I did not like the girls' rule; I never did, and I do not now. I enjoy basketball, but I love the boys' rule the best."[38]

Basketball fell short of being gender neutral in other ways as well. As prominent as girls' basketball became in the Indian schools, it could have been more so were it not for the biased competition with the boys' game for limited resources. Most of the Indian school superintendents, athletic directors, and coaches were men who took more interest in male teams, as did most of their counterparts at non-Indian colleges and high schools. U. S. G. Plank, for example, agreed to let Haskell's women play the University of Nebraska in 1903 only because he unexpectedly had time to coach them after canceling a men's team trip. And at Flandreau Indian School in 1933, the girls managed to cobble together a 5–7 season record against area high schools despite having access to only one ball for practice, unlike the boys, who had access to several. Even when girls and young women were coached by female employees, they were constrained by funding, equipment, and practice space limits imposed by male athletic directors and the school superintendents supervising them.[39]

Superintendents also had financial incentives for favoring male teams. Female teams cost more to operate because, with the notable exception of Fort Shaw, they drew smaller crowds—a reality made worse when they were fettered by less exciting women's rules. This problem meant fewer opportunities for female teams to play outside the schools because they could not recoup travel expenses. Flandreau superintendent George Peters was reluctant to host Mote's Bismarck team in 1931 for this reason. "We always lose money on the girls' games," he explained. Mote acknowledged the same problem the following year when seeking to play Flandreau. "I know of course that girls' basket ball games are not very profitable," he admitted, "and would not feel like asking you to pay very much towards our expenses." Fortunately for the Bismarck girls, Mote had his institution absorb this financial burden to maintain their competitive opportunities. Not all the superintendents were so willing. Bismarck was an exception, not only because of Mote's open attitude but also because it was an all-girls Indian school beginning in 1922.[40]

Overprotective administrators, funding inequities, and scheduling difficulties meant interscholastic basketball was unavailable to female students some years. But knowing the sport might be snatched away from them did nothing to dampen their enthusiasm for it. They knew basketball was their best opportunity to experience the joys and privileges their male schoolmates derived from a broader variety of varsity sports.

Basketball for All

Despite the external criticisms the Indian schools received for emphasizing varsity sports, athletics, including basketball, were always more accessible to the broader student population than was publicly recognized. This was the case, in large part, because students created their own opportunities to be athletic when these opportunities were not created for them. Whenever a new sport was introduced that sparked student interest, it quickly spread through the student body as a new obsession. This occurred with basketball in the early 1900s, as it had with baseball and football in prior years. School administrators and teachers encouraged broad involvement in basketball through formal physical education classes and intramurals, as well as varsity programs, but the students themselves were primarily responsible for the sport's dissemination through their ranks, as they eagerly organized their own pickup games and intramural teams and tried out for varsity squads in large numbers. It did not matter how fast, tall, strong, or old a student was or whether they were male or female; if they wanted to play basketball, they found a way.

Chilocco school bugler Albert Makescry (Ponca) knew that dreams of making varsity sports teams were unattainable for most students, but anybody could be athletically active. Makescry attended Chilocco in the late 1900s and early 1910s, at a time when varsity football ruled the Indian schools and star players like Carlisle's Jim Thorpe were American icons. The closest brush Makescry ever had with that kind of fame was when he met Thorpe during a visit to the Chilocco print shop where Makescry worked. There were also the times he and his schoolmates basked in collective glory when their varsity teams triumphed over a rival. But looking back sixty years later, what Makescry remembered just as fondly about sports at Chilocco were the pickup basketball games students played without employee supervision. Nobody read about these informal competitions in the newspapers, and superintendents rarely reported on them to their superiors, but these were some of the most frequent and foundational interactions Indian school students had with basketball.[41]

Indoor court time was hard to come by at Chilocco, Makescry recalled, so some students made their own places to play, thus expanding opportunities for their schoolmates to take up the sport. The "dairy boys," remembered Makescry, "had an extra place there [in the dairy barn]. They had a goal, you know, just right height . . . and regulation ball. And they do all that, shooting goal, move around." Built by male students assigned to that work detail, the dairy barn court was open to all interested comers: "Everybody used to get out there and practice, you know. That's how most of them got started. Yeah, they didn't get started in the gym. They got started over at the dairy barn."[42]

The Chilocco dairy barn became a student-managed proving ground. A group of younger boys from the young boys' quarters played together as a unit for years on that court, developing the skills and group cohesion that eventually earned them varsity privileges in the main gym. Those who never made varsity still had ample opportunities to put the skills they honed in the dairy barn to the test as members of Chilocco's many intramural teams. What Makescry most appreciated about all the informal and intramural play was that no one needed to be an "expert" athlete—it was just a "way we have a lot of fun, you know."[43]

Few higher ups in the Indian Office realized that basketball and other sports were as democratically accessible in the schools as Makescry knew them to be. This was an unsung success story, largely realized through student initiatives. Native students fulfilled the Indian Office's athletics-for-all policy without the Indian Office fully realizing it or doing much of the heavy lifting. To satisfy their superiors, local superintendents had always talked the talk when it came to the athletics-for-all ideal. A 1914 issue of the *Chemawa American*, for example, included an extended editorial preaching this democratic philosophy. "Many of our students have been endowed by a Merciful Creator with a body strong in wind and limb and it is hard to down such a youth," it said. "But, after all, the person most in need of athletics is the weakling—the one of puny body and little strength. Here is the fellow who needs athletics the most. Alas! He gets the least, for his feeble strength keeps him from shining as a bright particular star."[44] Indian Office superiors read such words, but they were dubious about the local superintendents' follow-up assertions that sports were indeed broadly participatory in the schools. In fact, government investigations called out the big Indian school athletic programs multiple times between the late 1900s and early 1930s for alleged abuses and breaches of policy and for overemphasizing intercollegiate sports while neglecting most students' needs for recreation and physical education.[45] Such reports eventually prompted the Indian Office to take concerted action. According to John Bloom, fallout from the Meriam Report in 1928 and determined efforts by the Indian Office led to the deemphasis of college-level competition by the large Indian schools during the 1930s and an increased emphasis on intramurals and other forms of recreation.[46]

These top-down reforms were based in part on the biased and often flawed assumption that varsity and intramural sports were mutually exclusive pursuits. Although the off-reservation Indian schools did put extensive resources into intercollegiate sports—especially football—and the desire to win did lead to some inequities in their treatment of students, none of this prevented less physically gifted pupils from being athletic. A lot of them played sports and played them often because they loved to and aspired to become varsity players themselves. Superintendents after 1930 complied with the Indian Office reforms by more commonly using the term "intramurals" in their reports and by claiming to increase their emphasis on that form of competition, but these activities had been going on for decades. As early as 1915, for example, Haskell's Athletic Director Alfred M. Venne (Chippewa) reported that 260 boys and 126 girls—about half the total student population—were regularly playing basketball in various forms, the vast majority at the intramural level.[47]

By the 1910s, intramural basketball was readily available to students at most off-reservation Indian schools and was widely accessible to students of different ages and physical builds. So were other sports, although not always to female students. Some intramural basketball, baseball, and football teams were catered to students of specific ages or sizes.[48] Basketball came with names like Juniors, Middle Weights, and Babes. It is not always clear whether students' ages or physical sizes were the determining factors in team membership, but the latter was the case for Chemawa's basketball "Midgets" in 1916, who were boys of any age weighing ninety pounds or fewer.[49] These teams gave boys who were not on the varsity first or reserve teams chances to play competitive ball. On occasion, they played interscholastic games against outside YMCA lightweight and junior teams, college freshmen, high school, and junior high teams. The Indian school smaller-sized and younger teams usually stayed on campus and played schoolmates in short "curtain raiser" or halftime matchups during varsity games.[50] These specialty teams continued through the 1930s for the boys and increasingly included the girls.[51]

These age and size-based teams expanded basketball's reach without necessarily leveling the playing field. Quite often, the young, small athletes competed against larger schoolmates. At Haskell, the Midgets, Lightweights, Middleweights, Giants, Reserves, and YMCA teams played each other in the same intramural leagues.[52] Although these mismatches were arrangements of practical necessity, they also gave smaller students chances to prove that athleticism and well-practiced teamwork could overcome size disadvantages. The Haskell Midgets made this point in 1916 with a 29–10 win over a team of schoolmates made up entirely of six-footers, called the Slats.[53]

Other intramural basketball teams were organized irrespective of age or physical size. These shop, society, YMCA, and class teams emerged in all the team sports. They were encouraged by school officials, but students often organized them. They performed functions beyond the welcome entertainments they provided. From the superintendents' perspectives, they increased athletic participation while encouraging students to identify with the various vocations and organizations that facilitated assimilation and maintained campus order. Regarding basketball, the school newspapers made special note of boys' and girls' shop teams with names like the Carpenters and the Seamstresses; debating and literary society teams like the Websters and the Invincibles; and often more than one YMCA team per institution.[54] During the 1910s, Haskell students were even encouraged to form teams representing the band and each of the military-modeled companies into which they were placed to maintain campus order and discipline.[55]

For students, intramural teams served other purposes. They were welcome opportunities to play ball, but, just as importantly, they fostered a group solidarity that emotionally sustained students during hard years spent away from home. Older Native students in particular commonly adjusted to the boarded environment by self-identifying with groups or cliques that conferred identities supplemental to their tribal or family identities.[56] Membership on these intramural squads further proved that a student *belonged* somewhere within an Indian school's complex social environment.

Shop teams in particular enabled older students to express the pride some took in pursuing chosen or appointed trades.[57] These shop basketball teams were among the most common found on Indian school campuses, Chemawa alone having teams in 1910 representing "the printers, carpenters, black-smiths, tailors, harness-makers, dairymen, gardeners, farmers and engineers."[58] Students organized their own shop teams and called out their opponents, occasionally via school publications. Young men working in Haskell's print shop were in an especially privileged position to taunt rivals through the *Indian Leader* school newspaper they helped issue. "The Printers would like to challenge the Tailors for a game of basket ball," they wrote in a December 1905 issue. "Wake up, Tailors. See Captain Harris of Printers, for a game."[59] This school-sanctioned but student-driven process continued in later decades. In 1929, for example, Genoa Indian School's Nurse Trainees called their female schoolmates from domestic science to the court.[60]

Still other types of student-formed basketball teams allowed them to express group identities that transcended the schools' organizational structures, like one assembled by male students from Oklahoma tribes at Haskell in 1903, simply named "Oklahoma."[61] Carlisle's Whirlwind Five, Haskell's Fighting Five, and Concho's House Cats alternatively chose names that gave no hint about what players had in common beyond an interest in basketball.[62]

Class teams, representing each grade level from the fifth grade up, also proliferated through the off-reservation schools in all team sports. Class teams often competed in intramural leagues and tournaments against each other and sometimes against other types of teams.[63] These mixed competitions would have been entirely lopsided were it not for the fact that each grade level was populated by students of diverse ages. While many Indian school students were about the age of an average American student at a given grade level, some were much older. Quite often, these older students had not enrolled in primary grades until they were well into their school-age years. Some had never attended a school before enrolling off-reservation, or they had begun their schooling on a reservation, and sometimes spent years languishing at a single grade level, before transferring to an off-reservation institution. This complicated reality made for some interesting age distributions on varsity and intramural teams. In 1928, for example, the ninth grade girls on Bismarck's team ranged from sixteen to twenty-one years old, while ninth grade boys on Concho's 1929 team ranged from fifteen to nineteen. One of Chilocco's varsity "boys" during the 1910s had first enrolled in 1909 as a seventeen-year-old first grader![64]

This broad age distribution within each grade, and the hard work some teams put into practicing, made interclass basketball contests more competitive than one might have predicted. In many cases, the higher grade levels prevailed, but this was far from guaranteed. Haskell's interclass tournament in February 1923 had numerous surprises. In one day of competition, a team named "Junior High" predictably defeated the sixth grade 30–10, but the seventh grade beat the seniors just as handily. The eighth grade also played the Junior Commercials in such a tight contest that student spectators chose to ignore the supper bugle to see its end. The eighth grade won narrowly and went on to finish second in the tournament, behind the sophomores, but ahead of the other high school–level teams.[65] The highly competitive tournament reflected how serious students were about intramurals. Assistant Superintendent Sharon Mote reported that "during the basketball season, some class teams practice late at night, while others get out early in the morning before breakfast, the class rivalry is so keen." The junior boys' "All Stars" team spent so much time practicing in the "over-busy" gymnasium that they were said to "virtually live" there and were nicknamed the "gym rats."[66]

Intramurals thrived even at schools where superintendents strongly advocated varsity sports, because the two types of competition could exist symbiotically. Both Chilocco and Haskell (and presumably some other Indian schools as well) relied on intramurals to scout talent for their varsity basketball teams, which was part of the reason younger students were so eager to get involved. As stimulating as it was to play intramurals for their own sake, doing so could also be a stepping stone to something more. Athletics-for-all was not a meaningful philosophy to some students if it meant they could only play schoolmates. Their dream was to make varsity, as they proved by trying out in large numbers. This was evidenced in the 1909–10 season when forty girls tried out for Chilocco's varsity basketball team, and again in 1915 when at least fifty young men vied for positions on Haskell's first and second team rosters.[67] The level of interest was just as intense at Chemawa in 1926, with fifty-seven boys trying out, exceeding the "30 or more" who came out for baseball that spring. The girls matched this enthusiasm the following year, when fifty-seven veterans and newcomers competed for a few prized spots.[68]

Intramurals also supported varsity play in other ways. Although Chilocco prohibited first team players from continuing in intramurals, other Indian schools used these internal competitions to train varsity teams in the preseason. While serving as Bismarck's superintendent in the 1930s, for example, Sharon Mote refused to schedule any girls' interscholastic games until players honed their skills in an intramural tournament.[69] The Indian schools also used intramurals as vehicles for placing varsity players in leadership roles so they could inspire up-and-coming athletes. For example, in 1910, Chemawa's varsity boys each captained a separate intramural squad in the "Happy Six League," hand-selecting teammates from the forty-eight students who signed up. Bismarck had a similar arrangement for girls later in the 1930s, permitting the six varsity starters to each coach a different intramural team, which then competed against each other for bragging rights.[70]

The Most Played Game

Multiple sports were popular and accessible in the Indian schools, but basketball's cogender availability put it over the top. During the 1920s and early 1930s, it became the leading game in participatory numbers even as football remained the top spectator sport. A prime illustration of its broad appeal was the response Albuquerque Indian School's superintendent Reuben Perry gave to a letter he received in 1930. It asked if he had "discarded" basketballs to donate to neighboring public schools. "I beg to advise that we do not have any discarded basketballs," he replied. "We keep the good ones for our first, second and third teams and allow the fourth to twentieth teams to use the old and worn out ones. We have over five hundred boys in the school and I think every boy plays basketball somewhere and in some way."[71]

The Indian schools rarely kept statistics about how many students played which sports, but evidence suggests that basketball was extremely popular system-wide during the 1920s and 1930s. At Chemawa in 1926, for example, the gym was said to "fill up" every winter afternoon with girls

Figure 5. Boys' intramural teams at Pierre Indian School in 1939. The first row displays a variety of basketballs ranging in age, style, and condition. Courtesy of NARA, Kansas City, Missouri, identifier 35294633.

belonging to class and literary society teams. At Concho, in Oklahoma, sixty-four boys and fifty-eight girls signed up for intramural basketball in 1928, equaling half or more of the enrolled students. Interest was just as high at Chilocco, where, in 1932, one hundred boys signed up for interclass basketball compared to eighty-nine who went out for interclass track. And 46 percent of Haskell's male students volunteered for intramural hoops in 1938.[72]

Yearbooks also provide quantifiable clues about basketball's popularity relative to other sports. Graduating seniors at the larger Indian schools usually listed extracurricular activities next to their photographs, including favored sports they had played. Even though male graduates had frequently played three or more varsity sports, they afforded basketball a prominence in their yearbook entries second only to football. At Haskell in the 1920s, for example, twice as many males listed basketball and football next to their photos as listed baseball and track. Basketball featured even more prominently in female entries. The majority who listed any sports next to their graduation photos at Haskell and Chilocco exclusively listed basketball.[73] Application forms for various Indian schools asking students about their previous "athletic experience" demonstrate similar trends. Applications from Kaw, Otoe, Pawnee, and Ponca students in the early 1930s reveal that more had played organized basketball in their previous schooling than any other sport. This was narrowly the case for boys but overwhelmingly so for girls. Some had received this prior exposure at day or public schools, while others had played basketball at sister Indian schools before applying to Chilocco, Genoa, or Haskell.[74]

One source is perhaps the most telling about the popularity basketball had achieved in the Indian schools by the mid-1930s. Haskell's Commercial Department issued a questionnaire to 590 enrolled students in 1936 asking about their interest in various extracurricular activities. In addition to soliciting their opinions about everything from glee club to puppetry, it listed all the major sports. The students' responses indicate they were far more interested in athletics than any other school activities, and basketball led the way. More of them—279 in total—said they had experience playing basketball than participating in any other activity, athletic or not. Baseball trailed close behind, with 247 claiming playing experience. The male-only sports of football and boxing came in at 118 and 43, respectively. More also said they were currently playing intramural or varsity basketball at Haskell than any other sport—264 compared to 240 respondents who said track, 161 baseball, 150 football, and 105 boxing. A much larger number also listed basketball as the sport they *wanted* to play if they did not already—a total of 137 compared to baseball's 82, football's 63, track's 60, and boxing's 50.[75]

The Haskell survey was a snapshot in time that was no doubt influenced by recent developments. The decline of intercollegiate-level play in football and the total absence of a baseball program at that school for a few years during the 1930s led to the overrepresentation of basketball in certain categories. The results nonetheless made clear that, in the four decades since it was introduced, basketball had become a quintessential Indian school sport, second to none in participatory interest. The number of Native basketball enthusiasts the Indian schools produced each year was thus large enough to facilitate the sport's dissemination, through them, to all corners of Indian country.[76]

Supporting the Game

Native students also did their part off court to make basketball a fixture of Indian school life. As the sport gained greater presence in the schools, it became more complicated to manage and support, especially at the interscholastic level. Because the Indian Office did not directly fund school athletics, superintendents had to make their programs financially self-supporting, and this invariably necessitated their enlisting student assistance.[77]

One way they did this was by establishing student athletic (or "activities") associations and selecting students and employees (Native and non-Native) to serve on their executive committees. Most of the off-reservation Indian schools had these associations in place by the early 1900s, and reservation schools did as well in following decades. In addition to handling athletic funds, the associations were booster organizations meant, as Albuquerque's athletic association charter explained, to "promote sports by any legitimate means." They were not entirely "student" associations, however, as the ultimate authority lay with the athletic staff members, principals, and superintendents who were usually ex officio committee or advisory board members. In carrying out their fiscal duties, the associations pooled revenues from athletic ticket sales, movie nights, plays, and other entertainments into special accounts. They also took in funds traveling teams earned by splitting gate receipts and negotiating advanced guarantees with their hosts. These athletics and activities accounts were then used to cover a variety of athletic expenses, including purchasing sporting goods from national retailers.[78]

The associations normally operated on tight budgets. During the 1910s, Carlisle's football team generated enough revenue to support the school's other sports on its back.[79] This was the exception, however, as few Indian school athletic programs were ever net profitable. Athletic budgets were always tight and became particularly so during the Great Depression. Haskell's athletic program especially struggled in 1932, for example, incurring a $6,718 loss.[80]

Basketball offered yet another institutional advantage in these financial environments of being one of the least expensive sports to operate. In 1901, the student manager of Haskell's baseball team commented on basketball's inexpensive nature with a hint of jealousy. "With a small admission 10, 15, or 20 cents," he explained "basket ball can more than make its way, but base ball costs more and therefore cannot be maintained on the same cheap basis." This was still the case during the 1920s, when basketball's per-player and per-game costs were notably lower than football's and baseball's. Varsity basketball required travel expenses for only five to eight players, basic uniforms costing around five dollars, one ball costing about ten dollars, and knee pads for each player costing about three dollars a pair. Home teams in the 1910s and 1920s also hired local referees for about five dollars a game, paid out guarantees to their opponents of ten to fifty dollars, and usually boarded and fed the visiting teams. By comparison, in 1920 it cost Flandreau Indian School, in South Dakota, twenty dollars to outfit each football player. Baseball could also get pricey. Balls with limited lives cost about a dollar each, uniforms seven dollars, and fielders gloves two dollars or more (not to mention bats and catcher's gear). These sports' larger teams also cost more to transport and board.[81]

Basketball was a comparatively less expensive means to expose large numbers of students to athletic competition, but it was not a consistent money maker for the schools. With the exception of boxing at Chilocco, no sports consistently generated the large ticket revenues football could.[82] Though expensive to operate, football pulled in by far the most revenue. Indian school basketball, in contrast, either made or lost money by small margins.[83] Most often, the boys' interscholastic programs roughly broke even. Concho's team discovered as much on a nineteen-day road trip in 1930, which cost $230 while bringing in $227.[84]

Indian school basketball and other sports operated so often in or near the red that superintendents reduced costs however they could. Some transferred surplus sporting goods between each other's schools or took competitive bids from retailers to get the best prices on new goods.[85] The most common cost-saving measure, though, was to call upon the students to support athletics themselves, including through unpaid or low paid labor. These were not unusual demands as far as superintendents were concerned. The general use of student labor was in fact a common nationwide practice in the Indian schools, officially justified as a form of vocational education but largely motivated by the government's need to sustain the day-to-day operation of chronically underfunded institutions.[86] Although the students did not likely regard the labors they performed to support basketball as odious tasks, it must be noted that they were not always *voluntarily* promoting the sport in performing them.

Students thus supported basketball by the sweat of their brows off the court as much as on, and they did so on virtually all fronts. They toiled in the kitchens and bakeries preparing generously portioned meals for the home and visiting teams using the produce of student farmers and dairy workers. Female students in domestic science acted as wait staff at athletic banquets. Student seamstresses and tailors occasionally made basketball uniforms, gym shoes, and the athletic banners that heralded intramural and interscholastic championships. Meanwhile, the printers issued the school papers that advertised intramural tournaments, reported the varsity teams' accomplishments, and encouraged students and townspeople to buy game tickets—which they had printed of course. At Chemawa, student blacksmiths fashioned dumbbells and rings used in physical education and team training, while the carpenters built lockers, spectator benches, and new front doors for their drafty gymnasium. Their counterparts at Phoenix even made the schools' iron basketball hoops.[87] In fact, students were called upon at times to produce about anything basketball required, except the balls.

Many basketball players also paid to outfit themselves. Although the

Figure 6. The Chemawa boys' team in 1913 wearing basketball trousers. Girls' coach Reuben Sanders (Siletz) stands at the top-center. The others are unidentified, but among them is boys' coach Joseph Teabo (Chinook from Grand Ronde). Photograph by Trover Studio. Courtesy of the Oregon State Library.

schools usually provided the varsity uniforms, students commonly purchased their own shoes and attire for intramural sports and gymnasium classes.[88] These policies saved the schools money and enabled student tailors to pocket something for themselves by taking special orders from their schoolmates. "For up-to-date basketball trousers see Nick Hatch and Arthur Van Pelt, merchant tailors," two students advertised in the *Chemawa American* in 1910. "For samples look at the printers' trousers."[89] Realizing that these extra expenditures were burdensome for many students and their families, Haskell began providing gym shoes to all male and female students in 1916. This was also done, in part, to encourage more students to play intramural basketball.[90]

Native teams also did their part to self-fund basketball through performances and fund-raisers when their institutions could not, or would not, cover all their expenses. This was especially true of female squads. The young women at Fort Shaw famously raised money for their team travels in 1904 by playing exhibition games and entertaining paying crowds with club swinging routines, theatrical recitations, and musical performances.[91] Girls at other schools in the years that followed commonly played exhibition games as well, in addition to hosting basket socials, luncheons, and auctions. In 1910, the girls' varsity team at Tulalip used a combination of these fund-raisers to pay for their own uniforms, as did Rapid City's girls' team in 1927.[92]

Some student athletes also covered portions of their basketball teams' expenses out-of-pocket. This is what a student-organized all-Native men's team at Hampton Institute (Virginia) had to do in 1911. Unlike most student-organized teams, this one competed externally but was not funded directly by the school. Team member Joseph Metoxen (Oneida) sent a well-crafted letter to Commissioner of Indian Affairs Robert Valentine asking for direct funding support from the Indian Office. "Our situation is rather embarrassing, having only a few boys to back on financially," Metoxen explained. "When the basketball and suits were bought, one of the boys, a member of the team, put in four dollars. While another boy, the captain of the team, has always paid our car fare." He plucked a chord he believed would resonate with Valentine, referring to the positive interactions his team had with "white people" in the area and the "better understanding" they had reached with them through basketball. This elicited from Assistant Commissioner Frederick H. Abbott a friendly and encouraging reply but no check. He explained that Indian Office procedures prohibited him from directly funding the team.[93]

Students also supported basketball financially as paying spectators. Some schools, including Carlisle and Fort Belknap's agency school in Montana, allowed their students free admission to athletic events. So did Hampton, which helps explain why Metoxen's team lacked funds.[94] But at most Indian schools, student ticket sales were a significant source of revenue for the athletic programs. Native and non-Native employees also did their part by paying admission for their family members. Haskell's students in 1915 were charged five cents per basketball game, and Chemawa's a quarter in 1931, or they could opt for season tickets to attend all athletic events. Chemawa tried various methods to get students and employees to opt for this latter route, urging them to purchase a season ticket in 1914 as their "duty" to "further the cause of athletics." In 1916, the school granted automatic membership in its athletic association to any student, employee, or alumnus who purchased an athletic season ticket for two dollars. By 1931, Chemawa had dropped the price for students to one dollar and sweetened the deal by adding admission to the "picture shows" and an "operetta."[95] In 1933, Flandreau avoided the incessant sales pitches by simply requiring all students to purchase a one-dollar "activity ticket" upon registration that would admit them to "all football, basketball games and track activities."[96]

By far the most expensive line items in Indian school basketball were the gymnasiums themselves. As the first-generation facilities fell into disrepair, burned down, or otherwise outlived their usefulness, they began to be replaced by more elaborate and costly successors. These newer gymnasiums were the only significant federal expenditures directly related to Indian school basketball, as they were funded through congressional appropriations. The superintendents played their parts by lobbying Indian Office superiors and congressmen for the financing while student workers were sometimes called upon to aid in their construction (outside contractors did the bulk of the work).[97]

These second-generation gyms were basketball venues, constructed around the game itself, with more consistently sized and shaped playing surfaces and more room for onlookers in elevated seats that replaced the older running track balconies. They were physical manifestations of the central role the sport had come to play in campus life. Between 1914 and 1919, Indian schools at Crow Agency (Montana), Flandreau, Haskell, and Mount Pleasant (Michigan) all received new gymnasiums, with price tags ranging from Flandreau's modest $7,500 building erected in 1914 to Haskell's more elaborate Hiawatha Hall, built in 1916 for $35,000 on a foundation excavated by student workers.[98] During the 1920s and 1930s, more basketball gymnasiums went up at Indian schools across the country, including at Albuquerque (1923), Chilocco (1926), Fort Peck (1928), Pipestone in Minnesota (1931), Phoenix (1938), and Stewart in Nevada (1938).[99]

Chemawa waited longer than other schools to get its new gymnasium, but this patience was rewarded with one of the grandest facilities. In 1930, Superintendent Oscar Lipps secured funding for a new building meant primarily for basketball but also to house a band-room and serve as the school's general social center. It would be the most expensive gymnasium yet constructed in the Indian Service, at an estimated $50,000, but Lipps assured his superiors that it could be brought in under budget by using "a good deal of student labor for which we will pay less than one-half the usual rate." Lipps was determined to make this a first-class basketball

Figure 7. Boys' teams at Chemawa in the 1950s. First opened in 1931, this gymnasium was considered expansive, but an imposing wall loomed along the baseline. The projection booth and electronic scoreboard sit above the backboard. RG75, Chemawa Photographs, 1907–71, 1364. Courtesy of NARA, Seattle, Washington.

venue with removable bleachers to allow the incorporation of crosswise practice courts. For three months in 1930, he negotiated with his Indian Office superiors to resist their cost-saving modifications that threatened to reduce the main court to less than the forty-two by seventy-two feet that he considered minimal.[100]

Ultimately costing $60,000, Chemawa's new gymnasium opened in 1931 as the envy of the Indian school system. It had a high ceiling, room for one large main or two smaller cross courts, 884 spectator seats, and a maple floor specially designed to withstand western Oregon's damp climate. A large theater stage, flanked by a massive portrait of Mt. Hood, and a movie projection booth in the balcony were the only indications that this was anything other than a basketball arena. Lipps's push and pull with the Indian Office had forced him to accept two design flaws that gave the modern court some awkward character, reminiscent of its first-generation predecessors. The prow of the stage jutted out nearly even with one baseline at waist level, and a thinly padded wall encroached within about one foot of the other, endangering anyone driving in for a layup and forcing players inbounding balls to paste their backs to the wall. They had to get intimate with officials who were plastered to the wall alongside them to monitor the inbound pass.[101]

Such design flaws aside, these more spacious gyms stood as testaments that basketball had become an institutional constant—that it had truly become an Indian school game. They also changed the nature of that sport by imparting a more open feel and, with their multiple hoops, provided opportunities for more teams to practice more often. They made basketball more of a spectacle by increasing seating capacity, thus allowing hundreds of spectators to ratchet up the excitement while buying twenty-five cent tickets to make it all possible. As students, employees, and townsfolk filled these seats, each in their assigned areas, they collectively expressed a passion for basketball. But the gyms and the sport itself could do only so much to bring these people together beyond the physical sense. They cheered for the same teams but had different ideas about what this experience meant and why Indian school basketball mattered.

4

Bonding with Basketball

Native youths of many tribes formed their first social and emotional connections to basketball within the Indian schools. The sport became so meaningful to many of them during their school days that a passion for it stayed with them throughout their lives. In later years, they would look back fondly on their basketball experiences as positive memories from a time that was, for many, traumatic. They would remember this game as something they embraced on their terms, even though others used it to try to change who they were as Native people.

Through the first half of the twentieth century, Indian school administrators and employees were more effective at encouraging student interest in basketball and boosting their morale with the sport than they were at using it to modify behaviors or identities. This was the case because student athletes were resilient, innovative, and at times rebellious; because employees failed to monitor their play as strictly as policy dictated; and because administrators frequently acted counter to their own stated principles. And so the Indians schools unintentionally permitted Native students to exercise more personal and group autonomy while playing basketball than was prescribed. Students thus discovered they could largely disconnect their participation in the game from distasteful agendas that the schools attached to it.

Given the leeway to do so, Indian school students related to basketball in ways that were relevant to them as youths coping with difficult environments. Not all of them disdained taking the path their superintendents, coaches, and teachers hoped they would. Some accepted that playing organized basketball made them better pupils with brighter futures as economically productive and morally upright American citizens. These students were held up as exemplars of everything administrators said Indian school basketball was about. Not so for the many students who grasped onto the sport just as tightly while rejecting everything the schools stood for. These youths were branded incorrigible but were nevertheless allowed to play. The majority of Native basketballers fell between these poles, staying out of trouble while using the sport as a refuge inside institutional walls and as a means to carve out a better existence for themselves.

The Basketball Spirit

Indian school administrators believed basketball benefited their students in numerous ways beyond improving their physical fitness. Primary among these were the sport's power to instill school spirit and boost morale, whether the students in question were players or spectators. Achieving these objectives would aid student recruitment and make for more contented, compliant pupils. In using basketball and other sports for these purposes, the Indian schools modeled themselves after American high schools and colleges, which had similar incentives for promoting sports among non-Native students.[1] Indian schools thus encouraged students to wave school colors, be they Haskell purple and gold, Chilocco red and white, or St. Francis scarlet and maize. Students also belted out school cheers and sang school songs they were to know by heart, like "Onward Haskell" and "Chemawa We'll Love Thee Forever." Basketball players earned letters they were told to display with pride and with a heightened sense of institutional responsibility. Chemawa "wearers of the C," for example, were told they were public representatives who were not to do or say "anything that would in any way disgrace the name of the school."[2]

To elicit the maximum response, basketball games were grand events, accompanied by waving banners and resounding brass. At Tulalip Indian School in the 1910s, Saturday afternoons in wintertime were designated "half holidays" so students could attend home games. Meanwhile, at the boarding school in Leupp, Arizona, on the Navajo Reservation, basketball was accorded all the pomp of affairs of state, as student motorcades escorted visiting teams to the campus entrance, where they were met by "the reception committee of the day" and "the full school band of twenty-eight pieces."[3]

The rituals surrounding Indian school sports were intended to inspire American patriotism as well. Student athletes played under the American flag and sang patriotic lyrics inserted within school songs. They were taught to be like non-Native students, cheering for their home teams with pride in their hearts for school and country. So when asked by a journalist in 1903 how he inspired Haskell's basketball team, Athletic Director Plank gave the stock reply: "We are training youths for American citizenship. The tune 'America' and the flag, symbols of true Americanism, give us inspiration in such training."[4]

These attempts to bolster school spirit through sports succeeded to a degree. Administrators were pleased to see that students indeed packed the gyms, cheering for their basketball teams as fervently as other American sports fans. School publications reveled in these shows of enthusiasm,

Figure 8. Chemawa's boys (in darker uniforms) center jump against a visiting opponent in the 1950s. The school's cheerleaders sit near center court in a specially designated "Pep" section. RG75, Chemawa Photographs, 1907–71, 1368. Courtesy of NARA, Seattle, Washington.

reporting on Native students at various schools "yelling and cheering" for their varsity teams, making "enough noise to send vibrations to the rafters" and rooting "like fiends." Pupils were just as enthusiastic about interclass games. A nationally syndicated newspaper article reported on Carlisle students in 1904 constituting a "sea of faces" along the elevated running track, watching "every move of the players with intense interest." And at a Haskell interclass tournament final in 1926, a "thousand frenzy [*sic*] students" were said by the *Indian Leader* to have gone "through more states of emotion in five minutes than a motion picture actor does in five reels."[5] As overblown as this latter description may have been, it was an appropriate metaphorical pairing given that, as Agnes Picotte (Lakota) recalls, watching movies and basketball games were two of the most common and anticipated entertainments in the Indian schools.[6]

Many Native students acquired lifelong affinities for their alma maters' athletic teams. They fervently followed them throughout their academic careers and maintained this interest after graduation. Hundreds of them over the years wrote letters to the school superintendents, individually or as representatives of alumni associations, inquiring about the progress of their old teams, urging schools to retain college-level sports schedules, and extending their well-wishes to the younger generations of players.[7]

How satisfying it was for Haskell's Hervey Peairs in May 1917 to open one of these letters postmarked from Cass Lake, Minnesota. It contained pressed Trailing Arbutus flowers picked by elementary schoolchildren and their teacher, Mamie Setter (Chippewa), the former forward and captain of Haskell's inaugural women's basketball team. She told Peairs that her school days had not always been "flowery," but Haskell had prepared her well for life. "I hope these flowers will show a deep, sincere, and cherished memory to my former superintendent and family, and my dear old Alma Mater," she wrote, closing with Haskell's customary cheer: "Sizzle Crackers, Fire Crackers, Sis-Boom-Bah, Haskell Indians, Rah! Rah! Rah!"[8]

To be sure, there were other Mamie Setters out there, but a superintendent could easily be misled by hope to think most former students shared her sentiments. School officials saw how hard their teams played and fervently their students cheered, but the more experienced understood these actions did not necessarily reflect institutional loyalty or, less so, national patriotism. The loudest cheers swelled from the allegiance the young people felt to each other as Native people going through a shared, and often difficult, experience. Within the schools, students from different tribal communities developed shared identities separate from the overarching American identity the schools aimed to impart. As they worked, played, and at times schemed together to get around official restrictions, they put their collective stamp on the schools and sometimes developed a sense of ownership.[9] The pride some took in their school teams, therefore, reflected the bonds they had with each other—a solidarity that both reinforced tribal identities and helped construct new pan-tribal experiences. Many others took no pride whatsoever in the institutions, but they still cheered for their school teams. For them, it was about the Indian people, not the place.[10]

When they applauded and shouted for their shop and class teams, many Native students were also expressing new group identities that while products of the institutional environment were no less meaningful to them. The Haskell sixth grade girls demonstrated such affinity for the sixth grade boys when they inserted a brief note in a March 1900 issue of the *Indian Leader.* It lamented a boys' loss to the ninth graders in an interclass game

Figure 9. Creek and Seminole students enjoying playground basketball at Wewoka Indian School in Oklahoma, ca. 1905. LAB FILM S143:1. Courtesy of Labriola National American Indian Data Center, Arizona State University Library.

as a shared heartache and ended with: "We are just as proud as ever of our boys for they played like professionals." These were kids from different tribes who had come to identify with and care for each other, and with a few words of solace, they showed it.[11]

Even school officials who understood how resistant many students were to appeals for institutional loyalty and American patriotism had another, more cynical reason for serving up basketball; it was a means to maintain sanity—the students', the employees', and quite often their own. They hoped basketball would allay their students' homesickness and malaise, making them easier to recruit, manage, and retain. Superintendent Horace E. Wilson at Fort Berthold Agency (North Dakota) viewed all sports as essential in this regard, linking athletic enticements to the maintenance of boarding school enrollment rates and the annual funding the institutions thereby received. "It is vastly better to keep up the attendance of the school by means of school attractions that tend to absorb and interest the youthful mind," he argued in 1903, "than to drag pupils to a school by police force for the want of such attractions." It was on this logic, he said, that he approved the introduction of "basket ball for the girls and baseball for the boys."[12]

In 1916, Athletic Association Manager Leo Frachtenberg employed the same line of reasoning in an editorial for Chemawa's newspaper. His intent was to rebut critics who said sports were wasteful trifles. In surprisingly candid language for a school publication, he told naysayers they would be wise to consider that few Native students "fully appreciate the value of acquiring learning":

> Not a few of them are sent to the school against their will. This condition must be borne in mind . . . for it will fully explain the desire for play and a good time on the part of the students. Were play and good times withheld from them the probabilities are that the students will not care to return to the school to avail themselves of the opportunity of acquiring knowledge. To many students, knowledge is a bitter pill which, in order to be taken, must be sugar-coated. Athletics offers a good coat of sugar for such a pill.[13]

Basketball continued sugar coating the Indian schools' bitter pills during the 1920s and 1930s. In 1924, Florentine Digmann of St. Francis Mission, in South Dakota, reported that Lakota boarding school students had gone "crazy" for the recently introduced sport and linked this response to a sharp decline in runaway rates.[14] Superintendent Carl Stevens at the government school in Wahpeton, North Dakota, was of the same mindset, regarding basketball as a basic institutional necessity for maintaining morale. "We schedule more games than the average high school," he reported in 1932, "because in a boarding school, we need the entertainment for our children." Stevens especially struggled to keep his boarded students occupied during Christmas break. When their non-Native high school opponents were off for the holidays, Stevens scheduled as many basketball games as possible with independent teams like the Fergus Falls Masonic Temple. These contests effectively consumed the students' interests but also reminded them, inadvertently, that they lived different lives than most American youths. White kids spent Christmas with their families while Native kids were playing basketball.[15]

Basketball was not just offered up for the students' benefit. Administrators knew employees who felt overworked and socially isolated craved entertaining distractions, and so they too were encouraged to salve their spirits on the court. It took little prompting to get Indian school employees to organize their own teams. Female employees at Haskell (both Native and non-Native) were exceptionally eager to start playing in 1900, taking advantage of an opportunity to compete full tilt and let off steam. They appeared at the breakfast table the morning after their first interemployee game with assorted combat injuries: one with a black eye, another with a broken arm, and a third with what a local reporter referred to as a "dislocated vaccinate." Whether in defiance of standard procedures or signaling that the safety of female employees was not as protected as that of female students, these women had thrown caution to the wind and loved every minute. It also became common for employee teams to play against student pickup or varsity teams to promote positive student-staff relations. Chilocco and Albuquerque employees played outside independent teams as well, occasionally traveling away from their home schools for these matchups. These forms of competition had the added benefits of keeping Native employees involved in the sport after graduating from the Indian schools themselves, as well as making them role models for the next generation of student athletes.[16]

Some superintendents personally experienced basketball's power to invigorate and captivate and themselves became aficionados. This personal investment made them more resolute in their belief that basketball benefited their students and employees, but it also blinded them to certain institutional failings in carrying out athletics policies. They were all in for basketball regardless of evidence that suggested it fell short of performing certain assigned tasks.

Often socially isolated and frequently moving from one posting to another, the superintendents and principals craved entertainment as well as contact with their counterparts at distant schools. Scheduling inter-Indian school matchups by mail allowed them to connect through good-natured banter. Basketball talk became a sort of wintertime lingua franca of the Indian Service. Fairly typical dialogue included exchanges like: "Your team plays our team tomorrow night, and I want to give you the opportunity of doing (perhaps?) some plain and fancy gloating;" or "We will show you a good time . . . and in fact be real nice to you in every way except that our girls will give yours a good trimming on the basket ball court." Occasionally, administrators and their spouses traveled with the teams, not only to demonstrate their support but also to enjoy a post-game dinner, a cigarette, and some Indian Service gossip with their hosts.[17]

Some also showed their enthusiasm for the sport by acting the part of cheerleaders. Superintendent Peairs was particularly demonstrative at Haskell, as he was in 1921 when the women's team hosted an opponent from Kansas City. The student spectators were uncharacteristically quiet most of the game, but with the score tied in the final minute, Peairs and two coaches suddenly "appeared on the sidelines and helped turn in a victory by means of their leather lungs." With the crowd finally behind them, Haskell's players eked out the 15–14 win.[18]

Some superintendents even demonstrated their school spirit as players in faculty-student or interstaff games. Peairs and Sharon Mote both took to the court on occasion, as did Standing Rock Agency's superintendent Eugene Mossman, who played one game in 1932 a little too vigorously. He wrote to his peers—"friends in crime" he called them—explaining how he had seriously injured himself in a "good basketball game." "It was a yearly classic which we stage between the employees of the agency and the school here," he said:

> I played guard on the agency team and while my accident happened in the second quarter I played the entire game and you will know that I did the job up properly when I tell you that we beat the school, twelve to nothing. The third vertebrae was smashed and out of place and the fourth vertebrae was cracked. I wore a cast for twenty nine days and if any of you want a taste of the hereafter which all Indian Service employees are expected to experience, just wear a cast from the top of your head to your waist for that long and there will be nothing new when you cross the River and are cast into utter darkness where there is wailing and gnashing of teeth.[19]

Even accounting for his wry humor, and his suggestion that Indian Service employees were headed south in the afterlife, it was obvious that basketball appealed to Mossman on a gut level. The sport was a coping mechanism, helping him deal with life in a stressful and often discouraging job.

School administrators largely succeeded at using basketball to boost morale among the employees and students. The same is true of team athletics in general. Historians have found sports-related memories to be among the most positive that Native alumni have of their Indian school days, including for the many who had negative school experiences overall.[20] The enthusiasm students acquired for basketball and other sports, however, was a complex emotion, varying from one individual to the next. The following accounts of former students highlight both the strong emotional bonds that athletes frequently formed with basketball and with their teammates and the diversity of their attitudes, from the very positive to the very negative, toward the institutions in which they played the sport. These accounts illustrate that while acquiring an affinity for basketball could positively affect student attitudes about their schools, by no means was this always the case.

No former students expressed more positive feelings about the institutions where they had played basketball than Overton "Buck" Cheadle (Chickasaw). He attended Chilocco from 1935 to 1938 and, like most athletic boys in that era, excelled in multiple sports. Basketball and baseball were his favorites, and his experiences playing them contributed to his favorable impression of the school. As a retiree many years later, he used the word "love" when describing both basketball and the place where he learned to play. "Chilocco was the best thing that ever happened to me," he later wrote. "Chilocco gave me some direction to plan for my life. . . . I will always love Chilocco and also remember what it did for me." Basketball's rewards were enduring for Cheadle. His skilled play at Chilocco earned him basketball scholarships to Oklahoma City University and Central State College (future University of Central Oklahoma). He then parlayed this experience into a decades-long career coaching high school basketball in Iowa. None of this meant that he forsook his indigenous identity. Cheadle never forgot the institution that gave him his start, but neither did he lose devotion to his Chickasaw community, which he served for many years as a Tribal Council member. It was with equal measures of pride that he spoke in retirement of his inductions to the Chilocco Indian School Hall of Fame, Iowa High School Basketball Coaches Hall of Fame, and Chickasaw Nation Hall of Fame.[21]

Like Cheadle, Lucille Winnie (Seneca-Cayuga) felt more at home in an Indian school than most Native youths, perhaps because she was the daughter of an Indian Service teacher. Basketball was nonetheless a source of comfort for her, not only as a student at Haskell during the 1910s but also in her subsequent position as a teachers' assistant at Mt. Pleasant Indian School. "There were times when I grew very bored [at Mt. Pleasant], and when I did, I'd take off for the gymnasium and join a physical education class in a game of basketball," she recalled. "The teachers were always understanding and, if they needed me, would send a messenger to the gym to get me." She joined the students playing basketball so often that she became intimately acquainted with the varsity girls' team and its inexperienced, overwhelmed coach. She leapt at the chance when her colleague asked her to take over girls' coaching duties, which allowed her to draw on the in-depth knowledge of the game that she acquired at Haskell. "We went to the boss and discussed this with him," she remembered. "He was in favor of the switch and I was elated. I now had a basketball team . . . as my sole responsibility."[22]

Most students had a much harder time adjusting to Indian school life than Cheadle or Winnie did, but many nonetheless fared better emotionally with basketball than they had before taking up the sport. It changed

Irene Stewart's school life for the better, for example, even though it failed to erase traumatic memories of a childhood spent away from home. She had completed her elementary grades during the 1910s at a boarding school on her home Navajo Reservation to which she was dragged by a tribal policeman. After graduating the sixth grade in 1922, Stewart left the four sacred mountains of Diné Bikéyah for far away Haskell in the rolling green hills of eastern Kansas. Though she had chosen to go willingly, she was overcome by culture shock when she arrived on campus. "When I saw the old grey stone buildings of Haskell, I felt disheartened," she said. "They were far from my happy imaginings about my new school." For two years, Stewart struggled with deep loneliness until she joined a glee club and the basketball team. These activities thrilled her and gave her new friends and the sense of belonging she longed for. Basketball and singing played twin roles in a transformative experience, as they did for thousands of Indian school students who were both athletic and musical.[23]

Countless other Indian school basketballers never acquired Stewart's qualified tolerance of the institutions in which they played. For them, basketball was instead a means to mentally and, for brief periods, physically escape confinement. Those who had the most traumatic school experiences were often unable or unwilling to speak about them in later years. Many died of disease in the schools or vanished while trying to run away for home. Others survived the experience but returned home forever scarred. Peterson Zah's personal insights help explain why many of these students, whose voices are not heard in these pages, chose to play basketball.

Zah was from a later generation than the early Indian school athletes, having attended during the 1950s, and he did not struggle academically, as many youths did. After his time at Phoenix Indian School, he earned a college degree and distinguished himself as one of the most influential leaders ever to serve the Navajo Nation, including as tribal chairman and the first ever tribal president. Like Stewart, Zah experienced a new vitality when he took up organized basketball and other sports in the tenth grade, but these positive emotions did little to alter his opinion of the school. "Boy was I happy, thinking this will keep me sane at this terrible boarding school," he later recalled. "Sports occupied my mind and time. Because going to a boarding school was difficult. You're isolated, you live in a dormitory, you live in a compound. You don't really have access to the outside world. And participating in sports and all of these school activities keeps you occupied and does not allow you to go crazy. It was kind of like my way out of the boarding school system."[24]

Most Indian school administrators failed to understand that for students like Zah, and even for many who spoke less critically of their overall experiences, basketball provided a mental refuge from the institutions they attended rather than imparting a sense of connectedness. Playing basketball and other sports allowed them to enter a world within a world, in the mental, social, and physical senses, where they felt happier, safer, and freer to express themselves as indigenous people than elsewhere on school grounds. This is how Sydney Beane, Jr., a member of the Flandreau Santee Sioux tribe describes his father's experiences as an Indian school athlete in the 1920s, as well as his own during the 1940s and 1950s.[25]

Sydney Beane, Sr., was born on the Yankton Reservation in 1912 and attended two Indian schools in South Dakota—first Rapid City and then Flandreau. Taking up athletics in these schools provided him with teammates and a sense of family and belonging. This was vital for Beane, as it was for other Native students who came from communities that valued family above all and had been wrested away from their own. Although he was fortunate to have his younger brother Orville with him, Sydney bonded so tightly with these teammates as surrogate family members and spent so much time with them that they exercised a profound influence on him. Remarkably, he was from a Nakota-speaking community but became a fluent Lakota speaker while at boarding school. Whether the players spoke this tribal language directly in front of Native coaches at Rapid City and Flandreau his son Sydney, Jr., does not know, but somehow, secreted in the gymnasiums, he learned it by practicing and socializing with Lakota teammates. Everywhere else on campus Native languages were forbidden, as they were in other Indian schools, and so Sydney's future wife, Lillian, who was not an athlete, was losing her tribal language while he was *learning* another.

Just as Sydney Beane, Sr., found a family refuge among his teammates, so did he provide the same for his students and players after graduating and becoming a boys' adviser and coach at Flandreau in the 1930s. He also raised his own family there, including Sydney, Jr., born in 1942. With his father's encouragement, Sydney, Jr., became an exceptional athlete and took great joy participating in track, field events, and basketball. He learned from personal experience how basketball could mentally transport students to a better world and how the gymnasiums where it was played became sanctuaries.[26]

For just a while, says Beane, Native students when they entered the gym to play basketball were freed from the traumas consequent of assimilation policy and life in the boarding schools. The same impulse drove students to participate in other sports. As John Bloom puts it: "When confined within the walls of an Indian boarding school, one must take advantage of any chance to escape."[27] The gymnasiums built to accommodate basketball were happy places for Beane, as they had been for his father, for Lucille Winnie at Mt. Pleasant, and for the so-called gym rats at Haskell. The peculiar smells of those places evoked positive feelings for Beane back then, as they do still: "I mean, I can still smell the gym. There's a certain smell, regarding the powder, and the tape, and the medicine ball—just the floor—I mean that never goes away. It was a special unique place. Nowhere else like it that I could describe . . . just the smell, of the sweat and the other players—almost spiritual. The smell of sage—I mean the smell of a *gym* is like that."[28]

In places where many Native youths experienced deep loss and disconnectedness, what it meant to have access to basketball, teammates, and the physical spaces where they played cannot be overstated. Playing a sport they loved, as well as having all-Indian teams and often Indian coaches, gave Native youths the feeling that "they could more be themselves," says Beane. "It was a refuge. It was a place to find family—that they were familiar with—and reconnect with family that they were being drawn away from. It was just the *joy* of it. Just the *joy* of it."

Shaping Minds, Changing Behavior

Some school administrators and employees believed basketball could do more than inspire institutional loyalty or make students happier. Their views were best communicated by John Keeley, the athletic director for Pierre Indian School in South Dakota. In 1916, he wrote an article for *Spalding's Official Basketball Guide* explaining how the Indian schools used basketball to mold Native youths into model American students. "The Indian is only commencing to learn the white man's customs, his language and his games," Keeley said. "He is by nature a stoic individual and very susceptible to ridicule. It takes several years to make a good basket ball player of him." But with proper coaching, he said, basketball could do wonders for these youths. When the "Indian boy once grasps the true method of the game he makes an excellent player, and I know of nothing that develops his mind and 'brings him out' like this game. A boy may enter basket ball with a lethargic mind and a reticent disposition and come out in a few years well developed bodily, with an active mind and a keen intellect."[29]

In postulating that basketball sharpened the intellect by developing quick thought and mind-body coordination, Keeley and other Indian Service careerists were expressing a physical education philosophy that was common in their day. They added to this the race-based notion that Native youths were particularly in need of a confidence boost to make them assertive Americans, blaming their social reticence on inherent deficiencies rather than acknowledging differing cultural values or the alienation many students experienced in a boarding school. These men also believed that basketball instilled discipline and made students more receptive and compliant. Native basketball players, they contended, were thus learning to think, be assertive, and take direction like model American students.[30]

The Indian schools used basketball to promote discipline in three ways: positively by relying on the orderly design and rules orientation of the game to teach teamwork, sportsmanship, and obedience;[31] passively by keeping youths occupied and out of the mischief bred by idleness;[32] and punitively through threats to withdraw the sport from disobedient or inattentive students who had been encouraged to rely on it. This latter method hinged on students fearing lost opportunities to play the game as well as enjoy its perks. As Concho superintendent Leo S. Bonnin explained to his athletic staff in 1929, all players should be reminded of the "many privileges" enjoyed by varsity athletes so they would feel compelled "to be proficient in all of their studies and in the industrial departments," lest they lose them.[33]

School administrators touted their success translating these educational and disciplinary theories into reality even though they never developed quantifiable measures as proof. They offered only qualitative evidence in the form of student-authored essays in school publications. These pieces reinforced messages the superintendents wished to convey while attesting to the positive influences sports had on the young athletes who authored them.

One of these student pieces appeared in a 1901 issue of the *Indian Leader*, penned by Omer Gravelle (Chippewa), a left fielder in baseball and "back" (guard) on the first basketball team Haskell assembled. "The athletic training the Indian is receiving in the Indian schools," Gravelle proclaimed, "is doing much to elevate him mentally, morally and physically to a height which in a few years will be equal to that of the whites." Sports did so, according to the young Gravelle, by encouraging Native players to think quickly while mastering the use of the English language. Sports also taught "the Indian" to control an inherently "quick" temper so not to surrender a competitive advantage. "When a man is training he is under very strict rules," Gravelle continued, "and this training has a great deal to do with the behavior of the man. He must keep his body in a sound and healthy state in order to accomplish the very best work and a man that has a clean and healthy body can hardly help but have good clean thoughts."[34] A related perspective was provided by a Pawnee student basketball player named David Wright in an article for Chilocco's 1919 *Senior Class Annual*.

He said nothing about inherent indigenous deficiencies but, like Gravelle, asserted that sports promoted a "quick-thinking mind," school loyalty, good sportsmanship, and productive relations with white society.[35]

It is unlikely that Gravelle and Wright developed such ideas and the particular phrasings they used in these essays solely on their own, given that these were internal publications overseen by school employees and administrators; but this does not mean these writings were entirely coerced or insincere. There were many students like Gravelle and Wright, as well as highly educated Indian school graduates like Charles Eastman, who valued what they learned in the schools and truly believed the best way forward for Native people was to seek progressive solutions and accommodate with American society.[36] They were more receptive than most of their schoolmates, therefore, to theories about sports as forms of self-improvement.

Superintendents took heart in what they heard and read from students like Gravelle and Wright and happily gave them a public voice, but they knew many student athletes strayed down different paths. Although it is true that many Indian school athletes did well in their studies and stayed out of trouble, school records fail to demonstrate that basketball or other sports had any profound influence on general academic performance or discipline.[37] Varsity athletes were as likely to struggle in their studies and run afoul of school regulations as other students, if not more so at some institutions. School administrators were well aware of this, yet spoke publicly of the wonders sports were doing for their charges. They did so in large part because they were determined to please their superiors and prove they had practiced what they had preached about athletics, but many were also true believers in the value of organized team sports and were fervent fans. Therefore, they naturally focused more on student athletes who lived up to their high expectations while mentally dismissing problem cases as exceptions to the rule.

Difficulties that Indian schools had molding student behavior through sports participation were the combined results of unreasonable expectations and chronic mismanagement. Students were not so impressionable if they viewed a game like basketball as a refuge, or were especially defiant and determined to retain their personal and group identities. Schools might force a degree of compliance, for what it was worth, by following through with threats to hold such athletes accountable by denying them access to basketball, but administrators were inconsistent enforcers of their own rules, in regard to both informal and varsity forms of play. As a result, ironically, many students regarded basketball and other sports as opportunities to escape or subvert the institutional discipline that those activities were meant to enforce.

Plans to use Indian school sports to mold youth behavior and enforce compliance through institutional rules began unraveling whenever students practiced or played sports without supervision, which was quite often. Through the first third of the twentieth century, superintendents in both the reservation and off-reservation schools commonly reported to superiors their inability to adequately monitor athletic and playground activities due to understaffing. What was a cause of concern for them was a blessing for their students, who took advantage of this lax supervision to escape an otherwise regimented existence, play freely, and bond with peers.[38] Basketball played in seclusion was a powerful experience that contrasted with the military drills, calisthenics, and rote classroom recitations they performed under strict supervision.

Indian school students typically got their first taste of freedom as young children on the playgrounds, participating in the simplest forms of recreation. Adam Fortunate Eagle (Ojibwe), for example, remembers Native boys at Pipestone Indian School in Minnesota during the late 1930s doing what kids often do when left to their own devices, namely, engineering their own playing spaces to test each other's courage. The Pipestone boys gleefully modified the swing sets with boards from the carpentry shop and dared each other to attempt dangerous stunts. School administers and faculty would have been horrified to see this, but they were oblivious. This same playfulness and inventiveness carried over to the dairy barns, outdoor courts, or wherever students erected makeshift basketball hoops. Even though girls were typically monitored much more closely than boys, they too experienced the occasional freedom of playing basketball and other sports under lax supervision. In an interview with Tsianina Lomawaima, a female alum later recalled participating in free play at Chilocco during the late 1920s and early 1930s. "We just went out in the yard, we'd play basketball and different games just kind of like, exercise out there," she said, "but nobody to supervise you or nothing like that [in the sense of directed physical education]. You're just on your own." In these brief moments, playing basketball imparted a thrilling sense of freedom that female students were rarely permitted to experience.[39]

School administrators worried less about the physical injuries students might suffer from unsupervised athletics than about the bad behavioral influences they might have on each other. Positive character-building activities, under such circumstances, could turn morally corrosive; so said an editorial in the February 1915 issue of the *Chemawa American*. Its anonymous author (presumably an athletic staff member or school administrator) preached at great length the gospel of organized athletics. These activities were invaluable in developing "the right kind of tastes" in Indian boys who were "full of vim, and possibly mischief." Unsupervised play at Chemawa, however, was a different matter. When it had been allowed to occur—which had been far too often, the author confessed—it caused "all classes of character and temperaments to intermingle" without direction, enabling less disciplined, more aggressive students to dominate their schoolmates. "It is like corralling a man with a man-eating animal," the editorial warned.[40]

The "man-eaters" of concern to administrators at some reservation boarding schools were not wayward students but older Native boys and men who visited campus unannounced to play pickup basketball. Some were former students who superintendents feared had not taken to heart the lessons they had been taught as Indian school players. At Fort Belknap in 1930, Principal L. E. Dial acted to blunt any insidious influence such interlopers might have. To prevent them from disrupting discipline, he barred older reservation-dwelling boys from playing basketball with his pupils on school grounds. Hoping, on the other hand, that basketball would continue to do these older boys some good, he opted not to cut them off completely. After all, these were former students who Dial did not wish to see stray from the straight and narrow. Instead, he opened the school gymnasium to them two nights a week with the understanding that they would keep clear of the student team practices, conduct themselves decorously, under supervision, and bring their own ball. Whether they complied with these conditions, he never reported.[41]

An account from Paul Moss (Arapaho) suggests that Dial's concerns about losing control of students who played unsupervised basketball with outsiders were not entirely misplaced. He attended boarding school during the late 1910s and 1920s at St. Stephens Mission on Wyoming's Wind River Reservation. Although a Catholic institution, St. Stephens and many of its church counterparts promoted basketball for the same reasons the government schools did and had similar staffing problems supervising informal play. Moss fondly remembered "outsiders," likely boys and young men from the reservation, coming onto school grounds for pickup games. "There were no rules," he said of these games:

> No. On the whistle, we would jump. If you got a hold of the ball, you would take it and run with it. There weren't no dribbling in those days. You would run over there and then you would run with it. No rules. We would go from end to end. You would go and take it and run over there. There used to be somebody just a little bit faster than you. By the time you got to the brick wall, they'd push you. You got a bleeding nose. Start fighting. You had fist fights. They said it was a good game. Outsiders

Figure 10. Navajo boys playing pickup basketball outside the Presbyterian Mission in Ganado, Arizona, during the 1930s. Clarence G. Salsbury Collection, 90-1152. Courtesy of Arizona State Library, History and Archives Division.

> would come in and fight. There was a little circle there. Go ahead and fight. Bleeding. Best ball game we ever had. Now, you can't do nothing. Touch someone, "Technical!" "Personal!"[42]

Here was a sport Native boys played with speed, toughness, and freedom of movement. Here was a way for students to take out aggressions in the shadow of an oblivious authority.

Indian school administrators could not blame every instance of students straying from discipline or succumbing to bad influences playing basketball on inadequate supervision. When varsity athletes were the ones misbehaving, superintendents were often well aware and bore some personal culpability. Whether out of a consuming desire to win or a belief in the power of second chances, these men often let transgressions slide. This was one of the dirty secrets the employees knew to be true despite the superintendents' denials when confronted by Indian Office inquiries. Sometimes varsity athletes were let off the hook in cases where other students would have been severely punished or expelled.

Chilocco's disciplinary problems in the late 1930s and early 1940s serve to illustrate the hypocrisy Indian school administrators were often guilty of when managing their student athletes. One evening in early November 1937, fifteen school employees sat down across the table from Superintendent Lawrence E. Correll. This meeting focused on a cliché subject that educators grappled with across America and that the Indian schools had been hashing out for decades: whether varsity sports encouraged good behavior or bad. "Daddy Correll," as the students called him, had earned a reputation as one of the more compassionate superintendents in the Indian Service, but now he was distraught about a downturn in student discipline.[43] "What is the matter with our students that there is so much unrest?" he asked his staff. "There must be something in the leadership of the boys that isn't quite right. Is football the hub of this unrest? We have two or three good ones. The percentage of dependable boys on the team is quite small!" He spared mention of the basketball team, but they were implicated by the fact that the best athletes played both sports. The curious thing was that athletes were meant to be role models of good behavior, but here they were Correll's leading suspects.[44]

No long-term solutions came of that meeting, and in 1940, Correll and his employees met again, this time focused on athletes' grades and work requirements. Teachers began to ask whether it was true that football and basketball players needed to maintain a "C" average or be cut from the teams and, if so, why the school had been letting them "get by on D's." They asked why players were not being held to the standard of maintaining passing grades in at least three subjects. They shared stories of athletes "sleeping all day" instead of doing required work details. Correll dodged, saying he was unaware of some of these problems, before turning it back on them, telling his faculty and staff they could enforce existing standards. Other employees came to the players' defense, arguing that they "should be given every consideration and an opportunity to make up grades." Another bluntly laid things on the table. "Suppose you have a boy on the athletic team who is an excellent basketball player," he said. "To bar him from playing basketball is depriving him of doing something that he can do." To this, Correll responded, "in that case he should be classed as a special vocational," allowed to make up his work and stay in school. Basketball was supposed to make better students, but here Correll was condoning the uncoupling of sports and academics.[45]

Indian school superintendents were not always so easy on athletes. Varsity basketball players who got in fights on campus, drank, philandered, ran away, or committed other major infractions were sometimes suspended from teams and expelled from schools. Quite often, though, athletes got off with a reprimand, and those who were expelled might subsequently be readmitted after apologizing and agreeing to accept the consequences. There was, for example, the Albuquerque Indian School basketball player in 1927 who, as the conditions for his readmittance after deserting campus, was suspended from the team for a year and put to work operating a concrete mixer to help build a school hospital.[46]

Female students could be expelled for similar reasons, but the names of varsity female players appear far less frequently in Indian school disciplinary and desertion records than do males'. This may not be unusual given that there were fewer female players to begin with and male pupils generally got into more trouble, but it raises a question, unanswerable by written records, of whether female players took something different from basketball than did their male counterparts. Perhaps basketball promoted better discipline among them because they were more closely monitored and chaperoned than males on campus and on the road. The male-female discrepancy may also point to the fact that stardom rarely descended on female basketball players the way it did on male students who excelled in multiple sports, and so they were less influenced by the social pressures and temptations accompanying such a status.[47]

On the many occasions when school superintendents let male athletes get by with disciplinary infractions or low academic performance, they followed through only on the first half of their basketball carrot-and-stick schemes. Varsity basketball became a valued privilege, but one the best athletes knew would not be taken away if they strayed from discipline. Some school administrators who broke their own rules when star athletes were involved may only have cared about institutional glory and been negligent or corrupt in their duties. At least a few, though, were compassionate hypocrites who treated their student athletes as the complex and resilient young people they were. They developed personal sympathies for male athletes with whom they were better acquainted than most students because of their local celebrity status.

Lawrence Correll's pronounced leniency toward Chilocco's athletes in 1940, for example, is not surprising given how compassionately he spoke about his school basketball players earlier in his career. In 1908, for example, Correll received a disciplinary report on one of the varsity players from his disciplinarian, who referred to the student as a "good athlete" with a "bad disposition." Correll was more nuanced and paternal in his response. He referred to the young man as "real bright" and a "capable student" who just happened to have a "hot temper." While acknowledging that this exceptional player had been hard to control and "stubborn and head strong," Correll counseled that "you can accomplish most any end by appealing to his sense of honor and justice but cannot get results by commanding him to do anything."[48] One wonders if he would have been so aware and understanding of a Native student who was not a varsity athlete. Correll was one of many superintendents, notably including Hervey Peairs, who formed personal bonds with athletes (especially males) and maintained these relationships for many years thereafter. They commonly wrote references for their employment, often times regardless of how disciplined they had been as students.[49]

The Indian schools also had difficulty controlling basketball's behavioral influences because athletic staff members had their own agendas and philosophies. In theory, the athletic and physical education programs operated through a chain of authority headed by the superintendents, but as has been noted, most superintendents deferred week to week operations, including disciplinary matters, to their athletic staff. The chain of command was especially loose when superintendents could not afford to assign permanent employees to these positions and relied instead on outside volunteers or contract staff to coach their teams. The best known of these outsiders, when it came to basketball, was Forrest "Phog" Allen, the man who would later be known as the "father of basketball coaching" but who in 1907 was still a young man looking for any opportunity to develop his craft. He spent just a season coaching Haskell while simultaneously coaching the teams at Baker University and the University of Kansas. Spending only two hours of each busy day on Haskell's campus, he scarcely had time to learn about or enforce institutional policies, even if he cared to.[50]

When superintendents did assign permanent employees coaching duties, they tended to follow consistent logic. The close association they made between discipline and sports often led them to appoint school disciplinarians, who were responsible for supervising male student conduct, to supplemental posts as athletic directors and coaches. U. S. G. Plank, at Haskell, was one of many Indian school careerists who simultaneously wore three hats as disciplinarian, athletic director, and multisports coach. In the 1930s, the disciplinarians were rebranded "boys' advisers," but their tasks remained the same. Although the disciplinarians' female equivalents, known as matrons, were less commonly associated with athletics, at least at Chemawa, supervising girls' basketball was an official part of their job description.[51]

Many disciplinarians who were assigned coaching responsibilities were former Indian school athletes. More than a dozen male graduates served in these dual capacities at various schools between 1900 and 1930, including ex-superstar athletes Wilson "Buster" Charles (Oneida) and John Levi (Arapaho), as well as Sam McLean (identified only as "Sioux"), a talented artist who served as athletic director and boys' basketball coach at Pierre

Indian School. Sydney Beane, Sr. later held coaching positions under the boys' advisor title.[52] Superintendents favored these arrangements because they assumed these were men who young Native athletes would naturally admire and obey.[53] To formalize things Haskell even instituted a two-year physical education course in the late 1920s to specifically train "boys for positions as disciplinarians and coaches in the Indian Service."[54]

Having Natives in these positions, as opposed to non-Natives, did not necessarily alter the intensity or structure of school discipline. Many of these Native athletic directors and coaches believed in the importance of an education and viewed sports in ways similar to the superintendents under whom they served. In fact, they were sometimes more insistent that varsity athletes abide by the rules than superintendents were. They were not, however, mere pawns in the Indian Service. Native coaches did not discard their indigenous identities or follow orders blindly. As Cathleen Cahill has argued, Native people had diverse reasons for seeking employment in the Indian Service and many were critical of assimilation and other aspects of federal policy to various degrees. They often valued American Indian identities, argued against abusive practices, and acted as mediators between their communities and the federal government.[55] The same can be said of Native athletic directors and coaches who were commonly very protective of their athletes (perhaps explaining why some were stricter with them) and advocated on their behalf. The Native men, and occasionally women, who held athletics positions, aware of the considerable authority they often exercised in the athletic realm, tended to be assertive both in their dealings with students and with school administrators.

Among the Native men who acted simultaneously as disciplinarians and athletic staff members, none was a stronger presence or served longer than George W. Bent, Jr., the part Southern Cheyenne-Kiowa grandson of famed trader William Bent. After graduating from Haskell's Normal Department in 1899, the star quarterback began a thirty-five-year career in the Indian Service, acting as a disciplinarian, bandmaster, teacher, Boy Scouts leader, athletic director, and coach at many of the largest Indian schools. Although he struggled with a chronic throat ailment that forced him to quit various postings, he was assertive in applying for new ones, arguing that Haskell's graduates were as capable as Carlisle's of handling demanding jobs. One such job he was tasked with by virtue of being a disciplinarian was tracking down and returning student runaways. While working at Chilocco in 1910, he was said by a Topeka reporter to carry out this duty "just as diligently as a sheriff hunts a criminal."[56]

Bent was indeed a strict disciplinarian and dedicated coach who enthusiastically practiced what school officials preached. At his graduation from

Haskell, he gave an address titled "Education through Self-Activity" urging students to capitalize on any opportunity to improve their stations in life. He stuck with this philosophy throughout his career, consistently demanding that his charges fly right and arguing against any laxity in discipline for star athletes. For example, when one of Chemawa's expelled basketball players asked to be readmitted after punching another student in 1925, Bent urged Superintendent Harwood Hall to remain firm. "If we are going to establish a rule that those expelled should not be allowed to re-enter school," he argued, "we should stick to it." Nor was he afraid to scold the administration for allowing athletes to skip out on required marching drills or pull "thru the school year without accomplishing very much."[57] Bent's athletes knew he expected much but also that he was a concerned coach who would take heat for them. He did exactly that in 1922 following a boxing and wrestling meet at Salem Senior High School. After the opposing coach accused him and his athletes of shouting insults at a referee, Bent accepted full responsibility to deflect criticism from his boys, even though he had, in fact, done nothing wrong. He sent a letter of apology before Superintendent Hall had time to tell Salem's principal that Bent was innocent of the charge. The true culprits, Hall said, had been Chemawa's student cheering section.[58]

Bent's assistant disciplinarian at Chemawa, Reginald Downie (Klallam), proved just as diligent a coach after he took over that duty under Bent's direction. The two men had known each other since Downie played for Coach Bent on Chemawa's basketball team. Fifteen years Bent's junior, Downie—known to Bent and his friends as "Reggie"—had been a multisport star at the school. In 1914, he had been class president while simultaneously captaining the football and basketball teams. Four years after graduating, Downie was drafted to serve in Europe during World War I. While there, he was caught in a German gas attack that left him suffering from a chronic respiratory illness. Both he and Bent had difficulty speaking without pain during their Indian Service careers, but this did not stop either from asserting themselves with their athletes and supervisors.[59]

The two men maintained a good working relationship at Chemawa, but Downie was the softer touch. He was no pushover to be sure, even recommending on one occasion that a star basketball player be expelled for being a "continual disturber" off the court.[60] Downie was inclined though, to show leniency to athletes he deemed worthy of second chances. In 1926, for example, he kept his composure while one of his baseball players shouted profanities in his face and challenged him to a fight in front of the entire team. Downie managed to reestablish "amicable relations" with the player and dissuaded Superintendent James McGregor from expelling him. This was a good boy, he argued, who should be forgiven for his occasional bouts of anger.[61] In this case and others, Downie may have acted more deliberately as a buffer between institutional authority and his players than he let on. Years later, in 1937, he revealed his true feelings about the assimilation policy that held sway during his coaching years at Chemawa. He sent a letter to *Indian Education* in response to an article titled "Why the Boarding School Fails," which detailed the harms that forced assimilation had done to Native youths. Downie simply wrote: "The truth in this article . . . is the reason for this note of appreciation."[62]

It may have been out of similar disdain for the institutional mission that some Native employees allowed student athletes to stray further from discipline than even Downie considered prudent. Some were far from strict, instead permitting basketball players to subvert rules they deemed irrelevant or offensive. One such incident occurred at Rapid City in 1925, when three employees allowed some boys to skip their required religious instruction period to play pickup basketball in the gym. This drew Superintendent Sharon Mote's sharp rebuke. How could he maintain order and impart Christian values, he reasoned, if students were granted sanctuary on a basketball court? Henry Flood, the Lakota coach at Flandreau during Sydney Beane, Sr.'s playing days, may also have permitted, or encouraged, players to speak their forbidden language in the gym. Who was to know if he did? After all, this physical space was a coach's domain.[63]

The superintendents thus got more than they bargained for when they made former Native students their athletic staff. They were the role models superintendents hoped they would be and were invaluable in maintaining a semblance of discipline and consistency within school athletic programs, but they had an independent influence over students that was difficult for the superintendents to check. So many Indian school coaches were Native—no fewer than fifty serving at multiple institutions between 1900 and 1950[64]—that students' memories of the game were inevitably intertwined with those of athletic men like Sydney Beane or women like Lucille Winnie, who were a big presence in their lives during hard years away from their own families.[65]

Agnes Picotte remembers Bob Clifford (Lakota) being this sort of presence for kids at the Holy Rosary Mission school on South Dakota's Pine Ridge Reservation. Clifford built the basketball program there from scratch and oversaw it at all levels between 1925 and 1962, including coaching the highly competitive girls' and boys' varsity teams. There was no doubt who was the face of basketball at this Indian school. When it came to that sport, "whatever he said went," remembers Picotte. "He called the shots." "Did players like Clifford?" I asked her. "Oh, they loved him, oh yes," she responded. "If he came around, you know, he was like a star. And in physical education class, if he talked to you, everybody thought that was great. . . . And on the playgrounds, they all came around him. The little kids would go and grab his hand or they'd hug him. But us, the bigger ones, we would just be in his presence. We thought that was great."[66]

Basketball's Rewards

Indian school students knew the many ways that playing basketball made life in these institutions more tolerable and at times rewarding. There were the many benefits described in the preceding pages: the opportunities to perpetuate athletic traditions in new forms and be competitors as their ancestors had been; the camaraderie and sense of having surrogate families; gaining refuge within a difficult environment, even if only temporarily so; and most of all, the pure joy of playing a good game and feeling free while doing so. Gender as always altered the experience. Male single-sport athletes used basketball as their sole means to acquire these benefits, while multisport players relied on it only to maintain access to them between football and baseball seasons. For female students, basketball was all there was, and it came in the late fall and melted away each spring.

There were still more benefits that came to those who played at the varsity level, including better food. It smacked of inequity to Indian Service critics and students alike that varsity athletes ate well while their schoolmates were often malnourished. Carlisle's training tables were designed specifically to fuel its football and track teams to victory, but as the top athletes at that school played three or four varsity sports, a large percentage of the basketball and baseball teams were also represented at the tables.[67] Students blessed to eat at one of them enjoyed the company of their teammates as they consumed a greater quantity and variety of foods than did students in the dining hall. Haskell maintained a training table for basketball as well as football. So did many other off-reservation schools after 1900. Located in a separate room with a specially detailed cook, Haskell's table allowed the athletes to eat anything they requested pending their coach's approval.[68] Lucille Winnie remembered the good fortune she had to have an athletic sibling at Haskell during the 1910s. "During my first month there, I would have died of malnutrition had I not had a big brother on the football team," she said. "They had a special training table, and I always found my way there for the evening meal. . . . The football team was served juicy steaks and other 'good eats,' and brother and his teammates always saved something for me."[69]

If they were not lucky enough to have kin on one of the boys' teams, female students were denied access to these tables, except in the rare instances when the girls' basketball team had their own. There is scant evidence of these girls' basketball tables existing, but at least one Indian school had them. In 1905, Superintendent Harwood Hall, who was at that time stationed at the Sherman Institute in California, instructed the cook to set one up to make the team more competitive. "It is desired to have a training table in the children's dining room for the [girls'] Basket Ball team, consisting of six members," he said. "I wish you would arrange it, and give these girls plenty to eat; steak, potatoes, rice, hominy, and everything that tends to make them strong, out of such materials as you have issued."[70]

There was even better food and more excitement available at the athletic banquets. These were grand feeds like nothing Native youths had experienced since leaving home. If they were a form of bribery, used by school officials to entice students to play sports and mold their behavior once they did, so were they means for students to get what they needed to cope with school life. Multiple times a year, varsity athletes attended these celebratory dinners where awards were distributed and speeches made to impress on them the importance of success and sportsmanship. The Haskell boys' basketball team began to attend these at Peairs' invitation around 1900. Before that, this sort of gala event, complete with "old gold and royal purple" centerpieces and oysters from Wiedmann's store on the west side of Lawrence, had been the football team's pleasure. Now it was the basketball players' turn to feast while sitting through obligatory speeches about sportsmanship and instrumental selections from the school band. Basketball players attended similar banquets at other Indian schools, including at Chemawa in 1927 where they enjoyed a multicourse meal with pork roast, ice cream, and coffee.[71]

These banquets also provided prized opportunities for young men to impress young women at schools where dating opportunities were restricted. In the first place, the players could enjoy being guests of honor in front of female students from the domestic science departments who commonly served as the waitstaff. They were also, on occasion, allowed to invite dates to these events, making for potentially awkward situations where female students who were not asked out served female friends who were. Female varsity players were sometimes included in cogendered multisport athletic banquets, starting in the 1920s, but they more commonly attended modest suppers with guest teams and coaches—and without dates.[72]

The Indian schools went to great lengths to disconnect basketball from romance, but the two rewarding activities often went hand in hand. This policy reflected the strict gender separations that the schools endeavored, but chronically failed, to maintain. The campuses created physical barriers between male and female students through the use of separate dormitories with no-man's-land green spaces in between; separate seating areas in dining halls; and separate gymnasiums, when possible, for each sex.[73] These demarcations carried over to athletic spectators as well, as students were commonly required to sit in gender-specific sections at outdoor sporting events and indoor basketball games. The strict gender lines characteristic of the turn of the century were still drawn well into the 1930s. In 1937, Chemawa boys sat on the west side of the gym for basketball games and girls on the east. The boys had to remain seated at the end of each contest until the girls had been escorted by adult chaperones out of the building.[74]

As they often did with any school restrictions, many students found ways around these rules. They could do something as innocent as Asa "Ace" Daklugie (Apache) did at Carlisle football games when he and his love furtively exchanged a "silent greeting" each time the female students were escorted past the boys' section.[75] Or they could try to get away with a serious infraction, as two young couples from Chemawa did in 1931. The four students snuck out of the stands for the duration of an away basketball game to have some alone time, only to be caught trying to sneak back onto Chemawa's return bus—school spirit and love for the game obviously not being the only passions that drew students to sporting events.[76]

Athletes were also known to break dating regulations. Although vigorous sports were said to relieve sexual energies, administrators knew the two pursuits were sometimes connected. They let slide the fact that some male athletes had numerous love interests and went on unsanctioned dates, so long as they did not desert or commit other serious infractions. The basketball player that Bent finally helped expel in 1925 for fighting, for example, had long been known for his amorous exploits. In response to Correll's questions about disciplinary problems at Chilocco in the late 1930s, one employee made a telling juxtaposition: "Unless such subjects as *sex*, *crime*, *athletics*, and a few others are discussed, it really is a difficult matter to determine just what constitutes each student's interests" (emphasis added).[77]

Whether they stayed within the lines the schools drew for them, students inevitably sought out their love interests. Basketball could bring them together, as this was the sport where varsity male players most commonly shared experiences with female players. Reginald Downie was among those who met his future spouse in the Indian schools. He and schoolmate Rose O'Brien were forwards for their respective teams at Chemawa before he left for the Great War. They were married a year after he returned. The Downies thereafter modeled marital partnership for their students; she was a school matron and coached the girls while he coached the boys. The two stayed together, a basketball family, until Reginald passed away in 1943.[78]

Basketball also won its most skilled players acclaim from their peers. This school fame may not have been something that everyone wanted or that served well everyone who received it. Frequently told stories of sports legends like Louis Sockalexis and Jim Thorpe confronting their fame, and too often public abuse, point to the difficulties stardom could bring Native professional athletes who were accustomed to kind expressions of kinship and community.[79] Some basketball players may have struggled silently with their local celebrity on Indian school stages as well, but many clearly took pride in their accomplishments, and their fellow students freely expressed admiration for them.

Signs of the local fame many athletes achieved included the nicknames they carried through their school years and saw used in school publications to hype their individual accomplishments—although normally only if they were boys or men. Whites only used "Chief" as a nickname for Native sports stars, but in the schools, students gave each other names like John "Skee" Levi, Harry "Hambone" Jones, Egbert "Eg" Ward, and "Push 'em up" Tony Wapp. The best of them were also selected as team captains by their teammates, an honor they wore as public badges signifying their peers' respect for their athletic and leadership skills. Beyond these honors, there was the cheering the standout players heard in their ears, the words of praise students wrote about them in school publications, and the crowds of youngsters gathering around them whenever they walked down the hall or across campus grounds.[80]

Sean Patrick Sullivan argues that the celebrity status that student athletes sought out and achieved at the Albuquerque and Santa Fe Indian schools represented a departure from indigenous cultural traditions. This status-seeking, competitive behavior was a manifestation of the "individualistic mindset" they developed through athletic participation, expressing American values the schools imparted to serve the assimilationist agenda.[81] This is an important argument, especially concerning students from tribal communities where individualistic behavior was particularly taboo (like many Southwestern groups that had youths attending Albuquerque and Santa Fe). Native students may have been acting like other twentieth-century Americans when they elevated their sports icons and lavished them with praise, but there is another way to look at things. While some Native students and employees viewed athletic status-seeking in the Indian schools as counter to tradition, others regarded it as a perpetuation

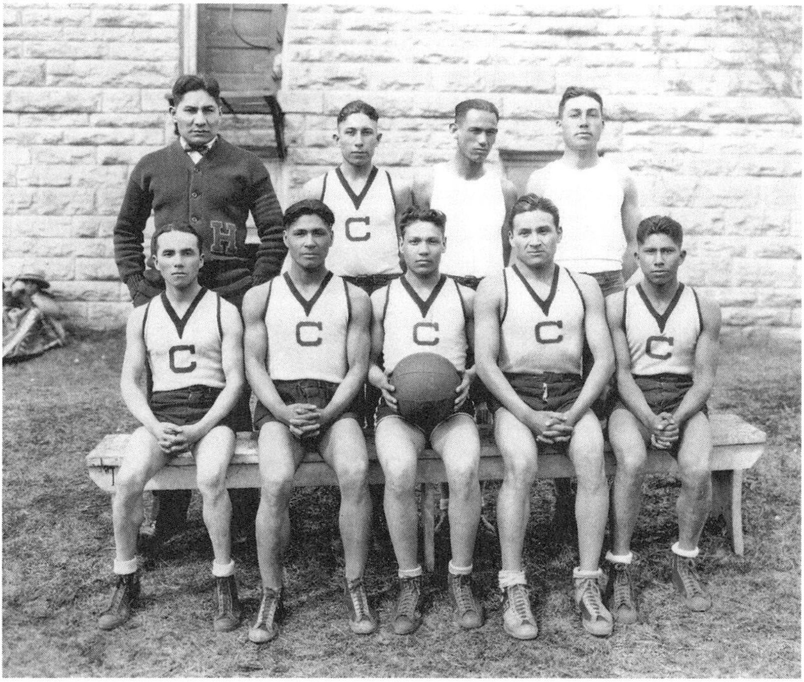

Figure 11. Chilocco's 1926 team with new Coach John Levi still wearing his Haskell letter sweater with pride. Florence Correll Collection. Courtesy of the Gateway to Oklahoma History, Oklahoma Historical Society, ark:/67531/metadc1079866.

of traditional social reciprocity. The praise Native players received from their schoolmates was not the superficial sort people showered on professional athletes. Absent the role models of success Native youngsters would have had in their home communities, older student athletes performed vital social functions. If these local stars abused their celebrity, as some did, then their behavior ran counter to traditional values, but many of them, like John Levi, understood that being honored by their peers obligated them to give something in return.

Coach Frank McDonald, for example, remembers the way Levi mentored and cared for younger athletes who idolized him at Haskell during the 1920s:

> Whenever possible John would be available when they came running from the school building and when they saw him the shouts would go up "Skee-Skee-Skee." He would always give them a pat on their back, ruffle up their hair, or pick them up and hold them high in the air with

a big boyish smile. Yes, John was good for the young "Gym Rats." I honestly believe he kept them from becoming homesick as it was apparent the affection that normally would go to their parents was poured out to John. He returned it in kind—and in doing so he was giving them something they needed.[82]

Like so many Native athletes in the schools, John Levi was loved, and he gave love in return to youngsters who desperately needed it. John and the other varsity athletes were also getting something they needed from these exchanges. As they searched for ways to gain their bearings and social acceptance in the Indian schools, basketball and other sports proved essential. Success in athletics increased their self-esteem and allowed them to be somebody worthy of admiration. This especially mattered after they had been torn from their home communities and denied access to traditional means to earn respect. Perhaps more than any other activity, sports provided a path to acceptance and respect in schools where age, tribal affiliation, and one's degree of Native heritage could otherwise make a student feel the outsider, even among all-Native schoolmates.[83]

Played within campus confines, basketball proved deeply meaningful to students. The schools were unable to fully dictate this meaning. Instead, on their own terms, Native people of all ages bonded with basketball and, through it, with each other. It became a multitribal, multigenerational cultural phenomenon within the schools, but everything was taken to another level when teams ventured beyond campus to compete against white opponents. In the world outside, they would enjoy still more rewards basketball had to offer but also experience its darker side.

5

The World Outside

Indian school administrators believed their students benefited even more from playing interscholastic basketball than from playing the sport as an intramural. Only by competing against whites, they said, did this activity expose students to the dominant society and promote their integration. In this context, the sport served both public relations and educational functions. Through demonstrations of "clean playing" and "gentlemanly behavior," Native basketballers proved the merits of an Indian school education and convinced white Americans they could be productive citizens.[1] The involved travel, social interactions, and competitions were also said to provide them with real-life experience and instill the confidence necessary to succeed in the world.

What the administrators failed to acknowledge was that the American public was not fully supportive of this integrationist scheme, nor were Native athletes. Some non-Native teams greeted their Indian school opponents with compliments and smiles; others with insults and thrusted elbows. Reporters praised their abilities while using racist stereotypes to market them to the public. Referees tasked with giving them a fair chance at success appeared to be biased against them. In these ways, the non-Native sports world welcomed Native basketball players partway through the door, seeking them out as athletes while refusing to embrace them as social equals.[2] This conflicted reality encouraged Native youths to regard interscholastic basketball not as a pathway to assimilation but rather as a means to win some peoples' respect while remaining outsiders.

Indian school students also valued interscholastic basketball for reasons having nothing to do with pleasing non-Natives. In addition to the practical and social privileges varsity basketball brought them on campus, they appreciated the opportunities it gave them to get away from the schools and see places and things they otherwise would not have, including parts of Indian country that were unknown to them. They particularly relished the chances basketball gave them to visit bustling cities like St. Louis and Chicago. This did not mean, however, that they desired to become culturally non-Native. Just as older relatives had joined Wild West shows in the 1880s searching for opportunity and adventure, so did Indian school athletes use football, baseball, and now basketball to explore their surroundings. American Indian people had always journeyed to experience the world. Now they did it with basketballs in their hands.[3]

Interscholastic basketball did provide Indian school athletes with a real-world education, even if the results were not exactly what the superintendents hoped for. Many of its lessons were bitter, but players made the best of their situations and found the thrill of competition empowering. Playing basketball allowed them to stand up to prejudice in ways they would have been punished for in other contexts. Within gymnasium confines, they argued and fought back at times or simply silenced their critics by posting wins. By enabling them to transcend conflict in an interracial context, basketball took on still greater meaning to American Indian youths. It became a valued means for them to prevail in the face of adversity and to assert Native pride.

Home and Away

In the same 1916 *Spalding's* article where John Keeley raved about basketball's power to shape Native student intellects, he also emphasized the sport's ability to promote racial integration. It did this, in part, by making Natives confident that they could succeed in a white man's world. "It is in the excitement of a contest that the Indian is at his best," Keeley said. "He feels that here he is an equal with all, as his race has been known as a race of athletes for generations." In Pierre, South Dakota, and its environs, Keeley said, interracial basketball had also brought about "a much closer relationship between the white and Indian youth, as the fact that the Indian is holding his own, mentally as well as physically, has caused the white man to look upon him more as an equal, while the Indian feels more as a brother to his white neighbor."[4]

The majority of Indian school administrators who shared Keeley's perspective believed interracial competition was beneficial whether played at home or on the road. Hosting home games allowed them to create opportunities for white and Native youths to socialize on Indian school courts, in their dining halls, and overnight in the dormitories. Hosting white teams also allowed the schools to show off their operations to these visitors who, it was hoped, would relay positive reports back to their communities, thus eliciting more public support for the institutions.[5]

Away games, despite the travel costs involved, were nonetheless considered more beneficial to Native pupils than playing home games. Only on the road, administrators said, did Native youths experience the advantages of American society and learn to make their way. Pop Warner at Carlisle even argued that sports travel was "as much, if not more" beneficial to Native students than the "steady grind of school work." These road experiences better prepared them "to fight the battles of life," he said, because the athletes were compelled to navigate the outside world in real time, with only their coaches to guide them.[6] The schools thus sent their teams on the road for much the same reason they sent students to live and labor in white households for extended periods through formalized "outing" programs. One in play, the other in work, both initiatives were designed to immerse Native youths in white society and thereby ease their social and cultural transition to citizenship. Basketball did this less intensively than the outings, through many short forays rather than through prolonged stays, but it exposed students to an even broader expanse of the country and emboldened students by allowing them to taste the thrill of victory.[7]

When venturing out, most Indian school basketball teams went by automobile, putting thousands of miles on aging sedans each season. Native students were more than happy to go on these extended journeys. They usually meant enduring bumpy roads while crammed together in a backseat, but they were worth the discomfort to escape the drudgery of work details and to get out and do something enjoyable. During the Depression, the Bismarck girls' team motored in a 1928 Willys-Overland Whippet that their superintendent said was "disreputable in appearance and very unreliable in performance." Every pot hole sent shocks up their spines and sapped their pre-game energy. Bigger school teams had it better, often traveling in buses like Albuquerque's spacious Diamond T built to seat twenty. On the Washington coast, Tulalip's girls avoided the roads altogether, traversing Possession Sound in a launch called the Ranger. The boat carried them, shivering across winter waters, twenty miles or more to play high schools on the outskirt of Seattle. Male and female teams from Chemawa and Haskell had it best, often taking trains and sometimes overnighting in Pullman coaches to big-city games hundreds of miles away.[8]

On longer journeys lasting more than a day, students were meant to benefit from the passing wonders they saw out their windows, the sites they stopped to tour, and the social interactions as much as they were from on-court experiences. Even dining and lodging arrangements served dual practical and policy functions. To socialize Native and white youths, visiting and host schools often had their players eat together in the cafeteria. Although lodging was usually secured in local hotels, Native athletes occasionally boarded with white students in college dormitories or, when playing at high schools, in opposing players' family homes. Such arrangements made these visits ideal opportunities to promote interracial friendships and, for female teams, to impart an appreciation of Victorian domesticity.[9]

Meetings between Native and white female teams were meticulously planned affairs that were meant to ease members of both races into accepting racial integration. The young Native women were met at train stations by opposing teams and whisked away for town tours and receptions held in their honor.[10] A game against Topeka High School in March 1901 thus spelled a busy two days for Haskell's team. A Saturday morning train ride gave way to an afternoon of tea and guided tours. Then came an evening game beginning at 7:30 and ending at 9:30 in a 19–15 Topeka victory. Haskell's players then split up for late dinners and sleepovers in their counterparts' homes, waking Sunday morning for breakfast and services—one of their denominational choices being a Methodist church where they were shown the mechanical workings of a newfangled electric pipe organ.[11]

On these trips, for female athletes, there was no escaping strict supervision. Whether they were teenage girls or young women in their early twenties, female players were closely chaperoned by their coach, who could be a man or a woman, and one or more female school employees to keep them safe and on script. School officials insisted that players maintain a womanly decorum in all interactions with the non-Native public. This was the case throughout the first half of the twentieth century. Early in the 1930s, for example, Superintendent Sharon Mote regularly gave the Bismarck girls and their chaperones pre-trip lectures to remind them there was to be no smoking, gum chewing, or "rolled stockings" on the road. "Let it be said after we are gone—'Bismarck girls were the best behaved,'" he always exclaimed, adding: "Rather have that than medals and cups."[12] As constricted as they were on the road by gender-biased rules, these travels still provided young Native women with rare opportunities to see the world and assert themselves in non-Native society. Many would look back fondly on these forays throughout their lives.[13]

Traveling rules for the boys or men were more lax. Their teams had smaller entourages, usually consisting of just the players and their head coach. When the coaches were former students, this meant the entire contingent was Native with no white authority figures present for days or weeks. To an even greater degree than within the home gymnasiums, Native coaches were autonomous on the road and loomed large in their players' lives.[14]

As with the female teams, there were efforts to maximize the educational value of longer trips for male teams through side excursions meant to impress on them the benefits of American civilization. In February 1907,

Figure 12. The Haskell Indians visiting Chicago in 1907. *Seated left to right*: Alex Baird, Levi Dupuis (team captain), Joe Crotzer (in Juniors uniform), and Frank Fish. *Standing left to right*: Coach George Shawnee, Napoleon Barril, Frank Means, Louis Dupuis, William Prophet, and Leonard Gillenwater. Captain Dupuis's well-worn sole hangs lose from his right shoe. Chicago Sun-Times/Chicago Daily News Collection, SDN-005499. Courtesy of Chicago History Museum.

for example, Coach George Shawnee (Shawnee) took his nine Haskell varsity players on a three-week, three-thousand-mile train journey throughout the Midwest. Along the way, they made scheduled tours of the Loose-Wiles Biscuit factory in Kansas City; the US Post Office, Art Institute of Chicago, and Board of Trade in Chicago; the World's Fair grounds and Art Museum in St. Louis; the National Cash Register works in Dayton; and the Ohio State Capitol building in Columbus. All highlighted America's business, cultural, and political might. Their additional tour of the Ohio State Penitentiary perhaps sent a different message, reminding players of the fate awaiting young men who strayed from the straight and narrow.[15]

School administrators calculated that the public relations, socialization, and educational benefits of sports travel outweighed the financial and human costs. They were thus willing to break even or lose modest sums to tour their basketball teams and to risk the physical dangers involved in dispatching them over treacherous winter roads. They knew that placing poorly maintained vehicles on icy highways was a recipe for trouble. Breakdowns and slide-offs left some teams stranded, shaken, and bruised in below-freezing temperatures.[16] At least one accident, in late January 1937, proved fatal. A bus carrying the Chilocco boys' varsity team to Dodge City, Kansas, was struck at a train crossing by a Santa Fe locomotive barreling out of the sleet and fog. Four players were injured and one killed instantly, while driver Jefferson Mouse (Cherokee), who was also the assistant coach and physical education director, died the following night from massive head trauma. Buck Cheadle was one of only three team members who came through unscathed. The tragedy ended the school's competitive year, but they were back on the road the following winter.[17]

Superintendents also permitted basketball trips to interfere with players' vocational and academic instruction for extended periods, although they usually avoided scheduling games midweek.[18] The sport was especially demanding on male students. Their teams traveled frequently during seasons lasting from late December through February or early March. Schedules were erratic in the 1890s and early 1900s as Indian schools struggled to locate opponents in years before the sport's full blossoming throughout the West. During the first decade of the 1900s, only Chilocco and Haskell consistently played ten or more games a year, evenly split between home and away. Other male Indian school teams did not develop consistent interscholastic schedules until after 1910, but most were playing between ten and thirty games annually by the 1920s.[19]

Most weeks, male teams missed only Friday classes and were back on campus within two days after departing for away games. This was not always the case however. Early in the century, Chilocco and Haskell sent their teams on extended barnstorming treks throughout the Midwest to play college and independent competitors. Haskell's 1908 tour lasted two months, traversing seven states before the team returned mid-March. The large off-reservation schools gave up these extended journeys after 1910 and, like the smaller schools, began scheduling regional tours within a radius of about two hundred miles once or twice a season.[20]

Concho, in Oklahoma, broke from this post-1910 trend by setting out on a 1930 barnstorming trip reminiscent of those that its larger sister schools once took. Riding in two cars, its boys' team covered two thousand miles in nineteen days, winning seven of twelve games played in three states. Along the way, they spent nights at three host Indian schools, a few hotels and private homes, and, in Tulia, Texas, an unheated courthouse jury room. When not in transit or practicing for an evening game, they went sightseeing. They spent a night at the movies in Albuquerque, visited the Palace of the Governors in Santa Fe, and watched a Corn Dance at Isleta Pueblo. Although the Isleta visit occurred when references to tribal traditions were no longer taboo in the Indian schools, it still had an assimilationist purpose. Coach John Kirk happily reported to Superintendent Leo S. Bonnin that his players noted that they spoke better English than their Southwestern hosts. "The knowledge alone of actually seeing how the New Mexico Indians live, look, talk and act will be of use to them as a comparison of their own achievements," Kirk said.[21]

At most Indian schools through the 1930s, basketball alone accounted for an average of ten to twenty days away from campus each year for male players—not too excessive—but these days added up for the multisport athletes. Even accounting for the portion of baseball season extending through summer break, these unremitting sportsmen spent significantly more time away from school than their classmates did. More than a few went from wearing football cleats, to gym shoes, to baseball cleats with no breaks between. It was unrealistic to expect the most involved athletes to excel in their academic work given their exhausting athletic schedules. That many of them did was a credit to their abilities and determination.

Female basketball was not as disruptive to academics. Between 1900 and 1905, girls played more extensive interscholastic schedules than boys at Albuquerque, Fort Shaw, Phoenix, and Sherman, but this brief period gave way to decades of male-dominated basketball. A combination of factors periodically disrupted female interscholastic schedules through the 1910s and beyond and limited their travel opportunities. Some Indian schools, like Haskell, repeatedly suspended and restarted their varsity programs as opinions fluctuated about the appropriateness of female competition or its financial feasibility. Scheduling also became more difficult for off-reservation schools that preferred college-level competition, as many western colleges and universities eliminated their women's teams altogether by the 1920s.[22] Even schools like Chemawa and Genoa that consistently sent girls' teams out to play rarely let them go more than a weekend's distance away, and they sent them out less often than the boys' teams, scheduling about half as many games a season.[23] Only all-female Bismarck bucked this trend into the early 1930s. Under Mote's authority, its team covered one thousand miles on a single road trip in 1931, playing three games in four days.[24]

Interracial Relations

Indian school administrators frequently argued that interscholastic basketball was worth its costs by pointing to evidence that it was positively influencing interracial relations. Most encouraging were the crowds. Haskell's men's and Fort Shaw's girls' teams attracted record audiences in many small towns they played in during the early 1900s.[25] In the years that followed, non-Natives turned out by the hundreds for other Indian school teams as well. This response paralleled the enthusiasm white fans displayed for Indian school football and baseball teams.[26] Many of these spectators came to root for Indian school basketball teams from the outset, and those who did not commonly applauded them for their spectacular plays.[27]

Non-Native spectators also treated Indian school teams as local favorites in the towns where those institutions were located, which municipal newspapers encouraged through positively biased reporting.[28] The *Albuquerque Citizen* in the early 1900s even claimed virtual ownership of the local Indian school team with headlines referring to them as "Our Indian Girls."[29] Well-to-do residents and small businesses also supported boarding school basketball programs financially by purchasing season tickets and vending them out of storefronts downtown. Some merchants even donated small sums to allay travel expenses to distant tournaments and donated trophies for the winners.[30] The Indian schools encouraged this philanthropy to reduce athletic expenses and promote positive town and gown relations. As they did with their football teams, brass bands, and theatrical productions, school officials used their basketball teams as ambassadors for local community outreach. They hoped in this way to garner political and moral support for the institutions and their students.[31]

Indian school newsletters and journals also publicized the many compliments and well-wishes Native teams received from the white teams and coaches that hosted them as evidence of a narrowing racial divide. The superintendents most appreciated it when observers used adjectives such as "gentlemanly," "sportsmanlike," and "clean-playing" to refer to their players' civilized demeanor. School publications and municipal newspapers also made special note of displays of mutual respect and friendship between white and Native teams.[32] Among Haskell's feel-good stories reported in the *Indian Leader* was one telling of the women's varsity team's visit to Omaha, Nebraska, in 1905. The article spoke of their cordial relations with their YWCA opponents and highlighted a lunch room exchange illustrating basketball's powers to promote cultural assimilation and interracial acceptance. "Why, they speak English and dress like the rest of us," a Y player said to one of her white teammates sitting next to her. Overhearing this, one of the Haskell players was said to have "smiled in a dignified way" and murmured to her friends, "Wonder if they thought we still wore blankets."[33] A later story from 1915 told of Kansas Wesleyan students in Salina applauding Haskell's basketball men at chapel the day after a game in recognition of "the friendliness and good fellowship manifested by the Indians."[34]

Although these pleasant vignettes simplified a more complex reality to promote an institutional agenda, they should not be dismissed as mere propaganda. These interactions spoke to basketball's real power to provide common ground and initiate dialogue between Native and white youths. It indeed would have struck Haskell's players as profound to see white students applauding them, given how poorly treated Natives usually were in non-Native towns. Albeit to a limited degree, basketball and other sports did what the school administrators said they would: they helped Native youths make some social inroads into the dominant society.[35]

As the Omaha YWCA story illustrates, though, interracial basketball had at best a mixed influence on race relations, on the one hand, promoting cordial relations while, on the other, reminding Native players they were still regarded as outsiders and oddities. If the Omaha story is to be believed, it said more than the *Indian Leader* intended, demonstrating an absence of understanding between young Native and white women after four years of consistent relations between their basketball programs.

What the Indian school administrators failed to recognize, or refused to say, was that non-Natives who pleasantly greeted and supported their teams as hosts, donors, and spectators did not necessarily accept them as social equals or support assimilation policy. Non-Natives were in fact drawn to these teams for many reasons, ranging from true admiration and a modicum of social acceptance to economic self-interest and the desire to exploit them as racial novelties. As a result, basketball could as easily reinforce the racial status quo.

Local interests in host towns like Albuquerque, New Mexico, Lawrence, Kansas, and Salem, Oregon, benefited financially from the popularity of their Indian school teams and supported them even if they scoffed at the notion of racial integration. Athletic boosterism was a quid-pro-quo relationship, politically beneficial for the schools and financially for local whites, all made possible by Native athletes' sweat and toil. Indian school teams drew out-of-town spectators by the hundreds to patronize city shops, hotels, and eateries. Business donors also received free advertising when local newspapers and school publications thanked them publicly for their generosity. Haskell took things further in 1919, opening their new gymnasium, built with federal dollars and some Native student labor, to Lawrence high school to use for its home games—evidently free-of-charge. Being a good neighbor, Superintendent Peairs told the public school principal he was happy to extend this courtesy to improve the quality of education for all students in Lawrence. Taken together, the revenues and facility savings that townsfolk gained from Indian school teams far exceeded what they spent to help support them.[36]

The print media also capitalized on the public popularity of some Indian school teams to sell newspapers. Many reporters indulged in racial stereotyping to do so, depicting Native athletes as exotic outsiders to pique reader interest, while others treated them more respectfully as modern athletes.[37] The former stories were more widely distributed, appearing mostly in big city newspapers and as syndicated columns.[38] These reporters presented Indian school teams as racial and historical novelties to readers who had rarely seen them in action. They trafficked in imagery borrowed from Wild West shows and dime novels, rendering Native players tomahawk-wielding warriors reenacting frontier conflicts of old. Native and white teams became "Redskins" and "Pale Faces" and wins were termed "scalps." This narrative style had been perfected in press coverage of Carlisle football in the 1890s and early 1900s. David Wallace Adams argues that this martial metaphor had been particularly effective there because of the easy analogy drawn between an expanding frontier and a team slogging its way down a field.[39] The media extended this narrative to baseball and later basketball as well, minus the territorial dimension. This enticing imagery enabled whites to glory in new victories over Indian villains, to romanticize a quintessentially American past, or to root for underdog Indians to prevail in an age-old struggle without real-world consequences for white consumers.[40]

This sensationalized approach could cut two ways depending on how readers received it, either undermining federal Indian assimilation policy by portraying Native teams as exotic antagonists or reinforcing it by illustrating how civilized sports were gradually controlling and absorbing them into American society.[41] The narrative style endured for decades, the *Chicago Tribune* laying it on especially thick when announcing St. Francis Mission's (composed of Lakota players) arrival for a national Catholic basketball tournament in 1940. The headline for the story read, "A Smoke Signal Warns of Indians on Basket Warpath." Next to this was a cartoon of a tomahawk-wielding warrior chasing a terrified Pilgrim who somehow found himself transported from Plymouth to the Windy City. But this was just in good fun, said the reporter, because this was not really a "hostile tribe of Pottawatomie," but instead "a friendly little band of Indians." They would "not be equipped with tomahawks. Their only weapon will be a basketball."[42] Even though Indian school athletes varied widely in tribal membership and degree of Native ancestry, every one of them became a "full-blooded Indian" for the purpose of such narratives, lest the racial metaphors be too complicated for non-Native consumers to grasp.[43]

Newspapers covered Indian school female teams less frequently than male teams, but when they did in the early years, they were sensationalized for their gender as much as their race. In the 1890s and 1900s, they were inevitably referred to as "dusky maidens" or "Indian lassies," usually absent the warrior metaphors used with male players. A Salem, Oregon, newspaper story proved the exception in 1898, filtering the frontier warfare motif through a sexist lens. In reporting on Chemawa's 13–11 loss to the Oregon Agricultural College in Corvallis, it opened with the headline, "Scalps Dangle at the Belts of the Pale Faces." The journalist likened this particularly rough matchup to a feminine version of football. Both groups of "maidens," seven to a side in this version of the game, played with "dash and force." "The collisions and mix-ups, too, reminded one of football," he wrote. "At times there would be seven pretty fair faces and seven as equally pretty dusky faces down on the floor at once and pointing straight upwards, would be twenty-eight cute little feet mingled with a perfect labyrinth of orange colored shoe strings and well shod pedal extremities."[44]

Nuance and accuracy were never the goals of this sensationalist, racialized, and sexist journalism. The frontier warfare motif was not about social commentary or in-depth sports analysis. Neither was it intentionally about supporting or subverting the schools' integrationist efforts, even though on the latter score, it was racist to be sure. With the male teams in particular, it was about making Indian school basketball a marketable commodity.[45] And it was about lazy journalism. This was formulaic copy written by reporters who had never seen these teams in action and who failed to do their research.

The second journalistic approach contrasted with this crude sensationalism, transforming historical villains into modern athletes. Players were still "Indians," "Red men," or even "Redskins" in these stories, but they were less caricatures. These reporters only hinted at the racial novelty of whites spectating Native teams, by commonly referring to them as "colorful" attractions. Beyond that, the writing style was more honest and informative, approaching that of modern sports journalism.[46] Most of these stories were produced by local newspapers in towns where white fans saw Indian school teams play on a regular basis.[47] They were therefore more likely to portray those teams as legitimate competitors existing within regional basketball cultures, thus reinforcing the Indian schools' racial integrationist message. Native teams were made basketball insiders but situated on the outer perimeter of that sphere, as even these newspapers occasionally slipped into sensationalism. It was too hard to resist adding a little flare once in a while to titillate readers and sell more papers, perhaps saying that a local team had returned from the road with "scalps in its belt."[48]

Only a smattering of articles covering Indian school basketball teams in any detail fell outside of these two stylistic categories by commenting directly on the degree to which Native players had assimilated. These were produced in earlier years before basketball became an established sport, at a time when readers were less concerned with game outcomes. In 1901, a Scandia, Kansas, newspaper went the furthest by announcing that "the assimilation of basket ball by the Indians of Haskell Institute seems to point clearly to the enervating influence of civilization." And the *Great Falls Tribune* in Montana referred to the young women at Fort Shaw in 1905 as "cultured, quiet, and refined as any of their white sisters."[49]

Even as sports coverage fell at different points along this interpretive spectrum, there is no denying that Indian school teams had a racial novelty appeal to white spectators and that the frontier motif sold more newspapers and tickets. White spectators were clearly drawn to see Indian school teams play *because* they were Indian teams, not in spite of that fact. This did not always reflect a lack of understanding or respect. Some non-Native spectators recognized the Native pride with which Indian school teams carried themselves and were thrilled by the distinctive up-tempo style they often employed (as discussed in the following chapter). Many truly admired them for their talents and accomplishments.

Other spectators, however, only wished to see "real live Indians" doing something unusual. White Americans in the early twentieth century were generally fascinated with things Indian. This was especially so as indigenous peoples were no longer perceived as military threats. They saw in Native cultures and athletes the special qualities they wished to see at the heart of the national character, while ignoring past atrocities. Native athletes were embodiments of an idealized past. As Dakota historian Philip J. Deloria explains, they "gave spectators a timeless (if fuzzy) sense of Edenic nature sometime before the Fall, when natural men walked the earth." The perceived impermanency of Native cultures, and perhaps the people themselves, was part of the appeal for some Americans. Thus a reporter in Sedalia, Missouri, could still write in 1930 about what a "novelty" it was "to see people of a vanishing race" play basketball.[50]

Both reporters and non-Native basketball programs profited from this American fascination with things "Indian" and so developed a symbiotic relationship to feed it. The Indian school superintendents occasionally received requests from opposing teams seeking Native-themed content they could relay to local reporters to hype upcoming games and sell more tickets. Most superintendents responded politely with basic information about their players' tribal affiliations and hometowns. Wahpeton's superintendent Carl Stevens seemed annoyed, however, when Hatton High School's principal asked him specifically for his players' "Indian names" in 1935. The Indian Service had gone to great lengths in previous decades to eliminate students' traditionally given tribal names, considering them uncivilized, and so Stevens either believed none of his players still had them or preferred not publicize them. "I am afraid we will have to disappoint you if you have an idea that our boys have Indian names," he wrote back. "They do not so probably there would be no advantage in publishing their names in your advertising."[51]

Although they may have been annoyed by the particulars of certain requests, Indian school administrators did not wrangle with journalists or their opponents over their stereotypical portrayals of Native teams. They welcomed coverage that brought attention to their basketball programs so long as it did not attack the players' reputations or the institutions they represented. Nor were school administrators or employees averse to tapping into the public's fascination with things Indian. With basketball programs operating on shoestring budgets, anything that made the teams more marketable kept them in the field and allowed basketball to perform its positive functions. They were, however, usually more subtle in their race-based promotion than Bert Berry, Haskell's physical director. In 1903, while trying to book a game with a college in Greencastle, Indiana, he wrote, "I have no doubt that there are many young people in your school who have never seen a real live Indian. To such people this alone would be a treat, to say nothing of seeing one of the best teams in the country play a game of basketball."[52]

Another way to highlight a team's Indian identity was to encourage players to dress the part on the road. Some administrators sent their players to high-profile events with both traditional tribal attire and their basketball uniforms. They wore the traditional clothing for pre-game photographs and, in some cases, while performing halftime dances at center court marketed to crowds as "war dances." Fred Campbell may have been the first to employ this strategy, dispatching Fort Shaw's girls' team to the 1904 Louisiana Purchase Exposition in St. Louis with buckskin dresses their families provided. They wore them there to perform a scene from *Hiawatha* and pose for publicity photos. Many years later, in 1925, the Jesuits of St. Francis Mission sent their boys' team to a Chicago tournament in their traditional Lakota attire to wear before taking the court. And Chemawa's male players posed for photos at the Oregon state tournament in 1929, half of them in basketball warm-ups and the others in hide leggings—one in a ribbon shirt and three bare chested.[53] In these cases, the attire fit the traditions of the tribes to which the players belonged and so would not have been culturally uncomfortable for the athletes themselves, but this was

Figure 13. Fort Shaw's team tours in their traditional attire again in 1905. *Kneeling left to right*: Emma Sansaver, Gertrude LaRance, and Rose LaRose. *Standing left to right*: Nettie Wirth, Genevieve Healy, Josephine Langley, Belle Johnson, Minnie Burton, and Sarah Mitchell. Pac 80-79 M3. Courtesy of the Montana Historical Society Research Center Photograph Archives, Helena, Montana.

not so with Albuquerque Indian School's team. When they took publicity photos before a Chicago tournament in 1928, they wore Plains-style headdresses that were alien to their Southwestern traditions (most were Navajo or members of Pueblo tribes). School employees and Albuquerque merchants had them wear these to promote tourism, hoping to entice a national audience with the Plains imagery they were accustomed to seeing in Wild West shows and media depictions.[54]

Child "mascots" also proved useful means to advertise teams' Indian identities. These mascots were younger students or employees' children who occasionally traveled with the teams and posed beside them in promotional photos. Some just wore sweaters displaying school emblems like Haskell's purple "H," while others donned buckskins and headdresses. Probably the first basketball mascot to be attired in traditional garb was ten-year-old Louis Youpee, who appeared in 1902 alongside the Fort Shaw girls' team. Little John Papakie also dressed the part for Haskell in 1907. And eight-year-old Collins P. Jordan put on his Lakota regalia for St.

Francis in 1925, wearing it while accompanying his teammates during their halftime "war dances" in Chicago. Jordan was a hit with crowds. A Jesuit publication exploited his Indian star power when announcing his return to the city in 1926. "The drum carried last year was twice as big as he was," it said, "but reports say that the little redskin has put on a few pounds by eating South Dakota beef."[55]

Indian school administrators and athletic staffers encouraged Indian-themed displays mainly to feed the paying public what it wanted. As Haskell's coach, Frank McDonald, explained in the 1920s, white football fans back East "almost demanded seeing Indians as they knew them from pictures and publicity," and so he had his players dress up and dance for them the same as Native basketball teams.[56]

The administrators also had other reasons for encouraging teams to dress and perform in traditional attire. Some believed these displays accomplished two tasks simultaneously, selling tickets while also serving as assimilationist propaganda. The key was the contrasting imagery; the traditional clothes Native basketball players performed and posed in represented an indigenous past, while their game uniforms represented a "civilized" present. This practice fit with the Indian Office's established public relations tactic of juxtaposing displays of traditional culture alongside Native youths in school uniforms at parades and fair exhibitions—the old giving way to the new. Hervey Peairs employed the same contrasting imagery in the 1910s when he permitted Haskell's musicians to perform alternatingly in traditional dress and standard band uniforms. Posing child mascots in buckskin alongside uniformed basketball players was the ultimate form of this tactic, cultural progress being visually represented as a transition from childhood to maturity.[57] Not all administrators used traditional imagery on the court for the same purpose however. Especially by the late 1920s and early 1930s, some may have wished simply to inspire their athletes by allowing them to express indigenous identities within defined limits.[58]

There is little evidence that Native athletes took issue with being asked to wear traditional clothing for publicity photographs or to dance at halftime. What was novel imagery to the white public were expressions of cultural pride for the athletes, as it was for the Fort Shaw players whose families still prize the traditional dresses they wore on their basketball journeys. But how Native athletes felt about the crass language and racist cartoons representing them in newspapers was a different matter. There were different ways to mentally process and respond to this racist imagery. As discussed below, some Indian school students adopted and repurposed the publicity for their own needs, while other Native students, educators, and reformers condemned it as insulting.[59] Native athletes who were similarly offended or wounded by this coverage, however, typically remained silent in public forums. Even Louis Sockalexis, who was the target of intense media scrutiny and racial stereotyping in baseball's major leagues, did not protest, appearing outwardly unaffected until the reporting became overtly cruel in 1897, during a downturn in his career.[60]

Sydney Beane, Jr., recalls that Indian school athletes of his father's generation in South Dakota usually ignored or "laughed off" media coverage that athletes of his generation, and of today, would condemn as racist. They did this both "to deal with it" as a defensive mechanism, he says, and because the coverage confirmed what they already knew: non-Natives lived in another world and knew little about them. Rather than internalize the hurt or lash out, says Beane, his father and other Native athletes of that generation became more determined to prove on the court that they were better, as both athletes and human beings, than others depicted them to be. One of the empowering things about basketball, as well as other sports, was that it allowed Native people to safely retort by action rather than just words.[61]

Harsh Receptions

Basketball, of course, had as much power to facilitate racial conflict as to transcend it. Indian school administrators could not have thought the goodwill that athletics spread would easily overcome endemic anti-Indian sentiments. All they had to do was look to baseball's recent history. Native professional baseball players had been confronting open hostility for many years before Indian school basketball came to prominence. Even whites who rooted for these players as home team stars unleashed racist insults when they faltered. Native baseball players also dealt with poor treatment as midwestern barnstormers during the early 1900s—the same territory that basketball teams from Chilocco, Haskell, and Genoa were beginning to cover. These teams were often met by criminal accusations, physical assaults from drunken spectators, and hoteliers refusing them lodging.[62] Indian Service superintendents thus realized their basketball teams would, and did, encounter some hostility, but they rarely acknowledged this to Native students or publicly in written records. To report on racial conflicts risked displeasing their Indian Office superiors and irritating the YMCA associations, colleges, and high schools that hosted them. Whether the superintendents failed to address bigotry in basketball because they were negligent, were racist hypocrites, or believed their students would be emboldened by standing up to this negativity is uncertain because of their silence.

What evidence there is of Indian school basketball teams and players being mistreated was reported mostly outside Indian Service records. A few accounts appeared in municipal newspapers that reported conflicts matter-of-factly without rendering moral judgements. One local Salem, Oregon, paper even fomented the tension. The incident in question occurred after Dallas College, of Oregon, defeated Chemawa's boys in a very physical contest played in late March 1903. The white visitors were particularly upset about having to leave one of their injured teammates behind in a Salem hospital. On their way out of town, they aired their grievances to a reporter for the *Statesman Journal*, which the reporter and the editor saw fit to print. The racist insults cut straight to the bone. "Although Dallas was able to lift the scalps of the Chemawa braves," the *Statesman* reported, "the verdict of the team is that the wards of Uncle Sam are very much lacking in the element of decency to visitors and that possibly the old gentleman could devote a few dollars profitably in teaching these untutored savages a few common courtesies, as well as the rules of the game of basketball."[63]

Another account of racial hostility appeared years later in a 1909 Wichita, Kansas, newspaper. The incident would have gone undocumented had George W. Bent not been such a strong advocate for his boys. While he was serving as an assistant disciplinarian and coach at Chilocco, Bent's basketball team was denied use of the Wichita YMCA's locker room after a game against the Y team that had been marred by an astounding forty-eight fouls. It was hard for anyone to believe that the association director would have made this spiteful decision had the opposing team been white. This so infuriated Bent that he vented to a reporter, making public something that Indian Service employees were no doubt told to keep quiet. "At Arkansas City we were allowed to dress and take shower baths in the YMCA, but we were refused that privilege here," he said. The decision was particularly galling, he explained, because "all of our players belong to the student YMCA too."[64]

Neither were female Indian school teams immune to such treatment. Hostility particularly tarnished one of Fort Shaw's visits to Fargo, North Dakota, in 1904. The opposing team accosted the Native girls with a chorus of racist slurs before the tip-off. Fort Shaw responded to this not with physical aggression or verbal retorts but with a determined spirit. They crushed the North Dakotans on the court 34–0. The next year, news circulated through the Indian Service of a women's team from "a very prominent college in Kansas" that had been "debarred from playing basket-ball off their own grounds because of their rude manner and abusive language

Figure 14. Chilocco's 1908–09 Oklahoma state champion team. Coach George W. Bent, Jr., sits at the top alongside an unidentified child mascot. Their jerseys display the school logo, borrowed from American Indian cultures. Courtesy of NARA, Fort Worth, Texas, identifier 251717.

to a visiting team from Haskell Institute." The implication was that this college was either Kansas State Agricultural College (future Kansas State University) or the University of Kansas. The former makes sense given the frictions known to exist between the Haskell and Aggie men in that era, but the latter possibility is more intriguing. The women from KU and Haskell were very familiar with each other, as their teams had been frequent opponents since 1901. In 1903, they also traveled together to Lincoln for games against the University of Nebraska, with U. S. G. Plank and his wife chaperoning. Rather than promoting harmony between them, perhaps these extended interactions had bred racially charged frictions that later boiled over.[65]

On top of the racist slights, female players were also subjected to sexist insults when playing on away courts. The paucity and brevity of media coverage they normally received obscures this reality, but a 1917 account in a North Carolina newspaper offers a glimpse. During a clash between the Cherokee boarding school and a high school in Asheville, a group of teenage boys in the risers relentlessly taunted the players on both teams. They shouted out one sexist joke after another, drawing a mixture of laughs and disgusted looks from the other spectators. The Cherokee team lost that game 12–7. The only positive thing they could take away from the otherwise humiliating experience was knowing that their determined play had reportedly won over "fully half of the spectators" in the Asheville crowd.[66]

Even though reporters and Indian Service administrators maintained their silence on such matters, there is no reason to believe Indian school teams confronted less overt bigotry as the decades progressed. We know of one egregious incident that occurred in 1940 only because a high school principal sent a rare letter of apology to an aggrieved Chemawa player. While going for an errant pass during a road game in Silverton, Oregon, the player had lost his balance and fallen into a spectator's lap courtside. The man shoved the nineteen-year-old away while shouting a racist insult, prompting the player to throw a punch, which he landed square to the man's jaw. No doubt to his amazement, the Native player was not expelled for this. Instead, Silverton's principal barred the offending non-Native spectator from future games between the two schools. The Chemawa player stayed on his team and, one year later, was elected student body president.[67]

There is no doubt that Indian school teams, prior to mid-century, experienced overt acts of bigotry far more often than these few examples suggest. One only need listen to the many stories Native people tell of experiencing such hostility during public high school games from mid-century to now. They speak of people shouting racist insults at Native players on the court or as they exit arenas, holding up offensive signs in the risers, making crude gestures during handshake lineups, and even fist fighting on the court and in parking lots.[68]

All of this is to say that the old Indian school athletes would have been under no illusions that they could fundamentally alter peoples' racial attitudes by playing basketball. This does not mean, however, that most of their interactions, in most places, were negative. When white reporters commented on the physical tenor of play between Indian school and non-Native teams from 1900 through the 1930s, they judged that a slightly higher percentage of these games were "clean" as opposed to "rough" affairs. Although they no doubt ignored many egregious acts of hostility, this reporting suggests that most athletes respected the game and its rules regardless of how they felt about each other. Native and white players expected aggressive play and accepted the possibility of injury so long as their opponents were not overtly dirty or insulting. And when they were, Native players responded as they could, sometimes with fists but more often by striving harder to win. They nevertheless experienced enough harsh receptions through their Indian school careers to know that the integrationist propaganda that Indian Service employees produced was based, at best, on half-truths.[69]

Officiating

Indian school players were as concerned about biased referees as they were about offensive reporters and unfriendly opponents. One of basketball's greatest appeals was its potential to give Native people a fair shake in non-Native society. In basketball, things were meant to be structurally equal, with two teams of the same size playing on a surface divided into two mirrored halves. Introducing human subjectivity into this mix was bound to threaten this perfection. There were already Indian agents on the reservations, police officers in the border towns, and teachers and disciplinarians at school—all embodiments of authority upholding and at times abusing rules written by non-Natives. Now, on basketball courts, there were referees.

American Indians were not the only ones who suspected that basketball referees were corruptible, or at best unreliable, during the early decades of the sport. Even James Naismith acknowledged that too many of them were undermining the integrity of the game. This was not entirely their fault, he said. Officials might be forgiven for displaying some bias, as American crowds so relentlessly pressured them that they frequently feared for their own safety. There was even one referee, he recalled, who made a habit of exiting games through a locker room window to avoid spectator retribution.[70]

The processes through which officials were procured also undermined their legitimacy across America. Basketball umpires had always been able to call fouls, but after 1895, referees gained this power as well, enabling the two types of officials to better assist each other on the court and theoretically to check each other's biases.[71] Under this arrangement, most Indian schools, as well as non-Native school and YMCA teams during the 1900s used in-house staff as part-time officials. This seemed fair and expedient so long as one side designated the referee and the other the umpires. Coaches were often selected to double as officials because they had little else to do in an era when many were mere chaperones, the coaching profession still being in its infancy. The predictable result of this was that everyone became more suspicious, not less so, because they knew there were no impartial actors on the floor, just opposing arbiters with varying levels of bias. This checks and balances approach never satisfied anyone, and matters did not improve after 1910, when host teams began to hire outside officials, because they were assumed to be beholden to those who paid them.[72]

Under either of these arrangements, many teams and spectators assumed that any bias ran toward home team partisanship, but when one team was primarily American Indian and the other white, questionable calls took on racial implications. Indian school players and fans often feared they were being adjudicated against not only because the other team was a favorite but also because of the color of their skin.

Basketball officials were not the only ones Indian school students or other Native athletes worried about. Natives competing in other sports during the late nineteenth and early twentieth centuries were just as leery of white arbiters who were determined to rob them of their victories. Carlisle football players in the 1890s were convinced that some referees called games against them to favor their opponents, and many white reporters and spectators agreed. Native barnstorming baseball teams after 1900, knowing that hometown umpires stood in their way, negotiated to add their own to the field as counterbalances. And Native rodeo competitors, convinced that white judges were prejudiced against them, transitioned during the 1920s to timed events, such as calf and team roping, and away from judged events, like bronc riding.[73]

Usually, Indian school spectators and athletes held their tongues when they felt cheated by basketball officials, but not always. With their schoolmates at their side, they sometimes found the confidence to cry foul when things went too far. Sometimes they got their way within the context of the game, and sometimes not, but they discovered they could take action without disciplinary consequences off the court. Basketball therefore afforded a certain leeway for calling out injustice that other realms of Native student life did not—most particularly in the classroom or on forays into town.

Numerous times during the first decade of the twentieth century, Haskell's student cheering section howled in protest at the poor treatment they believed their varsity basketball teams received from biased officials, particularly when their men played the Blue Diamonds team from the

Kansas City Athletic Club. Not only did the fan protests go unpunished by school officials, but on at least one occasion, in 1909, they succeeded in prompting the Blue Diamonds to pull their offending referee at halftime. On this and other occasions, the anonymous authors of the *Indian Leader*'s sports columns sided with the student body, alleging that the officials had an anti-Haskell bias.[74]

Indian school players also protested on their own behalf at times, and occasionally they got their way. In 1905, for example, Rapid City Indian School's boys stood in solidarity against a perceived injustice. When their team drove into Lead, South Dakota, to take on the local high school, they did not expect to receive a fair shake from fans or officials. This was the territory of white people, who perceived these contests in a racial context. Two local newspapers suggested as much by later reporting on Rapid City's loss with competing headlines, one reading "Whites Victorious" and the other "Indians Defeated." Surprisingly, though, the local reporters and many white spectators began to sympathize with the Indian school team as it became obvious that they were being cheated. "Those who understood the game and those who were near the players declared that foul after foul was committed by the Lead team, which were allowed to pass by without any penalty whatever," reported the *Lead Pioneer-Times*. Having had enough, Rapid City stopped in their tracks, refusing to take another center jump until the most biased official was removed. To their amazement, Lead's school administrators pulled him out, and the game continued. The rest of the contest passed without incident, but Rapid City still lost 23–13. For Native boys to succeed in this protest, and have whites applaud them for it, was unexpected. Albeit through complicated circumstances, basketball achieved that day what Indian school administrators hoped it would. It allowed Native players to assert themselves while winning over a white crowd. Then again, it came at the price of confirming their suspicions that many white officials were biased against them.[75]

Even though basketball afforded Native student spectators and players a degree of freedom to protest, they could not help but notice that white spectators got away with crasser accusations against American Indian referees when situations were reversed. Haskell's Coach George Shawnee found this to be true on at least one occasion while doubling as an official. Athletic Director Plank considered his coworker one of the best part-time officials around and many non-Native opponents concurred, praising Shawnee for his impartiality. But this reputation did not extend to Manhattan, Kansas, or stop people there from publicly humiliating the man. When Haskell edged out Kansas State Agricultural College 28–27 on the road in January 1907, the *Manhattan Mercury* ran the headline: "Colored Referee

Assists Red Skins in Winning the Victory." Shawnee's work was "exceedingly bad during the last half," the text of the story explained. "At one time it seemed as if the crowd would go out and divide him up for souvenirs."[76] One imagines how disheartened and angry Haskell's players must have been reading this diatribe, joking about violent retribution against a Native man they admired. If this is how white opponents talked about an Indian referee, why should they treat every white official they encountered as someone who was unimpeachable and worthy of their respect?

When Phog Allen arrived as Haskell's men's basketball coach for the 1907–08 season, he indeed found a team of Native players who were deeply distrusting of white officials. A dedicated young coach who knew the game well, Allen nevertheless had little capacity for understanding his players' perspectives as Native people. He dismissed their suspicions out of hand. He called their notion that white referees were biased a paranoid "complex" that was "an inheritance of their race," and he aimed to dispel it. During preseason practices, he told the players to forget the feeling they were being "legislated against" every time a foul was called. They were not being intentionally penalized to cause them shame, he insisted. They were fouling excessively because they were "overrunning themselves" and forgetting their fundamentals. When other players fouled them, they should not take offense, nor should they feel shame if they committed one themselves. It was all part of the game. "When you leap at the ball and grab an opponent's arm rather than the ball, you are not a dirty player," he said. "You have just made a mistake." During their eastern tour in 1908, he pulled the team aside before a road game against the Detroit Athletic Club. "Boys, I want you to have confidence in the white man official," he told them. "He wouldn't steal a ballgame even if he did steal your land." Allen claims the team "got a big wallop out of this."[77]

The young coach believed his players internalized his sermons and were the better for it, providing as evidence a story about Frank Means, the team's right forward.[78] Allen described Means, from Pine Ridge, as "a giant Sioux from the Dakota hills, standing 6 feet 2 inches," who had "all the fire and daring of his forefathers pent up in his powerful bronzed physique." As Allen told it, Means won the game in Detroit through a spectacular display of athleticism and self-control:

> No goal, that night, was too difficult for [Means] to cage. He shot them from all angles. He was the life and the inspiration of the team. With the Indians leading by a single point near the finish of the game, which they finally won, the referee called a foul on Means . . . "On you. Holding!" . . . Suddenly a savage ferocity flashed across this player's

countenance. With beads of perspiration popping out on his magnificent body he fixed his fierce eyes on the arbiter. But, in an instant his countenance changed from ferocity and to meditation. After a moment of reflective silence, he evidently, remembered his previous instruction and realized that he had unintentionally erred. Immediately, in a voluminous voice that filled the hall he drawled out: "Humph! I made a mistake."[79]

Allen recalled that the crowd roared with laughter in response, perceiving Means as unsophisticated rather than acknowledging his act of self-control.

Whether or not things happened the way Allen described, there are two ironies to this story. The first irony was his pleasure in criticizing Detroit's fans for failing to see that Means was a complex individual when Allen himself could never get past racial stereotypes. The second was that Allen's players would not have initially regarded him as an impartial authority on the subject of unfair officiating but rather would have associated him with it. His first meeting with the team had not been the day he arrived as a twenty-two-year-old coach, but a year before when he had been a player on an opposing team. He had been the designated free throw shooter for the Blue Diamonds when they played Haskell in December 1906. Means had played against him that night, scoring late in the game to tie it up when the referee, a friend of Allen's, began calling foul after foul against Haskell. Allen stepped to the line each time and sank the free throws, securing a 24–20 win for his team. Haskell's players and students believed the referee had cheated them that night, as the Blue Diamonds' favored officials so often did in their opinion. Although Allen had not made the calls, he had sealed their fate from the foul line. Means had not forgotten this as the rookie coach preached to his Indian players about white officials who would never "steal a ballgame."[80]

When it comes to questions about biased officiating, perception is everything of course. Whether or not white officials commonly cheated Native teams because of their race, the belief that they had an anti-Indian bent made many players feel like outsiders fighting uphill battles. Too many variables make it is impossible to determine what percentage of basketball officials in the country may have treated Indian school teams unfairly. Many Native observers who remember basketball at mid-century are convinced there was bias against Indian teams then, as they say there is still today.[81] But if this impartiality existed during the pre-1940 Indian school era, how widespread and egregious had it been? Statistical evidence is informative but inconclusive. A sampling of 120 box scores from 1900 to 1939 fails to show that Indian school teams received more fouls on average than their non-Native opponents, arguing against widespread bias but in no way disproving it. There is much these statistics leave unsaid.[82] If either Indian school or non-Native teams tended to commit more uncalled fouls, then benign-looking box scores are deceiving. The statistics, for example, were mute regarding a 1921 game where one of Haskell's forwards was knocked out cold by Creighton University defenders three times in one half without a single foul called (and for that matter, without Haskell's coach taking him out of the game).[83] Aggregate statistics also fail to tell us whether officials deliberately timed calls to favor one side or whether certain teams played beneath their potential for fear of overeager whistles.

Asserting Identity

Although they were confronted by offensive media coverage, some hostile receptions on the court, and officials who they believed were racially biased, there is little evidence that Indian school students were deterred from playing varsity ball out of fear or frustration. There is evidence, however, that some students resisted playing because they believed doing so endorsed institutional policies with which they disagreed. This concern may have pitted Native students against each other at St. Francis Mission in the 1930s, for example. Collins Jordan recalled schoolmates there criticizing him and his varsity teammates for representing the Catholic boarding school in a positive manner. The disagreement over basketball there, said Jordan, was also intertwined with frictions between certain "full-blood" and "mixed-blood" students, with the majority of players at the time being the latter. One of John Bloom's collaborators who attended Flandreau much later, in the 1960s, had his own criticisms of varsity athletes, who he believed acquiesced to assimilationist pressure. How widespread such opinions were during the first half of the twentieth century is uncertain, but some students no doubt preferred to play basketball informally, or not at all, rather than for white-run institutions. Many others, however, believed they could participate without forsaking their tribal identities. Rather than thinking they were bowing to someone else's agenda, they competed to proudly assert themselves as Native peoples. This was true for hundreds of Indian school athletes over many decades regardless of their tribal affiliations, degree of Native heritage, or gender.[84]

Many Native students could appreciate the fundamental simplicity of interracial basketball. Despite the unfriendly receptions they often encountered, they knew this game gave them a chance to gain positive recognition from the non-Native public, and they could take satisfaction in earned victories regardless of how they were treated by outsiders and regardless of how the press reported on those triumphs.[85]

When they competed interracially, many of these players and teams were playing for family, community, tribal, and Native pride. A former Navajo student who boxed for Santa Fe Indian School in the 1930s told John Bloom that when he competed against boxers of other races, his strongest motivation was "to show what an Indian can do." Other historians have also found that Indian school athletes were driven by this desire to prove themselves as Native people. Even Pop Warner understood this drive and relied on it to motivate his football players. In 1909, he wrote: "The Indians know that people regard them as an inferior race, unable to compete successfully in any line of endeavor with the white men, and as a result they are imbued with a fighting spirit, when pitted against their white brethren, that carries them a long way toward victory." Unlike John Keeley, at Pierre Indian School, who emphasized sports to bring the races together harmoniously, Warner more cynically cast racism as something that motivated Native athletes to win games. Regardless of what this says about Warner the man, his take likely came closer than Keeley's to the way most Native players viewed things.[86]

Indian school athletes competed to prove to non-Natives, and to each other, that all of the hurtful things said about them were lies. A few may have done this, as Richard Pratt and other superintendents intended, to show they were capable of American citizenship, but most wanted to prove they were worthy of respect for who they already were as Native people. In addition, athletics enabled them to exact symbolic revenge for past and present wrongs. It was for this reason that Carlisle football players especially relished the opportunity to defeat the US Military Academy in 1912. Regardless of the fact that Natives also served in the Army, and would so in the future in disproportionally large numbers, that particular victory was a small measure of vengeance for white atrocities at places like Sand Creek and Wounded Knee.[87]

Indian school student spectators also expressed Native pride and sought symbolic revenge by adopting the same frontier warfare rhetoric that whites employed. This was perhaps an alternative to internalizing, ignoring, or "laughing off" what these students read about their teams in the press. What is seen now as a pejorative narrative peddled by white reporters likely seemed more appropriate to some Indian school athletes than the assimilationist platitudes they heard from their teachers. A basketball court *was* a warrior arena, if only symbolically so. Carlisle students therefore co-opted the martial rhetoric for use at football games during the early 1900s, shouting "we will scalp you!" to white opponents from the stands.

They did similar things at Haskell. Recalling her days there in the 1910s, Lucille Winnie likened the football team to warriors on a raid, returning to campus each time with "another scalp to place in our Hall of Victory." They were welcomed home by other students as "winning warriors," she says: "It was always a noisy welcome when the Iroquois, Comanches, Sioux and Apaches gave their warwhoops [*sic*], and the Haskell band played 'Onward Haskell,' which was our war cry."[88]

This warrior language carried over to basketball as well, as students and Native employees frequently called wins "scalps" and players "braves" in school publications beginning in the 1900s. In an anonymously written and reprinted letter from 1904, a Chemawa student exclaimed how proud everyone was of "our basketball girls who took twenty scalps from their pale-faced sisters of Albany College"; and in 1915, Haskell's Athletic Director Alfred M. Venne (Chippewa), who was himself a former Indian school student, wrote that his basketball boys were "determined to get their scalps" from Kansas Wesleyan.[89]

Natives adopting language others used to marginalize them may appear tragic, evidencing how deeply outsiders had affected their sense of being and robbed them of some tribally specific modes of expression, but they clearly felt empowered to write and speak this way, proudly asserting that these were *Indian* teams. It may have been an example of what Lisa K. Neuman refers to as "Indian play," which Native students at Bacone College in Oklahoma engaged in before World War II. They appropriated stereotypically Indian terms and phrases from whites—fully aware of what they were doing—as a form of social commentary and a means to reinforce Native identity. As they did elsewhere in the context of sports to mean "victories," Neuman finds that Baconians used the word "scalps" to refer to romantic exploits.[90] When Native teams backed up tough talk about raiding white opponents for their scalps with high point tallies, the whole experience became more satisfying. In re-creating a long-lost diary entry from his time as a Pipestone Indian School student, Adam Fortunate Eagle used a final basketball score as an exclamation point. "Pipestone High School says they will 'heap wallop' the Indians," he said about a game in 1937. "They must not remember what happened to General Custer at Little Big Horn. Tonight, our Indian boys 'heap walloped' the boys of Pipestone: 38 to 14." This tongue-in-cheek prose allowed Fortunate Eagle to bask in triumph while turning frontier rhetoric back on white society.[91]

By the 1920s and 1930s, Indian school players were also members of teams carrying "Braves" and "Warriors" as nicknames. It is not clear what role Native students and employees had in adopting these sobriquets. White reporters had been referring to the "Carlisle Braves" and "Haskell

Braves" informally since the early 1900s. It did not become standard for the Indian schools to use these warrior names themselves until the 1920s, but they had become so ingrained by the early 1940s that Albuquerque Indian School's teams stitched the word "Braves" in big block letters across their basketball jerseys. When they took on Santa Fe Indian School in those years, spectators were given the option of either rooting for the Braves or the Braves, as both teams carried the same nickname. Meanwhile, Rapid City Indian School and St. Francis were both taking the floor in South Dakota as the Warriors. St. Francis added some extra flair, alternating from year to year during the 1930s between the names Scarlet Warriors, Scouted Warriors, and the more specific Sioux Warriors. In the same era, St. Stephens Mission in Wyoming broke from this martial trend, invading the court under the decidedly less fierce name, Galloping Antelopes.[92] Even though non-Natives had originally applied warrior names to Native teams as novelty hype, this seemed to make little difference, as Indian school players carried them with pride. Many still do at all-Native public schools that use these warrior names today, understanding that they mean something very different in these contexts than when appropriated by non-Native college and professional teams.[93]

By the late 1920s, a few Indian school basketball teams in South Dakota were also stitching Native-themed iconography on their jerseys. Prior to this, most Indian school uniforms were either blank or were adorned with a block letter initial for the school. Haskell was one of only a few teams in the early 1900s that displayed its Native status by spelling out "Haskell Indians" on the players' jerseys. The Printers' shop team at Haskell may have been one of the first Native teams to design their own symbol when they ordered basketball trousers with an "Indian head" on them in 1910. This same head, wearing a war bonnet, then appeared on the varsity men's jerseys in 1919. Chemawa's first team boys also commissioned a student to paint or stitch an "Indian head" wearing a war bonnet on their warm-ups and shorts in 1927. They paid for these logos out of their own pockets. Teams proudly wore these symbols, displaying for all to see that they were teams of modern warriors.[94]

Then again, Indian school athletes did not always focus their energies on impressing or defying non-Natives. They competed just as fiercely and proudly against other Native teams, vying for recognition across Indian country. As their communities had always done through traditional sports, they used basketball to share something in common with and distinguish themselves from each other and to forge bonds and settle differences between localities and tribes.

Indian school teams rarely played each other interscholastically. The majority of their outside opponents were non-Native—mostly all-white teams, but in some areas African American, Asian American, and Mexican American, as well. This was the case, in part, because school administrators emphasized interracial play but also because Indian schools were usually too distant from each other to play consistently. Opportunities did, however, arise from time to time. Reservation boarding schools with sister institutions and Indian day schools nearby did so more often, but even the off-reservation schools played each other on special occasions, with Haskell taking on Carlisle and Chilocco once a year beginning in the 1900s, and other Indian schools more commonly taking part in all-Indian tournaments by the late 1920s and 1930s.[95]

Indian Office superiors did not object to inter-Indian school play so long as it did not displace competitions with whites.[96] The local superintendents also preferred interracial competition, but they more valued all-Native play than their superiors for a variety of reasons. Most of all it was about convenience, since it was easier to arrange lodging with sister institutions. Beyond this, they believed these games fostered interinstitutional cooperation and that students benefited intellectually and emotionally from socializing with Native students attending other schools. This allowed them to see how things were *just a little better* where they attended than it was for the other guys, or alternatively to aspire to greater things. *See how exciting it is to play sports for Carlisle or Haskell? Maybe if you behave, study, and play your best ball, you can get there some day.* In this spirit, Haskell's *Indian Leader* extended thanks to Chilocco's boys' team after their maiden visit in 1906. "We all hope that this may be the beginning of athletic relations between these two Indian schools," the paper wrote. "Situated as they are, games of different kinds could be exchanged, and a new interest in each other would be aroused." Superintendents also regarded inter-Indian school games as recruitment opportunities. Teams from the bigger schools wowed players at smaller schools, enticing them to transfer or matriculate there. Off-reservation school administrators and coaches likely regarded these games as scouting opportunities as well, locating future talent for their programs.[97]

Students and employees especially looked forward to these inter-Indian school games. These were opportunities to converse about shared experiences from home and growing up in boarded environments. The attendant social festivities were also more elaborate than they were with non-Native visitors because the stayovers were longer. This was the case because the opposing basketball teams used each other's institutions as temporary base camps on the road while playing non-Native schools in the vicinity. In addition to the obligatory oyster suppers and building tours, there were holiday parties and dances to enjoy when Indian school teams came together. During Concho's epic 1930 road trip, for example, the team celebrated Christmas with other Native students at Albuquerque Indian School before moving on to Santa Fe Indian School. In both places, the players and their entourage were treated royally. At Santa Fe, "two dancing parties were given in honor of the boys," Coach Kirk reported. "These parties they were able to enjoy even though they did not dance as dominoes, checkers and other games were to be played. On our last night there, a bridge party was given by a couple of the employees, for the Santa Fe employees and visiting employees, which was very much enjoyed."[98]

During their long trek, the boys from Concho felt more at ease with, and were more intrigued by, other Native students at Albuquerque and Santa Fe than with their non-Native hosts. They also became more aware of the diversity of Native America through their basketball travels. Having never been to the Southwest, the players were especially interested in noting differences in height and physical features between Native people there and in Oklahoma. While Kirk was mostly interested in comparing the facilities at Albuquerque Indian School to his own school, the first thing a player said when they drove onto campus was, "These Indians don't look like we do." This observation was a pleasant revelation for him but was unflattering to his gracious hosts. In contrast, the boys had little or nothing to say about non-Natives they met along their journey. These were the people to whom the Concho boys were to culturally aspire, but all Kirk could report was that the boys felt "embarrassed" whenever they were taken to non-Native homes or nice hotels.[99]

Games between Indian school teams also took on added excitement as they competed passionately against each other. Some of these rivalries were just as heated as those they had with non-Native schools, if not more so. It is uncertain how often these oppositional attitudes were rooted in long-standing intertribal, interband, interfamily, or intercommunity rivalries. They must have been to a degree, especially when the involved teams were from smaller Indian schools that drew heavily from specific reservations or cultural regions. The biggest off-reservation school teams, on the other hand, were intertribal, which subsumed other tensions into heated interinstitutional rivalries, most notably between the Haskell and Carlisle men. Carlisle's basketball players derided Haskell's as Indian school bush leaguers, so to speak. Some Haskell players competed to either disabuse Carlisle of this notion or to catch their eye as a future prospect. When the two teams met for an unofficial "Indian championship" in

1903, for example, the tension was palpable. Haskell's center Pete Hauser, who was parts Cheyenne, Arapaho, and German, reminded his opponents that night that basketball could be a contact sport. After he committed numerous fouls and watched one of Carlisle's forwards sink one free throw after another, Hauser reportedly leaned-in toward the player on the line. "Throw another basket like that and I'll split you open," he hissed. The threat's recipient was so shaken the rest of the game that his shots flew erratically. Hauser must have been pleased with himself, having brought this lofty Carlisle man down to Earth.[100]

In the end, basketball neither exclusively brought the races together nor drove them apart. It did both, which Native players understood and addressed on the court. Interracial basketball was a complex phenomenon, and whether the social encounters were cordial or downright nasty, Indian school students conducted themselves as determined competitors. The school administrators were right about some things and wrong about others. Playing basketball *was* about getting a real-world education, and it did instill confidence, but mostly it was a confidence to stand up as proud American Indians. Native youths were out there making friends, defending themselves, and settling old scores in ways that only athletes could appreciate. They had no illusions that basketball would remake society and their place in it, but they could play it to score victories amid the injustices of the white man's world and to befriend or battle other Native youths as their ancestors had through indigenous sports.

Basketball was also a sport stylistically flexible enough for athletes to assert themselves as Natives not only in how they presented, carried, and stood up for themselves but also in how they played; together they created a distinctive style later called Indian basketball and later still Rez ball.

6

Indian Basketball

Indian school teams typically played basketball in a distinctive fashion regardless of which institutions they represented, the tribal membership of their players, or their gender. The Indian school style—or "Indian basketball" as it would be dubbed in the early 1940s—began developing as soon as Native students took up the sport at the end of the nineteenth century, and it gained greater definition through the first third of the twentieth century. In decades thereafter (discussed in this book's conclusion), rules changes would allow Indian basketball to evolve into the style popularly referred to as Rez ball, or alternatively Indian ball. And so, just as Native peoples' contemporary passions for the sport can largely be traced back to the Indian schools, so can the Rez ball style that many Native teams favor today.

The Indian basketball style, as it existed by the early 1900s, was characterized by sharp, accurate passing, pronounced agility off the ball and on the dribble, ambitious, long-range shooting, well-coordinated teamwork, high endurance, and above all foot speed. The style was not unique to Indian school teams in terms of its constituent elements but was nevertheless distinctive and modern when contrasted to the methodical, slow-but-sure approach most non-Native teams employed before mid-century. Indian school teams typically frustrated their opponents using fast-breaking offenses that rapidly moved the ball down court before defenders could set up. They ran their opponents ragged, beating most of them in the full court sprint and outlasting them in the game-long marathon. On defense, they were typically less stylistically distinctive, but the best teams were noteworthy for their ability to shift quickly from open attacks to tight defending.

The Indian basketball style developed both as an extension of Native peoples' existing athletic traditions and as a product of the boarded environment. Although they were culturally diverse, Indian school students collectively and organically created the style by drawing on shared athletic skill sets and expressing shared cultural values. Their running, sporting, and community-centered ways provided the Indian basketball style with its foundational skills and core values. These were its makings. The boarded environment then served as an intensive incubator for developing and refining these ingredients into a finished product; and so out of the Indian schools, came Indian basketball.

This style emerged in multiple locations within a short window of time, arguing against a single point of origin. The cross-pollination that spread the sport itself throughout the Indian school system, however, also lent geographic continuity to the playing style, as Native athletes and coaches transferring from one school to another shared tactics and techniques at stops along the way. Dozens of Indian school students who played basketball this way also went on to become coaches in the schools, teaching the next generation the established style while adopting new tactics and techniques to keep up with developments in the overall sport and to keep winning.

The Roots of a Style

Understanding how Indian school athletes developed a collective basketball style begins with the nature of the sport itself. It was more stylistically adaptive than other team sports that students commonly played in the Indian schools and so was more able to fit the preferences of athletes of diverse cultural and social backgrounds. This was especially so in contrast to baseball, a sport where players stand alone at pivotal moments, allowing for less direct group interaction. Baseball is also less fluid than basketball. As coaching legend Phil Jackson has explained, "Baseball is a simple, linear game, while basketball is a complex, ever-changing flow."[1] Basketball thus allows greater personal and group expression than does baseball because players are less physically constricted. Football exists between these extremes. It involves more direct team interaction and expressive movement than baseball but still is more stylistically rigid than basketball because it has more stops and starts in action, places greater emphasis on physical force, and relies more on pre-drawn plays. As will be explained, football nevertheless provided sufficient interpretive space for Indian school teams to develop a somewhat distinctive approach, related to the approach they developed for playing basketball.

The notion that basketball is, to a high degree, a culturally expressive and adaptive sport is well-established. As sportswriter Alexander Wolff has explained, it is an essentially open and "improvisatory" game. Of the world's major team sports, arguably only soccer equals or exceeds it in this regard.[2] It is therefore not surprising that ethnically diverse groups in the United States and around the globe developed their own discernable styles, some overlapping others in key elements but each a distinct expression of identity. In 1970, for example, Pete Axthelm described Jewish youths in New York City playing a "defensive-minded," set-shooting game in contrast to the African American style emphasizing "flamboyant moves." The distinct cultural experiences of growing up urban verses rural were also reflected stylistically in the game, Axthelm claimed. Small-town midwestern kids became superb players "by developing accurate shots and precise skills," while "in the cities, kids simply develop 'moves.'"[3] Basketball was thus a sport in which Indian school students could carve out their own stylistic niche.

At its foundation, Indian basketball, as played in the boarding schools, was about footracing faster and for a longer duration than the opposition. It was rooted in a running tradition shared by Native students from many tribes. Everywhere in the Americas, Native communities had relied on runners for their spiritual and physical existence. For millennia, they had run for ceremony, to hunt large game, as a means of distance communication, and as a form of self-sacrifice and betterment.[4] Life had changed by the boarding school era, and running was no longer as important to political and economic survival as it had once been, but many of the youths entering the Indian schools were still being raised as runners. They honored running as a tradition and had the physical ability to go faster and farther than many non-Native youths of their time. Although competing at white-administered Indian schools, American Indians like Carlisle's famed distance runner Louis Tewanima (Hopi) ran to express timeless traditions and honor their home communities.[5] They ran to remember who they were as indigenous people, and they infused this tradition and determination into their school sports, from footracing to basketball.

Many of these athletic youths also came from reservation communities where some traditional team sports involving running endured despite the constant assault from external forces. They had experience running at sustained speeds for long distances and, what's more, their participation in lacrosse, double ball, and other traditional sports had trained them how to cut, block, spin, dodge, and react quickly to the flow of action. The throwing and aiming skills students acquired in these team sports, as well as in games like hoop and pole, were also transferable to basketball. Not every youth who left for the boarding schools in the early twentieth century was still active in all, or even *any*, of these running and sporting traditions. Some came from urban areas or other predominantly non-Native communities where they had little or no connection to the traditional ways. They were not all athletically experienced or in prime physical shape from day one, but enough were that they could push their teammates to excel. They could teach by word and example how to run and react quickly.

Modern-day Blackfeet athletes Ryan Wetzel and Jesse DesRosier agree that the speed Native basketball players were renowned for in the Indian school era, and still are today in high school and college, reflects their cultural heritage. They see a seamless continuity between Native peoples running to live off the land, as they have since time immemorial, and Native players running on basketball courts. "You know we grew up hunters and gatherers, we were running the Plains and feeding our family through running—constantly moving, going," says Wetzel. "And with things changing, basketball became a way of keeping that alive, and continually staying active and running, and in a sense hunting and scoring and defeating the opposition." DesRosier, who took up the game on the reservation in the third grade, sees things similarly. "We're known for running," he says of Native peoples. "Running has been a long tradition of our culture since before the horses. And we're known for running on a basketball court."[6]

Timeless traditions of running and living off the land imparted not only foot speed but also an exceptional physical endurance and mental drive that showed through in the Indian basketball style. Sydney Beane, Jr., who played in the Indian schools during the 1940s and 1950s, believes that emphasizing outdoor living as an indigenous youth was fundamental to his personal athletic development. Like many Native athletes of his day, Beane spent a portion of his younger years on the reservation hunting, trapping, fishing, and swimming daily, which influenced him both physically and emotionally as a budding basketball player. "Just that connection to nature, and that conditioning by nature," he explains, "those were the fundamentals . . . that you carried into sports." Native athletes not only came into the Indian schools well-conditioned, says Beane, but also wanted to train hard once they got there because this form of physical activity gave them a "sense of being free with nature and being more of a natural person." When journalists and other non-Native observers referred to Native players as "natural" athletes, as they often did in the early twentieth century, they engaged in racial stereotyping, but there was some truth there in terms of many peoples' upbringing.[7]

The athletic and running heritage that many Native students shared thus imparted speed, agility, stamina, and competitive drive to their mode of play, but it took more to create their playing style in full form. The boarding school environment also played a role, because this is where students pooled their talents and channeled them into a new context. Boarding schools were ideal places for this. There was much that these institutions took from these students culturally, linguistically, and emotionally, but their emphasis on sports was conducive to producing well-practiced, well-conditioned, and highly coordinated teams. Varsity, intramural, and informal forms of basketball play were so accessible and sought after in the Indian schools that their students tended to be better versed in the game than many non-Native contemporaries. They also gained more competitive experience at it than did most high schoolers of their day because of the extended road trips they took and additional games they played during holiday breaks.

Indian basketball's signature emphasis on well-coordinated teamwork was also the combined product of a shared heritage and the boarded environment. As diverse as Native communities have always been in structuring their kinship, socioeconomic, and political systems, the vast majority have stressed the primacy of the group over the individual. Team-oriented thinking was thus prized by many Indian school athletes. As Sydney Beane explains, "there was a natural sense of teamwork through the culture." But this is not the only reason Native players worked so well together on ball courts. In their efforts to cope with boarding school environments, Native students clung to each other for emotional support and built a strong sense of group solidarity. On top of this was the fact that they were together more than athletes who competed for public school or even most college teams. They studied, ate, worked, and slept alongside their teammates virtually twenty-four-seven. All of these factors translated into some extraordinarily tight-knit basketball teams. When players bond as a family, live together for years, and practice together incessantly, they can produce a magic on the court that few other teams can match, no matter how well-coached.[8]

The Indian schools' notoriously lax supervision of playing spaces and the relative absence of intensive basketball coaching during the early 1900s also permitted teammates to bond on their own terms and engineer their own stylistic approach. This was not, however, one of the factors that separated their experience from that of the average non-Native athlete or gave them a leg up. Players everywhere exercised more control over the game in the early 1900s than they do in today's world where coaches rule supreme. Player captains commonly directed practices and game-time action on Indian school teams, as well as on non-Native public school and college teams.[9]

Given the freedom to do so, Indian school players worked at honing their fast, bold style while practicing inside gymnasiums and informally elsewhere on campus. They proved themselves as individuals, learned to coordinate their movement as a group, and identified their leaders all in seclusion, working out many of the kinks that might later divide a team against itself. They coached their own intramural teams, and their varsity team captains controlled the flow of play during games. In these ways, as

Figure 15. Lakota boys taking direction from their coach (unidentified) at a day school on the Pine Ridge Reservation in the early 1940s. Courtesy of NARA, Kansas City, Missouri, identifier 12460876.

well as through physical education course work, they were taught to think like both players and coaches. They were taught to lead by example and look up to each other. Phog Allen was one of a handful of strong, controlling coaches in the early years, but he did not stay at Haskell long. Some non-Native coaches like Ray Colglazier at Chilocco (there from 1920 into the 1950s) stayed at a single school for more than a decade, but they did not squelch the fast-breaking game their athletes were accustomed to playing; and even they were far more hands off than head coaches and their troupes of assistant coaches would be later in the century.[10] As coaches rose in prominence over time, many of the longest-tenured and influential in the Indian schools were themselves former Indian school players. They were strong authority figures with their own ideas, but they rarely tried to repress the Indian basketball style, most likely because it was the style they had played in their youths. At least the Native coaches who Sydney Beane knew in the Indian schools, including his father, actively reinforced the style. They emphasized conditioning and speed in practice, as well as ball handling fundamentals.[11]

The larger than average off-reservation Indian school gymnasiums also contributed structurally to the Native game's stylistic development. Even the smaller, first-generation gymnasiums were large compared to counterpart facilities of that time and so better accommodated a more open mode of play where teammates could gain the separation necessary to receive sharp passes and break for the basket. Because many non-Native high schools had inferior gyms in the early 1900s, or none at all, they were often ill prepared and outmatched when they played on Indian school courts.

In turn, Indian school publications frequently blamed road losses on the inadequate host facilities their teams were forced to play in rather than crediting their opponents' abilities—a face-saving measure to be sure, but with some basis in fact. The *Indian Leader* attributed a Haskell women's loss to Topeka in 1903 to the Y gym there being "so small" and baskets being "arranged so differently from those in the large gymnasium here, that they could not play their usual game." Chemawa's school publication similarly blamed a boys' loss to the Salem YMCA in 1910 on the Y court being "too short and narrow" to allow their teamwork to shine. Teams from both schools also blamed road losses on away floors that were "slick as glass," alleging that their non-Native opponents over-waxed them. Indian school publications did not accuse host teams of purposely slickening their playing surfaces to blunt the Native players' speed advantage, but neither did they rule out this possibility.[12] As the bigger second-generation facilities like Chemawa's 1931 gymnasium came on line in later years, they provided still larger, better-lit spaces, as well as more reliable playing surfaces for the Indian school style to continue evolving toward speed and open play.

Stylistic qualities that Indian school basketball teams exhibited during the first third of the twentieth century were also evident in the way they played football, as exemplified by the marked speed, quickness, agility, and stamina both Carlisle and Haskell were known for on the gridiron.[13] This was, by and large, a reflection of the fact that indigenous athletic, running, and group-oriented traditions carried over to both sports, but for the men, the two sports also stylistically reinforced each other. They were closely related activities for most male athletes in the Indian schools. In fact, Carlisle's varsity basketball team during the Pop Warner era *was* the varsity football team, or part thereof, in the sense that the majority of its players were on both rosters. The same was true to a lesser extent at other Indian schools, including Haskell.[14]

The two sports likely influenced each other by way of their common players in various ways. Most obviously, the conditioning the athletes received in one sport paid off in the other. Realizing this symbiotic potential, Pop Warner relied on basketball as a tool to keep his football players in shape. Even though he cared far more about football glories, he encouraged them to join varsity basketball in the winter and play pickup basketball during football road trips to keep them fit.[15]

Baseball, track, and other sports were also mutually reinforcing with basketball in terms of maintaining foot speed and physical endurance; but other athletic skills and tactics crossed over more readily between football and basketball. For example, the backfield moves and laterals Indian school teams deployed on the gridiron easily carried over to the court in the form of quick cuts, spins, and passes—long and short. Not all of this cross-influence was necessarily deliberate or in all ways beneficial, however, as football's physical aggressiveness also bled over into basketball at times in disadvantageous ways. In January 1923, for example, the *Indian Leader* noted the difficulty Haskell's players had transitioning from full-contact football to low-contact basketball, which rendered one of their early season hoops games a virtual "wrestling match," marred by incessant fouling. "A number of the players had just washed off their football paint and had not spent much time on the court, so it was not wholly unexpected when some familiar football tactics were introduced," it reported. "However, this will all disappear when the boys become used to the feel of the basketball and spend more time on the courts."[16]

To a degree, Indian school teams may also have relied on similar tactics in both football and basketball to overcome physical size disadvantages, but this factor should not be overemphasized on the hardwood. Size was much less a driver of stylistic innovation in basketball than it was for Carlisle's or Haskell's football teams, which were dramatically outweighed by many of their university opponents. At least at Carlisle, Pop Warner was known to compensate for his football team's smaller stature by emphasizing speed, agility, deception, and clever formations to evade big defenders. Carlisle used leverage to turn their opponents' weight against them or flew around the ends, which proved amazingly effective.[17]

Some historical observers perceived a similar dynamic on basketball courts, assuming that Indian school teams were relying on their speed and agility to counteract their opponents' height and weight advantages. A *Philadelphia Ledger* reporter covering an early basketball game between the Carlisle men and Germantown YMCA in 1897 noted a connection between the Native team's physical size and its playing style. "The Indians on the whole were not big men," he said, "but they made up for this by their agility and speed and played with all the dash and fire which characterizes them in all athletic contests."[18] Decades later, James Naismith made a similar observation regarding Native basketball players. In his memoirs, completed not long before his death in 1939, he wrote that Native teams were "usually made up of comparatively small men." "This fact is a distinct handicap to them," he continued, "but their ability to move quickly and their art of deception overcome the disadvantage of their height, so that wherever these teams play they are assured of a large crowd of spectators."[19] In the intervening years between the 1897 Carlisle reference and

Naismith's analysis, a variety of reporters told similar tales of smaller Indian school teams besting bigger foes using superior speed, agility, and well-coordinated teamwork.[20] These included some girls' teams as well, like Albuquerque Indian School when they played and defeated Mesilla Park College in 1902. The college women were larger, one reporter said of that game, but their "advantage gained in size was handicapped by the quickness of the Indians."[21]

It is evident from such accounts that when Indian school teams were outsized by their opponents, their playing style provided ample compensation, but broader analysis reveals that size discrepancies between Indian school and non-Native teams were not as extreme, on average, as observers like Naismith reckoned. The fact that Indian school players could often defeat larger opponents using their speed and agility did not mean they developed their style primarily for that purpose.

The vast majority of newspaper reports of games between Indian school and non-Native teams said nothing about size mismatches. This is not surprising, as a sampling of eighty-five varsity players from multiple institutions (fifty-two male players and thirty-three female players) between 1900 and 1940 suggests that Indian school athletes were of average to slightly below-average stature and weight compared to non-Native basketball players of their day. The male players between the ages of sixteen and twenty-one averaged just under 5'8" and 147 pounds and the female players between sixteen and eighteen averaged 5'3½" and 118 pounds.[22]

If these athletes were playing high school or college basketball today, they would be at a decided competitive disadvantage, but they were not during the height of the Indian school era. By Naismith's own measurements, the University of Kansas varsity men in 1914 averaged 5'9" and 149 pounds, with their best player standing just over six feet.[23] Robert Peterson also maintains that before World War II, most professional basketball players, of any race, "were not much taller than the average American male—at that time, 5 feet 8 inches." He may underestimate average player sizes for later years, as six-foot players had become common even at the high school level by the late 1930s.[24] It is nevertheless the case that basketball during the first half of the twentieth century was much less a tall person's game than it is today. Weight, not height, was often considered to be more determinant of a team's success in that era; but by this measure, too, Indian school teams were at only a slight disadvantage.

There were some Indian school players and teams that were actually larger than most of their opponents. Although it was rare for any of the Indian school boys to top six feet by their late teens, some did. According to Phog Allen, Haskell's 1908 team was extraordinarily large. "Our Indian team was of unusual size," he recalled twenty years later. "Every man with one exception stood at least 6 feet tall and weighed from 180 to 210 pounds."[25] Even if Allen's tendency to exaggerate added a few inches and pounds, Haskell's 1908 team would have been significantly larger than the Jayhawk's of 1914. Schools drawing most of their students from Southwestern tribes tended to have smaller players than the northern schools, but even they had their big men. Albuquerque Indian School's largest player in 1928, its center, Richard Milda (Akimel O'odham), stood 6'1" and weighed 172 pounds.[26]

Most of these average- to above-average-sized players and teams still employed the same up-tempo, agile approach, which further argues against physical size being the key factor determining the Indian basketball style. This does not, however, mean that size played no role, particularly at the individual level. Some of the best Indian school basketballers were smaller athletes who relied heavily on their speed and agility to compete not only against bigger opponents but also alongside bigger teammates.[27] These diminutive dynamos may also have inspired their larger teammates to play faster, with more flair. Among them was five-foot-five forward Edward Dominguez, who first learned to play basketball by throwing a carpet rag ball at a hoop in his dormitory room at Chilocco. Identified in school records simply as "Pueblo," with no further clues as to his tribal affiliation, he went on to start for the school's varsity team during the 1910s and became its standout scorer. Dominguez was said by journalists to be a brilliant player "who shoots goals from any corner of the lot, whether facing the basket or not," and once, in 1913, he scored thirty-five of his team's forty-five total points to defeat the University of Oklahoma. This high of an individual point tally would be impressive today but was astounding in that era.[28]

Another smaller player with above-average moves was Collins Jordan, who transitioned from team mascot to star player for St. Francis Mission during the early 1930s. Three five-foot-eleven teammates towered over his five-foot-four frame, but he inevitably stole the show. Although offensively referring to him as the "little papoose of the redskin band," a reporter complimented the guard on his amazing play during a 1935 Chicago tournament. He was the "spark plug and the whole motor in the Indian war machine," the reporter said, "baffling the easterners with his tricky ball handling, passing and dazzling shots."[29] He and his Lakota teammates had added a few inches by 1937, with three six-footers bringing the squad's average height up to 5'8½. Although this only made them half an inch shorter on average than their non-Native opponents in that year's tournament, Jordan's small yet fierce presence must have made them feel like Davids slaying Goliaths. St. Francis used their athleticism to roll off defenders on screens when they encountered man-to-man guarding. "And since we were short and we had a lot of speed, it was advantageous," Jordan later recalled. "We'd go and pass-off and roll-off, just keep going like that and had the whole middle aisle open."[30]

Together, these factors contributed to the development of Indian basketball within the Indian schools: tribal running and sporting traditions; intensive physical training and practice; team cohesiveness consequent of shared cultural values and life in a boarded environment; comparatively spacious gyms; some cross-influence with football; and, to a lesser extent, the athleticism some players and teams employed to overcome size mismatches. But their style was about more than talent, techniques, and tactics. Playing the Indian basketball style was also about attitude—the pride that comes from representing something greater than yourself or even your team. Their indigenous pride pushed them to train and play harder, further explaining why they displayed such skill and endurance. They worked to secure every possible competitive advantage to outplay white teams at the same games. Some historians have expressed this impulse in other Indian school sports as their desire to beat whites "at their own game," but at least in basketball, what Natives were really doing was using their own playing style, their own *version* of the game, to win on common ground.[31]

As will be seen in the following chapters, the stylistic innovations that students developed in the Indian schools later carried over to predominantly Native barnstorming and reservation public school teams. Through these types of teams, the style would live on through mid-century, after the Indian school programs declined in prevalence and significance. These teams played similarly to earlier Indian school teams because they were influenced by the same competitive drives and athletic traditions that helped spawn the Indian school style. Tribal youths growing up living in the same reservation towns, often as blood kin, also replicated the tight social bonding that Indian school youths previously developed with peers from other tribes.[32] Indian school players also caused the style to carry over directly as they transferred to public schools as students, or as coaches, and as they formed independent amateur and professional teams as adults.

It should be reemphasized here that the Indian basketball style of play was not in all ways unique, though it was distinctive. There were other teams, from other racial and ethnic groups, that shared certain stylistic qualities with the Indian boarding school, barnstorming, and public school teams. Prominent among them, before World War II, were Chinese American playground and barnstorming teams based in San Francisco, Mexican

American high school teams in San Antonio, and various African American teams in Chicago, which all relied on foot speed, adroit ball handling, and rapid passing. In some but not all of these cases, historians documenting these groups' stories attribute their playing styles to their physical size disadvantages, but one wonders what else is there. Perhaps the similar sense of empowerment that peoples confronting prejudice attained through basketball motivated them to play a more fluid, vigorous style, or perhaps similar concerns about biased referees, eager to call personal fouls, may have encouraged them to privilege evasive speed over physical brawn.[33]

Indian school teams did not single-handedly inject speed and flair into the sport of basketball, but they were prominent among the early pioneers who helped make it the exhilarating game it is today, in contrast to the more methodical sport it was at the turn of the twentieth century. They were innovators and were recognized as such by non-Native observers of their day.

Streaks of Lightning

The Indian basketball style began to emerge soon after the sport was introduced to the Indian schools. Key elements of it were already on display when Carlisle's varsity men played the Germantown, Pennsylvania, YMCA in March 1897. A thousand spectators packed the Y gymnasium eager to see if Carlisle's football prowess would translate to this new sport. No one thought the Indians had much of a chance against the unbeaten Y team, which was widely regarded as the strongest in the Northeast, and so it was to no one's surprise that they lost 28–10. What everyone left the arena talking about, though, was Carlisle's determined effort and distinctive approach. A reporter writing for the *Philadelphia Ledger* identified their "dash and fire" on the court as uniquely Indian while his counterpart at the *Philadelphia Inquirer* simply referred to Carlisle's play as "innovative," specifically citing their amazing "passing, leaping, and jumping."[34] Neither called what they saw a playing "style," as such in-depth analysis was then rare in sports reporting, but they understood that Carlisle was showing them something new and compelling.

Indian schools farther west soon eclipsed Carlisle competitively, dominating many of their regional competitors using the same stylistic elements as their Pennsylvanian sister institution but executing them with greater precision. In 1901, Lawrence townspeople watched in wonder as Haskell's men ran Lincoln, Nebraska's YMCA team off the floor. It was the "prettiest and fastest" game they had seen all year, said one reporter. "The game was furious from the first, but the red man's miraculous wind was too much for the Nebraskans," he wrote. "There was no letup with the braves, but the Lincoln boys tired and became disheartened." In a remarkably high scoring game for the day, Haskell prevailed 52–24. Being "longer winded" also enabled them to grind down William Jewell College in 1902, on their way to a 35–19 victory. Haskell also distinguished itself in 1902 by its "excellent team work" and "superb form," said reporters, but it was their quickness and stamina that most impressed. They kept their feverish pace going into 1903, dazzling spectators in a game against the Sioux City YMCA by unleashing their fast-breaking speed. A reporter declared that "for all around, speedy play, the equal of the Indians has probably never before been seen [in Sioux City]. . . . Time and again, when the ball had narrowly escaped the Sioux City basket, was it whisked to the other end of the court with lightning-like rapidity and dropped deftly in the yawning basket before anyone realized that it was done."[35]

That word, "lightning," began to appear in many journalistic references to Indian school teams, communicating to readers just how fast they were. It was applied to Native female and male teams alike. One of these was a Native girls' team from Sherman Institute, in Riverside, California. They showed off their remarkable speed and endurance in 1904 in taking down previously undefeated Los Angeles High 12–5. There was a "lightning-like rapidity" about them, said the *Los Angeles Times*, "the game being one of the fastest ever played here." They maintained this pace throughout, appearing "not to tire" and exhausting their opponents. Sherman's ability to emphasize speed was aided by their playing men's rules at that time, as did Fort Shaw, another Indian school girls' team known for its whirlwind presence on western courts. Fort Shaw was fast in all forms of movement—running, passing, juking. "It is said that [Fort Shaw's players] are very fast and quick with the ball and they play the game with a vim and dash that are lacking in many girls' teams," an Anaconda, Montana, reporter wrote in 1902. Emma Rose Sansaver (Chippewa-Cree and Métis) was especially renowned for quickness. Playing in St. Louis in 1904, she was said to dodge "here and there with the rapidity of a streak of lightning."[36]

As the years progressed, many Indian school teams maintained this reputation for superior speed and endurance. Chilocco's varsity boys were perennially listed among the fleetest squads in Oklahoma during the 1910s. They were also known for their quick action in all respects, outplaying competitors through seamless teamwork, dexterous ball handling, and all-out hustle. One reporter marveled at Chilocco's "uncanny ability to pull the ball back in bounds" whenever it seemed headed out. One of the best known referees in the Midwest, E. C. Quigley, extended a greater compliment to Haskell's men in 1918, declaring their team the fastest in the country.[37] During the 1920s, other male teams from Chemawa, Flandreau, Genoa, Phoenix, and Stewart Indian School in Nevada were also praised for their fast floor work.[38]

Some of these teams, however, proved more adept at moving the ball than sinking it. Most were capable, if not extraordinary shooters, but there were exceptions to both ends of the spectrum. Carlisle's varsity men particularly struggled with accuracy in the early 1910s. During the 1920s, Chemawa, Haskell, and Phoenix were among the teams adopting a live-and-die-by-the-sword approach, thrilling fans with their unorthodox tendency to shoot both on the run and from long distance, and too frequently missing in these attempts. They were basketball pioneers, foreshadowing a more exhilarating era yet to come, but also proved there was a downside to privileging speed and audacity over fastidiousness.[39]

At the other end of the spectrum were Indian school teams that were both fast and keenly accurate, playing with pronounced élan while still taking care to shoot straight. These were the deadliest Native squads, and they awed spectators and intimidated competitors. Fort Shaw was the most notable female team fitting this bill in the early years. In the 1930s, a later generation of girls from Pierre earned a similar reputation, though this was in large measure the work of one extraordinary player: Marcella Crow Feather.[40] She scored 362 of Pierre's 401 total points in 1930–31, leading them to a 15–1 season record. "Her speed has often been the means of overwhelming her opposition and running up big totals," wrote a reporter for Pierre's *Capital Journal*. "She was a scoring machine all by herself, and her ability to shoot from any position made her an extremely valuable player."[41]

Many male Indian school teams demonstrated this same potent combination of speed and shooting accuracy, including Haskell's early lineups during the 1900s, Wahpeton in the 1910s, Genoa in the 1920s, Albuquerque and Santa Fe in the 1930s, and St. Francis consistently from the 1920s through the early 1940s. Some of these teams had spectacular outside shooters, especially Haskell and St. Francis. Even during their more erratic 1920s, Haskell's forwards had some fantastic nights, like on January 7, 1927. In their 40–11 victory over the University of Kansas City, they sent balls sailing from near mid court, "thrilling the crowd as they floated in the air and dropping through the net with a singing switch." This long-range shooting was equal parts bravado and tactics. Although this was decades before the three-pointer entered the game, hitting the target consistently from long range enabled Indian school teams to overshoot zone defenses put up to counteract their speed advantages.[42]

Even James Naismith was struck by what Indian school teams were doing, thinking their play was both distinctive and attractive. To his eyes, Natives were playing basketball as ideally as anyone ever had. They made such an impression on him, in fact, that they were the only American racial or ethnic group he singled out for lengthy discussion in his basketball memoirs. He had first become enamored with Native players while refereeing games at Haskell in 1900. Once hooked, he kept returning to watch them play from the sidelines. "During each winter I made it a point to see several games at Haskell," Naismith recalled, "because I delight in the agility of the Indian boys."[43]

Naismith no doubt had Haskell's teams in mind when he wrote more generally about the way Native teams relied on the "art of deception." He meant nothing negative by "deception," but instead was referring to their quick action and evasiveness on the court, which he regarded as ideal characteristics.[44] Naismith once wrote in 1914 that he designed basketball to demand instantaneous thought and action rather than relying on preplanned plays. When the sport is played properly, he explained, "there is not time to think out a play, but reflex judgement must control, and the action must be performed with lightning rapidity."[45] Seeing Native players move their bodies and the ball so quickly with such precision and apparent ease thus enthralled him. He much preferred it to the way most non-Native teams moved, ploddingly throwing their weight around or going through preplanned motions. Here, instead, were indigenous streaks of lightning, animating his sport.

Naismith was among many commentators who noted how Indian school teams reacted in unison to the flow of play so quickly that their perception seemed to slow the passage of time or be extrasensory. From the early 1900s forward, journalists everywhere complimented these teams on their ability to pass the ball quickly from player, to player, to player without hesitation and with little to no verbal communication. Non-Natives were often mesmerized by this dynamic. Haskell's men, it was said, left the YMCA team from Evanston, Illinois, "completely mystified" by their rapid-fire passing in 1907. In similar fashion, Adam Fortunate Eagle remembers his schoolmates at Pipestone stunning non-Native teams during the 1930s. The Pipestone boys passed the ball around the courts so swiftly, he said, that the "white boys" could "hardly get their hands on it."[46]

Non-Natives unaccustomed to dealing with Indian school teams, and ignorant of their life experiences, failed to understand that this lightning quick, silent teamwork was a culturally and socially learned skill. Sydney Beane, Jr., remembers his father and his players at Flandreau in the 1940s communicating effectively on the court while saying very little, which he attributes to their shared cultural emphasis on nonverbal communication. "My dad wasn't really highly verbal," he explains, "but his non-verbal sense of self and who he was, and the pride of who he was; he was always able to convey that through just a look. He always had this whistle in the gym. All he'd have to do is whistle and people would look at him; and there was a look that he gave, and people automatically responded to that."[47] This cultural emphasis on conveying meaning nonverbally and accurately reading each other was only heightened by a boarding school's social environment. These student athletes spent so much time together and practiced so intensively that they did not have to yell to get attention or crane their necks about searching for their teammates on the floor. They could anticipate each other's actions, signal quietly, and be depended on to give up the ball to the right person at the right time.

Non-Natives also marveled at how quickly Indian school players instigated and reacted as individuals, running circles around their opponents. Phog Allen later wrote about one of these special talents who played for him at Haskell in 1908, another athlete small in stature who electrified his team. The coach recalled the player only by his family name Little Old Man and said he was a member of the Iowa tribe. It was a fitting name for a player towered over by teammates and opponents alike. In a game against a non-Native team from Fort Clinton, Ohio, said Allen, this five-foot-five forward hoodwinked a six-foot-six defender. "The giant guard drove toward Little Old Man, who pivoted away," Allen recalled. "The guard spread his massive form over the pivoting Indian. He was going to reach clear over the little fellow and entirely encompass him. . . . Just as the big Ohio guard reached down and over the Indian to take the ball away from him, the little fellow quickly darted between the big fellow's legs, dribbling the ball with one bounce and laid it up against the backboard for a goal." When this occurred "pandemonium broke loose" in the non-Native crowd, said Allen, as they cheered wildly for Little Old Man.[48]

In his book, Naismith singled out for special praise another Haskell alum named Louis Weller, otherwise known as "Rabbit" or "Little Rabbit." This Caddo forward from Anadarko, Oklahoma, who was also five feet five, is best remembered for his agility as a football halfback during the 1920s and 1930s; but his contemporaries knew him almost as well for his feats on the basketball court. Descriptive terms like "crossover dribble" were not used in his day, so it is not known what exactly Weller was doing to impress, but Naismith thought it extraordinary. "I have often said the most expert dribbler that I have ever seen was Louis (Little Rabbit) Weller," Naismith later wrote in his memoirs, repeating a claim he had been making since at least 1928. "I have seen him take the ball under his own basket and weave his

Figure 16. Louis "Little Rabbit" Weller demonstrates his shooting stance at Haskell in 1931. Oklahoma Publishing Company Photography Collection. Courtesy of the Gateway to Oklahoma History, Oklahoma Historical Society, ark:/67531/metadc630708.

way in and out the entire length of the floor. It always amused spectators to see Little Rabbit take the ball and, by dribbling, challenge the much larger players to take it from him."[49]

Although quick in all aspects of play, Indian school teams were best known for their speed on the fast break. This was not because they were the only teams using the tactic before mid-century, nor because they were credited with inventing it. Teams of diverse ethnicities had been sprinting

Figure 17. Chemawa's boys in their home gymnasium during the 1950s. A well-worn mat protects players driving in for layups, unless they hit one of the metal supports. RG75, Chemawa Photographs, 1907–71, 1366. Courtesy of NARA, Seattle, Washington.

and throwing the ball down court to beat defenders to the hoop since the earliest days of the game. Indian school teams like Haskell's 1903 men's varsity squad were not alone in doing so, even if they did get it done faster than most. The use of the synonymous terms "fast-breaking," "quick-breaking," "race-horse," and "fire-engine" to describe basketball styles relying on the tactic did not emerge until the early 1920s when sports analysis became more technically descriptive. A variety of teams with players of diverse ethnicities used variations on the fast break in the early 1920s, mostly in the West and Midwest. The technique then fell out of favor briefly in the mid-1920s before reemerging in the early 1930s after being popularized by Coach Frank Keaney at Rhode Island State College.[50]

Even though Indian school teams were not the sole purveyors of the fast break, their skill running it was noteworthy. Amongst the best "fast-breaking" teams in the American West during the 1920s and 1930s were male teams from the Chemawa, Flandreau, Haskell, and Phoenix Indian schools.[51] In some areas, like South Dakota, Indian boarding school teams were singled out as trailblazers in their innovative use of the technique. Catholic Indian mission teams in that state were often recognized for deploying the fast break consistently and successfully during the 1930s. They did so at a time when the tactic was still generally uncommon in South Dakota—so much so, says historian Dave Kemp, that white opponents took umbrage at the way Natives broke protocol, refusing to walk each rebound to the center to set up an offense as custom dictated.[52]

The best fast-breaking team in South Dakota during the 1930s was the St. Francis team Collins Jordan played for. "It was the best ball club I ever refereed," former official Harold Schunk recalled. "Way ahead of their time. It's amazing how fast those fellows moved. They knew *when* to move." In 1934, St. Francis amazed Chicago crowds by playing what one reporter described as a "wide open and fast moving" style "with passes that amaze even the sideline coaches." Vincent Brewer, who played for St. Francis in the early 1940s, later referred to their approach as "fast break off the backboard." "If it bounced in any direction," he said, "we had three men going down. We tipped it. We didn't catch it, we tipped it. We played the fast break constantly."[53] As Brewer's comments illustrate, many Indian school teams took the fast break to another level, adding measures of athleticism and teamwork that few opponents could match.

Defense

Although the Indian basketball style was most recognized for its offensive elements, this was not a reflection of chronically poor defending on the part of Indian school teams. The style relied so heavily on outrunning and outmaneuvering opponents on offense that the teams' defensive skills and innovations usually went unsung.

James Naismith was one of the few observers who noted that the athleticism Native players demonstrated on offense carried over to their defensive play. One individual stood out in his memory as proof. He had first seen five-foot-nine guard Chauncey Archiquette (Oneida) playing varsity ball at Haskell in 1900. A Wisconsin-born renaissance man, Archiquette had great athletic careers at both Carlisle and Haskell, excelled in his studies, and was a celebrated singer. He entered Carlisle in 1895 while in his mid-to-late teens and played guard for the first men's basketball team formed at that school. He was thus on the court for the game against Germantown in 1897. His "beautiful passing" in that contest helps explain why Carlisle made such an impression on spectators and reporters that evening. Archiquette then enrolled at Haskell in the fall of 1899, just after Jim Thorpe arrived there as a student. Thorpe idolized Archiquette, who was at that time the football team's star player.[54] Archiquette also played baseball at Haskell, alternating between catcher and center field. His strong arm and keen accuracy served him well in that sport and also on Haskell's basketball team, as he once demonstrated by scoring twice in a single game from the backcourt against the Kansas City YMCA. Both times he launched the ball from beneath the opposing basket—an impressive feat even considering that most courts were considerably shorter in 1900 than they are today. This was no fluke for "Archie," as friends knew him, because he and his illustrious teammate Pete Hauser both had reputations for distance accuracy.[55]

Although Archiquette's offensive talents were outstanding, Naismith was more taken with his defensive play. If Louis Weller was Naismith's archetypal offensive player, Archiquette was his defensive counterpart. The two men did not play in the same era, but to Naismith they were as the sun and the moon, two basketball luminaries who dominated their spheres. "How well I remember his superb guarding!" Naismith wrote. "To me this player, named Archiquette, had embodied all the requirements for a perfect guard."[56] In a double header against the University of Kansas during the 1900–01 season, Archiquette was paired in an opening game against Fred Owens, who, according to Naismith, was "as expert at eluding the opposing guard as Archiquette was at intercepting forwards." In the second game, when the Jayhawks shifted Owens to guard, Archiquette began defending both Owens and a new player shifted forward by patrolling his area of the court. Naismith biographer Rob Raines cites this as the first time a player is known to have single-handedly employed a zone-guarding technique. Archiquette took over basketball coaching duties at Haskell just before his departure midway through the century's first decade and, according to later reports, taught some zone-defending techniques to his players. Never a fan of zone defense, Naismith remembered him instead as the ideal man-to-man defender.[57]

Most Indian school teams eventually adopted zone defense as a standard approach, as did most non-Native teams, which explains why the Indian basketball style was less distinctive on that side of the ball. The University of Pennsylvania's men first popularized zone defense as a conservative substitute for man-to-man guarding in 1911. The scheme was neither flashy nor something purists appreciated, but it was effective, and so high school, college, and Indian school teams increasingly adopted it during the early 1920s and 1930s. The five-player zone entailed players abandoning individual assignments and falling back to create a semipermeable formation near the goal. The athletic equivalent of an infantry square, the zone was meant to stymie penetrating attacks. Its rise frustrated many basketball purists who said it undermined the integrity of the sport by slowing its pace and inhibiting athleticism. Naismith also complained the scheme led to offensive stalling as teams sat back with their throttles at idle, waiting to attack. If they already had the lead, they simply ran down the game clock (the shot clock not yet existing). When offenses could not afford to loiter, their other option against a tight zone was to shoot the long ball over it, like Haskell and St. Francis often did.[58]

When their opponents relied on the zone, Indian school teams were slowed down on the offensive side of the ball as well, because they were not averse to stalling when defenders refused to challenge them. Even some lightning-quick squads did so when it was to their advantage, proving that they were adaptable and not always wedded to speed. Agnes and Norbert Picotte recall Lakota and Yankton Sioux Catholic mission teams—St. Francis, Holy Rosary, and Marty—playing each other in the late 1930s and early 1940s. In general, they and other Indian school teams were a lot faster and more "showy" on offense than white teams in South Dakota. They were, however, disciplined enough to mix things up. In contrast to what Brewer said about St. Francis ceaselessly fast-breaking, Norbert Picotte remembers them once beating Marty Mission 25–24 by methodically retaining possession once they secured a narrow lead. "They could just stall and hold that ball and the only way they could break that stall, the guy had to go after and use the foul," says Picotte. Both St. Francis and Holy Rosary employed this stalling tactic when they needed to, he recalls, "but Marty, we hardly ever stalled the ball. We always kept it moving."[59]

As uninspiring as zone defense was, Indian school teams deserve credit for the discipline and adaptability they demonstrated in mastering the practice. Chemawa's boys were especially well-known for their impenetrable zone during the mid-to-late 1920s, earning them a regional reputation for having a "stonewall defense." They held some opponents to scores in the low teens or single digits while their hard charging offenses consistently put up mid-double-digits. Halfway through the 1926–27 season, Chemawa had scored 390 points while surrendering only 161.[60]

In spite of Archiquette's early zone experiments, Haskell's men were known for their man-to-man defense during the 1900s and 1910s. Their speed and aggressiveness made them particularly effective at this approach. Phog Allen encouraged this go get 'em attitude, telling his players that "it was their ball" and their job to attack for it. "They had to get it to play with it," he said, and the young men eagerly complied. Basketball's

Figure 18. Chemawa (in the darker uniforms) plays what is likely zone defense against a visiting opponent. They close to trap a driving opponent at the top of the key. RG75, Chemawa Photographs, 1907–71, 1370. Courtesy of NARA, Seattle, Washington.

historical currents, however, eventually proved too strong. Under non-Native coaches Pat Hanley and Tus Ackerman, Haskell intermittently relied on zone defense in the mid-1920s before adopting it religiously in the early 1930s.[61] Albuquerque Indian School's boys relied on man guarding even longer, as they were still credited for their capable execution of that defense through the early 1930s. Santa Fe Indian School made the transition sooner, giving their larger New Mexico sister institution a hard fight in 1933 by deploying an "airtight zone." They baffled Albuquerque with it for three quarters before Albuquerque finally broke through in the fourth, prevailing 22–14. After this, Albuquerque experimented with the zone as well and began earning accolades for their skilled execution of it after mid-decade.[62]

Flandreau Indian School's boys in South Dakota also had adopted zone defending by the early 1930s but nevertheless stood out as more defensively

Figure 19. Chemawa's boys give their all in an intramural contest or perhaps a practice session. RG75, Chemawa Photographs, 1907–71, 1343. Courtesy of NARA, Seattle, Washington.

innovative than most Indian school teams. This was due to Coach Henry Flood (Lakota). Hailing from Pine Ridge, Flood attended both Haskell and Carlisle, where he excelled in football, basketball, and the classroom before graduating and taking employment at Flandreau. He was a gifted coach with years of experience playing the game against strong western and eastern competitors. He had studied all styles of play, and he put this knowledge to good use, designing a robust zone defense he called the "alternating X." Flood complemented this with the fast break on offense to devastating effect, opening the 1930–31 season with a 9–0 run. Flandreau scored thirty-five to fifty-five points a game during that streak without surrendering more than a dozen points an outing to their opponents.[63]

St. Francis Mission's teams also made their defensive mark beginning in the mid-1930s. They bucked the prevailing trend by reverting from zone defense back to a preference for man-to-man guarding. They also relied more heavily on the full-court press than most teams, but only as situations dictated. "We didn't press all the time," recalled Vince Brewer. "We only pressed when it looks like the other team relaxed. If they're taking the ball out a little slow under the basket, we press. . . . As long as we had them going, stay, then get off."[64] St. Francis may have been one of the first Indian school teams to begin the transition toward the full-court pressing defenses that later became characteristic of Rez ball play.

The more perceptive observers thus realized the Indian basketball style, as played by Indian school teams over the course of decades, was about more than offensive innovation and exuberance. Many of these teams also distinguished themselves on defense by demonstrating aggressiveness, fluidity, tactfulness, and well-practiced teamwork.

Replicating "Indian basketball"

By the early 1940s, sports analysis had matured to the point that some observers began referring to the way many Indian school (and by that time reservation public school) teams played as a distinct style of basketball, most characterized by the fast break. A few non-Natives even tried to copy it, including Albuquerque High School's coach Tony Wilson, who may have been the first person to use the term "Indian basketball" as a stylistic descriptor. He applied the term in early February 1942 while speaking to a reporter about preparations for a game against a rival team from Albuquerque Indian School. Wilson began the conversation by speaking of his team's uncharacteristic struggles to date. His players had not been shooting accurately that season, he said, because they lost composure whenever they set their feet to take aim. If they went up-tempo, the coach said, maybe they could block out the crowd distractions and improve their scoring. "I don't know," Wilson told the reporter, "we may play 'Indian basketball' against the Indians!" "But what is Indian basketball?" people asked when they heard of this plan. "To Coach Wilson, it is the fast-breaking floor game which most Indian teams in New Mexico use," the *Albuquerque Journal* reporter explained. "They abandon set plays, making it their sole object to get the ball down the floor and thrown at the basket. The Indians are adapted to this style of play because they generally are inexhaustible. They can run all night without stopping."[65]

What Wilson did not tell the reporter was that he had been studying this "Indian basketball" style for many years, learning through hard experience how successful it could be. During the 1930s, his Bulldogs had played dozens of closely contested games against the Albuquerque Indian School Braves, who were one of the best fast-breaking teams in the West.[66] Wilson had also encountered a similar style when playing the Fort Wingate Bears.

That all-Navajo Indian school team made a habit of blowing past opponents on the fast break during the decade, their bright green and orange uniforms a blur. When Wilson was preparing to play Fort Wingate in 1939, the *Albuquerque Journal* had embarrassed him by running the headline "Bulldogs Fear Fast-Break." Readers were told he was "trying to think of the proper medicine" to combat this tactic, which made it all the more humiliating when the Bulldogs lost badly. Led by undersized forward Willie Tsosie, Fort Wingate trounced them, 46–34. The Bears "demonstrated the art of basketry to five bewildered Bulldogs," a reporter wrote after that game. "Tired of chasing Les Lavelle's Redskins down the floor, the Bulldogs stood by panting to watch the Indians run, pass and shoot with the regularity of a machine."[67]

Tony Wilson was not the only New Mexico high school coach who had come to admire the way Native teams played—and who dreaded facing them. Soccorro's coach Duck Dowell told a reporter in 1939 that "playing an Indian team is an entirely different matter from facing any other quint of basketeers." As explanation, he cited Fort Wingate's strong fast break and their "fast rushing defense all over the floor," which allowed opponents no time to set screens. Coach Ralph Bowyer at Grants High School also considered the Native fast break a distinct and effective stylistic approach and preceded Wilson by two years in trying to reproduce it. According to the *Gallup Independent*, Grants "copied the Indians' fast break" and "added a tactic of its own" to defeat Albuquerque Indian School 33–29 in January 1940. Bowyer's version was not a true facsimile of the Indian basketball style, however, as his "added tactic" appears to have been a reliance on "bruising" defense to knock the Natives off their game.[68]

Wilson began his own experiments with what he called "Indian basketball methods" in late January 1942, just a week before his team was to play the Braves. He first tried these methods against some predominantly non-Native high school teams, barely losing to Raton 43–41 and then beating Las Vegas 35–30.[69] Encouraged by these outcomes, Wilson eagerly anticipated his chance to unleash the new offense against the local Indian school. The Bulldogs would have the upper hand, he thought, because this was not the Braves team he had faced in the past. They had recently hired a new coach—a Native basketball star who deemphasized the Indian basketball style. Jesse "Cab" Renick had grown up in a mostly white part of Oklahoma, playing the game in public schools and junior college before becoming a two-time All-American at A&M in Stillwater. He had little in common with his athletes at the Indian school other than a passion for basketball. Renick had never been part of a predominantly Native team, and although biographer Paul Putz says he was proud of his mixed Chickasaw and Choctaw ancestry, he "also seemed perfectly content to live completely within the customs and norms of mainstream white society."[70]

Under no-nonsense Coach Henry "Hank" Iba at A&M, Renick had learned a slow-paced offensive style emphasizing ball control. When he once strayed from the formula and attempted two quick transition shots in a row during a close contest, an irritated Iba exclaimed, "Get that Indian out before he shoots us out of the ball game!" The message got through, and a budding star previously nicknamed "Point-a-Minute Renick" transformed into a more disciplined and lower-scoring player. This was the style Renick tried to develop when he was hired as coach and athletic director at Albuquerque, making him one of the few coaches who tried to train the speed out of an Indian school team.[71] The role reversal of Wilson's non-Native team playing Indian basketball against a team of Pueblo and Navajo athletes playing Iba-ball was too rich for the *Albuquerque Journal* reporter to pass up: "The situation is something like the tourist who wears beads and a blanket in New Mexico while the Indians, dressed in overalls and sports shirts, stare at him."

The game, alas, did not go according to Wilson's plan. Relying on strong perimeter work from Navajo forward Isadore Begay, the Braves overshot the zone Wilson deployed against them, and they hit six of seven free throw attempts. Renick, on the other hand, used the zone to great effect against the Bulldogs' driving attacks. Albuquerque High finally mustered a run in the waning minutes of the last quarter, but to no avail. The Braves took the game 24–17 and the lead in the citywide high school series. It had been neither the exhilarating nor the rough contest spectators were accustomed to seeing when these teams met but rather a low-scoring and low-fouling affair—a "clean" outing for old rivals who had borrowed each other's ways. At least one Bulldogs fan had expressed his displeasure with the unexpected flow of the game. To remind everyone there was still no love lost between the two schools, and that racial animosities persisted, he hurled a soda bottle out of the stands at the end of the third quarter, shattering it at the Native players' feet.[72]

Tony Wilson discovered that "Indian basketball" could be mimicked but not easily replicated. As the Braves demonstrated that evening, it was never just about fast-breaking speed. The best Indian school teams were well-rounded operations that beat opponents with their stamina, practiced fundamentals, skilled ball handling, and seamless teamwork as much as they did with their quickness. Knowing this, they were always confident in their ability to win games and, ultimately, championships. Whether the non-Native organizations that governed the sport would allow them chances at the most sought after titles, however, was another matter.

7
Champions

Indian school teams excelled in the early years. Playing in their preferred style, they defeated some of the best amateur teams in the country to claim multiple championships before 1910. This was varsity basketball as the superintendents had intended, allowing all-Indian teams to achieve solely on merit in interracial competition; but their freedom to achieve had less to do with harmonious race relations than with the underdeveloped state of the sport. Competitors were so sparse west of the Mississippi River that amateur teams from various institutions and organizations had to play each other. They vied for the same king-of-the-hill championships, where challengers dethroned titleholders over the course of a season rather than through playing tournaments. This was an accessible, chaotic process, with reporters debating the merits of multiple teams that often claimed the same championship titles simultaneously. In this disordered environment, the Indian school teams had as much chance to fight their way to the top as the YMCA, company, high school, and college teams they competed against.[1]

Then things changed. As basketball fell under more structured governance during the 1910s and early 1920s, newly established college conferences and state high school athletic associations excluded most Indian schools from membership, thus denying their teams access to the most sought after championships.[2] Once again, it seemed Indian school athletes were being told they were socially unequal to their white counterparts. Undeterred by these slights, Indian school superintendents, coaches, and athletes strove to maintain their winning traditions in a variety of ways. Those institutions that eventually gained membership in the state associations began to achieve at the high school level. Others found alternate pathways to success by competing in parochial all-Catholic tournaments or claiming all-Indian school titles in tournaments sponsored by their home institutions. These varied pursuits propelled Indian school basketball teams along two competitive tracks: one that allowed them to prove their mettle within the mainstream athletic culture and another that encouraged them to participate in a solely pan-tribal experience.

Early Triumphs

Haskell's men broke out first. The school's program emerged as a perennial state championship contender in the very early 1900s, not long after students began playing basketball at that institution. Carlisle's erratic scheduling and inconsistent performance never allowed its men's basketball program to be as competitive, and it took longer for other boarding schools to build strong programs for either male or female teams. Haskell was also the first Indian school to agree to outside basketball governance, albeit a loose form that had little bearing on their pursuit of championships. After initially playing independently, Haskell's varsity men joined with the Topeka and Lawrence YMCAs and the University of Kansas to form a small league midway through the 1900–01 season. The league was not a strict regulatory body, had no end-of-season tournament, and awarded no trophies. It simply made it easier for league members to arrange season schedules with their rivals. Haskell's men performed well their first year under the organizational scheme, finishing second to the Topeka Y in the four-team standings and winning two of three games against the James Naismith–coached Kansas Jayhawks. They also dominated most of their nonleague opponents, beating some by twenty-five points or more.[3]

Haskell's competitive prospects were brighter still as the 1901–02 season approached. The *Lawrence Daily World* speculated in early November that the team would "make a strong bid" for the Kansas state championship, an informal title open to all amateur teams regardless of league affiliations. Haskell appeared well-positioned because the starters were all returning except top-scoring center Simon Payer (Ho-Chunk), who had graduated from the Commercial Department and now played amateur ball for the Sioux City YMCA. Chauncey Archiquette, then in his mid-twenties, stayed at guard and twenty-year-old Herbert Fallis (Lakota) at forward. Both had thrived the previous year alongside Payer, as had forward James Oliver (Chippewa), who now shifted into the center position.[4] James Edward Shields (Arapaho) and Pete Hauser also emerged from the practice squads to join these veteran teammates.[5]

Haskell's players began the new season in prime physical shape and quickly gelled as a unit. Relying on foot speed and strong cooperative play, they defeated a string of opponents by wide margins. After opening with a 28–13 home win over the University of Kansas on December 20, they defeated the Kansas City Athletic Club, Kansas City Schmelzer Arms Company (the "Schmelzers"), Topeka YMCA, and William Jewell College. One of their biggest wins was a 73–29 trouncing of the University of Nebraska, which elicited the headline "Cornhuskers Slaughtered" in the *Lawrence Daily Journal.* Playing "like tigers from start to finish," Haskell outran, outshot, and outlasted the highly esteemed Nebraskans, handing the program its worst defeat in history to that point. The Indians lost only twice that season, both in return games against previously beaten opponents. One was a 27–22 away loss to the Jayhawks and the other a 31–18 loss to the Schmelzers, a company team with no recruitment restrictions to consider. The Schmelzers had restocked their team with short-term ringers after their prior defeat, calling into question whether this game was truly a rematch.[6]

Two games remained in early February to decide the Kansas state championship—a third and deciding meeting with the Jayhawks and a second meeting with the Topeka Y. Haskell eliminated the university team first, beating them decisively at home, 31–9.[7] They then traveled to Topeka midmonth as the odds-on favorites to secure the title. They had made a strong statement since last meeting Topeka, not only by beating the Jayhawks but also by dismantling the Kansas City Athletic Club, 65–0, and Third Regiment of Kansas City, 69–7. Haskell's James Oliver was at peak performance, scoring thirty-two points from the field over his last two outings, while Archiquette, Fallis, and the rookie Hauser were all contributing consistently. Out of desperation, the Y team brought in three ringers, hoping to counter Native speed with Topekan brawn. Played before a rowdy crowd hungering for a victory against the Indians, the tenor of the contest quickly soured. While doubling as the referee, Haskell's Coach Plank was subjected to "catcalls and hisses" from the stands. Meanwhile, the Y players were busy thrusting their shoulders and elbows at Haskell's players, who responded to this in kind. The Y lost 27–23, which the *Topeka Daily Capital* blamed on Plank's poor officiating. Topeka had also been disadvantaged from the start, the hometown reporter argued, because the Natives were heavier, older, and more experienced not only at basketball but also at football.[8]

Although Haskell could have rested on its laurels as undisputed Kansas state champions, they wanted more. They set their sights on an independent team stocked of six-footers from Independence, Missouri, representing the Modern Woodmen of America fraternal organization. Beating them would be no simple feat, but a national championship title would be the reward. Although they took no pay, the Missourians were expert players as good as any professional team in the country. Through all the convoluted calculations journalists made to determine who held which titles, the Woodmen had been awarded the poorly defined but high-profile basketball championship of America. They had secured this in March 1901 by defeating a team from Fond du Lac, Wisconsin. That team had in turn claimed the title a few weeks before by beating some of the strongest college and YMCA teams in the Midwest and Northeast, including the vaunted Yale University Bulldogs.[9]

Having realized that the national championship was held tantalizingly close to Lawrence, just across the Missouri border, Plank first issued a challenge to the Independence-based team in late March 1901. He was rebuffed at the time, but in early March 1902, he sent another challenge. This time the Woodmen grudgingly accepted because Haskell had earned too strong a regional reputation to casually brush off. The matchup was scheduled for March 8 with Haskell, playing at home, considered the favorite by most observers. Even James Naismith declared the Indians were the best team in the country.[10]

Things got physical as soon as the players took the court in front of a Saturday night capacity crowd of Lawrence townspeople and Haskell students. Numerous fouls were called on both teams early on, but the Woodmen benefited more. As a visiting Topeka reporter explained, the two Independence-sponsored umpires were "calling fouls on the Indians at every opportunity they had of throwing a goal, thus preventing their frequent scoring in the first half." Plank, serving as the referee, must have rallied his team and dressed down his fellow officials during the break, because Haskell surged in the second half while the umpires fell silent. The Woodmen, dazed by this shift in fortunes, lost their composure. Down ten to fifteen at the half, Haskell surged into a 17–15 lead and, at that moment, the Woodmen abandoned the court, forfeiting the game because they said they were being treated unfairly by the officials. The record book listed a 5–0 Haskell win because of the forfeit, wiping out the game-high nine points Herbert Fallis scored before the game prematurely ended.[11]

This was no storybook ending to the season to be sure, but the Woodmen's protests could not diminish Haskell's accomplishment. If the Missourians thought they could retain their title despite the forfeit, they were wrong. The 5–0 score satisfied journalists on both sides of the state border that there was a new national champion. After all, Haskell had gone 12–2 on the season, averaging thirty-seven points a game to their opponents' sixteen (not counting the 5–0 forfeit), and the Woodmen had been back on their heels when they left the court. "By winning this game the Haskell team became the champions of America," reported the *Kansas City Star*. The *Lawrence Daily Journal* claimed an even greater prize for the team in whose glory its readership reveled. "If anyone should happen to ask you what we have in Lawrence," it said, "mention among other things that we have the champion basket ball team *of the world*" (emphasis added). This honor came with no trophy for Haskell, just the pride of knowing they were the best team anywhere. The Woodmen of course challenged them to a rematch but were refused.[12]

Of course, Haskell could not retain the title indefinitely. They had to surrender it to the first team of strong reputation that could beat them the next season. Although they performed well in 1902–03, winning the opener against Kansas 24–11 and most games that followed, they did not go unbeaten. One of their losses was in early January to the Schmelzers, who had absorbed some former Woodmen in the off-season. But these nomad players were too late to reclaim their national title under this new banner. The Missouri Athletic Club of St. Louis snatched it away first by beating Haskell a few days prior by an unreported score.[13] Haskell's men's program remained a regional power in following seasons but was never again crowned national champion. The closest a Haskell team came was a nebulously defined "championship of the West" in 1907, won by a string of victories over big-name university teams on their epic midwestern tour.[14]

As good as Haskell's young men were, Indian school girls' and women's teams were generally more dominant than their male counterparts in the early 1900s, outpacing them by winning numerous championships. Albuquerque Indian School's girls were the first to do so. Playing the five-player version of the game, they defeated the University of New Mexico and New Mexico A&M multiple times to capture the territorial championship in late January 1902. They held the title until surrendering it back to A&M in early January 1903.[15] Chemawa in Oregon and Fort Shaw in Montana soon followed, both winning state titles in 1903. Chemawa got theirs by beating Albany High School and Albany College numerous times before beating undefeated Oregon Agricultural College (future Oregon State) in Corvallis 8–6 in mid-February. In a show of good sportsmanship, Albany College's team warmly greeted their triumphant Native rivals when they stopped at Albany's train station on their return trip. They toured them around town as honored celebrities before seeing them off to Salem.[16]

The following May, Fort Shaw won Montana's championship through a two-game playoff in Great Falls against the Butte Independents (formerly the Butte Parochials). Things had not looked good for Butte going into those contests. Fort Shaw had dominated the regular season, winning nine of eleven contests against high school and college opponents, as compared to Butte's 5–2 record. Fort Shaw's starters were also household names to thousands of Montanans and to members of the diverse tribes they so proudly represented. Ranging in age from sixteen to twenty-two, they were Pikuni Blackfeet guards Belle Johnson and Josephine Langley (the team captain and oldest player), sharp-shooting Assiniboine center Nettie Wirth, speedster Chippewa-Cree and Métis forward Emma Sansaver, and

Figure 20. Fort Shaw's 1903 Montana state champions. *Seated, left to right*: Delia Gebeau, Josephine Langley, and Emma Sansaver. *Standing, left to right*: Nettie Wirth, Belle Johnson, Minnie Burton, and Genie Butch. Pac 2016-27.1. Courtesy of the Montana Historical Society Research Center Photograph Archives, Helena, Montana.

Lemhi Shoshone forward Minnie Burton, whose offensive talents inspired the rallying chant, "Shoot, Minnie, Shoot!" Predictably, Fort Shaw took both games, 35–6 and 17–12, to become undisputed state champions. Chief Rocky Boy and other Montana Chippewas were there for the final game, having accepted an invitation to attend sent by Fort Shaw's superintendent Fred Campbell. It was the first time they had ever seen the sport played in person and they became instant converts, cheering "in hearty enjoyment" whenever the Native team made a good play.[17]

Already regionally renowned, Fort Shaw next ascended to national fame by competing at the 1904 St. Louis World's Fair, known as the Louisiana Purchase Exposition. The opportunity arose serendipitously from the Indian Office's decision to erect a Model Indian School on the fairgrounds as part of an exhibit depicting indigenous peoples. It was meant to stand in modern contrast to surrounding displays of indigenous cultures as a demonstration of how successful the federal Indian schools had been assimilating Native youths.[18] Chilocco's superintendent Samuel McCowan was put in charge of overseeing and populating the exhibit, and he asked Fred Campbell to help recruit students. Naturally, Campbell thought of his basketball team, because they were the sort of well-mannered and accomplished youths McCowan wished to showcase. In addition to demonstrating basketball to fairgoers, Fort Shaw's players were to conduct physical culture demonstrations with batons and perform musical and theatrical selections. The players were thrilled at the prospect. Although they understood they were there to promote federal Indian education policy, and may have been discomfited by this assignment, they were eager to see the fair and to perform and compete before an international crowd.[19]

Campbell also recruited a second girls' squad from Fort Shaw to scrimmage against his starters at the fair, increasing his basketball contingent to ten. Langley would not be going. After her betrothal, she left the team and Genie Butch (Assiniboine) took over as the fifth starter. Leaving in early June 1904, both teams and a small group of schoolmates and adult chaperones wended their way from Montana to Missouri, performing and playing exhibition games in towns along their route. Their fame preceded them, spanning farther afield than they could have imagined. Honolulu's *Hawaiian Star* even printed a blurb in May saying Fort Shaw's recent victories over white college women attested to Native peoples' "advances toward citizenship and equality." The assimilationist rhetoric aside, Fort Shaw's athletes looked forward to seeing exhibits along the Fair's Pike and playing basketball. They did both after arriving in St. Louis on June 16. Their descendants later told authors Linda Peavy and Ursula Smith that the Fort Shaw girls had some of the best experiences of their lives those following months.[20]

Twice weekly, between other assigned duties and performances, Fort Shaw's first and second teams scrimmaged for fairgoers on the plaza outside the Model Indian School. Scores of onlookers were so engrossed by the thrilling competitions that they forgot many considered it indecent for young women to play sports in front of mixed-gender crowds. But these girls had not come this far just to scrimmage. They also wanted to prove themselves against other teams. A friendly game on July 4 against some of McCowan's Chilocco students was a bit of a letdown in this regard, as Fort Shaw won easily, 36–0.[21] Things got more interesting on July 28 when they played the Illinois state champion O'Fallon High School team away from the fairgrounds at Belleville, Illinois. This was a more challenging pairing, but the game's outcome was never in question. Playing on a roped-off court before a large crowd, Fort Shaw won 14–3.[22]

Fort Shaw's final opponent at the Fair was an alumni team from St. Louis Central High School called the All-Stars. These former holders of the Missouri-Illinois championship had reassembled to prove Fort Shaw was beatable. They issued a challenge to play a best-of-three series to decide the championship of the World's Fair, which Fort Shaw gladly accepted. The first game, played on September 3 in Kulage Park, ended in a blowout 24–2 victory for the Indian school. After a few weeks' pause, the second game was played at the fairgrounds on October 8. It went Fort Shaw's way from the start. As the *Great Falls Tribune* reported, when the ball descended from the opening tip-off "Nettie made one of her phenomenal leaps into the air and sent it spinning far toward the Indian girls' goal. Belle caught it and, skillfully evading her opponent, threw it to Minnie, who smiled as she dropped it into the basket, while the audience went wild with enthusiasm." Fort Shaw won the game 17–6 to claim the Fair's championship. Some Montana newspapermen extrapolated from this that they were also national and world champions. Other reporters stopped short of acknowledging those titles, but all agreed that Fort Shaw was an extraordinary and probably unbeatable team.[23]

Fort Shaw's girls and young women kept competing, and winning, at basketball until the school finally closed in 1910, but there were to be no more national or world championships. A squad traveled to another world's fair in Portland, Oregon, in 1905 but did not compete for a title there. They did, however, play a much-anticipated game against Chemawa on an August side trip to Salem. With Emma Sansaver as the new captain, Fort Shaw beat the former Oregon champions convincingly, 38–13. Chemawa's girls' program, though, had the better years ahead. Its teams won another Oregon championship in 1908 and just missed out on a third in 1913, losing their final game to McMinnville College (future Linfield), 24–16.[24]

Meanwhile, the girls' basketball program at Euchee boarding school in Sapulpa, Indian Territory, was an ascendant power on the Central Plains. After learning the sport from Superintendent Charles L. Garber the year before, Euchee's girls beat every high school team they faced in 1906–07 to claim the championship of Indian Territory—the eastern portion of the soon-to-be state of Oklahoma. The team's Yuchi (or Euchee) players came from a small community with a proud heritage. Together with their Muscogee (Creek) neighbors, the Yuchi were removed from their southeastern homeland to Indian Territory during the 1830s. Although the US government did not recognize them as politically separate from the Muscogee, they retained a distinct identity.[25] Perhaps as a conspicuous display of their Yuchi pride, they played their games in moccasins; or this may have been a utilitarian choice, the soft soles allowing them to move faster than some of their white opponents, who played in hard-soled street shoes. The downside to this footwear, however, were the injuries they inevitably suffered to the tops of their feet. "In one match game with a team of white girls the Indians were badly trampled," Muskogee's *New-State Tribune* reported in June 1907, and yet they showed "not a whimper of pain" on their path to victory.[26]

Belonging to a small and often overlooked community may have bound the Yuchi players closer together than most teams—Native or non-Native—and made them determined competitors. Their affinity for each other was evident. "Their strongest point is in team work, backed up by incredible swiftness of foot," the *Osage City Free Press* said of their 1907 squad. Their passes were so sharp and well-coordinated that in one game they scored from the center jump "without ever letting the opposing team touch the ball or allowing the ball to touch the floor."[27] Adding to the media mystique surrounding them, their sixteen-year-old team captain, Grace Olive Vanest, gained individual fame in 1907 for shooting accuracy of a different sort. Newspapers across the country named her the "best woman rifle shot in Indian Territory." Using a .38 Winchester repeater, she rarely missed a silver dollar from a range of 100 yards.[28] This and subsequent Euchee squads dominated most of their competitors through the end of the decade. Their signature season was 1908–09, during which they amassed an impressive 27–1 record against teams throughout Oklahoma and from surrounding states to become "champions of the Southwest."[29]

Although female Indian school teams usually held the spotlight between 1900 and 1910, Chilocco's boys emerged mid-decade as another strongly competitive male program, second only to Haskell's. Chilocco's teams were perennial contenders for the Oklahoma state championship against primary rival, Oklahoma University. The Sooners usually prevailed when the two teams clashed, winning thirteen of twenty contests between 1908 and 1919. On a few occasions, though, Chilocco won outright or split a series of games against Oklahoma while maintaining strong enough records to make bids for the state title. They did especially well in 1908–09, winning the championship by defeating Oklahoma 27–20 in their only meeting and dominating other state opponents. The title was blemished though, because Chilocco lost most of its games against teams from Kansas, including to the University of Kansas 39–9 and Haskell 88–23.[30]

Chilocco made another run at the Oklahoma championship in 1916 while under the direction of James E. Jones, the talented coach who would later shepherd Albuquerque Indian School's boys to greatness. Chilocco won fifteen games that season, including both against Oklahoma A&M. They would have gone undefeated had they not split two meetings with the Sooners, losing the first 34–17 and then winning 39–38. This left the championship in dispute—a reporter for the *Morning Tulsa Daily World* arguing it belonged to the 19–6 Sooners based on strength of schedule, while the *Wichita Beacon* anointed Chilocco.[31]

Doors Close

As many Indian school teams were peaking in strength during the 1910s, their championship prospects were nevertheless fading. The all-access titles they competed for were being replaced with sanctioned college conference and high school championships that were often inaccessible to them. Male teams from the off-reservation Indian schools were hurt by the emergence of college conferences that barred them from membership, while female teams at those schools were hurt by the dissolution of many college women's programs that had been their traditional rivals. For all Indian school teams, off and on the reservations, the best chance to win championships shifted toward the high school level, but this proved problematic as well because many state high school athletic associations barred them from membership. And so, as non-Native college teams went one way and high schools another in pursuit of well-defined championships, they closed the doors on Indian school rivals they had previously battled as peers.

The off-reservation Indian school basketball programs began to feel the effects of these organizational changes just before 1910. They became casualties of an ongoing movement to elevate the status of college sports through the establishment of regional athletic leagues and conferences. Through interinstitutional coordination and the enforcement of uniform regulations, these bodies facilitated consistent season scheduling and endeavored to remove the stigma of professionalism from college sports.[32] As misfit institutions that were neither state-funded nor private, the Indian schools had difficulty finding homes in this new order. If they were left outside as independents, conference member schools might still play them for profit but were no longer required to in order to fill out season schedules or claim regional basketball championships, which were now determined by conference play. Indian school basketball teams, in short, became nonessential opponents.

The establishment of the Missouri Valley Conference (MVC) in 1907 with the universities of Kansas, Nebraska, and Missouri as founding members was an ominous development for men's basketball programs at Haskell and Chilocco. The Indian school athletes and fans had always looked forward to competing against these big institutions for state championships, but those days were now numbered. The University of Kansas no longer scheduled the Haskell men after joining the MVC and only played Chilocco once more, in 1911. Kansas State retained Haskell a little longer until it too joined the MVC in 1914. The changes were deflating for Haskell, which had been the strongest college-level competitor of all the Indian schools. The program had a 13–10 lifetime record against schools that eventually joined the MVC. Chilocco had also performed well, especially versus Oklahoma A&M, which it had defeated eighteen of twenty-one times. The University of Oklahoma and A&M both retained Chilocco as a regular opponent through the 1910s but dropped them after joining the MVC—OU in 1919 and A&M in 1925.[33]

The loss of big university opponents came as less of a shock to Indian school basketball programs that had never been so competitive. Albuquerque Indian School's boys lost all five of their games against the University of New Mexico before the programs stopped meeting in 1917 and Chemawa all ten against Oregon and Oregon State. Both universities in Oregon stopped playing Chemawa in the early 1920s, a few years after joining the Pacific Coast Conference. Phoenix Indian School played against Tempe Normal (future Arizona State) a decade longer but won only one of twelve games before Tempe found its Border Conference home in 1931.[34]

With their days playing the state universities ending, some off-reservation Indian schools searched for league homes for their male varsity teams among smaller public and private colleges. Chemawa began doing so early on, finding a place for its teams in the newly formed Willamette Valley Basketball League (WVBL) in 1909. This collection of half a dozen private colleges seemed an ideal fit for the Indian school. The opponent institutions like Pacific College and McMinnville were roughly equivalent in size to Chemawa, which had an enrollment of about 550, and they were close in proximity. Although Chemawa went through only the eighth grade, its varsity players at this time were also the approximate age of their league counterparts, ranging from their late teens to early twenties.[35] The Indian school also matched up well competitively with other WVBL teams, neither dominating them nor being dominated. After hovering near the middle of the standings for three seasons, Chemawa claimed its first league championship, in 1912. Team captain Luther Clements (Mechoopda) also made his personal mark on the WVBL that year and again in 1913, leading the league in scoring. However, Chemawa's first college-level title was to be its last.[36]

In the fall of 1915, WVBL representatives restructured the league to better align athletics with their institutional missions and ejected Chemawa. This was necessary, said the WVBL, because Chemawa was not a college. It was not that the Indian school's misfit status had previously escaped their attention. For years, the league members had treated Chemawa as an athletic peer, even electing its school disciplinarian and team manager Charles Larsen (Chinook) as the first WVBL president in 1910. But increasingly influential college leagues like the WVBL no longer wanted Indian school members that were structurally dissimilar to their own institutions and were therefore deemed more difficult to regulate. In a last-ditch attempt to curry the WVBL's favor, Chemawa drafted an Athletic Association constitution in 1916. In the interest of promoting positive "athletic relations with other collegiate institutions and organizations," the document limited players' eligibility to four years and prohibited them from playing independent ball during school breaks, bringing Chemawa's policies into closer alignment with the WVBL's. But it was no use. Chemawa was out for good.[37] The league members did not cut the Indian school off entirely. Its basketball teams were still fan draws, and so WVBL teams continued scheduling them in nonleague games after 1915; but these arrangements offered Chemawa no chance at a second WVBL championship.[38]

Whether anti-Indian attitudes also motivated the WVBL and other college conferences to either exclude or expel the Indian schools is difficult to say. They never gave this as a reason, but of course they would not have. These colleges and universities had always been willing to play these teams in years past, which argues against this motivation, but perhaps the effort to make their governing bodies seem more reputable by expelling "misfits" brought racial prejudices to the surface.

At any rate, the Indian schools were left reeling, looking for a place for their athletic programs to land. Neither Haskell nor Chilocco could find organizational homes through the 1910s and 1920s. At various times, Haskell's men tried to gain admission to the MVC, and both Indian schools requested membership in the Kansas Collegiate Athletic Conference, which included their smaller college rivals Baker, Kansas State Normal (future Emporia State), and Kansas Wesleyan. In all attempts, both schools were rejected out of hand as noncolleges. After watching this struggle go on for years, the *Lawrence Journal World* came to Haskell's defense in a 1917 editorial, criticizing the MVC and Kansas Conference for not giving one of their oldest rivals "a square deal in athletic affairs." The paper singled out for special condemnation the church-affiliated Kansas Conference schools, "whose purpose is to prepare men to spread the gospel to all nations, irrespective of color" but who had nevertheless put up "bars to the Indian. The inconsistency in this may not have been considered, but it exists just the same." The editorial writer alleged the conferences had rejected Haskell mainly due to competitive jealousies. The Indian school had beaten Kansas Conference and MVC teams so often at football and basketball that title-hungry conference members found any reason to exclude them.[39]

The 1917 editorial neglected to say the Indian Office also bore responsibility for the crisis at hand. In its effort to integrate Native students into American society, it had, ironically, created a school system that was distinct in structure and operation and was thus isolated from the non-Native institutions it claimed to emulate. The government Indian schools were *not* colleges at the time, so why should they expect to be treated as such? The Indian Service superintendents also failed their students by naively assuming that college counterparts would, on good faith, accept the Indian school athletic programs as parallel to their own and be willing to compete with them on even ground. Although some may have been so inclined, most were not.

In spite of the organizational changes, Indian school coaches and players did their best to keep competing in college-level basketball as independents. Haskell and Chilocco kept playing Kansas Conference teams as nonconference members during the 1910s and 1920s. If they had been calculated into the standings, both schools would have finished around .500 most seasons through those decades. In 1923, while playing at Chilocco early in his basketball career, Louis Weller expressed the frustration he and other Native players felt knowing they were being denied access to big championships. "We had a team equal to any University team in the State," he wrote in Chilocco's school annual that year, but despite beating the majority of their opponents "with ease," the team had little to show for it.[40]

With the college conferences and leagues shutting them out, off-reservation Indian schools began focusing on high school–level play in the 1920s and 1930s, as did the smaller reservation schools, which typically had younger students. They were also pulled in that direction because high school competition offered some advantages. It created interinstitutional connections that advanced federal efforts to transition Native American students to the public schools, encouraged Native and white teenagers to regard each other as peers, and gave Native teams access to increasingly prestigious state high school championships. To complete this transition, though, the Indian schools had to come to terms with the emergent state high school athletic associations.

The state associations stemmed from a progressive initiative to reform high school sports after the turn of the century, driven by professional educators who regarded athletics as vital to youth development and so wished to regulate them. The statewide associations required members to accept standard procedures for scheduling games, determining player eligibility, and awarding state championships.[41] South Dakota, in 1905, was one of the first states west of the Mississippi to establish one of these bodies, and others followed through the early 1920s. The perceived need to sanction state basketball championships either helped prompt the creation of these associations or became a top priority soon thereafter. By 1912, Kansas, Montana, Nebraska, and South Dakota all had tournaments or other sanctioned means to determine high school basketball champions. Nearly every state did by World War I, but unfortunately for the girls, most only sanctioned boys' championships.[42]

Indian school superintendents pursued state association membership so their teams could play full high school schedules and be eligible for state tournaments, but this was no simple task. Although the associations aimed to bring all public school athletic programs under uniform governance, they tended to regard parochial, private, and federally operated schools as beyond their purview and pooled Indian schools with these ineligibles. The associations also had special reasons for singling out Indian schools for exclusion. They were mainly concerned that off-reservation Indian schools gained unfair competitive advantages by recruiting students across state lines. The associations also thought the Indian schools were harder to hold accountable to rules because they were federal or parochial institutions. Finally, there were the training tables and the boarded environments, which allegedly advantaged the Indian school teams by allowing them to micromanage player diets and sleep habits.[43]

Indian school superintendents denied that the competitive scales were tipped in their favor, insisting they maintained high ethical standards in athletics; but they knew some of the allegations against them had merit.[44] The big off-reservation Indian school programs did actively recruit across state lines, acting like university athletic programs in that regard, and they often appeared to care more about winning than about educating their students. It did not help that they were frequent targets of criticism from without and within the Indian Service. The state associations knew government-sponsored reports accused Carlisle and Haskell of athletic malfeasance numerous times over the years, including the Meriam Report's assertion in 1928 that Haskell was "harboring athletes of the most dubious kind."[45] Not all of these criticisms were fair. Indian schools that were actively petitioning for membership in the state associations generally strove to maintain strict player eligibility rules in accordance with public school regulations; but certain problems were difficult to overcome.[46]

The Indian schools had particular difficulty convincing the public schools that they could comply with maximum player ages, which were usually set at twenty.[47] Some schools such as Chemawa maintained reliable student birth records, but others did not, and this caused trouble. Albuquerque Indian School's athletic staff, for example, could not accurately account for player ages because many of its student files contained discrepant birth dates. There was one starter on the varsity boys' basketball team who may have been sixteen in 1928 or an ineligible twenty-one, depending on which part of his file one examined. The public schools also suspected that Indian school coaches lied about player ages on their rosters. They were not alone in thinking this. Indian Service employees sometimes accused each other of this ploy. In one 1927 incident, Pierre's coach Sam McLean charged Flandreau's Henry Flood with cheating him at football by violating age limits, which Flood denied. A similar dispute between the Albuquerque and Phoenix Indian schools in 1933 caused a flurry of angry accusations.[48]

Even though they denied charges of wrongdoing, it is likely that Indian school athletic directors and coaches did bend some rules. They knew some public schools hypocritically did so as well and were pressured by their superintendents, non-Native townspeople, and student alumni to win. What's more, many had been Indian school athletes themselves in years when it was acceptable to play varsity ball well into your twenties and when they and their classmates subverted a variety of school rules just to endure daily life.

After years turning them away, the state high school associations eventually admitted the Indian schools, but sporadically so and often over the objections of a sizeable portion of their membership. One of the first to get in was Genoa in Nebraska, a school of about three hundred students with a varsity team made up entirely of boys in their mid-teens. Like most others, Nebraska's high school association needed new members to boost its authority and, since 1911, had restricted access to the boys' basketball tournament to induce outliers to join. Genoa had nevertheless been barred from that tournament until 1921 when it was finally admitted to the association. Its teams were small fish in a big sea their first years in the tournament. The Nebraska association was so desperate to please its membership that until 1927 it made no effort to limit the number of member teams entering the postseason. The tournament had bloated so much in size by the time Genoa entered it that hundreds of competitors had to be broken into more than a dozen classes, each with a trophy to be won.[49]

Undaunted by the scale of the event, Genoa's boys were determined to seize this new competitive opportunity in the early 1920s. Before long, they made their mark in Lincoln. Their "fast floor work" and shooting accuracy, combined with the novelty of seeing a so-called "colorful" team in action, made them fan favorites from the start. In 1922 and again in 1924, Genoa advanced to the Class B final but came up short both times.[50] Getting demoted to Class C in 1927 pitted them against schools of more equivalent size, which helped them to finally get over the hump and win their first championship. It was a tough fight, especially for their starting center. Identified only by his last name, Parker, in the newspapers, the determined teen broke some ribs early in the second round game against Alma. Though he was wincing in pain, Coach Leroy Hall sent the boy back in for the second half to lead his team to a 19–6 comeback win. Hall played him the following two nights as well, in the semifinal against Milford and the final against Potter. In that last game, Parker soldiered through the pain to score five points, helping secure the 19–8 championship victory.[51]

More state associations opened their doors to the Indian schools later in the 1920s, as some off-reservation institutions added the full range of high school grades and were subsequently accredited by state departments of education. These developments, together with their renouncing college-level play and engaging in effective politicking, proved decisive.[52] Albuquerque and Santa Fe in New Mexico and Mount Pleasant in Michigan all gained membership to their associations during the decade. So did Chemawa, which was admitted in 1928 thanks to the administration's vigorous lobbying of Oregon's public school superintendents.[53] Indian schools in other states waited longer in spite of their best efforts to gain admission. Most were refused association memberships through the 1920s. Sherman waited until 1932 to join in California and Haskell until 1945 in Kansas.[54]

The Integrated Track

Becoming a state association member had upsides and downsides. Although these Indian school teams gained greater access to interscholastic competition, they were forced to discard their overaged players. These athletes had to either give up sports, transfer to an Indian school in another state, or be relegated to intramural competition. Member Indian schools also lost the freedom to schedule games against many independent teams they were accustomed to playing. Gaining membership was thus a two-steps-forward, one-step-back proposition for institutions wanting to expose as many students as possible to competition against a diversity of opponents.

The shift to high school–only schedules also created headaches for Indian school administrators because many of their students and off-campus supporters were upset about the cessation of college-level play (especially in football). This response threatened to reduce student interest in athletics, reduce ticket sales, and restrict outside donations. The move toward high school competition also increased animosities between Native teams and certain high school opponents who refused to accept them as institutional equals. School superintendents nevertheless believed the benefits of association membership far outweighed these costs. It was the best way to continue using athletics to promote racial integration and provide their students the competitive opportunities they needed and deserved.[55]

Chemawa's first year in Oregon's association, in 1929, was especially turbulent. School administrators and employees were unsettled as they feared violating one association rule or another and fretted about the blowback they would receive from alumni and Salem townspeople who preferred college-level athletics.[56]

It seemed that the boys' varsity basketball team would provide a welcome distraction from these concerns when they earned a bid to the state tournament that spring. This did not go over well with Salem High, however, the opponent they upset 26–23 in a district playoff to get to state. After the game, two hundred high schoolers rampaged across Willamette University's campus, where the game had been played, howling in protest and hurling rocks at windows. Salem had the better season record, they shouted, and should never have been forced into a playoff. That they had also lost to an *Indian* team may have further fueled their rage. The mob nevertheless bypassed the Native players and focused its ire on the state association for creating the situation. Two association board members who had exercised the poor judgement to be there for the game were apprehended, manhandled into a campus office, and held hostage. Their teenage assailants taunted them relentlessly, threatening to drag them outside by their lapels and dunk them "in a mill race." Fortunately for these terrified men, the city police restored order and freed them, shaken but unhurt.[57]

The following Monday, Chemawa's coach Reginald Downie feigned gratitude when Salem High's players offered their well wishes to his team, and apologized for the riot on behalf of their schoolmates, at a school assembly. It was the expected duty of any Indian school coach to make nice with the public school teams, lest a diplomatic breach interfere with the Indian Office's efforts to advance academic integration. Downie had agreed to attend the assembly in the high school gymnasium even though he knew it was a staged and insincere event, orchestrated by Salem civic leaders who feared the state association would move the upcoming state tournament from Salem to Portland as a punishment unless the local high school students appeared contrite.[58]

Meanwhile, Downie's boys shook off this controversy and entered the tournament two days later brimming with confidence. They played well their first game against Myrtle Point, winning 23–17. Stout, six-foot-plus center Eldred George (Klamath), and speedy forward Jesse Prettyman (Crow) were the leading scorers, each tallying seven points. Though they came from different tribal cultures, the two scoring dynamos played well together, perhaps expressing a bond forged while working long hours together in the school's painting trade. This interpersonal synergy, however, was not enough against a talented team from Washington High that trounced Chemawa 36–18 in the second round.[59]

Chemawa probably would have advanced further in the 1929 tournament had they not been a team of extremes. They lived and died by speed, playing a form of the Indian basketball style that was out of kilter. All season, they had exhibited a fast attack with accurate passing but also tended toward unfettered exuberance, heaving the ball at the goal "while running at top speed, from all angles." This frenetic pace wowed the tournament crowds but cost Chemawa in the end. Despite displaying "the flashiest floor work of any squad in the conflict," commented columnist Arthur Perry, their shooting in both games was "abominable and deplorable." "They would get the ball and race down the floor like greased lightning, then heave wild, and do this over and over, and over and over, and over and over, everlastingly without end," Perry wrote. "If their running during the tourney was placed end to end, they would have traveled across the continent and up to their necks in the Atlantic ocean." Things settled down for Chemawa in the following years. There were no more high school riots during the Depression and their shot selection improved, but neither were there any trips back to state until 1940, when they recovered from a shaky first round to win the consolation bracket.[60]

Of all the Indian school basketball programs, Albuquerque's had the most triumphant story to tell of its first decade as a state association member. Its boys' teams first appeared in the New Mexico state tournament in 1921, but none advanced far in the competition until the 1927 squad finished second overall. This strong showing reflected the positive influence Coach James E. Jones had on the team after transferring from Chilocco to Albuquerque mid-decade. His 1927–28 unit was even better than the previous year's, displaying a potent combination of speed, endurance, shooting accuracy, and solid fundamentals.[61]

Assembling and maintaining this championship-caliber unit was not easy for the veteran coach, who had a harder time retaining the young men than he did preparing them to compete. Although part Eastern Cherokee, Jones was born and raised off-reservation in Texas, and he had very different life experiences than did his players. Most were of full Native heritage and came from traditional rural families on the vast Navajo Nation or the Pueblo villages that dotted the western part of the state. His players knew their parents and elders were ambivalent or displeased with their attending an off-reservation Indian school and longed for their return. The same was true for athletes at any Indian school, but the gravitational pull homeward was especially strong here. On numerous occasions before and during the season, two of Jones's starters and one of his substitutes were beckoned home to help tend to their corn crops, sheep, and ailing relatives. Two deserted campus after Superintendent Reuben Perry refused to grant them leave, but they were restored to the team after returning to school. Another starter missed weeks of practice and conditioning, returning for the beginning of the season after overstaying the summer break by two months caring for his sick father. A fifth player habitually deserted campus for hours at a time to head into the city and was eventually caught with a friend joyriding in a school employee's purloined car. Jones convinced Perry to retain the twenty-year-old as a student and team member even though official policy dictated he be expelled for that stunt.[62]

Despite the off-court challenges, when Jones had these young men in a gym, they were a dream to coach—talented, selfless, and disciplined. The 1927–28 team, which by this time was known as the Braves, rarely committed turnovers or personal fouls, averaging five team fouls a game to their opponents' seven. They usually won with speed but could just as easily stall the ball to hold a lead.[63] The crew was shorter than Jones was used to coaching—only center Richard Milda topped six feet—but he squeezed every ounce of effort out of them. Most were five feet five, give or take an inch, including top-scorer and team captain Kee Kinsel, referred to by reporters as the "little pepper box." This right forward from Navajo country weaved through defenders with ease, scoring in close or kicking it out to his teammates, every one of them capable of sinking long-range shots with uncanny regularity. There was an intertribal symmetry to the starting lineup, with two Navajo and two Laguna players orbiting the Akimel O'odham center. Navajo guard Askie Legah was the pride of Fort Defiance, Arizona, while Martin Smith and Nelson Thompson represented different Laguna villages in west-central New Mexico. There were also frequent substitutes Santiago Lujan, from Taos, and Juan Aragon, also Laguna—both as capable of scoring as any of their teammates. By the end of the season, this talented group had amassed a 26–1 record.[64]

On March 9, 1928, the Braves entered the state high school tournament in Albuquerque favored to win, but it proved a tougher slog than anticipated. After beating Capitan easily in the first round, they ran into stiff competition from Menaul and Clovis. In the latter game, the Braves trailed in the second half until Kinsel hit a hot streak. One of Clovis's players tried to squash this by tripping the charging Navajo forward, sending him violently to the floor. The flagrant foul had no bearing on the game, however, other than drawing an ejection and a chorus of boos from the crowd, as the unflappable Kinsel led his team onward to a 30–24 victory.[65]

Albuquerque's hardest game was in the final against Las Cruces. Holding a small lead going into the last quarter, the Braves slowed their rhythm, stalling the ball until the game clock expired with them ahead 27–26. Reporters were amazed at how cool and collected they had been in the last minutes with the state championship on the line. The tournament run had been a team effort. Kinsel finished as the tournament's top-scoring player with forty-four points, earning him a coach's selection to the all-state first team together with tribesman Legah. Milda made the second team and Thompson earned honorable mention.[66]

By winning the New Mexico championship, Albuquerque Indian School earned a berth in the National Interscholastic Basketball Tournament (NIBT), which Amos Alonzo Stagg had been sponsoring at the University of Chicago since 1917. The NIBT was to high school basketball then what the NCAA tournament is to college basketball today, garnering significant national press coverage and public interest. In addition to at-large picks, Stagg invited state champions from across the country. African American teams were prohibited from competing, but no racial policy barred Native teams, and so the champion Braves were granted the honor of carrying New Mexico's banner to Chicago.[67]

The Braves's schoolmates, family members, and fellow New Mexicans were so proud of their accomplishments that many pitched in to get them the rest of the way to Chicago. After Superintendent Perry lamented that the estimated travel and lodging costs, totaling $1,500, was more than the school could afford, the *Albuquerque Journal* started a fundraising campaign on the team's behalf. So much money flowed in as a result of this that the Indian school ended up with hundreds more dollars in its coffers than the trip required. Among the donors were dozens of local merchants who hoped sending an Indian team would attract midwestern tourists to New Mexico, while others gave from the heart. Former governor Herbert J.

Hagerman did his part by sending in ten dollars. In a show of good sportsmanship, many students and employees from rival Las Cruces High gave as well. So did Navajo pupils and employees from Fort Defiance boarding school. Collectively, they donated $129 to show how proud they were of fellow tribesmen Kinsel and Legah. Not to be outdone, two dozen residents from five Laguna villages also did their part by mailing in sums ranging from twenty-five cents to twenty-five dollars.[68]

Before leaving for Chicago in early April, the Braves were treated to a grand send off by 1,200 students and city residents in their home gym. Kinsel, speaking on behalf of the team, promised to make the school and state proud. The same day, Perry received a letter from Assistant Commissioner of Indian Affairs Edgar Meritt congratulating the Braves on their accomplishments. Crowds of high schoolers and townspeople also cheered for the team from train platforms in Las Vegas and Raton as they passed through, destined for basketball's midwestern mecca. Some of these white, Native, and Hispanic well-wishers had driven twenty miles or more to be at the stations to see them off.[69]

Upon arriving in Chicago, Jones learned his boys would be playing tiny Carr Creek High in the first round. The NIBT organizers had made what they considered a novelty pairing, pitting Indians from the Old West against whites from the hills of Eastern Kentucky, cast in the role of country bumpkins. Carr Creek's team had been selected from a total male student population of just eighteen pupils. They had no gymnasium, practiced outdoors, and spent the first half of their season playing in overalls, but they were shockingly good. The Kentuckians posed a particular danger to Albuquerque because the two teams surprisingly had a lot in common. Carr Creek's boys were almost as fast as the Native players and they were just as tightly knit, no doubt because two of the starters were brothers and the rest were all their cousins. As evenly matched and talented as the two teams were, they both appeared overwhelmed by the enormity of the event when, on April 3, they entered the University of Chicago's large Bartlett gymnasium. Neither could mount much offense in the first quarter. Kinsel tried to spark things by hitting a spectacular half-court shot, but the Kentuckians swarmed and shut him down. Then Carr Creek's curly-haired forward Shelby Stamper surged in the second quarter, sinking shot after shot to build a 14–3 lead at the half. There was no way back for the Braves after that. They made a run in the third quarter but fell short in the end, 32–16.[70]

A *Chicago Tribune* reporter was surprised at how well-spoken these players from supposedly backward places were after the game. Stamper was as gracious and frank in speaking about the victory as Kinsel the defeat, the latter saying his team had "no alibi" for their performance. The Navajo stalwart then headed for the showers as Coach Jones stepped in to inform the reporter about his players' inner strength. "They act no different when they lose from when they win," said the coach. "Theirs is not the spirit to stay long under the pressure of humiliation. They look for the blue even as the thunder booms and the rain pours." As if to underscore this point, substitute guard Juan Aragon poked his head in to say, "Chicago's a good place even if we did come all this way to be beaten. . . . I noticed when we were taking this bus ride this morning that there's a ballroom named after me up here." This he joked in reference to the Aragon ballroom, opened on Lawrence Avenue two years prior. The reporter should have let that be the last word, but of course he did not. "A remarkable thing about these New Mexico Indians is that none of them says 'Heap-big,'" he wrote in conclusion. "It just isn't being done in the best wigwams."[71]

Uplifting as the year 1928 had been for the Braves on the basketball court, the boys' program was becoming too successful for some peoples' taste. Through the early 1930s, the school's squads were consistent entrants in the sixteen-team state tournament, along with their counterparts from Santa Fe Indian School, and this drew a backlash from rivals. On March 9, 1933, a caucus of public school administrators proposed an amendment to the state association constitution expelling all non-state-funded schools. Although the language included the state's parochial and private schools as well, it was widely understood that the two federally funded Indian schools were the primary targets of the new policy. As justification for the move, the draft cited unfair advantages the Indian schools gained by recruiting across state lines, using training tables, and allowing overage players to compete. One amendment promoter later admitted that some of his allies had also acted out of "prejudice" but refused to say whether this was just of an institutional nature or whether anti-Indian bigotry had reared its head.[72]

A livid Reuben Perry responded to the amendment with a flurry of letters to allies and opponents. The Albuquerque superintendent insisted that the complaints against the Indian schools were baseless and self-interested, meant to deny them access to state titles while retaining them as crowd-pleasing independent opponents. He reminded his association peers they should be cooperating to teach Native athletes to be "good citizens of the State of New Mexico and the United States" and said that marginalizing them this way was counterproductive. In the end, he got his way. A forty-four to twenty-seven association vote in late April defeated the amendment. The failed effort nevertheless left a bitter aftertaste. School administrators and coaches who favored the change believed Perry had pulled one over by arguing, against evidence, that his school kept an impeccable accounting of students' ages and gained no advantage from interstate recruiting. At the same time the Indian school players had been told in a most public and humiliating manner they were interlopers whose hard-earned triumphs were ill-gotten. Basketball was one of the few ways they could win in this white-dominated world, and these men had tried to take even that away.[73]

Meanwhile, those Indian schools that were still denied access to college conferences and state high school tournaments through the 1920s and 1930s pursued what other integrated titles were available to them. Haskell tried its fortunes in the AAU's national amateur tournament in Kansas City, open to a broad variety of entrants, including company and college-conference teams. Its men's teams received invitations to the event in 1923 and again in 1929 but lost in the first round on both occasions.[74]

A small government boarding school on South Dakota's Rosebud Reservation tried a different approach in 1924, sponsoring its own invitational boys' tournament for Indian and public schools. Only five other teams attended, including St. Francis Mission and a few nearby high schools, but Superintendent James McGregor judged it a success, not least because the home team claimed the trophy.[75]

Some Indian school boys' teams also did well competing in an invitational high school tournament held each year at Chadron Normal School in northwest Nebraska. The tournament's organizers were more receptive to them than were many of their own state associations, providing them opportunities to compete for championships against public schools. Two of the Indian school teams that played in Chadron during the 1920s won out. Oglala boarding school from Pine Ridge took the Class B division in 1924 and again in 1925, beating Nebraska teams in the finals both times, and St. Francis won Class A in 1928, edging out a team from Deadwood, South Dakota, 19–18.[76]

St. Francis also participated on numerous occasions in the National Catholic Interscholastic Basketball Tournament (NCIBT), held at Loyola University of Chicago. The annual competition was established in 1924 to provide Catholic high schools an opportunity to compete in postseason play despite being barred from most state tournaments and from the University of Chicago's NIBT. At its peak in the early 1930s, the multiday event attracted more than fifty thousand spectators. As a star attraction, St. Francis participated in about half of the NCIBTs, until the tournament ended in 1941, and would have played in more had travel costs not been prohibitive. The St. Francis teams were usually invited at large but earned a bid in 1937 by winning South Dakota's first all-Catholic state tournament, as they did

Figure 21. Navajo players (unidentified) at the Presbyterian Mission in Ganado, Arizona, ca. 1942. As many Native boys began playing in state high school tournaments, girls everywhere still lacked such opportunities through mid-century. Clarence G. Salsbury Collection, 90-3477. Courtesy of Arizona State Library, History and Archives Division.

in the three following years. The NCIBT organizers, the St. Francis Jesuits, and the team's Lakota players took different things from this partnership. The organizers recognized St. Francis's teams as big attendance draws, both because they were Native and because of their exhilarating style of play. They took advantage of this popularity to establish the NCIBT as a high-profile event, on par with Stagg's NIBT. The St. Francis Jesuits, for their part, used the Chicago tournament as a public relations opportunity to attract attention to their mission work, while the players simply wanted to compete on a national stage and visit the big city.[77]

St. Francis's first trip to the NCIBT in 1925 was the most eagerly anticipated by the Lakota players and Chicago crowds but not the most successful competitively. After Chicago's Knights of Columbus agreed to cover their train fare at the tournament organizers' request, Jesuit Joseph Zimmerman, Coach William Toomey, seven players, and then mascot Collins Jordan set out in mid-March. Zimmerman recalled the boys' excitement on their eight-hundred-mile journey. "Some of these lads had never seen or ridden on a train, and to all, the city was an unknown quantity," he reported. "When the great day came and the boys were on their way to Chicago they were a happy lot of children. With eyes glued to the windows they sat for hours watching the fields and houses and telephone poles whiz past in dizzy procession." Their tournament hosts just as eagerly awaited their arrival. They planned a grand reception for the team and advertised their visit through the university's *Loyola News*. The newspaper billed the group of mixed and full-heritage Lakota players as "five-full-blooded . . . descendants of the Sioux who massacred the troops of General Custer in his last historic fight."[78]

Chicago residents were already accustomed to hosting American Indian visitors as athletes, entertainers, and fair participants, but this did not dampen their enthusiasm for the St. Francis team, resplendent as the players were in the traditional Lakota attire they donned as their train pulled into the station. Representatives of Loyola University and the Knights of Columbus greeted them on the platform and drove them to meet Mayor William E. Dever, who formally welcomed them to Chicago. "The next few days passed as a dream," Zimmerman later reported. "They were carried all over the city, not as strangers, but more as old friends whom their hosts had not seen for years. Everywhere the lads drew large crowds of spectators who watched them until the last feather disappeared in traffic." St. Francis's failure to advance past the first round did not end this urban love affair with the team. At halftime during the championship game between Marquette and St. Mel's of Chicago, thousands of spectators chanted "We want the Indians" until the Lakota players finally appeared, no doubt by preplanned design, to perform a farewell dance at center court.[79]

In the years that followed, Chicagoans received other St. Francis teams just as warmly, but as well-liked and admired as they were for their basketball talents, there was no escaping the whimsical and often racist nature of the press coverage surrounding them. It is difficult to discern myth from reality when reading stories about St. Francis's off-court behavior during the 1920s and 1930s. On various occasions, these teams were said to joyride in downtown hotel elevators; dance around a bonfire beneath the arena floor "to the consternation of gymnasium fire officials"; and set a fire in their hotel room at the prompting of a mischievous reporter who said this was the norm on cold Chicago days.[80]

These were exaggerated stories, meant to sensationalize the players as wild Indians, but they also provided some true glimpses of exuberant youths sucking the marrow from the city, enjoying freedom away from the mission, and in private moments being who they were as Lakota people. St. Francis's players spent much of their youths within institutional walls, and confidential tournament records, year to year, evaluated them as "gentlemanly" and "orderly" in all their conduct, so surely there were no indoor bonfires. It is likely that any flames they lit were small ones used to smudge themselves with sage or sweet grass—asking a blessing while they were under intense scrutiny and pressure, far from home. Survive the pressure they did, time after time. St. Francis's teams after 1925 usually advanced past the first round and were always fan favorites, but as will be seen, they waited until the early 1940s to put on their greatest performance.

The All-Indian Alternative

Realizing that the Chadron and Chicago tournaments were hit-or-miss opportunities, and tired of being rejected by the state associations, some Indian school administrators decided to hold their own tournaments. None pursued this alternative course with more vigor than Rapid City Indian School's superintendent Sharon Mote. In September 1926, not long after accepting this new posting, Mote wrote to the South Dakota High School Athletic Association (SDHSAA) requesting that they admit his school. When the organization dismissed him out of hand, Mote decided instead to establish a Northern Indian School Association (NISA), which was to incorporate all the federal and Catholic Indian schools in the Dakotas, Minnesota, and Nebraska. Whether Mote devised NISA as a stepping stone to membership in the state athletic association or to thumb his nose at the organization he did not say, but he borrowed heavily from the SDHSAA handbook in composing his player eligibility rules and other regulations. Like most state associations, NISA's signature events were to be a championship basketball tournament and a track meet, the former serving as the occasion for NISA's annual organizational meetings.[81]

Mote hoped to hold his first basketball tournament in the spring of 1927 and to formally found NISA shortly thereafter, but to his dismay, few of his counterparts at the other Indian schools expressed an interest in his plans. They were reluctant to surrender control of their athletic affairs, unless it was to a state association, and were concerned about the financial entanglements their participation in NISA would entail. None of the superintendents told Mote they were opposed in principle to inter-Indian school cooperation or all-Indian interscholastic competitions, but they preferred to focus their limited resources on racially integrated athletics.[82]

There were two superintendents, however, who appreciated what Mote was trying to accomplish—Claude Whitlock at Pierre and James McGregor at Flandreau. They believed that pulling together in athletic affairs would foster greater cooperation among the Indian schools in all respects, athletic and otherwise, helping them better serve their students. But even with their support, Mote struggled to make his vision a reality.[83] Whitlock and McGregor were the only two who sent their teams to the inaugural 1927 basketball tournament and Mote canceled the 1928 event outright due to the general lack of interest.[84] He finally succeeded in his third attempt at the tournament, but only by cutting lose his broader NISA plan. Mote asked only that his peers commit their boys' and girls' varsity teams to one tournament, to be held in Rapid City in mid-March 1929, with no other strings attached. Most of the federal and Catholic Indian school superintendents agreed to this, including those overseeing Bismarck and Fort Yates in North Dakota, as well as Cheyenne River, Flandreau, Holy Rosary, Pierre, Pine Ridge, and Rosebud in South Dakota. Mote's greatest get was the vaunted boys' team from St. Francis, who agreed to attend after the mission failed to secure the travel funds to make that year's tournament in Chicago.[85]

Just as things were finally looking up for Mote and his tournament, nature intervened. He awoke Wednesday, March 13, two days before the tournament's scheduled start, to a foot of snow blanketing the West River region of the state. Six-foot drifts covered highways, trains were delayed, and telephone lines were down in many locations. Fort Yates telegrammed that they could not make it through and Bismarck said they most likely could not either, but Mote convinced all the South Dakota teams to forge on against their better judgement. This decision spelled more bad news. The Cheyenne River, Flandreau, Rosebud, and Pierre contingents became stranded in the snow near Wall, fifty-six miles to the east. While trying to breach the drifts, Pierre's bus also broke its driveshaft, leaving Coach Sam McLean fuming. He spent the last forty-five dollars Whitlock had given him

Figure 22. Boys' teams and administrators attending the 1929 tournament at Rapid City. Sharon Mote stands to the far left in the light suit with Bob Clifford off his left shoulder. Sam McLean is behind them, to the right, in a light suit and bow tie, while Henry Flood is to the far right of the frame, standing next to a small boy. The champion Rapid City team stands at the center of the second row. Holy Rosary is kneeling to the left while Saint Francis is likely the team kneeling to the right, with Flandreau in the second row behind them. Pierre is third row center in white with the remaining teams grouped behind. There is a puddle of melting snow along the sidewalk. Courtesy of NARA, Kansas City, Missouri, identifier 285698.

to send the girls the rest of the way by train while he and the boys bedded down in an unheated garage. "Mr. Mote should never had us come on," he complained in a dispatch to Whitlock. "I wish we had never started." By Friday afternoon, most of the teams finally made it to Rapid City only to learn that Mote had delayed the tournament's start until Saturday. This pushed the second round games back to Sunday and finals to Monday, which hurt ticket sales but allowed Pierre's boys and Bismarck's girls to arrive on time.[86]

This whole affair pushed Mote to his breaking point but gave Rapid City's well-rested, predominantly Lakota teams tremendous advantages over their travel-weary opponents. In Saturday's first round, the Rapid City boys upset heavily favored St. Francis 39–21 behind outstanding offensive efforts from Edward Quick Bear and Bert Afraid of Hawk. Then on Sunday, the girls beat Pine Ridge 28–8 thanks to strong play from Julia Black Fox and Cecelia Janis. Meanwhile, Henry Flood coached Flandreau past Pierre into the boys' Class A final against Rapid City, while Holy Rosary and Pine Ridge advanced in Class B, which Mote had set up for the smaller, younger reservation boarding school teams.[87]

The championship finals took place Monday afternoon at the South Dakota School of Mines, which had donated use of its gymnasium for that portion of the event. In Class B, Pine Ridge played Coach Bob Clifford's Holy Rosary team. Things looked good for Pine Ridge early. Joshua Wounded Head was accurate from long range in the first half, hitting four shots "from the center of the floor or further back," but Holy Rosary stayed patient, working the ball in close for easy baskets. They kept doing it in the second half, while Pine Ridge's accuracy from the perimeter fell off. Philip Brewer and Norbert Two Two played especially well for Holy Rosary down the stretch, leading their team to a 28–21 victory.[88]

The girls' final pitted Rapid City against the favored team from Bismarck. The North Dakotans had gone undefeated during the regular season, beating some high school opponents using women's rules and others using men's. In Rapid City, they played the six-player women's game. Mote and the other superintendents had opted for these more conservative rules even though they treated the girls as equals to the boys in other respects. Gone were the cumbersome dresses and bloomers of past years, as the Bismarck and Rapid City players strode confidently out of the locker room wearing the same style shorts and jerseys as their male schoolmates. McGregor described what happened next in a report to the Indian Office: "The Rapid City girls went on the floor with the greatest determination at their command, with the crowd cheering for them. During most of the game Bismarck led; but when the final whistle sounded the result was twenty-three to sixteen in favor of Rapid City." Cecelia Janis starred for Rapid City at forward, scoring fourteen of her team's points while forward Alice Slater (Chippewa) played just as well for Bismarck, scoring twelve. The other players on both teams battled hard throughout despite the officials' determined efforts to keep them in check, causing five to foul out.[89]

The tournament's last game—the Class A boys' final—pitted Mote's team against McGregor's before the largest crowd ever to fill the School of Mines gymnasium. McGregor later said both teams had been confident in their chances that evening, but his overly so. Under Coach Flood's direction, Flandreau ran a blistering fast break, but their "temptation to shoot from long range cost them any advantage gained from their speed," wrote a local reporter. Rapid City relied instead on "a consistent system which did not vary to any great extent." It entailed guards David Spotted Horse and Jacob Two Bulls bringing the ball past center court while Raymond Picotte "stood well within the Flandreau defense with Quick Bear and Afraid of

Figure 23. Girls' teams at the 1929 tournament pose with the donated trophies. Bismarck stands at the center flanked by Pine Ridge to the left of the frame and Pierre to the right. The champion home team stands at the top of the steps. Courtesy of NARA, Kansas City, Missouri, identifier 285699.

Hawk running in and out of the first and second line of defense." Repeatedly penetrating Flood's famously airtight zone defense in this manner, Rapid City cruised to a 25–14 victory.[90]

It was clear from McGregor's and Mote's later reporting that the two men cared more about the overall success of the tournament than the championships it determined. While McGregor wrote to the Indian Office saying the event was a resounding success, Mote gave a more mixed assessment, explaining that the event had taken a financial toll. "We did not have the crowd that we would have liked to have had on account of the storm and [because of] extra expenses the finances were not very satisfactory," he wrote in a thank you letter to School of Mines President Cleophas O'Harra. "In fact it cost each team participating including ourselves quite a little to participate in the tournament," he added. "However, we believe that the results justified the expense." Such was the case, he claimed, because the tournament had allowed the people of Rapid City "to see the class of basket ball our Indian schools play."[91]

Mote could not have known at the time how significant his 1929 tournament was to basketball's historical development as a pan-tribal experience. Never before had teams competed in an exclusively American Indian interscholastic tournament on this scale. The closest thing for Native players before this were the class tournaments the Indian schools ran internally. The 1929 event presaged the invitational all-Indian tournaments that would become prevalent in later decades throughout the West—basketball's ultimate expressions of pan-tribal community.

There were, however, to be no repeats of Mote's 1929 tournament. The following academic year, Rapid City Indian School was converted into a sanatorium school for students suffering from tuberculosis. It reopened as a regular boarding school later in 1930 before closing permanently in 1933. Mote had moved on to other postings by then but continued promoting inter-Indian school athletics wherever he went. As superintendent at Bismarck in the early 1930s he toured his girls' team around every year to compete against other Indian schools in the region.[92] Then, as principal of Phoenix Indian School in 1938, Mote took over administration of an all-Native junior high–level tournament that Superintendent Carl Skinner had established in 1934. The purpose of that event was to forge and maintain connections between Phoenix Indian School and the many reservation boarding and day schools in the state. By the time Mote took it over, the tournament had included Native boys' and girls' teams from most reservations in Arizona.[93]

A New Era

As Sharon Mote went about promoting basketball at Indian schools in other states, South Dakota's state association was finally loosening some of its restrictions. After Flandreau Indian School argued it was federally mandated to admit students from across state lines and could not reasonably be penalized for doing so, the SDHSAA admitted that school to membership in 1930. The other federal Indian schools in the state were incorporated a few years later. The Catholic Indian schools continued to be barred, however, along with other non-Indian parochial and private schools, until the mid-1960s.[94]

Pine Ridge boarding school was the first to win a championship in this new order. Relying on speed, "bullet like passes," and spectacular long-range shots, they beat Bridgewater 24–22 to capture the state Class B title in 1936. They were the only entrant that year to have two players selected to the all-tournament team: guard Dave Brewer and forward Sterling Big Bear. Upon their return to Pine Ridge, they were hailed as conquering heroes. Their school band greeted them in song and schoolmates cheered themselves hoarse as Coach Elijah Smith and his boys hoisted the trophy aloft.[95]

Flandreau followed in 1939, winning the South Dakota Class A championship in a tough final against the Rapid City High School Cobblers. The lead shifted back and forth all game until, with time expiring in the fourth, team Captain Norman Redthunder (Sisseton-Wahpeton) hit a clutch shot to send it to sudden-death overtime. About a minute in, Redthunder passed the ball long to forward Fred Demarrias, who set his feet near the corner and, as the *Rapid City Daily Journal* reported, "snapped in a sizzler," putting his team over the top 32–30.[96]

The skill Flandreau displayed in that game, and the team's ability to stay focused in the closing moments, reflected how cohesive it was as a unit under Coach Sydney Beane. As a former player who had captained his team to the tournament final at Rapid City in 1929, Beane knew the intricacies of this game, its pressures, and what his boys were feeling at any given moment. As boys' advisor, he lived alongside his players in the dormitory and developed a sense of family with them. His son Sydney, Jr., watched his dad coach later teams at Flandreau with the same caring and devotion—carefully diagraming every activity for them in practice; drilling them on fundamentals; and with the blow of his whistle and that particular look, getting them to move in unison without saying a word. Over the years, Sydney, Jr., came to know many descendants of the 1939 players, including Norman Red Thunder, Jr., who became a teammate of his at the Wahpeton State School of Science (future North Dakota State College of Science) in the early 1960s. He learned from these interactions how important his father had been in his players' lives as they moved forward and how important that championship was to them, their families, and the communities they represented. It never stopped mattering, says Sydney, Jr. It "was like it was yesterday and today. It's not forgotten to those families."[97]

By the end of the 1930s, some Indian school teams such as the boys' varsity squads at Albuquerque and Flandreau had established themselves within the high school athletic association fold as perennial championship contenders. In doing so, they carried forward a tradition of excellence that other Indian school teams had begun in the early 1900s. St. Francis, meanwhile, was still chasing its first national Catholic title. The mission teams' last best chance at it came in 1941, the NCIBT's final year.

It had looked for a while like there could be an all–South Dakota, all-Lakota championship game that year in Chicago, as St. Francis from the Rosebud Reservation was joined in the later rounds by Holy Rosary from the neighboring Pine Ridge Reservation. It would be a remarkable pairing because the two Lakota teams had each other's numbers. St. Francis had beaten Holy Rosary twice during the regular season before losing to them in the state Catholic tournament. They shared interpersonal connections as well. Holy Rosary, which went through only the tenth grade, had traditionally matriculated some of its best players to St. Francis. Holy Rosary's Coach Bob Clifford could also get into St. Francis's heads, having coached the team in the NCIBT four years earlier while on hiatus from his usual job. He had even taught St. Francis the only pre-drawn play they still used in 1941. But this dream matchup was not to be, as Holy Rosary was eliminated in the quarterfinals by Central Catholic of Fort Wayne, Indiana, leaving St. Francis to face Leo High of Chicago in the March 31 final.[98]

This last ever NCIBT championship game was also one of the most competitive, played in the Loyola gymnasium in front of 3,500 spectators. St. Francis looked good all game. They opened with a 7–0 run and maintained the lead to the half. The Leo Lions fought back in the third quarter and were within one point until St. Francis's star forward Ben Tibbitts sank one from the field to stretch the lead to three as the clock expired. In the fourth, Leo guard Henry "Babe" Baranowski and Tibbitts battled shot for shot, but the Chicagoans slowly edged forward and pulled ahead by five points with two-and-a-half minutes to play. St. Francis countered, and with regulation expiring, guard Vincent Brewer sank two free throws to tie it up. The Lakota players stole the ball with the score even and ten seconds remaining, and then pulled out Bob Clifford's old play. It had never failed them. It was a "double screen from the two forwards to the guards and pass to the center and hand off," Brewer recalled many years later. "They faked it to me and handed it to the next guy, and he blew it, landed under the basket," Brewer said with a chuckle. The name of the player who muffed the play Brewer either did not remember or did not care to say, but the missed master stroke sent the game into overtime for the first time in NCIBT finals history. St. Francis never got things going again in the extra period. They surrendered eight unanswered points to Leo and watched their last shot at a national championship slip away.[99]

It was no longer just about the Indian school teams anyway by the 1940s, as great as some still were. By then, it was clear that basketball had moved beyond those institutions to take a wider hold of Indian country. This was the result of a gradual process that had been unfolding for decades. Since the sport's earliest years in the boarding schools, Native students had been carrying it away with them—this game that had provided them a refuge, an escape, a way to express Indian identities, and be champions. They carried it with them as they left for the military, occasionally to college, increasingly to the cities, and inevitably to the reservations.

8

Collegians and Servicemen

After leaving the Indian schools, former students stayed active in basketball in a variety of ways. Most returned to their tribal communities and played there, but hundreds spent their young adulthoods competing in organized formats away from home. They played basketball in college, as soldiers and sailors in military service leagues, and as barnstormers on the professional circuit. In these situations, they kept drawing value from the sport beyond its simpler joys. Basketball provided them with teammates who helped them adjust socially to alien places and emotionally to stressful situations. It allowed them to connect with non-Native society and distinguish themselves there while expressing pride in their indigenous identities, and it helped some make a modest living for themselves and their families. Competing in these off-reservation venues, Native athletes detached basketball from its Indian school taproot and caused it to blossom in the diverse and rapidly changing contexts that constituted twentieth-century Indian country.

Thus it was that basketball did not only travel from the Indian schools to tribal home communities by direct routes. In many cases, former students kept bonding with the sport and gained more playing experience while traveling or residing elsewhere before returning to their tribal communities to stay. While away, they served as athletic inspirations for their tribespeople, and once they returned, they drew upon their broad experiences to nurture basketball's development as a part of community life.

This portion of the story is too rich to be told in one chapter, and so it is told over the course of two. The first focuses on Native players in college and the military from 1900 to 1960, and the second on professional barnstormers over approximately the same period; but in fact, many Native men (albeit not women) competed in all three venues, staying in the organized game any way they could, as long as they could.

Collegians

American Indian men and women who played college basketball before 1960 overcame significant obstacles to participate at that level. Not many could succeed in the effort, and thus far fewer played college ball than one would expect, given how competitive the Indian school teams were. A few dozen former Indian schoolers played football and baseball for major universities in the early decades of the century, and some gained national celebrity doing so, like former Carlisle student Joe Guyon (Chippewa), who played football for Georgia Tech during World War I. No Native men or women, however, gained national notoriety playing college hoops in Guyon's day, and only a handful competed at that level. Not until the 1920s did a dozen or more American Indians play college basketball anywhere in the country, at any one time. These numbers grew through mid-century, but only gradually, and mostly within small college programs that had direct connections to a tribal community or off-reservation Indian school.[1]

One reason so few American Indians played college basketball before 1920 was that it was not a premier college sport in those years. Although basketball emerged early on as a university-sponsored activity, it trailed football and baseball in terms of spectator appeal, institutional prestige, and profitability through the 1910s. Basketball did not gain firm standing in college athletic programs until the 1920s or become a big money maker for these institutions until the 1930s, when it finally became the second-most profitable sport, next to football.[2] Indian school athletes who were talented enough to be recruited by colleges or universities early in the century were therefore brought in to play football or baseball—not basketball.

Even if they were not recruited, there were so many Indian school basketball stars by the 1910s that dozens should have walked on to college rosters, but this rarely happened, in large part because very few Natives attended college at all. Very few Indian school graduates wanted to spend additional years away from home, or could financially afford to. Nor were they made to feel welcome in these non-Native-majority environments. The Indian schools had also focused so heavily on making their pupils into productive farmers and laborers that little was done to prepare them for college. Few even acquired high school diplomas. Those who never went beyond reservation-based federal schools received nothing more than an elementary education, and far fewer than half of the students attending off-reservation Indian schools accredited as high schools graduated. More attended college-prep-oriented public schools on or near the reservations as decades progressed, exceeding the number enrolled in Indian Service schools by the 1920s, but the quality of education they received was often poor, and so they too struggled to get to college.[3]

Indian education improved somewhat over time, in terms of both quality and accessibility, which led to gradual increases in the number of Natives attending college and playing college basketball. The federal government's focus on high school–level Indian education in the 1920s nudged post-secondary enrollments upward, as did reforms in the early 1930s that provided limited college loan support. The GI Bill and tribal funding efforts after World War II further increased Native college enrollments nationwide, from an estimated 385 in 1932 to about 2,000 in the late 1950s. Even these increases were modest, though, and so Native representation in college basketball remained small relative to the size of their population and deep pool of talented players.[4]

Few American sports fans noticed that the Indian schools were producing scores of talented basketball players every year through mid-century, yet only a handful were transitioning to college rosters. Most erringly assumed the top Indian schoolers already were college players, because Carlisle, Haskell, and other big Indian schools often competed against college and university teams. Sports writers contributed to this misconception by commonly referring to Carlisle and Haskell as universities, which they were not. People failed to realize that many of the Indian school greats they cheered for on college courts were at most high schoolers by grade level, even though they were approximately the same age as their white opponents. To become true college athletes, Indian schoolers had to matriculate to predominantly white institutions, and that was no easy task.[5]

The only American Indian athlete to play college basketball as a college student before 1910 may have been Thomas St. Germaine from the Lac du Flambeau Chippewa Reservation in Wisconsin. He got as far as he did because he was an extraordinary athlete and intellect, but even he found this a hard road to travel. Born sometime in the early 1880s, St. Germaine enrolled at Haskell in the late 1890s, where he played first team football and joined the school's inaugural basketball team. After graduating in 1901, he studied law at Highland Park College in Des Moines, Iowa, where he continued playing varsity football, baseball, and captained the basketball team. He kept at his studies, and at sports, after returning to Haskell briefly, and then transferred to the University of Wisconsin in 1904.[6]

Along his path, St. Germaine inevitably encountered anti-Indian bias, which was a significant, if usually unacknowledged, obstacle impeding the entrance of Native athletes into college sports. Whereas some college recruiters sought out American Indian players for both their athletic talents and novelty appeal, these attractions failed to sway their more bigoted colleagues. St. Germaine ran into this blatant discrimination while attending the University of Wisconsin in 1905. The *Janesville Daily Gazette* reported in March that the up-and-coming athlete was bound to become a football star for the Badgers unless newly hired coach Phil King prevented this. King had coached the team in prior years and earned a reputation for racial exclusivity. "It is a tradition here that no colored or red-skinned athlete can have a place on a team if Phil King is coach," the newspaper reported. King must have stayed true to this policy, because St. Germaine failed to appear in the starting football lineup that fall, or on any sports rosters before he departed Madison in the summer of 1906. This harsh experience may have been the reason St. Germaine returned to Indian school athletics, yet again, for a few years before pursuing his law studies at Yale. As hard as life could be at Haskell and Carlisle, at least there he was treated as a social equal to his teammates.[7]

As basketball gained popularity in American colleges through the 1920s, so did Native opportunities to play at that level, but not at a directly proportional rate. In addition to racial prejudice and other factors that made it difficult for them to make it to college, former Indian school athletes began to run afoul of conference eligibility rules. Paradoxically, although organizations like the Missouri Valley Conference (MVC) barred Indian schools from membership because they were not colleges, they commonly ruled that Indian school athletes used up their college eligible years playing *against* colleges. These policies were favored by conference member institutions that worried about rivals gaining a competitive edge by recruiting Indian school graduates who were as athletically experienced as most college upperclassmen. They feared that rival institutions located near the Indian schools—as the University of Kansas was to Haskell—could better identify and attract these athletes.[8]

Having some or all of their eligibility revoked also derailed Indian schoolers' academic aspirations by restricting their access to college athletic scholarships. In effect, the universities profited financially from pitting Indian school athletes against their own teams in non-conference play and then cut these Native talents off at the knees once they graduated, constricting their ability to earn college degrees or participate in college athletics as a stepping stone to a professional sports career.

These rulings barring their graduates struck Indian school superintendents as absurd and unjust. They failed to acknowledge their own culpability for the situation in scheduling university opponents for their teams, but some did what they could to rectify the eligibility problems these decisions created for their graduates. Chemawa's Oscar Lipps did so successfully for his former football and basketball star Coquille Thompson (Siletz) in the late 1920s. After much wrangling, he convinced the Pacific Coast Conference to restore Thompson's eligibility so he could compete for Oregon State University.[9] Superintendent Clyde M. Blair, meanwhile, tried to convince the MVC to ease eligibility restrictions against Haskell's graduates. In 1927, he wrote a letter to the conference representatives, hoping to pluck at their heartstrings. "The Indian race might rightfully be termed the 'human football,'" it said. "History proves that they have been kicked from east to west, forced to give up their homes—making way always for the white man. May your decision deal justice, not only to the schools of your conference, but to Haskell and the Indian people as well." Unfortunately for Blair's students, the recipients of this dramatic prose were unmoved and refused to alter their policy.[10]

For all these reasons, many talented Native athletes wishing to play college basketball never had the chance, but there was a sweet spot for some centered on Oklahoma's Indian Territory. Most Native college players during the first half of the twentieth century belonged to tribes that had been removed to Indian Territory during the mid-nineteenth century, including the Cherokee, Chickasaw, Choctaw, Creek, and Seminole. Those communities had long emphasized the value of western education, taken an interest in basketball, and produced standout teams early on. As examples, the Oklahoma Cherokees organized some excellent girls' teams at their Female Seminary in the first decade of the twentieth century; the Euchee girls excelled at that same time; and the Presbyterian-operated Dwight Indian Training School in Marble City produced some outstanding boys' squads during the 1910s.[11] Members of other Native communities who came to Oklahoma to attend Chilocco, or were indigenous to the area, also became immersed in this burgeoning basketball culture.

Oklahoma thus had produced scores of talented Indian players from diverse communities by the 1910s, most of whom were better prepared than Native youths elsewhere to play college basketball, academically if not always athletically. It also worked to their benefit that some of the colleges where they played, like Henry Kendall and Oklahoma Presbyterian, were founded to serve tribes in Indian Territory. Most subsequently opened enrollment to non-Natives, but they continued receiving tribal donor support through the first half of the twentieth century. These colleges neither had an anti-Indian bent nor were members of conferences enforcing strict eligibility standards, so they eagerly dipped into the indigenous talent pools surrounding them.[12]

Two of the first Indian school graduates to benefit from Oklahoma's amenable college sports environment were Haskell's big center William Louis Pappan (Kaw) and previously mentioned speedster Edward Dominguez—a transplant from the Southwest who had played for both Haskell and Chilocco. They were recruited within a year of each other to play for Coach Francis Schmidt at Henry Kendall College. Later to evolve into the University of Tulsa, Kendall began in 1882 as a small Presbyterian school for Creek girls in Muskogee. It had since relocated to the booming oil town fifty miles to the northwest and was becoming predominantly white by the 1910s, but Natives were still welcomed.[13] Pappan, who had been a leading scorer for Haskell, was brought in for the 1915–16 season and soon earned a reputation as "the best basket tosser" in the state. Dominguez joined him the next season, helping Pappan and his non-Native teammates improve to an 11–7 record. What more they could have accomplished there would never be known, because both enlisted for military service that spring. They survived World War I, but Pappan was later killed in 1935 serving in the line of duty as a federal law enforcement officer.[14]

The early 1920s witnessed a further influx of Native basketballers into small two- and four-year colleges in Oklahoma and bordering states. One of the standout talents during these years was Haskell graduate Fait Elkins (Caddo), a multisport sensation who played basketball for Southeastern State Teachers College in Durant, Oklahoma, beginning in 1924.[15] No Native players of this era shined brighter, though, than Clyde LeClair James, who played for Southwest Missouri State Teachers' College (future Missouri State University) in Springfield. He was the grandson of Modoc warrior Shacknasty (Shkeitko) Jim, who had removed with his tribespeople following the Modoc War in the early 1870s, journeying nearly two thousand miles from their homeland on the California-Oregon border to Oklahoma Indian Territory's Quapaw Agency. The surname "James" that Clyde made famous on the basketball court was an elongated version of the "Jim" in Shacknasty Jim, first used by Clyde's father, Clark.[16]

Born in 1900, James began his education and sports career at Seneca Indian School, a boarding institution in Missouri, just across the Oklahoma state line.[17] Thereafter, he continued his studies at Seneca High School, where he developed exceptional skills playing multiple sports. He became a regionally known phenomenon in 1921 when, just short of his twenty-first birthday, he wowed crowds with his bold and highly accurate shooting at the Southwest Missouri high school tournament, hosted that year at the college in Springfield. Playing left forward, James scored one hundred points during the multiday event, shattering the previous record and helping his team win the combined Class A and B championship.[18]

Southwest Missouri's head coach Arthur Briggs witnessed James's stellar performance at the 1921 tournament and quickly snapped up the five-foot-eleven, 170-pound dynamo to play for the Bears. He made room for him in the starting lineups for basketball, baseball, and football. Various injuries, including to his pitching arm, shortened James's baseball and football careers, making him a basketball specialist. He became a local hoops celebrity while at Springfield, and like many successful Native athletes of his generation, he was admiringly, but insensitively, dubbed

Figure 24. Clyde LeClair James (*center*) poses for a Southwest Missouri State Teachers' College yearbook in the early 1920s. Courtesy of Cheewa James.

"Chief" by his teammates and local reporters. By the start of the 1923–24 season, he had been elected team captain and was playing better than ever. "Chief James appears . . . to be in the best condition and all set for his best year," a reporter said, further complimenting "the big Indian forward" on his "smooth easy style that makes a game a pleasure to watch."[19]

James was indeed the Bears' leading man that season, with movie star looks to match his athletic talents. He was the team's top scorer, regularly achieving double-digits at a time when most college players were lucky to have two games a year in that range. On some occasions, he single-handedly scored more on a night than the entire opposing team. His fifteen against the Rolla Miners the last game of the season brought his total to 190 points, setting an all-time season record for the Bears. He also helped his team capture the Missouri Intercollegiate Athletic Association title, while earning himself election as captain of the All-League team. Thereafter, James remained a legend in both Seneca and on the Southwest Missouri campus.[20]

During the 1930s and early 1940s, the flow of Native men into Oklahoma college basketball continued to increase as products from the Indian schools converged with Native athletes coming out of public high schools—the two streams represented by Buck Cheadle, the Indian schooler, and Jesse Renick, the high schooler. Based on his athletic achievements at Chilocco, Cheadle earned basketball scholarships in the early 1940s to Oklahoma City University and Oklahoma's Central State College. Renick's renown as a high school player earned him a basketball scholarship to Murray State in 1937, which he used as a stepping stone to Hank Iba's Oklahoma A&M program. He twice gained selection there as an All-American and led his team to a third place finish in the 1940 National Invitational Tournament (NIT).[21]

Renick, who grew up attending predominantly white schools, achieved greater fame than any American Indian basketball players who came before him. He may have had an easier path to college than most Native athletes because of his integrated upbringing, but, as Paul Putz explains, whites still thought of Renick as "that Indian" throughout his college career. This quasi-outsider status motivated him, as Native athletes elsewhere, to "show that I can do anything that anybody else could do."[22]

Outside Oklahoma, the handful of American Indian men who broke into college basketball before World War II usually did so at smaller institutions that had historic ties to a particular Indian school or were located close to rich pockets of talent, as the Oklahoma colleges were. A few top athletes from Chemawa, in Salem, Oregon, for example, benefited from established institutional connections with neighboring Willamette University. Numerous ex-Chemawa students played football at Willamette in the late 1920s, and a few tried out for Coach Spec Keene's basketball squad. Brothers Reginald and Charles DePoe (Siletz-Cheyenne) both made the cut at the end of the decade and equated themselves well on the court against the University of Oregon and other regional opponents.[23]

Late in the 1930s, Nettleton Commercial College in Sioux Falls, South Dakota, also acquired some Native basketball talents. Because of its small size, Nettleton was less able to attract recruits from outside its region than big university programs could, and its athletic staff members were well-familiar with the state's best Indian school players. Nettleton's athletic program was thus more open to offering Native men a chance at success than were its university counterparts. In particular, Nettleton attempted to capitalize on St. Francis Mission's national fame by recruiting some of the school's former players for the 1938–39 season. It is uncertain who initiated this effort, but it hinged on the participation of Willard Iron Wing from the Rosebud Reservation. He had played for St. Francis mid-decade, graduated, and then coached the team to the second round of Chicago's NCIBT in the spring of 1938. He was also honored by a selection committee as the NCIBT's best coach that year. Soon thereafter, Nettleton's administration reached out to Iron Wing, knowing it would be a boon to acquire the newly minted celebrity.[24]

Iron Wing agreed to be Nettleton's player-coach in the fall of 1938 and, soon thereafter, was joined by former St. Francis teammates Ernest "Spec" Blacksmith, Leonard Quick Bear, and Charles Tibbets, as well as Townley Hare, a six-foot-five center that Iron Wing had played with at Haskell in 1937.[25] The Nettleton "Netts" were thus transformed into an Indian team, and presented themselves as such to the Sioux Falls public. Through the first third of the season, the white players on the squad were permanently relegated to the bench except for part-time center Clifford Jansa, a Sioux Falls sports hero who had attended Cathedral High School. In one game early in the season, Iron Wing ran his Lakota players ragged, neglecting to substitute any whites other than Jansa, who came in only for the fourth quarter after Hare fouled out.[26]

Caring more about ticket sales than easing the rookie team into its year, the Netts's athletic staff booked games against high-caliber four-year college teams and professional barnstormers through the first weeks of the 1938–39 season. This resulted in a string of embarrassing defeats, including to the barnstorming Harlem Globe Trotters and House of David Bearded Aces in mid December. Both of these teams were crowd-pleasers but, at this time, played to win rather than following a script like today's Globetrotters. Another home game spectacle against a professional women's team called the All-American Rockets was canceled because the visitors were involved in a minor bus accident.[27] The Netts's schedule normalized after that, and they trounced numerous junior college opponents to end with a 16–8 season record. Although Iron Wing retained stewardship through this run, the Native character of the team eroded, Blacksmith and Hare disappearing from the lineup by early January and Jansa increasingly stepping forward as a team leader. After the season, the remainder of the Native players left, including Iron Wing.[28]

The mass departure of every Native player from the Netts suggests either they had never intended to stay, Nettleton had never intended to retain them, or they had succumbed to similar pressures—academic, financial, cultural, racial. It is unknown whether any of them earned a degree, and none showed up on other college teams in the fall of 1939. Blacksmith may have opted out for a professional barnstorming career, as he soon appeared on a team stocked of St. Francis alumni called the Sioux Travelers (see chapter 9). Some of his Netts teammates followed him there after World War II. As for Coach Iron Wing, he was back in the Indian schools the next season, overseeing a Catholic mission team from Stephan, South Dakota. Nettleton's foray into Indian basketball thus ended as abruptly as it had begun.[29]

As a modest but growing number of Native males realized their college basketball dreams during the 1920s, 1930s, and early 1940s, they left their female counterparts behind. If it was difficult for a Native man to make it as a college player, it was nearly impossible for a Native woman. Professional physical educators and recreation leaders, who were mostly women, largely succeeded at snuffing out intercollegiate women's basketball during the 1920s and 1930s. These reformers were opposed to young women of any race competing in the game beyond the intramural level. They worried that basketball and other sports, when played too competitively, endangered their physical well-being and compromised their womanly qualities—in effect, masculinizing them—and they criticized varsity-level sports for excluding less athletically talented students from healthful participation. These reformers also resisted the rising influence of male-dominated athletic organizations (e.g., the AAU), male coaches, and business interests, who they said exploited female athletes for financial gain and too often sexualized them. Through their participation in the Committee on Women's Athletics (later renamed the National Section on Women's Athletics) and the Women's Division of the National Amateur Athletic Federation, the reformers pressured many high schools and most colleges in the country to drop their female varsity basketball programs. By the 1930s, only small business colleges that trained women for office work and an assorted smattering of two- and four-year institutions persisted in the sport beyond the intramural level.[30]

These developments largely barred American Indian women from following their male tribespeople into college basketball, but there were a few exceptions. One of the schools bucking the trend was Oklahoma Presbyterian College for Girls (OPC) in Durant. Not only did it stay committed to women's intercollegiate basketball, but as one of the institutions that had historical connections to tribes in the state, it welcomed Native athletes. So it was that parts Cherokee and Irish Doll Harris, the daughter of a sharecropper, found the opportunity to play college basketball.[31]

After graduating from Cement High School in 1930, Harris was offered a scholarship to play for the OPC Cardinals. There, she competed alongside a few mixed-heritage Native teammates on a predominantly white squad. Race was never a divisive force for this tight-knit team. They steamrolled the opposition in the 1931–32 season, winning twenty-five games in a row over mostly non-college teams and earning an invitation to play in the AAU's national women's tournament in Shreveport, Louisiana. Harris, who had been the team's most outstanding player, lived up to her strong reputation while in Shreveport. In the final game, she led her team to a 35–32 victory over the Dallas Golden Cyclones (a company team featuring famed athlete Babe Didrikson) to take the national title, while earning selection for herself as captain of that year's AAU All-American team.[32]

After World War II, the college basketball world opened a little wider to Native men, but still not to Native women, as athletically talented war veterans returned stateside determined to pursue economic and educational opportunities. Aided by the GI Bill, which made them less dependent on securing athletic scholarships to pay for their schooling, they enrolled in college in greater numbers. This trend continued after the Korean War as well. And as more Native men went to college, there was a consequent bump in the number playing basketball at that level.[33]

In Oklahoma, Native collegians picked up where they had left off before the conflict. One of the standouts of the period was Stacy "Bub" Howell (Pawnee), a public high school player who went on to earn distinction as an All-American in 1950, playing for East Central College in Ada. Kenneth Jerry Adair, of Cherokee heritage, demonstrated his twin basketball and baseball talents at Oklahoma State University (OSU) later that same decade. He averaged eleven points a game as a guard for OSU and was a virtual lock from the free throw line.[34]

At Oklahoma City University (OCU), Coach Abe Lemons proved his keen eye for spotting up-and-coming American Indian talents by recruiting Kiowa marvels Joseph "Bud" Sahmaunt and Fred Yeahquo. Sahmaunt had accepted an offer to play for Kansas State University in 1958 but transferred to Lemons's program at the urging of his cousin Yeahquo. Their first year together, the two helped carry the OCU Chiefs to a 20–5 season record and a 1959 NIT berth. Kiowa-Comanche guard Eugene Tsoodle joined them the next season and later developed into one of OCU's top scorers, averaging fourteen points per game in 1961–62. All three parts of this Native trio made their indelible marks on OCU basketball history, but Sahmaunt was

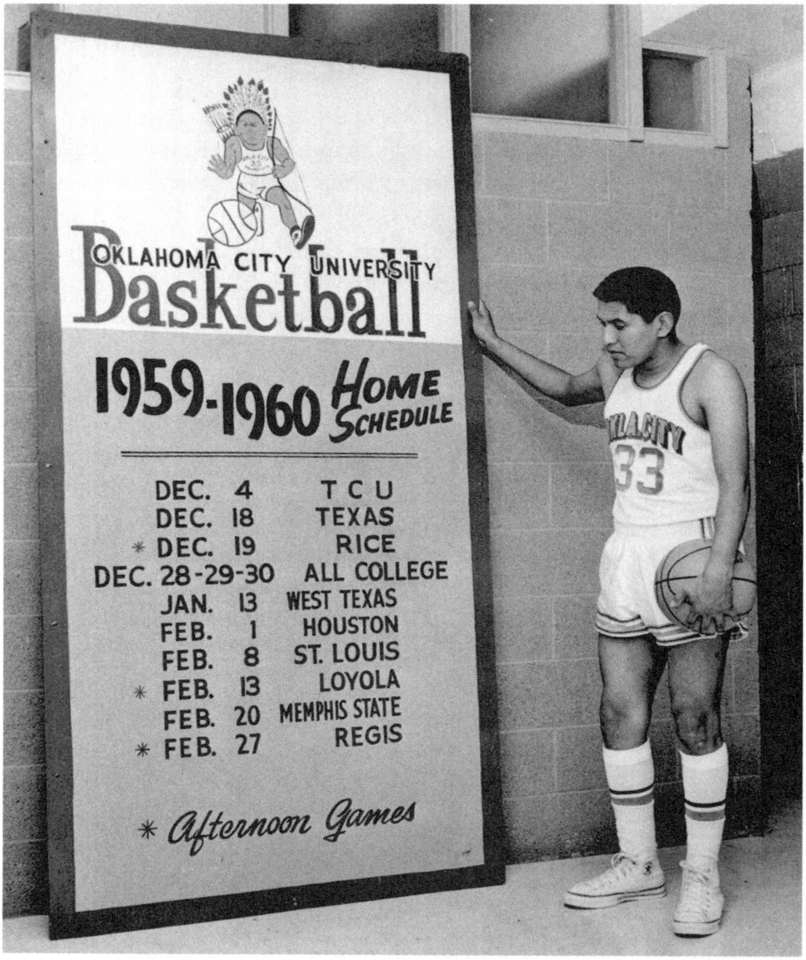

Figure 25. Joseph "Bud" Sahmaunt looks over Oklahoma City University's 1959–60 season schedule. Dick Cobb photographer, Oklahoma Publishing Company Photography Collection. Courtesy of the Gateway to Oklahoma History, Oklahoma Historical Society, ark:/67531/metadc580828.

remembered just as well for his off-court accomplishments. After graduating, he earned his doctorate at the University of Minnesota, returned to OCU as a professor of education and later a dean, and, in 1987, became the university's athletic director.[35]

In the years that followed, Coach Lemons, believing they were talented, "hard-nosed" players he could rely on "in a clutch," kept recruiting exemplary Native high schoolers who many of his counterparts had overlooked

Figure 26. Oklahoma City University guard Eugene Tsoodle poses for a publicity photo in 1961. Dick Cobb photographer, Oklahoma Publishing Company Photography Collection. Courtesy of the Gateway to Oklahoma History, Oklahoma Historical Society, ark:/67531/metadc659366.

or ignored. This inclusionary attitude paid off for OCU again in 1964, when Lemons brought in guard Gary Gray (Delaware) from Fort Cobb, Oklahoma. Gray went on to score 1,710 points in three seasons with OCU. He also did the program and Lemons proud by making it as a pro when the Cincinnati Royals selected him in the third round of the 1967 National Basketball Association draft. Gray played in Cincinnati for one season until the

Milwaukee Bucks acquired him in an expansion draft and subsequently released him.[36]

A growing number of Native men also played basketball for small colleges outside Oklahoma after World War II. The Oregon Institute of Technology in Klamath Falls, which focused on educating military veterans, recruited a number of Native players during the 1940s and 1950s. The program scouted Native players as far east as Montana, including seventeen-year-old Crow standout Larry Pretty Weasel in 1958, who a Klamath Falls reporter said had "more hard driving ability and brilliant shooting touch than we have ever seen on a boy of his age." He rejected the offer, however, opting to play closer to home for Rocky Mountain College in Billings.[37] More colleges in South Dakota like Augustana and Huron were also recruiting homegrown Native players during the late 1940s and early 1950s. One of the best was Ed Manydeeds from the Standing Rock Reservation, who played center for the Northern State Wolves in Aberdeen.[38]

There was also a concentration of Native collegians playing in North Carolina during the 1950s. Most were from Robeson County and were exceptions to the rule that college basketball required Native players to leave their tribal communities. Pembroke State College for Indians (future University of North Carolina at Pembroke) primarily served the Lumbee population there, offering them a chance at a four-year degree (beginning in 1939) while staying close to home and playing a sport many had loved since childhood. Pembroke State never competed against the big universities, but it produced local basketball heroes like the fast-breaking pair James Howard Locklear and Forace Oxendine in the mid-1950s. John W. "Ned" Sampson also graduated there in 1953. An accomplished player and coach in his own right, he was also the father of Kelvin Sampson, who was destined in later decades to coach top-tier university teams like the Oklahoma Sooners and Indiana Hoosiers.[39]

Robeson County was not just home to great male athletes. It was also one of the few places in America that was supportive of women's basketball. The county sent some great high school players to small colleges in the state during the 1950s, including Pauline Bullard Locklear. After graduating as valedictorian from Prospect High School in 1950, she attended and played basketball for Pfeiffer College in Misenheimer, a small Methodist-affiliated school. About the same time, Pembroke High School's gifted and aggressive guard Katrina Locklear moved on to Pembroke State, where she played college ball for two seasons.[40]

Another American Indian man playing college basketball in North Carolina during the 1950s was Phillip Smith, an Eastern Band Cherokee. Smith never became a regional star, but he held local distinction as the first Cherokee to play for Western Carolina College, located three hundred miles west of Robeson County. Smith had no scholarships, instead paying for school through the GI Bill. He walked on to the basketball and baseball teams, a stranger to virtually everyone, but playing varsity sports made him a "big man on campus." He enjoyed the experience. Smith never felt mistreated at Western Carolina even though he knew some people thought of him as a novelty because he was Indian. The only thing that irritated him was needing to explain to teammates who insisted on calling him "Chief" that "we had a chief [back in Cherokee], but it wasn't me."[41]

Although there remained a dearth of Natives playing for big universities in the 1950s and 1960s, basketball was making a difference in the lives of more college-bound Indian youths than ever before, including Navajo athlete Peterson Zah. Upon graduating Phoenix Indian School in 1958, Zah discovered that he and his classmates had been ill-prepared for college, and most could not afford to attend. There seemed no one to turn to for encouragement and assistance. "You had to be determined and find your own scholarship, to find your own way to a university," Zah recalled. "No one really helped you." Under these circumstances, most Natives failed at their college dreams. He might have too were it not for his basketball coach at Phoenix Indian School, Joe Famulatte. Native players loved and respected this Italian-American skipper because he truly cared for them, as he proved to Zah at a critical juncture in his life.[42]

Famulatte urged Zah to take advantage of the proximity of Phoenix College as an entry point to higher education and spoke to his counterpart there on Zah's behalf. Basketball helped Zah get into college, by way of his intermediary Famulatte, and also provided him with the assistance he needed to establish himself once he got there. "And when I enrolled, I met the basketball coach, and he put me on the team," Zah recalls. "And for that, I got tuition waived and I was able to negotiate a good price for my meal ticket and purchase books. Phoenix College treated all of us good as long as we were on the team." Beyond this, basketball gave Zah a sense of community. While he was attending college, he formed bonds with teammates, all of whom were non-Native save for Rodney Lewis, who came from the Gila River Reservation, just south of the city. Zah's teammates helped him succeed by driving him to class while coach Famulatte saved him boarding expenses by opening his home guest room to his former player.[43]

A nagging ankle injury forced Zah to quit basketball midway through his first season at Phoenix College, but the sport had already given him a helpful boost. Once in the door, Zah proceeded to earn his associate's degree in 1960 and then a bachelor's in secondary education from Arizona State University (ASU) in 1963. After many decades serving the Navajo

Nation, he returned to higher education as a special advisor to the ASU president in 1995, helping the institution meet Native students' needs.[44] In this position, he assisted younger generations as Coach Famulatte had once assisted him.

Servicemen

Before 1960, young Native men leaving the Indian schools were far more likely to carry their passion for basketball into military service than they ever were into college. Such was not the case for most women, whose only real options to stay in the game were to play informally or in adult amateur leagues (see chapter 10). The number of American Indian men playing military hoops reached into the thousands because they enlisted at exceptionally high rates, particularly during the two world wars, and were encouraged to play recreational and competitive athletics while in uniform. In this military context, basketball took on the added functions of providing thousands of Native servicemen temporary relief from the boredom, strain, and terror of a life at war while helping them adjust socially to a regimented, multiracial environment. And so it was that the military, to a greater degree than colleges, nurtured Native peoples' love for basketball and helped facilitate that sport's dissemination from the Indian schools to Indian country.

American Indians were twice as likely to serve during World War I (1917–1918) as other Americans—12,500 in all by the end of the conflict. Indian school students were especially apt to volunteer, in large part because the schools strongly encouraged them to enlist as their patriotic duty.[45] So many joined the military, in fact, that many Indian school basketball programs suffered competitively for loss of talent. Teammates often joined in groups and were dispatched to the same Army training camps before being shipped overseas. While preparing for duty, they discovered that the Army was pleased to provide them with opportunities to stay active in basketball and other team sports. And so they played alongside their old teammates a while longer before heading into harm's way, offering each other the moral support they needed to adjust to the stress of this new environment.

The military did not encourage Natives to play sports in these camps out of any concern for them, in particular, but rather because leaders believed all troops benefited from these activities. Coincidentally, though, military officers used much the same logic as the Indian school superintendents did for promoting sports. Specifically, the Army and the Navy hoped that playing team sports would help troops stay physically fit, morally upright, and well disciplined while imparting a competitive, fighting spirit. The YMCA had its hand in all this, assisting the military by sponsoring recreational activities for new recruits at training camps across the United States. This naturally meant the Y's signature sport, basketball, was readily accessible in the camps.[46]

The military's sparse reporting on athletics makes it impossible to know how many Native men learned to play basketball for the first time while stationed in these World War I training camps. Surely hundreds did who had neither attended the Indian schools nor encountered the game elsewhere before enlisting or being drafted. Because Indian school newspapers commonly updated their readers on alumni in uniform, more is known about their athletic activities in the Army camps. These servicemen were indeed eager competitors because they already enjoyed sports and knew they could impress their fellow troops by playing them well. They also understood from their Indian school experiences how sports could help them adjust to alien environments in times of stress.

Former Indian school students organized dozens of all-Native sports teams in these World War I training camps. Military records and publications rarely commented on this, but Hervey Peairs did, reporting that Haskell's students-turned-servicemen "made camp teams everywhere and later were prominent in groups competing for championships in the [American Expeditionary Force] in all lines of sports."[47] Thanks to Indian school publications, we also know that Haskell's former athletic director Alfred M. Venne (Chippewa) helped Natives stay athletically active in the camps. He organized multiple all-Indian athletic teams late in the war while serving as the YMCA's physical director at Camp Travis near San Antonio, Texas. Among them was a football team he supervised in October, 1918, that grouped Haskell alumni with athletes from the Anadarko, Carlisle, Chilocco, Concho, and Pipestone Indian schools. Of nineteen players on the all-Native team, bound for service in six different Army units, all but two were former Indian school athletes.[48] How many of these all-Native teams played basketball is uncertain, but at least one hoops squad competed at Camp Logan in Houston just after the Armistice. It was entirely composed of Chilocco alumni and was known to local reporters as the "Oklahoma Indians."[49]

Once shipped overseas, Native troops served in integrated units where they could not as easily play basketball with other Natives. Instead, they played it to blow off steam behind the lines and bond with their new non-Native comrades. Future Flandreau coach Henry Flood (Lakota) even used sports to become an informal leader of sorts within his mostly-white machine gun battalion. While serving in France, he drew on his former experience captaining track and basketball teams at Carlisle to organize a number of battalion teams in various sports that competed during periods of rest and relaxation.[50]

Native men again carried their passions for basketball into the service during the Second World War. While wartime restrictions on gasoline and tires were forcing the Indian schools and reservation public schools to scale back competitive hoops, military leagues provided twenty-five thousand Native men in uniform with ample opportunities to stay in the game.[51] As their fathers had during the previous conflict, these servicemen relied on basketball and other sports to help them adjust to life in the military and to impress their comrades.[52] Buck Cheadle and Jesse Renick did so playing on Navy service teams—Cheadle while stationed in San Diego and Santa Cruz from 1943 to 1946, and Renick as a Navy lieutenant stationed at an air station in Norman, Oklahoma. Renick was made a physical instructor there even though he had left his position at Albuquerque Indian School hoping to get into the fight and personally avenge Pearl Harbor. His experience as a college player and Indian school coach made him more valuable to the Navy as an athlete, however, because its teams were used as advertisements to boost recruitment. And so he was kept stateside, where he became high scorer for the air station's Zoomers team from 1943 until war's end. Twice in the winter of 1943–44 he was lauded by the national press for leading the Zoomers to victory over his former Oklahoma A&M team.[53]

Basketball kept Renick out of danger during the war and could have spared the aptly named Soldier Sanders from the fight as well, but he insisted otherwise. Sanders was born in Stillwell, Oklahoma, in 1918, speaking Cherokee as his first language. As an infant, he was given the first name Soldier by his uncles who had fought in the Great War. Sanders then attended a small boarding school in Tahlequah, where he engaged in the obligatory military-style drills to which Indian students of his generation were subjected. His name, and that drilling, he believed, destined him to lead a warrior's life; but when he entered military service soon after the onset of World War II, he was assigned to the relative safety of England as a staff sergeant in the Army Air Force.[54]

After arriving in England, Sanders became the sole American Indian player on an Army basketball team competing in a Red Cross–sponsored league. He could have stayed with that team until they advanced through a series of basketball tournaments, safe in the British Isles, but instead requested immediate combat duty. "I did not come here to play basketball," he told himself, "I came here to help win this war." The Army granted his request and sent him into action as a B-17 gunner with the 390th Heavy Bomb Group. On May 28, 1944, his plane was shot down over Magdeburg,

Germany. He bailed out, was captured by angry civilians, and spent nearly a year in prisoner-of-war camps. He escaped while being marched to a new camp late in the war, evaded capture, slipped into France, and was ultimately sent home. Thereafter, he held jobs as a baker, postmaster, and teacher. He also made his way back to the sport he had loved in his youth by coaching basketball in Oklahoma and North Carolina public schools.[55]

Most Native servicemen during World War II were not offered the chance to dedicate themselves as wholly to basketball as Renick did, or Sanders could have, but many played the game behind the lines. Hundreds more played basketball, in more formal league contexts, for longer periods of time, during World War II and the Korean War than had during World War I. These prolonged experiences deepened their emotional connections to the sport and helped them hone their skills against diverse opponents from all races and from all regions across the United States, Europe, and East Asia. When they returned home, they were more determined than ever to promote the sport's development in their home communities. Navajo veterans of World War II and Korea, for example, did this in the late 1940s and early 1950s, working alongside returning Indian school students to build outdoor basketball courts across the Navajo Nation, including one that educator Robert A. Roessel, Jr., watched veterans construct in the town of Round Rock in 1953.[56]

Military basketball also contributed to the rise of Native professional barnstorming basketball in the years following both world wars. Some of the greatest professional, as well as amateur, Indian barnstormers of the 1920s and late 1940s had played on service teams in wartime, which kept their skills sharp during these tumultuous years. They were as primed for the professional game coming out of the military as they had been leaving the Indian schools. A few had played in college as well, either before or after their military service. Playing in the military and college alongside and against a diversity of athletes, drawn from around the globe, increased their tactical knowledge of the game and gave them the added confidence of knowing they could hold their own against anybody, anywhere. In the decades before 1960, many of them went on to prove their skill and determination, competing at the highest levels of play against the best professional teams in the country.[57]

9

Barnstormers

After leaving the Indian schools, some former students made an immediate living in basketball. A few dozen did so by accepting Indian Service coaching jobs, while scores more played for pay. Most competed professionally for all-Indian barnstorming (also known as "touring") teams between 1914 and the late 1940s. This barnstorming life allowed them to travel the country part of the year while maintaining residences in their tribal communities. Some Native barnstormers played for racially integrated teams as well, and an elite few transitioned to semiprofessional company teams, achieving financial security by working salaried jobs year-round contingent on their playing basketball.

The barnstormers and company team players helped facilitate basketball's transition from an Indian school activity into something of broader significance to Native people. On the personal level, these activities extended and intensified players' basketball experiences, making them lifelong supporters of the game within their communities. Those barnstorming teams that were based in the home communities also became sources of tribal pride and exemplified grassroots entrepreneurship. Like the Indian school teams, they traveled and competed against the best non-Native teams in the country, but they had more immediate social connections to their tribespeople. They returned home after each tour to tell their stories and glory in shared triumphs. Multitribal barnstorming teams, on the other hand, were less often Native-owned and less connected to specific communities. These teams, as well as integrated touring and company teams, nonetheless provided a modest living for Native athletes and their families and allowed them to compete with pride after their Indian school days ended.

The Barnstorming Life

For Native men, the only way to go pro in basketball during the first half of the twentieth century was to join an independent team that played most, or all, of its games on the road, a form of play known as "barnstorming."

Competing for urban-based professional league teams was out of the question for most of them as a matter of geography. What leagues there were before the National Basketball Association (NBA; established in 1949) existed east of the Mississippi River and rarely recruited west of it. Many barnstorming teams, on the other hand, had bases of operation nearer the Indian schools and western reservation communities and were eager to recruit American Indians. Because barnstorming teams cost less to start up than franchise teams, Native players with limited resources could also establish and manage their own, if they chose.

Barnstorming teams operated differently than league-based teams. They competed incessantly from late fall to mid-spring, playing almost every evening or twice nightly. Days were spent traveling from one town to the next, sometimes on trains or in buses, but usually in sedans just large enough to fit five or six players, with their luggage strapped to the roof. There were no set schedules or in most cases home courts, and games were normally billed as exhibitions, with no championship implications. These teams competed against town or company teams (also known as industrial teams), local all-star squads assembled for the occasion, or other touring teams, and they played anywhere host towns could find the space, be it a high school gymnasium, an armory hall, an empty barn, or a theater stage.[1]

Barnstorming was a tough life for Native athletes, offering them nothing like the comforts, fame, or fortune NBA players later enjoyed, but it was a way to see the country and earn cash. They made calculated choices like the hundreds of Wild West show performers—or "Show Indians"—who traveled throughout America and Europe from the 1880s to the early 1930s, seeking adventure and a living wage during hard economic times on the reservations.[2] Like the Show Indians, the Native barnstormers made money at something they loved and that was fundamental to who they were as individuals and as Indian people. The fact that white entrepreneurs often exploited them for profit did not preclude them from taking pride in their expressive or athletic performances and seizing rare opportunities.

Taking part in epic barnstorming tours was the adventure of a lifetime for Native hoopsters like William Sazue (Dakota). Conversing with a journalist later in life, Sazue spoke of his days touring with the Sioux Travelers in the late 1930s and early 1940s. True to their name, the South Dakota–based Travelers spanned the country, coast to coast. They saw every corner of America, wowing spectators of all races in big cities and small towns. Sazue remembered the joys of the road, like the time his teammates sang and gave "war whoops" while driving over the Hudson River into New York City. He gained a sense of pride and accomplishment from seeing children standing in line "holding out sheets of paper" to get the players' autographs; and he remembered pulling in between fifteen and twenty-five dollars a game, which was "good pay" he said, in an era when lodging cost fifty-cents a night. Those were the "best of times," he recalled.[3]

No Natives got rich barnstorming, but the pay and adventure was worth their time. Kathleen Yep has estimated an average American barnstormer's earnings in 1939 at $135 a month—just shy of the average American's monthly income of $144. But few American Indians made an average income.[4] For those living on reservations, where a living wage was hard to come by, barnstorming made financial sense, even if it was not year-round work. Many came home to find that while the industrial skills they had learned in the Indian schools did not translate into steady jobs on the reservations, the athletic skills they learned did have economic utility if they were willing to leave the reservation for extended periods. The advantage of barnstorming was that these departures were only temporary. Touring at basketball, not unlike doing seasonal agricultural work, allowed Native men to earn the supplemental outside income they needed to maintain a reservation residence among their people. For many, the alternatives were to struggle in poverty or move to urban areas in search of wages.[5]

Some Native barnstormers did better than others financially. They earned enough to cover household expenses, or even made a tidy profit, while others just earned pocket change. The Sioux Travelers did very well compared to most. If they earned as much per game as Sazue said, they made three or four times Yep's monthly estimate for an average American barnstormer. Jack Little, who played for the Travelers in the 1940s, supports Sazue's recollection, remembering that he pocketed so much cash he did not know what to do with it and so sent it home to his mother. Although he eventually appreciated what that money could buy, neither a lust nor need for it drove him as much as the quest for adventure and love of the game.[6] Other Native athletes were likely motivated by all these factors, playing for the joy of it but also knowing their families sorely needed the money. Some even tried to make a modest living by interlinking seasonal incomes from barnstorming at both basketball and baseball.

To be sure, barnstorming had its disadvantages. It was no easy thing for Native players to spend a few months away from their families and tribal communities. It was also an unpredictable vocation, with no guarantees that either their teams or roster positions would last from one month to the next. Professional basketball before the 1950s was still a backwater of the American sports world. It had a much smaller fan base than college football, college basketball, and professional baseball. It was also much less profitable and stable than major league baseball. Even in the East where professional basketball was more firmly established, teams and leagues usually folded within a few years. All but the best managed barnstorming teams had similarly short existences, sometimes going bust in a matter of weeks. Things were also unpredictable for individual players, who usually lacked contracts to protect them from immediate dismissal, especially if they got hurt. And injuries were all too common in the pay-for-play game, which was generally rougher than college or high school basketball.[7]

The barnstorming life nevertheless attracted scores of Native athletes. Beyond the financial rewards, they were motivated by what famed basketball promoter-manager Frank J. Basloe referred to as the "lure of the road," the same lust for adventure that motivated all barnstormers, regardless of their race.[8] For former Indian schoolers, touring professionally was a chance to fully realize the freedom and pride in accomplishment they had enjoyed playing Indian school varsity. They could travel the country doing something they loved and did well and enjoy the camaraderie and sense of purpose that came with being part of a team. The same financial, emotional, and social impulses that compelled so many Natives to pursue professional careers in baseball and football beckoned scores of them out on the road with basketballs in hand.[9]

The Demand for Native Talent

Opportunities to play basketball for pay were more abundant for Natives in the barnstorming era than they would be later in the twentieth century. The Indian school programs were largely to credit for this, even though they did not purposely groom their students for this life. Their varsity players were sufficiently trained and experienced to become professional players and coaches, and their teams were well-publicized, increasing the likelihood that alumni would be recruited by non-Native team owners. This was especially true if these athletes attended Indian schools like Haskell or St. Francis that spotlighted them on extended national tours or trips to the Chicago tournaments. These Indian school team tours, while meant to expose Native youths to American society for assimilative purposes, had the practical effect of acclimatizing them to a barnstorming lifestyle.

Although Native athletes made it as basketball professionals primarily because they were talented and knew how to play an attractive style of ball, their general appeal to white spectators as Indians also contributed to their success. The same novelty impulse that attracted non-Native spectators to Indian school teams attracted them to professional barnstorming teams made up partly or wholly of Native players.

The barnstorming basketball business especially commodified Native athletes because it was an unregulated, volatile industry singularly motivated by profit. All athletes understood there was an ugly side to the business, but some experienced more indignities than others to attain personal rewards. Many white barnstorming outfits were league teams that toured periodically during the off-season or periods of league instability. They usually played straight basketball, with no added bells and whistles; but full-time barnstormers, of any race, often relied on some gimmicks to appeal to crowds of strangers who had no hometown loyalties to them. They commonly offered sundry halftime entertainments, trick ball handling demonstrations, and sometimes comedic gags. Many barnstorming games thus appeared part carnival, part sporting event. Some of the men who owned and managed these teams were equal parts sportsmen, vaudevillians, and con artist, looking for any way to turn a profit, even if it meant fictionalizing aspects of their players' backstories to attract attention.[10]

Among the most successful team promoters and owners were those who marketed their teams as novelty attractions based on their players' physical size, gender, ethnicity, or race. These entrepreneurs wanted talented athletes but especially prized those who could fill seats other ways.[11] Even some white male barnstormers were exploited for their appearance, like those competing for the House of David Bearded Aces baseball and basketball teams. The Bearded Aces were top competitors that barnstormed from the 1920s through the 1950s, directly associated with a religious colony of Christian Israelites in Benton Harbor, Michigan. The House of David faithful wore their hair long and grew facial hair for religious reasons, but the look was so marketable that noncolony members recruited to the teams also had to grow beards, or glue them on.[12]

Female barnstormers tolerated more offensive gimmicks, regardless of their race. A few basketball teams cornered the market on peddling sexuality and sexist stereotypes for profit, and thus offered women rare opportunities to play for pay. There were a number of these women's professional teams touring the country at various times from the 1930s through the 1970s, including the All-American Rockets, Texas Cowgirls, and All-American Red Heads. These teams were composed of talented players who took the game seriously but were sometimes compelled to do flirtatious gags during breaks in the action. They usually played all-male teams in "battle of the sexes" contests meant to make women's basketball more titillating for spectators. Although female athletes resented these antics, they appreciated the opportunity to earn money in a male-dominated sports culture and took pleasure knowing they inspired young girls to take up basketball.[13]

In addition to being the most famous women's team, the All-American Red Heads were noteworthy for launching the career of Hazel Walker, the only Native woman known to play professional basketball during the first half of the twentieth century. Walker's experiences exemplified how barnstorming basketball could, on the one hand, cost a measure of your personal dignity while, on the other, allowing you to break through societal barriers to attain financial success, celebrity, and a sense of accomplishment.

Born in 1914, near Ashdown, Arkansas, Walker was of mixed Cherokee-European heritage and was raised in a white community. According to Pamela Grundy and Susan Shackelford, she "lived a thoroughly assimilated life. But her [Cherokee] heritage showed clearly in her dark skin, hair and eyes, and she invoked it with pride throughout her career."[14] Walker had been an all-state selection in high school, played for Tulsa Business College in the early 1930s, and competed in AAU ball before joining the All-American Red Heads in 1946. Going pro meant dealing with certain indignities. Like that of most of her teammates, her natural hair color mismatched the team's gimmicky red shade, so she wore a wig on the court, preferring that over the dye other players used. She played well with the team but was eager to run her own operation, and so, in 1949, she left to found the all-female Arkansas Travelers, the first professional team ever owned and operated by a woman. It proved a successful venture, as the Travelers toured successfully for sixteen years. All the while, Walker insisted that her team play fundamentally sound ball with the intent to win, but even she felt the weight of public expectations and so had her team perform some obligatory ball tricks and flirtatious gags to entertain fans and stay in business.[15]

Some of the most commercially successful barnstorming teams profited from America's obsession with race, even if they were not conceived as novelty acts. Just as sports promoters and team owners pitted women against men for dramatic purposes, so did they match teams of color against predominantly white teams. This practice played to many white spectators' racial prejudices, by allowing them to root for white heroes against nonwhite foes.[16] Some of the attraction to nonwhite teams was also motivated by peoples' curiosity about anybody who appeared exotic in small-town America and by genuine admiration for their talents and playing styles—especially the Indian basketball style many Americans were accustomed to seeing from both Indian school and Native barnstorming teams.

The best-known basketball entrepreneur to cash in on America's interest in nonwhite teams was Abe Saperstein, founder of the Harlem Globetrotters, a Chicago-based team that added the misleading "Harlem" identifier to broadcast that they were African American. Neither the Globetrotters nor other African American teams touring during the first half of the twentieth century were novelty acts alone. They were serious competitors and were recognized as such, but they were also marketed as foils to local white opponents. Fans also expected them to do ball tricks and comedic gags—or "clown"—more so than white teams. The Globetrotters clowned for various reasons. The routines provided brief rest periods for the road-weary barnstormers, kept scores close for heightened drama, and entertained spectators who were not normally basketball fans. Some historians have argued, though, that the Globetrotters and other black teams also clowned to play to racist stereotypes and assuage whites' displeasure with their competitive dominance.[17]

All-Indian barnstorming teams were also presented to white audiences to satisfy racial expectations, but they clowned less often than African American outfits. Multitribal teams under non-Native management usually followed a standard script. Managers invariably billed the players as "full-blooded" Indians to the man, which was rarely true. Not only did "all-Indian" teams occasionally carry some white players, but a large proportion of the Native players also had some degree of non-Native heritage. The advertising was too simplistic to acknowledge that a player could be part European and still be Indian by culture and identity. Another commonly falsified claim was that a given team was the only "genuine" all-Indian team touring the country at any given time. This was rarely if ever true, especially during the 1920s, when numerous predominantly Native teams toured the Midwest simultaneously. Managers could easily manipulate the truth these ways because local reporters relied on them for their team information, and most spectators preferred not to know any facts that would spoil their experience.[18]

There was also the obligatory Indian dancing, and sometimes drumming and singing, that players performed at halftime. The all-Indian teams rarely announced what precisely these were other than "war dances," but one assumes that team members who performed them innovated them or chose specific tribal dances they deemed appropriate for a general audience. Singing and dancing exhibitions were practices that former Indian school players on the teams were already accustomed to doing and that white spectators expected to see after previously observing Indian school teams.[19]

Then there were the "Indian names" that team promotional materials either listed next to or in lieu of players' commonly used names. These were sometimes tribally appropriate kin-given or family names that players shared freely with white team managers. Players in these situations were no doubt struck by the irony of white men asking for the names the boarding schools had tried to wipe away. This would not necessarily have endeared those managers to them, however, as the players knew these men used their names only for commercial effect. These same managers also fabricated Indian names for Native players who had only non-Indian-sounding names or to conceal the racial identities of white players who were billed as Indians.[20]

Managers of all-Indian teams also distributed captioned photographs of their players to local newspapers, which could be innocent enough. This was not always racialized hype, as many were posed in shooting stances wearing standard uniforms, with nothing other than jersey markings advertising their Indian identities. Quite often, though, players were photographed wearing Plains-style war bonnets. Unlike the Indian school teams, they did not wear these along with full traditional attire. There was no need to depict contrasting images of players alternating from Native dress to fully uniformed, because team managers and sports promoters had no interest in the progress of assimilation. It was about marketing, plain and simple, and the stark juxtaposition of players wearing feathered headdress and sneakers was eye-catching. Players may not have minded in many cases, proud as they were of their Native identities and warrior image, but many were from tribes that never wore this style of headdress, and some were made to wear cheap facsimiles of the real thing.[21]

A few all-Indian barnstorming teams were also posed in photographs alongside people acting as Indian mascots of sorts, but unlike the Indian school teams that used children for this purpose, the professionals inverted the imagery by pairing the players with older men identified as chiefs or medicine men. To be fair, they were not always *called* mascots and the players probably did not regard them as such. These were often Native elders or inactive players who the active players liked, respected, and drew moral support from, but managers posed them in promotional photos wearing full tribal regalia to attract spectators. One twist on this theme was what an all-Indian, white-managed team called Al Seeger's Indians did. While touring Wisconsin in the late 1920s, they were accompanied by a man called Chief White Feather, who in addition to performing traditional dances and songs gave pregame lectures on "the history of the American Indians." This was all part of the team's advertised purpose of providing both "deluxe entertainment" and "an educational program for the entire family."[22]

In a world where sex and race were sensationalized for profit, it is curious that no all-Indian women's teams existed during the height of the professional barnstorming era, which extended through the 1940s. Not until the 1960s would Native women take to the road in large numbers as members of amateur independent teams. Their conspicuous absence may have reflected public ignorance of indigenous female talents post-1910, when Indian school girls rarely competed at the varsity level and when most barnstorming women's teams drew their players out of colleges (unlike the men's teams). It could also be that Native women, and their families, were less accepting of women touring the country for extended periods than they were of men. Or perhaps it was that basketball promoters were so invested in imagery of male Indian warriors that they had no script with which to market the women. At any rate, professional barnstorming was a man's pursuit in Indian country, save for Hazel Walker.

All-Indian Teams

The all-Indian barnstorming teams that emerged in basketball during the 1910s and 1920s followed in the footsteps of earlier baseball teams. A number of barnstorming Native baseball teams formed around the turn of the century, including the famed Nebraska Indians, established by non-Native Guy Wilder Green in 1897. Green devised the idea for the team after observing Genoa Indian School's first team in action. He recruited his players from that and other Indian schools, as well as some directly from reservations, and began touring the Central Plains states. Green took full advantage of the public interest in Indian-themed entertainments, adopting a Wild West show approach by attiring his baseball players in traditional Native outfits to advertise games and by camping out in an "Indian village" at stops along the way.[23]

Indian Service administrators objected to these professional baseball teams because of the corrupting influence they were said to have on their Native players. Men like Hervey Peairs, somewhat hypocritically, promoted Indian school teams for institutional profit while railing against the immorality of professionalism and the prospect of their students dropping out to pursue athletic careers. Peairs took Green to task on the subject in a 1903 letter. "I have never yet seen an Indian boy or any other man who is following the profession of baseball . . . who has amounted to anything worth speaking of," he wrote. Administrators much preferred that their Native students finish school and then engage in farming or some other acceptable vocation. They also fretted that unscrupulous team owners would fleece Native players of their earnings and strand them at distant locations when their services were no longer required. For years, the Indian Office had also expressed these concerns about unscrupulous Wild West show owners exploiting American Indians for profit. But as was the case in those instances, the government could neither stop white entrepreneurs from seeking out Native talents nor wholly prevent those talents from answering the call.[24]

The first American Indian to barnstorm at basketball, rather than baseball, was Charlie Young, who competed for a mostly white team in the early 1900s. Little is said about him in the historical record other than that he was Cheyenne and began playing right forward for the Crescent Five of Evanston, Illinois, in 1904. Young was technically an amateur because the Crescents played under AAU rules, but he had his immediate needs met during months-long tours throughout the Midwest. Where he learned basketball, how he came to reside in Chicago, and how his path intersected with the Crescent's is a mystery.[25]

Young was not subjected to as much racial hype as his successors would be on the all-Indian teams to come. Most newspaper stories referenced his Native identity matter-of-factly, with no added clichés, and his team never issued publicity photos with him in a war bonnet. There was, however, an exception to this straight media coverage in a January 6, 1907, issue of Iowa's *Des Moines Register.* Sensationalized as the reporting was, it hinted at the ambivalence Young must have felt about being the only American Indian on a white basketball team. According to the article, Young missed a team dinner in downtown Des Moines on the eve of a game and, after a frantic search, was found by his teammates socializing in a hotel lobby with "old friends." These were two Cheyenne men in town with a stage show reenacting Custer's Last Stand. The *Register* caught wind of the story and ran it under the headline "He Answered the Call of the Wild," claiming Young was discovered smoking a "peace pipe" with his tribesmen. Young was hustled to the arena in time for the tip-off, and the foofaraw was soon forgotten.[26]

The all-Indian barnstorming basketball teams began appearing some years after Young's playing days, just before World War I and peaked in number during the interwar period. More than twenty operated in various years, at both the amateur and the professional levels. The amateur variety played under AAU regulations that prohibited players from taking pay. Some of these teams are nevertheless included in this discussion because the line separating the two competitive categories was ill-defined and poorly enforced. Not only did amateur players of all races sometimes have their living expenses covered on the road, but it was also a poorly kept secret that many received under-the-table compensation.[27]

As well known as they were to basketball fans in their day, the all-Indian teams' stories are not easily traced, which helps explain why most have been forgotten by historians. Few people remember these teams today, and their records are not archived anywhere. Only scattered newspaper articles tell us who they were and what they did. Fortunately for historians, most all-Indian barnstormers attached the term "Indians" or tribe-specific identifiers to their team names out of pride and to attract spectators; but to muddy the waters, white teams frequently used the "Indians" sobriquet as well, taking advantage of America's fascination with Native themes.

Manager Frank Basloe took this latter practice to an extreme, accepting bookings for his all-white "Oswego Indians" from opponents who assumed they were truly Indians. He made no effort in his correspondence to disabuse opposing managers of this misconception. On one occasion in 1912, he even had his team paint their faces and prance around "like Indians" before tip-off in a game against a team from New York City. This, he said, was good fun at the expense of naive "city slickers" on the opposing team who had told everyone how excited they were to play "real Indians" for the first time. He claimed no profit motive for this stunt, though he hinted at it by crowing about the spectacle as something spectators would never forget.[28]

The real all-Indian barnstorming teams were stocked with Native players graduating or otherwise leaving the Indian schools, intermixed with a smaller number who had played in public schools.[29] These teams were essentially unofficial extensions of certain Indian school athletic programs in that those institutions were their best recruiting sources. Team owners also traded on the Indian school teams' famed reputations to sell their own squads in promotional ads, especially highlighting players who had competed for Carlisle or Haskell. These teams were not, however, officially connected to those schools or to their policy agendas. The only exception was a strictly amateur touring team known as the Dakota Eagles, coached by Henry Flood. Flandreau superintendent Byron J. Brophy sponsored the unit for graduated athletes in the early 1930s to maintain institutional engagement with them after their departure.[30]

A few of the barnstorming teams cut the Indian school cord more cleanly than others in that they were made up of former students but arose directly from the Native communities to which those students had returned. These teams represented specific tribal nations or confederations on specific reservations rather than identifying with the Indian schools where the athletes had once played. They functioned fully under Native management and were less racially sensationalized than the multitribal teams non-Natives organized. Historic accounts rarely said whether the reservation-based teams were amateur or professional outfits, but it is safe to assume that the players shared in the profits they generated from gate receipts and guarantees. At least one of these teams known as the Oneida Mission Indians signed players to formal contracts, suggesting there was financial compensation involved.[31]

The Oneida Mission Indians were from Wisconsin—a state especially fertile for community-based, Native-managed teams. Beginning in the mid-1910s and continuing through the 1930s, multiple teams were formed from Chippewa, Menominee, Oneida, and Stockbridge athletes in the state, most of whom were returned students from Haskell or Wisconsin's Tomah Indian School. These teams toured exclusively within the state's borders and played some home games on the reservations, but like dedicated barnstormers, they competed outside formal leagues. In addition to the Oneida Mission Indians, they included the more simply titled Oneida Indians, the Neopit Indians, and another team billed by the awkwardly long title "Wisconsin Indian basketball team of Lac du Flambeau."[32]

Another of these Wisconsin teams was a Chippewa squad based at Odanah on the Bad River Reservation. They were known simply as the Odanah Indians or, variously, as the Odanah Braves.[33] They hosted Frank Basloe's team in 1915, which was at that time known as Basloe's Globe Trotters rather than the Oswego Indians. The interactions between these teams, as described by Basloe, suggests that this and other reservation-based Native teams regarded basketball games not simply as entertainments but also as opportunities to engage in intercultural diplomacy and exhibit community accomplishments. This was evident from the way the Odanah manager toured Basloe's team around town like visiting dignitaries. Basloe, on the other hand, had little interest in the people of Odanah other than a superficial curiosity in them as Indians. "Imagine our astonishment when we found that the manager was a real Wild West Indian chief with beautiful black hair and scanty beard," he recalled. When his hosts took Basloe and his team to a local school, he was impressed with how "well educated" the children were, but during a scheduled visit to the home of two young women, he was more interested in flirting than listening to the lecture they gave him on "Indian history."[34]

At that evening's game, Basloe was amazed to witness his opponents' "physical prowess" on the court. Like most teams composed of former Indian school athletes, Odanah kept playing the Indian basketball style. "All the boys were nearly six feet. They started out running at top speed and never stopped," said Basloe. "We had never seen such speed and endurance." The Trotters nevertheless won 38–22. When Basloe and the opposing manager met to settle up afterward, it was evident that something, or somebody, had caused relations to sour. "When it came time for the payment of our guarantee, the [Odanah] manager and a couple of associates came over and the chief started to count out the money," Basloe recalled. "He looked at me as he might have looked at General Custer. I was just a bit nervous. He smoked his pipe and I smoked my pipe. He counted out

$90. We were supposed to get $135. The chief said, 'You get $45 tomorrow morning when you wake up.'"[35]

The next day, the "chief" failed to show at the train station to pay the remainder and Basloe moved on, peeved but also amused that, for once, he had been outhustled. "I got scalped for $45," he said. When he told this story to a Native passenger on the train ride out of town, the man supposedly replied: "Simple justice and honesty in the dealing of your ancestors would have prevented him from thinking of cheating you." Basloe was tickled by this explanation, especially since it allowed him to dismiss any personal culpability for spoiling relations with his hosts.[36]

Native athletes who played for multitribal barnstorming teams covering wider territories stood to make more money than those on reservation-based teams like Odanah, but they were less able to use basketball as a means to exhibit pride in their home community and normally had less say in how their teams operated and were branded. Some of these road teams had Native player-managers conducting their daily operations, but whites experienced with sports management and promotion usually handled the scheduling, accounts, and advertising. In some cases, these non-Natives acted only as sports agents for the teams, while others were true owner-managers, hiring and firing the talent, naming the teams, and reaping the lion's share of the profits.

One of the first multitribal pro touring teams, the Cheyenne Indians, was also one of the most successful, both financially and competitively, but its players learned a hard lesson about the perils of having outside management. Things ran smoothly for the team in the early years. Who founded them is a mystery, as is often the case, but they began competing sometime in 1914 or 1915 and lasted until 1920, apart from a hiatus during World War I. They wore through many tire treads driving about from "the Alleghenies to the Rocky mountains," with an emphasis on Iowa, Illinois, and Indiana. The Midwest proved prime barnstorming territory, because these were well-populated, basketball-savvy states, where a team name like "Cheyenne Indians" struck an especially exotic chord. Most of the all-Indian teams that followed favored this same territory over the sparsely populated West that was home to most of the players.[37]

The "Cheyenne Indians" team name was misleading in that only its top-billed member, Pete Hauser, was Cheyenne. The name may have been adopted simply because it was easily recognizable to white spectators and carried a warrior connotation, or it may have highlighted Hauser, whose Carlisle football fame made him the team's celebrity hook. It may be recalled that Hauser was also the former Haskell basketball player who threatened to "split open" one of his Carlisle opponents in 1903, before his attending that institution. Though Hauser was now in his early thirties and "old enough to be the father" of most opponents he faced, he was still a potent and aggressive basketball player, able to outrun and outmuscle most anyone. The other players were also recognizable, though less famous, alumni of Haskell or Carlisle representing diverse tribes. The 1920 lineup, for example, also included Edward Dominguez (of Haskell, Chilocco, and Henry Kendall fame), who, unlike most Native barnstormers, had college experience on top of experience playing in the Indian schools and military.[38]

Whomever assembled the team hit on a winning formula, as the Cheyenne Indians were deemed by reporters "one of the biggest drawing cards in the basket ball world." They booked games consistently and won the large majority, winning 102 of 112 contests their first season and staying around .900 in subsequent years.[39] The Cheyenne Indians achieved these heights in the style they had perfected as boarding school players, earning recognition as "one of the fastest travelling teams in the country." They were also accurate long-distance shooters and played solid defense.[40]

The Cheyenne Indians' fortunes took a turn for the worse in January 1920, however, thanks to Rexford T. Smith, who had recently taken over as team manager. Under his tutelage, they made consistent bookings, but a tension developed between Smith and the players that disrupted team synergy and triggered a losing streak. Things finally came apart at the end of the month during a game in Muncie, Indiana. While the players were on the floor during the second half, Smith slipped into the locker room, stole the cash from their wallets, and skipped town. Varying reports had him lifting between $400 and $700. All he left behind was twenty-five dollars to cover the team's travel expenses to their next game in Indianapolis. The players told the police Smith was the likely thief because they had notified him before the game that he was to be replaced.[41]

Inexplicably, Smith was back in his office in St. Louis, Missouri, that November booking games for the Cheyenne Indians, or at least trying to. This may have been wishful thinking on his part, or a scam, as there is no indication the team was still together. At any rate, he soon gave up and turned to managing all-white barnstormers. His most successful venture was a team he called the Denver Athletic Club, until it was discovered that he and his players were imposters who had no connection to their namesake organization or city. Why he faked a Colorado connection was anyone's guess.[42]

The Cheyenne Indians–Smith saga illustrates the control Native barnstormers often exercised over their relations with white managers—even one as conniving as Smith. They hired him and retained the right to fire him and were burgled only after he realized he was on the outs. That the players had somewhere between $400 and $700 on their persons at the time of the theft also illustrates how well barnstorming could pay. Like most touring teams, the Cheyenne Indians traveled with only five players (Smith was the alternate in case of injury) and so, if divided equally and adjusted for inflation to 2019 dollars, each man carried the equivalent of $1,000 to $1,800.[43] They were doing well financially for basketball players of that day, and especially well compared to most Native men.

Some other Native teams began touring around the same time as the Cheyenne Indians with varying degrees of success. Thomas Merritt, a basketball promoter in Detroit, Michigan, capitalized on Carlisle's athletic fame by recruiting some of its former players. Playing under the apt if peculiar-sounding name, "The Carlisle Indians of Detroit," the team went bust after one season in 1917–18.[44] Another team known as the Oklahoma Indian Quintet was also short-lived, lasting only the 1919–20 season. It was composed of, and self-managed by, former Haskell and Chilocco teammates who had served together in the American Expeditionary Force during World War I. Although they never confirmed it in their correspondence, the implication was that they had played together in the service before becoming a barnstorming team upon their return.[45]

The Tuscarora Indians from upstate New York proved longer-lived than most of the first generation all-Indian barnstorming teams. They began as a reservation-based, regionally competitive team like Odanah before going national. They formed on the Tuscarora Reservation near Niagara Falls around 1914, from male students returning from Carlisle and the Hampton Institute.[46] Calling themselves the Tuscarora All-Stars but known to reporters as the Tuscarora Indians, they scheduled games against independent teams in nearby towns and traveled short distances for return matchups, under the management of tribesman Willard Gansworth.[47]

After World War I, the Tuscarora Indians expanded their operations beyond their traditional territory, touring broader portions of the Northeast. To make this transition, they acquired the services of a non-Native sports-editor-turned-promoter from Syracuse named Birney P. Lynch. In the fall of 1921, he launched an advertising campaign and scheduled an extensive tour throughout the Midwest, covering the same territory the Cheyenne Indians had mined. This was a business partnership rather than a takeover by Lynch, as tribal member Harry Patterson managed the team's day-to-day operations while playing the center position.[48]

Newly uniformed in orange jerseys and shorts, with black tights, the Tuscarora Indians set out on their tour in late January 1922 with high hopes that fame and fortune lay ahead. On arriving in Indiana, though, they discovered the downside of teaming up with Lynch, who had marketed them broadly as "Indians" rather than specifically as Tuscarora. Indiana newspapers referred to them as full-blooded "redskins" and began printing Indian names alongside their surnames. The midwestern reporters knew nothing about the community they represented, one misidentifying them as the "famous Tuscarora Indians of South Dakota." The competitive advantage the Tuscarora gained by speaking their tribal language on the court—which they had retained through their Indian school years and now used to befuddle opponents—was marketed in the newspapers as them generically speaking "the Indian language" for the amusement of spectators.[49]

There was also some confusion about one of the team players named Tomahawk Allen. A Fort Wayne sportswriter identified him as Algonquian, while newspapers back East said he was the only white player on the team. In fact, this was Kenny Allen, a non-Native who previously starred for Niagara Falls High School. Patterson had met Allen playing together on a city-league team and later recruited him to fill a roster vacancy for Tuscarora. This was not the only time Patterson and his Tuscarora teammates employed an outsider when they needed extra manpower. They did again in 1924, hiring a non-Native to fill in for an injured teammate for one game, at the rate of fifty cents a basket. The temp sank five and went on his way, two dollars and fifty cents richer. Adopting white subs was common practice for all-Indian teams as a matter of practicality, especially when they were on the road and had no tribespeople or other Native players readily available to replace an injury; but it posed a dilemma for white managers and promoters because it disrupted the "full-blood" narrative they marketed. So Lynch rechristened Kenny Allen "Tomahawk" to pass him off as an Indian to unwitting audiences.[50]

Apparently dissatisfied with tour profits or the ridiculous press coverage, the Tuscarora Indians returned to their original business model after 1922, dropping Lynch and again scheduling games closer to home.[51] By that time, other all-Indian professional teams had arisen to tap the midwestern audiences the Cheyenne and Tuscarora squads had primed for them. Some Tuscarora talents stayed out on the road by teaming with Seneca players from New York's Cattaraugus Reservation and barnstormed professionally throughout the 1920s and early 1930s as the Seneca Indians. Their prime territory was New York, Pennsylvania, and Ohio, but on their 1930 tour they covered ten states and 5,600 miles, winning sixteen of twenty-four games. They were best known for their "marathon-like running tactics," which they employed to exhaust their opponents.[52]

Meanwhile, in Wisconsin, the best players from the reservation-based teams united in the 1920s to form heavy hitting multitribal touring contingents, beginning with the Plymouth Indian Aces in 1921. Their best player, as well as manager, was Louis Steffes, a top-rated center who had learned to play basketball outdoors on his Oneida Reservation. It was said that as a young boy "his agility and fleet footedness was a source of wonderment among the members of even his own tribe." Steffes was joined by some ex-Indian school stars, including John Leroy (Stockbridge), who had competed at Carlisle. To accent the team name, each member wore his own jersey emblem, one for each ace in a deck of playing cards, another with a one-spot domino, and a sixth player with snake eye dice. Over these they donned warm-ups with their personal names and tribal affiliations.[53]

Although sharply dressed and well experienced, the Aces disappointed competitively and disbanded after 1923. Steffes went on to play for mostly white professional teams for a few years until agreeing in 1927 to play for another multitribal team owned by Al Seeger, a Milwaukee-based sports promoter.[54] Although Steffes captained the team, there was no doubt who ran the operation. It was promoted under the name Al Seeger's Indians and the players wore the owner-manager's name printed in large cursive letters across their jerseys. Fortunately for the players, Seeger had managerial savvy to match his ego and provided them with ample opportunities to compete for cash. Though concentrating on Wisconsin and Michigan, and ranging only so far as Iowa, the team maintained an exhausting road schedule. In their first season, they traveled 9,375 miles and earned distinction as the "world's endurance basketball record" holders by playing 125 games in one season. They won 109 of them. Always crowd-pleasers with their aforementioned "deluxe entertainments," Al Seeger's Indians stayed in business until 1934, when Seeger gave up the team to organize a ten-piece traveling orchestra of non-Native musicians.[55]

There were still more American Indian barnstormers crisscrossing the Midwest between the world wars. The Navajo leaders of Albuquerque Indian School's famed 1928 team, Kee Kinsel and Askie Legah, stayed in the game during the early 1930s by playing for the First Americans (also known as the All-American Indians), a multitribal team under the management of J. C. Jordan, from Savonburg, Kansas. In 1933, after Kinsel and Legah left, the team acquired Louis Weller, James Naismith's quintessential dribbler.[56]

The Oklahoma Indians also operated in the later 1930s and again postwar in the late 1940s. Not to be confused with the earlier Oklahoma Indian Quintet, this team represented multiple tribes then residing in the state, as well as including some tribal players from elsewhere in the West. The late 1940s iteration traveled the Midwest and mid-Atlantic states in a bus with a bullhorn attached to the roof to announce their games in each town they entered. Wearing northern Plains-style war bonnets and clad in jerseys emblazoned with "Oklahoma," the newspapers marketed them as "real honest-to-goodness-Injuns" who had served their country honorably during World War II. Each of them had sharpened his hoops skills playing for regimental teams during the conflict.[57]

Thorpe's World Famous Indians

One of the most renowned of the all-Indian teams was the World Famous Indians (WFI), which had Jim Thorpe as lead attraction. Thorpe's professional basketball career was lost to history until 2005, when someone found a ticket to one of the WFI's 1927 games inside an unrelated book, purchased at auction. This discovery came as a surprise to all, including the book's buyer, Thorpe's grandson, and his biographers, none of whom knew about this chapter in his life.[58] It is striking that the WFI was forgotten for so long, because they were no flash in the pan. The team was in high demand during the three seasons it toured—two with Thorpe, and a third without—from the fall of 1926 to the spring of 1929.

The team's origin story began in 1922, the year Thorpe, in his thirties, relocated to little La Rue, Ohio. He did not go there for basketball but rather to start an all-Indian football team called the Oorang Indians on behalf of Walter Lingo, a wealthy breeder of Oorang Airedale dogs. Lingo financed the team as a vehicle for promoting his kennels, trading on Thorpe's celebrity and the marketability of Native athletes. The Oorang Indians belonged to the recently established National Football League but had no stadium in La Rue and so functioned as a touring team. In addition to competing at football, its Carlisle and Haskell alumni players danced in traditional Native attire at halftime and did stunts with Lingo's dogs. The team lasted only two seasons and was less than the sum of its parts competitively, winning only four games. Thorpe went along with this over-the-top sensationalized project because he needed the money, had an affinity for the dogs, and wanted to help other Native athletes succeed as professionals.[59]

What has gone untold about this story is its epilogue. Their football days over, Thorpe kept a pared down version of the Oorang Indians going through the winter of 1923–24 as a basketball team. This had nothing to do with his ambition to remake himself as a pro basketball player late in his career. He had played the sport at Carlisle, but it had never been his forte. All he planned to do was coach the unit and make brief appearances as a player to please spectators and turn a small profit. The team, however, was a flop. Oorang lost all the basketball games they played against local independent teams and called it quits in early January.[60]

This would have been an ignominious end to Thorpe's pro basketball career had Charles "Chic" Skelley not gotten involved. Skelley was a small-statured man with big ambitions. He was a sign shop owner and semipro baseball manager from Akron, Ohio, who was determined to make his fortune in sports business. Thorpe had met him in the winter of 1919, when he signed to play for Skelley's newly established minor league baseball team, the Akron Buckeyes. This team was so unprofitable its first season that the investors ousted Skelley in June.[61] Thorpe went his own way, playing baseball and football various places before landing in La Rue. While Thorpe was with the Oorang Indians, he stayed in touch with Skelley, who he seems to have regarded as both a friend and a potential business associate. In February 1923, Thorpe even presented himself as a potential player to help Skelley finance another baseball team representing the Ohio towns of Bucyrus and Galion. This too proved a bust, leaving Skelley $356 in debt to Spalding's for the useless team uniforms.[62]

That was the last anyone heard of a connection between the two men until the summer of 1926, when Skelley popped up in La Rue to help Thorpe revive the Oorang Indians—briefly, as it turned out—as a dual semiprofessional football and baseball team.[63] In October, Skelley also helped Thorpe give pro basketball another go in La Rue by co-organizing the World Famous Indians. The team name was represented in abbreviated form as "WFI" on the jerseys, set above the same-style Indian head that appeared on many Indian school uniforms of the time. Although the team was advertised to the public as "Thorpe's Indians," the aging celebrity was only a player-coach, talent scout, and perhaps coinvestor. As the business manager, Skelley called the shots off the court.[64]

The WFI got off to a rocky start in mid-December 1926. Despite having an all-star team on their debut tour that included John Levi, they lost four straight games in Indiana—the first of five states on their schedule. Levi and some of the other players quit over this embarrassment, and the opposing team manager in Newcastle, Indiana, used the opportunity to deal half his squad to the WFI as replacements. These additions were talented but also white, and so Skelley, or possibly Thorpe, assigned them bogus Indian names. Journalists in most places the team toured overlooked the ruse, but not in Indiana, where the WFI additions were homegrown commodities. One reporter in the state delighted in referring to them as Thorpe's "paleface Indians."[65]

The WFI never lost its dependence on supplemental white players after that—particularly its six-foot-three, high-scoring center Dale "Deak" Peters, who, like Kenny Allen years before, was rechristened Tomahawk. Thorpe and Skelley did what they could to recruit Native replacements when needed, but white athletes were more readily available in the eastern third of the country where they toured; and so the roster fluctuated between majority Indian and half white at various times. After the initial tour, Thorpe scouted his Native players primarily out of Haskell, the cradle of Indian basketball. He had connections there through Jesse Parton (Caddo), listed on rosters as "Swift Deer," and Leo Wapp (Sac and Fox-Potawatomi), listed as "Running Hawk." Both were Haskell alums who had stayed with the WFI through the early defections.[66]

The WFI became a majority Native team again in January 1927 when former Haskell teammates Dennis Hildebrand (Cherokee—"Eagle Feather") and Raymond West (Cheyenne—"Light Foot") signed on. Whereas the other Haskellites on the team had graduated, West dropped out midterm to answer Thorpe's call and never looked back. He thus fueled Indian Service administrators' fears that professional sports would lead their students astray. Then, when Parton and Leo Wapp left the WFI to pursue other opportunities at the end of the first season, Wapp's kinsman Anthony joined to keep the Native contingent in the slight majority. Nicknamed "Push 'em up Tony" during his days at Haskell, the younger Wapp was a hulking presence on the court at six feet five and 215 pounds. With the WFI, he became "High Sky."[67]

Anthony Wapp and West became the heart and soul of the team thenceforward, leading the scoring and receiving the lion's share of publicity after Thorpe's eventual departure. Wapp was marketed to fans mainly for his ball handling skill. As Skelley told reporters, he could "make a basketball do most everything but call him papa." He could duplicate any trick he ever saw anyone perform. On one occasion, he famously irritated Harlem Globetrotters wizard Inman Jackson by stealing a spinning ball off the tip of his finger and putting it on his own without interrupting its rotation. West, meanwhile, played the part of heartthrob. Reporters said he resembled Hollywood sex symbol Rudolph Valentino and gave him the nicknames "Indian sheik" and "dusky Apollo." Skelley fed this hype by telling reporters he requested police escorts in every town to protect West from mobs of crazed women.[68]

Even though the WFI was never the all-Indian team it claimed to be, few reporters or spectators cared. The team's larger-than-life persona, spirited play, and connection to Thorpe kept them in public demand. The Native members were some of the best the Indian schools ever produced, and they always controlled the flow of play. The WFI was *stylistically* an Indian team despite having several imposters in tow. They played a souped-up Indian basketball-style, winning with long-distance sharpshooting and a fast "driving attack." Few of the company, college, and professional teams they played could keep pace. Despite the WFI's weak start to the 1926–27 season, they finished fifty-one and eleven and followed in season two with fifty-four wins in seventy-two games. They did this while scouring the eastern third of the country, covering fifteen states by the spring of 1928. The team fared even better in its third and final season without Thorpe, winning sixty-two of sixty-five.[69]

The WFI did not attract big crowds by today's standards, but the attendance was respectable for barnstorming teams of that era, ranging from a few hundred spectators to nearly a thousand. Thorpe was the main draw even though he spent most his time on the bench. He turned forty just after the first season and had no interest in taxing his aging body to keep up with his younger teammates, especially since he wanted to showcase up-and-coming Native talent more than himself. When he did play, he stayed back on defense and never shot the ball. This satisfied most fans, who were happy just to see a living legend.[70]

Thorpe nevertheless showed his old competitive spark at least once with the WFI. It was in the first season finale against the Elks of East Liverpool, Ohio, on April 3, 1927. Wanting the season to end on a high note, he stayed in the whole game and only played his Native starters. Late in the last period, trailing hopelessly 41–31, Thorpe broke script and charged out of the backcourt toward hometown hero, Dick Larkins. "Big Jim Thorpe got loose . . . and began to ramble down the floor, dribbling, plumb into Dick Larkins' territory," wrote a local reporter. "Dick saw him coming, took a deep breath, a last look at the sidelines and stepped in front of the greatest all-around athlete of all time. The two jolted and the play was broken up. Big Jim grinned till his eye teeth showed as he trotted back up the court."[71]

Thorpe's proclivity for the bench did not betray indifference. He felt indebted to those spectators who were there to honor him. He proved as much during a visit to Harrisburg, Pennsylvania, on March 19, 1927. A small but enthusiastic crowd had assembled there to see the WFI and its legendary skipper take on a team representing the Pennsylvania Railroad. The WFI arrived as planned, only to discover that the host railroaders were no-shows. This was a crushing turn of events for the adoring fans who had come to see Thorpe in action. Skelley blamed the opposing manager for the mess, referring to this as "the worst deal ever handed to us in our career." With that, he wanted to move on, but Thorpe refused to leave town until they could play a replacement game. Thorpe took this stand, said a local reporter, because he wanted "to show Harrisburg fans that Jim Thorpe was not in the wrong and to prove that he is the same as of old, when he was in the hearts of all Harrisburg sports lovers." Skelley relented and booked a game two nights later against a cobbled together "all-star" team, who the WFI beat 41–33.[72]

As the WFI were preparing to leave Harrisburg for their next game in Lebanon, Pennsylvania, local papers reported that Skelley had lied. In his own defense, the Railroad team's manager had written the reporters to correct the record. He explained that Skelley had demanded such a large share of the receipts that negotiations had fallen through at the last minute and, rather than take the blame for canceling a pre-advertised game, Skelley feigned ignorance and deferred responsibility. Thorpe refused to impugn his associate in the press, but his body language said it all during their next game in Lebanon. The 700 fans in attendance saw the WFI manhandle the local Fraternal Order of Eagles team 43–29, boosted by Parton's sixteen points, but Thorpe never moved from his place on the bench. Late in the game, the fans began cheering for him to sub in for his normally scripted victory lap. Hearing this, Skelley stepped forward, called time out and waved Thorpe in, but the legend sat motionless, refusing to take off his warm-up jersey. Disappointing fans this time was a price worth paying to set Skelley straight and remind him that the team was known as *Thorpe's* World Famous Indians.[73]

Thorpe stayed with Skelley and the WFI the following season, but he missed a few games in December due to an injury suffered in a car accident outside Lodi, Ohio—or at least that's why Skelley said he missed them (I have found no other record of this accident). He played very little after returning in January 1928, riding the season out mostly on the bench or "detained" elsewhere. Thorpe probably stayed that second year mainly for the money. In addition to his share of the profits, he had a new endorsement deal with Studebaker. It was lucrative enough that he agreed to appear in a turkey feather headdress in a newspaper advertisement for Studebaker's seven-passenger President, which the company provided the team for its highway travels. His teammates often appeared in these headdresses for team promotions, but Thorpe did so only this one time.[74]

At the end of that season, Thorpe left the team to the younger, spryer players and to Skelley. During its last season in 1928–29, reporters alternatively referred to the team as both the World Famous Indians and "Chick Skelley's Indians." It is curious that Skelley gave up on the project. Even minus Thorpe, the WFI was competitive and profitable, attracting eight hundred spectators to one of their final games in Harrisburg. Instead, Skelley went back to managing semipro, all-white baseball teams and, in later years, became a major league scout for the St. Louis Browns and Cleveland Indians.[75]

Through its illustrious run, the WFI's story was one of exploitation and opportunity. In hindsight, Thorpe and Skelley both deserve criticism for shamelessly appropriating Native identities for their white players, but the WFI must also be acknowledged for the heavy dose of style and speed they injected into professional basketball and for advancing the careers of some supremely talented Native athletes. If Thorpe's primary motivation for the project was to use the WFI as a public relations tool to benefit younger Native players, he succeeded.

Anthony Wapp and West made the biggest splashes. When the WFI disbanded, both were recruited in 1929 to play for Olson's Terrible Swedes, which was one of the top professional barnstorming teams in the country. Owned and managed by C. M. "Ole" Olson, the team toured all regions of the United States. Their pay was never made public, but Wapp and West no doubt earned more with the Swedes than they ever did with the WFI; and although West still gave "war dance" exhibitions on occasion, they were marketed less for their Indian identities with the Swedes than they had been with the WFI.[76]

In January 1933, Olson also made Wapp player-manager of a side team he put together called the Giants. Unlike the Swedes moniker, this name was truly descriptive of the players. With an average height of six feet six, Wapp and his teammates were considered freakishly tall for their day. It must have seemed an odd turn for Wapp to be made a novelty because of his height rather than his race, but he embraced the assignment. Drawing on his prior experience touring with baseball's Nebraska Indians (he and Leo Wapp had played for them before joining the WFI), he developed a special trick to thrill crowds. Olson had them chant "Wind 'er Up Wapp" until he palmed the ball in his big right hand and pitched it down court like a fastball.[77]

Later that year, Wapp signed to play for the famed House of David basketball team. He barnstormed with them three seasons wearing the obligatory beard. He developed a new trick there, pitching balls up and headbutting them into the basket with keen accuracy. Wapp then returned to captain the Swedes, clean shaven (or *unglued* if the beard had been fake), until the fall of 1938. He opted to end his career barnstorming one season with the Oklahoma Indians. Wapp had gone full circle in the professional game, concluding his trek back with an all-Indian touring team. He received his last nickname there from his teammates, presumably meant to tease someone they admired. High Sky no more, he ended his career as "Flying Duck."[78]

Company Team Players

While Wapp stayed on the barnstorming circuit, Jesse Parton and Raymond West moved into industrial basketball. Parton did so first, leaving the WFI after the first season to play for the Akron Goodyears, one of the best company teams in the country. After his one season with the Swedes, West went in a similar direction, signing with the Tulsa Diamond Oilers—a team sponsored by the Mid-Continent Petroleum Corporation.[79]

As company players, Parton and West technically competed as amateurs, but this was no step down from their play-for-pay days. The best basketball players in the country often chose company over professional teams to achieve greater financial security. Company team players were technically paid for their nine-to-five day jobs with the sponsoring business, not for basketball. This made them amateur competitors even though it was widely known that many top athletes were brought in for their basketball skills and assigned factory or desk jobs only to get around AAU regulations. The sponsoring companies engaged in this practice because winning teams boosted employee morale and helped advertise their products, and the AAU looked the other way because company teams were lead attractions in its national basketball tournaments. For their part, the athletes were happy to make a living playing basketball. How they officially earned their pay was beside the point.[80]

One of West's veteran teammates on the Diamond Oilers was Clyde LeClair James, the Southwest Missouri State legend who made his way to industrial basketball by a less traveled route for a Native player. After graduating college, James played independent basketball various places until 1927, when he signed at forward for the Diamond Oilers (then called the Tulsa Eagles) at Coach William Miller's urging. Miller gave James the hard sell, telling him if he passed on the offer to join the team, he would be "throwing away the chance of a life-time." He meant this only in terms of the team's competitive prospects. No mention was made of which company job James was to take as part of the offer. James was likely the first American Indian to ever play industrial basketball, having signed with the Oilers a few weeks prior to Parton going to the Goodyears and three years prior to West becoming his teammate in Tulsa.[81]

The Tulsa Eagles-Diamond Oilers team was one of the best competing at any level during the years James and West played. They claimed the Oklahoma state amateur championship partway through James's first season in 1926–27 and then embarked on a 6,200-mile victory lap from Oklahoma to California and back, winning thirteen of fifteen games along the way. James led the team in scoring the next season before leaving in 1929 to play independent basketball in San Francisco. He then returned to the Oilers to play alongside West for the 1930–31 season. The team's talented Native duo were featured in team promotional materials neither wearing headdresses nor performing war dances, but both were listed with the title

Figure 27. Jesse "Cab" Renick coaching his former team, the Phillips 66ers, ca. 1950. No other Native athlete accomplished more in basketball as a high school, college, semiprofessional, and Olympics player. Oklahoma Publishing Company Photography Collection. Courtesy of the Gateway to Oklahoma History, Oklahoma Historical Society, ark:/67531/metadc554216.

"Chief" attached to their names on the Oilers' scorecards. These cards allowed fans to keep track of their game stats in a grid set above an advertisement for the parent company's Diamond 760 Motor Oil, "heat tested for motor protection to 760 degrees."[82]

In his long and diverse basketball career, Jesse Renick also played industrial basketball. After leaving the Navy, he played with the Phillips 66ers from 1945 to 1948. Sponsored by the namesake oil company based in Bartlesville, Oklahoma, the 66ers were the top AAU team in the country during Renick's time with them. His spirited play helped them win three AAU national championships and twice earned him selection as an AAU All-American. Playing for the 66ers proved advantageous for Renick, not just because the sponsoring oil company provided him steady employment in its sales department but because the arrangement allowed him to play at a high level while retaining his amateur status. This decision made it possible for him to cap off his illustrious career by captaining the United States Olympic basketball team to the gold medal at the 1948 London games.[83]

The handful of Native men who played on company teams were among the best of the best—competitors so talented at basketball that they did not have to lead an exhausting and unpredictable barnstorming lifestyle to make a reliable living in the game. As Renick was taking to the floor in his stylish 66ers uniform, there were nevertheless some Indian barnstormers still out there proving their ability perpetually on the road, and none did it better than the Sioux Travelers-Warriors.

The Sioux Travelers-Warriors

The Sioux Travelers-Warriors reached more spectators, in more places, over a longer period than any other Native professional touring team. Their operation was so talent rich that it ran two interconnected squads, the Travelers and the Warriors, which simultaneously toured the eastern and western portions of the country. They did so semi-randomly rather than assigning a squad permanently to one region or the other. The Travelers name usually designated the A-unit and was used exclusively during the few seasons when only one of the two teams was operating. The Travelers-Warriors stayed at this from 1938 until 1950, apart from a break during World War II. Later teams reviving the Sioux Travelers' name also toured sporadically from 1955 onward.[84]

As the WFI team acted as a de facto extension of Haskell's basketball program, so did the Travelers-Warriors become extensions of the top Catholic mission school programs in South Dakota. A virtual pipeline ran from Holy Rosary on the Pine Ridge Reservation to St. Francis on the Rosebud to the Travelers-Warriors, supplying these teams an endless flow of Lakota talent. These teams, in exchange, offered Holy Rosary and St. Francis alumni steady opportunities to earn income through basketball. Over the years, dozens of them played for one or both of the Travelers-Warriors teams. The Lakota athletes were also supplemented by Dakota players who were recruited on team visits to other reservations in South Dakota. William Sazue, for one, was discovered at Fort Thompson on the Crow Creek Reservation.[85]

The Travelers-Warriors business model was well-conceived to ensure competitive consistency, longevity, and commercial success. By concentrating the best Native players in the state in one operation and strategically shuffling them between twin teams, the Travelers-Warriors remained highly competitive without resorting to non-Native substitutes. They were therefore able to stay true to their advertised identity. America's fascination with the Sioux as legendary warriors and familiarity with St. Francis from its NCIBT appearances also made them the most marketable and recognizable of Indian teams.

The Travelers-Warriors also benefited from adopting a family-based approach to barnstorming, from top to bottom. They were comanaged by three brothers from Crookston, Nebraska, just south of the Rosebud Reservation: Bill, Jerry, and Francis Donovan. The eldest, Bill, was a sports promoter who handled the team's bookings and media relations, while the other two brothers served as road managers. Judging from newspaper reporting, the Donovans were non-Native, but they had attended high school on the Rosebud Reservation and were well acquainted with many of the Travelers-Warriors players, who were of their generation.[86] The fraternal nature of the operation extended to the players, too, as illustrated by the frequent occurrence of brothers on the team rosters, like the Blacksmiths, Cunys, Littles, and Valandras.[87]

It is uncertain who founded the Travelers-Warriors. It could have been the Donovans, a group of players, or an individual athlete like Ernest "Spec" Blacksmith. At the very least, Blacksmith deserves much of the credit for making the Travelers-Warriors a successful venture. He was the Travelers' lead attraction and scorer, he personally recruited many of the players, and he stayed with the operation longer than anyone. One of the initial members in 1938, Blacksmith remained to the end of the original Travelers' run in 1950 and served as player-coach of a revived version of the team in 1955.[88]

The Harlem Globetrotters and their owner, Abe Saperstein, also influenced the Travelers-Warriors, both inspirationally and more directly. Virtually everyone on the Sioux teams had encountered the Globetrotters during their formative playing years. Saperstein ran multiple Globetrotters units that simultaneously toured different parts of the country during the 1930s, including squads that competed regularly against American Indian teams in South Dakota.[89] St. Francis hosted them on multiple occasions in the early 1930s. So did other Indian school and predominantly Native AAU teams in the state, but St. Francis was the only one that occasionally defeated the esteemed professionals.[90]

Widely admired by South Dakota Native youths, the Globetrotters helped inspire future Travelers-Warriors to take up barnstorming. Agnes and Norbert Picotte remember how enthusiastically students received them on their annual visits to the Pine Ridge, Marty Mission, and Holy Rosary Indian schools later in the 1940s. Holy Rosary students had opportunities to socialize with their celebrity visitors, recalls Agnes, during classroom visits and while eating together in the dining hall. The Globetrotters and the students "just kind of accepted each other," she remembers, and "became friends." The Indian school athletes were nevertheless determined to defeat them on the court. "We can beat them! We can beat them!" the boys used to say. "They really did try to beat them," Agnes recalls. Sometimes, the Globetrotters let the Holy Rosary boys get the score close but never close enough to win.[91]

The earlier cohort of students who attended Holy Rosary and St. Francis during the 1930s must have been just as smitten with the Globetrotters, especially judging from the way they duplicated their tricks and tactics. Spec Blacksmith and other St. Francis alumni, for example, played basketball at Nettleton College in 1938–39 as though they *were* the Globetrotters. Whenever they built an insurmountable lead, the Netts began performing what reporters called "trick ball handling" routines to keep the audience engaged. This practice was straight out of the Globetrotters' playbook. They even showed off some of these tricks to the Globetrotters when Nettleton hosted them in December 1938. The Netts lost the game, but the experience of matching the Globetrotters move for move must have sparked something in Blacksmith because it was just a few days later that he dropped out of Nettleton and showed up barnstorming on the Travelers' debut roster.[92]

Abe Saperstein observed all these interactions between Indian school players and his Globetrotters and recognized the business value of acquiring a financial stake in some Native talent. Not only did these South Dakota Indians have all the right moves, he knew from St. Francis's NCIBT appearances in Chicago that they had poise under pressure and were crowd-pleasers. So, in the spring of 1941, Saperstein arranged a series of dates for the Globetrotters to play the Sioux Travelers in the more profitable barnstorming territory of Iowa and Illinois.[93] Just a few days into this mini-tour, St. Francis made headlines by finishing runners-up in the NCIBT finals. To capitalize on this, Saperstein either cut a deal with the Donovans or cherry-picked their players to form a composite team of Travelers and St. Francis NCIBT finalists he billed as the "St. Francis Mission Sioux Indians." Spec Blacksmith was included. Saperstein booked them to tour professionally down the East coast, which they did in early 1942 until war demands diverted most of the players into the service. Following the war, the Donovans regained full managerial control of the Travelers. Saperstein continued arranging annual dates between the Globetrotters and Travelers thereafter until a rift with the Donovans put a stop to this in 1948.[94]

These sustained interactions with the Globetrotters clearly rubbed off on the Travelers-Warriors. The twin-teams concept, attributed in the press to Bill Donovan, was an evident duplication of Saperstein's use of multiple Globetrotters squads. The close relationship with the Globetrotters also explains why the Travelers-Warriors were the only Native teams known to clown. They did this primarily in the late 1940s, including some elaborately staged gags very similar to those performed by the Globetrotters. The leader at this was "Chub Bear" Tibbitts, who was the advertised "top cage clown" of the operation. While other players were busy running up the score on their opponents, Chub Bear did a routine wherein he stole the ball from an opponent and ran it to the end line like he was scoring a football touchdown. After this, his teammates lined up to kick the ball at the hoop like an extra point. While traveling under the Warriors name in 1948, Chub Bear did the gag to roars of laughter from spectators in New Salem, Indiana, and then proceeded to sit down next to a woman in the stands. At this, said a reporter, "she fluttered, she screamed, and she flew, with the Sioux in pursuit of her through the bleachers." The Travelers-Warriors advertised their games that season as offering "side-splitting laughs," in addition to "Fancy Dribbling," "Trick Shooting," and "Spectacular Ball-Handling." When it came to the latter, Spec Blacksmith stole the show with his signature "slap-passing" and "ball juggling" tricks. On occasion, he even sank shots launched underhand beneath one of his outstretched legs.[95]

In addition to the gags and tricks, the Travelers-Warriors played up their Indian warrior image. Jack Little handled the job of singing tribal songs and dancing at halftime, and the usual promotional pictures were circulated to the papers with players in war bonnets. Sazue also remembers the players shedding their shirts, hanging towels down the front of their shorts, and putting on feathered headbands and war bonnets when they took to the court. According to Sazue's sister-in-law Charlotte Lambert, they did this not just to entertain but also because they knew spectators "expected them to be fierce." "They had that reputation to live up to," she explained.[96] They did not, however, list Indian names in lieu of their commonly used names. Instead, they tended toward flashy nicknames. Thus they had Spec and Chub Bear. Little was "Suitcase" Little, there was Calvin "Thriller" Valandra, and Spec's younger brother Wilbur was "Glamour Boy."[97]

The Travelers-Warriors' willingness to entertain did not detract from their drive to win. They had a proud heritage to uphold as Lakota and Dakota men and as former St. Francis players. Coaches like Bob Clifford and Willard Iron Wing had taught them to be winners in school and they were determined to remain so as professionals. Iron Wing reminded them of this storied tradition every night when he too played a stint with the Travelers in 1946. Both the Travelers and Warriors played every game full tilt, not unleashing their ball tricks and gags until they had built an unassailable lead. Their competitive drive showed in their consistently impressive record. The Travelers unit maintained an 85 percent win rate their first two

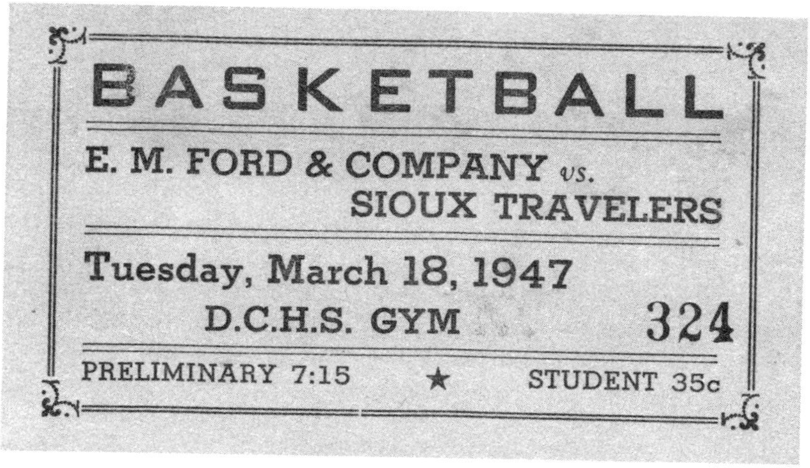

Figure 28. Ticket for a Travelers March 1947 game against an insurance company team in Owensboro, Kentucky. The Travelers won 72–54. In possession of author.

seasons, playing as many as 150 games a season. They were even better after World War II, winning nine out of every ten games in 1947. That year, the Travelers lived up to their name by putting 7,887 miles on their sedan, crossing seventeen states from South Dakota to New Jersey. The Warriors did just as well further south and west in 1948. They won sixty-one of sixty-nine games in one stretch of games played from Louisiana to California.[98]

Like the other Native barnstormers, the Travelers-Warriors played the Indian basketball style, which alone entertained most spectators. The gags, tricks, and dancing were icing on the cake. Just as they had at St. Francis, the twin teams relied on the fast break, earning accolades for so perfecting the "fire wagon" game that they hardly needed to mount any defense. They had the "fastest of fast breaks," it was said. The Travelers-Warriors amazed crowds not only with their speed but with moves that were rare for the time, including no look passes behind their backs and between their legs. In describing their passing and shooting, reporters applied adjectives such as "flashy," "fancy," "nifty," and "dizzying."[99] Spectators who may have come to see "real Indians" left amazed by the quality of basketball they had been privileged to witness. One letter to the editor of the *Rapid City Journal* in 1947 pleaded for more daily coverage of the Travelers, disparaging all other teams in the state as, by comparison, "a bunch of cold potatoes." That same day, the *Rushville Republican* in Indiana reported that its editorial staff had "been swamped for the past few days with requests for further information concerning the Sioux Travelers who were at the local gym the other night. Seems that everybody wants a crack at sponsoring a return appearance of the netters."[100]

The greatest of the all-Indian teams, the Travelers-Warriors outlasted most barnstormers, Native and non-Native, but their days on the road were numbered. Except for the Globetrotters and a handful of other teams that adapted to become scripted entertainers, barnstorming died off after the NBA was established in 1949. Those teams could not compete financially with a well-established league that had a national reach, nor with television, which provided small-town Americans with home entertainment.[101] As the barnstorming circuit faded, so did Native men's professional career hopes. None of the Indian barnstormers made the crossover to the NBA. The main reason for this was that NBA teams selected players from top-tier college programs rather than scouring the barnstorming ranks. Nor did the NBA necessarily appeal to former Native barnstormers. It could not offer the camaraderie of playing alongside their kin or the option of returning home between tours.[102]

One Native barnstormer *was* given the chance to play in the early NBA but declined. On the Travelers' tour through Maryland in 1949, Spec Blacksmith was offered a contract to play for the Baltimore Bullets just months before they became one of the original NBA teams. Although he was an aging player by then, Blacksmith had an extraordinary resume. He had been the perennial high point man for the Travelers for many years and had once scored more than three thousand points in a single season. He could no longer keep that pace in 1949, but the Bullets still liked what they saw. The reason Blacksmith gave for declining the offer was never publicized. Perhaps he saw more value in representing his own people on a team he had helped make legendary.[103]

In their time, the Native barnstormers and company players made their mark, not just on the basketball world but also in their home communities. This was especially true of the early teams like Odanah and later on the Sioux Travelers-Warriors teams that toured partly within Indian country. For the Travelers, this included their home South Dakota, where they were a source of intense interest to tribespeople, who came out in large numbers to see them play, and to the Lakota and Dakota basketball players they inspired for generations to come.[104] By the 1950s, many of the players they inspired were competing for public high schools, city league teams, or reservation-based independent teams. Many of them also participated in all-Indian tournaments organized by Natives themselves. A new era had dawned where basketball had wholly disconnected from the Indian schools to become a part of community sports traditions.

10

Communities

Native youths attending Indian schools and returning from them spread basketball to their tribal homelands in the early twentieth century, where it developed into a traditional community sport. These students taught many of their tribespeople how to play basketball and remained ardent supporters of the sport through their adult lives. As years progressed, they also received help. From the end of World War I through the end of the century, other individuals and organizations supported the game, inspiring more tribal youths to take up basketball, organizing adult teams and leagues, and providing the necessary equipment and facilities to make it a widely participatory activity. In addition to the previously mentioned Native collegians, military veterans, and barnstormers, these additional actors included Indian Service administrators, Christian missionaries, New Deal works programs, and, most of all, public schools.

Basketball did not, however, become an integral part of tribal athletic traditions all at once. What began as a minor pastime was woven into the social fabric gradually, year by year, so deeply in the end that it became difficult to imagine Native community life without it. The sport first found a foothold in a handful of communities in the 1910s before gaining a wider presence during the 1920s. By the 1930s, it was a commonly played and enjoyed activity in most tribal communities, and within two decades following World War II it achieved its pinnacle as Indian country's most popular team sport in both urban and rural settings.

Bringing It Home

Indian school students did not wait until they returned home to share their newfound appreciation of basketball with their families. Because they frequently set pen to paper to describe their eager involvement in basketball, many Native families had read about the sport before they saw it played. Some learned about it from letters they received, like the one that twelve-year-old Chippewa student Willie Jerome mailed from Haskell in 1900. "There is not much to think about in what extra time we have except basket ball," he told his family in North Dakota. Sure they had never heard of this odd-sounding game, he gave them a rundown of its rules. Portions of this letter, and others like it, were also reprinted in school newspapers that employees mailed to students' families on the reservations. They appeared alongside detailed sports reports authored by students in the print shops and by Native athletic staff members. Through these written modes of transmission, home communities discovered that their young people wholly enjoyed this game and also acquired a rudimentary knowledge of its structure and rules.[1]

Students attending reservation boarding schools also transmitted their basketball interests and styles of play to non-student tribespeople by playing with and against them on campus grounds.[2] This occurred through unauthorized pickup games students organized with tribal visitors, like the "no rules" scrum Paul Moss played at St. Stephens, in Wyoming around the time of World War I (see chapter 4). Although school superintendents disapproved of this unauthorized rough-and-tumble activity, some offered non-student locals conditional access to school courts when they were not in use, and they occasionally condoned, or even encouraged, supervised games between these outsiders and their students. They did so both to extend the benefits of sports participation to non-student populations and to promote positive institutional relations with host tribes. During the 1920s and 1930s, such open door basketball policies were in effect at numerous agency boarding schools, including at Fort Bidwell in California and Crow in Montana.[3]

Students also communicated their passion for the sport by playing hard to impress family members who came to watch their games. This happened most often at the reservation boarding schools, and later public schools, where community supporters traveled less far to see them play, but some of the off-reservation teams also enjoyed the backing of tribespeople who journeyed great distances to see teams they had read and heard a lot about.[4] Such was the case when Chief Rocky Boy and other Montana Chippewa made the one-hundred-mile trip to Great Falls to watch the Fort Shaw women play in 1903 and, again, during the 1920s, when scores of Oklahoma Natives traveled to various locations to cheer for Chilocco's boys.

Native people made these trips mainly to support their player relatives. Many, though, were also budding fans of the sport itself. An observer named Florence Mims noted as much while attending a 1922 Chilocco boys' game, played away in Tonkawa, Oklahoma. She could see how intently Native spectators in the crowd were following the action. It was clear that basketball enthralled them even though many were too old to have played it

Figure 29. Community members on Arizona's San Carlos Apache Reservation watch local schoolboys play basketball during the 1920s or 1930s. Francis Uplegger Photographs, CP SPC 187:5.29. Courtesy of Greater Arizona Collection, Arizona State University Library.

in their youths. Mims was particularly taken with an elderly man perched above her in the balcony. He first attracted her attention with his sharp attire—with his big black cowboy hat, bright white hat band, and brilliant orange tie—and he held it by the intense manner of his gaze, which he fixated on the Indian athletes. Mims wrote to her hometown newspaper, back in South Carolina, describing the man. "He sat during the first part of the game, stolid and staring, not relaxing a muscle of his face," she said. "During the middle of the game, his face thawed into a furrowed smile, and near the end, when some particularly striking feat occurred, his face melted into a broad laugh and he clapped his hands in delight."[5]

But the main way Indian school students transmitted their passion for basketball to the home communities was by teaching the game to their friends and relatives upon their return. Members of later generations owed a debt of gratitude to these pupils-turned-teachers who survived difficult times away and brought home this game to share. One of their many admirers was Dennis Smith, a high school scoreboard operator for Owyhee High School in Nevada. During the 1980s, he told tales of former Indian schoolers who planted the basketball seed in his Duck Valley Reservation generations before. They were pioneers, he explained, worthy of every basketball-loving Shoshone and Paiute person's respect. "They learned to speak English fluently. They learned about agriculture. They learned to play basketball," Smith said. "When they came back to the reservation, they had it (the love of basketball) in their blood. They taught it to the kids." Smith also spoke fondly of Earl Dunn, a legendary Paiute player from the Pyramid Lake Reservation, who had starred for Stewart Indian School during the 1940s. In the years after his return from school, Dunn taught others how to play the game and inspired them as a leading scorer on local independent teams. In the 1960s, he also helped administer a large all-Indian tournament hosted on the reservation, in the town of Nixon. Dunn "learned about basketball . . . he brought it home," Smith remarked. "It was like a flower that bloomed, blossomed. . . . What he brought to his people is still growing."[6]

The Indian Office hoped boarding school graduates would help people in their home communities assimilate by introducing modern ideas and practices they learned as students. Some hoped they would teach the sports they learned as part of this, for these were wholesome, all-American activities, but they miscalculated how eager many pupils were to impart athletic knowledge, on the one hand, while discounting lessons of supposedly greater import, on the other. Nor did they anticipate that community members would adopt these new sports and welcome home these athletes while still showing contempt for the schools. Other white man's ways were often rejected by the elders as useless or culturally threatening. Conflicts flared between the generations when returning students who had accepted aspects of the assimilationist agenda tried to make their families eat in a "civilized" manner, act on a profit motive, or pray differently. Speaking well of the YMCA as a Christian reform organization drew many scornful retorts; yet the sport the Y gave birth to was broadly accepted. Most people exempted it, and other introduced sports, from concerns they had about the schools' insidious influences.[7] They had fun participating in these activities, saw in them glimpses of the sports of old, and realized that playing them together reinforced community bonds. They saw that these sports could be made their own.

A Crowded Garden

The basketball "flower" that students transplanted to the reservations set its roots in a garden that was already occupied by the traditional games and sports Native people had played for centuries. Many of these activites had disappeared, including some traditional dice games and chungke, but others still bloomed in their seasons. Through the 1930s, many communities still played hand game and people struck balls with shinny sticks on western reservations. The Shoshone-Bannock tribes continued pitching quoits and playing hoop and pole at Fort Hall, in Idaho, and Zunis were still playing a traditional game in New Mexico, throwing stones at upright corn-cobbs to knock them over and claim the coins set atop.[8]

On many reservations, old and new sports coexisted, but as their roots intertwined, some old sports withered. Lacrosse and stickball were still played in many Native communities but shared the calendar with baseball. This was the first introduced team sport that Indian country embraced and was still very popular there in the early twentieth century. Baseball's premier status in American athletic culture had transferred to Native peoples, who played it extensively in schools, as barnstormers, and in professional leagues. Native communities adopted the sport as a supplement to, rather than a replacement for, their field sports, but as baseball became more established, it distracted attention from the old ways. This occurred, for example, among the Lake Superior Chippewa and Mississippi Choctaws in the 1910s and 1920s, as they focused less on their indigenous stick-and-ball games and increasingly gravitated to baseball as a modern means to compete within their communities and against whites.[9]

There were also other introduced sports occupying Native community interests at the time basketball arrived—especially rodeo and football. The former was coming on strong during the first two decades of the twentieth century in the personage of men like Jackson Sundown (Nez Perce) and Tom Three Persons (Blood), who both won bronc riding championships in integrated competition. The parallel emergence of all-Indian rodeos and the varied cultural activities tied to them made that sport an important part of tribal life during years when basketball was still a minor past time.[10]

Football was also gaining popularity in local Native communities during the first third of the twentieth century. It was played at reservation boarding schools as well as in the public schools in later years. Some reservation towns had their own adult teams, and many former Indian school students kept close tabs on their alma maters' gridiron exploits—especially Haskell's. However, rural Native communities never rallied around football to the extent that Indian school students did, perhaps because of the expensive gear it required and the difficulty smaller communities had fielding full teams. Some public school and town teams on the reservations adopted the more manageable six-man version, invented in 1934, but this never captured peoples' interest to the extent that five-player basketball did.[11]

As crowded as this garden was, there was an open patch where basketball could grow. Being a mostly wintertime activity meant it did not compete directly with the traditional or non-Native-introduced field sports for attention. Ice hockey might also have filled that seasonal slot, but despite shinny's traditional significance across Native North America, the skate and puck game never became a widespread activity south of the Canadian border.

Basketball was also well-suited to small, economically depressed populations, as many reservation settlements and towns were. Teams of varying size could play the game almost anywhere, on dirt courts or indoors in relatively tight spaces, and any equipment people could not afford to buy, they made. Its minimum requirements were nothing more than a ball of rags; a barn wall or flat board elevated on a wooden pole; a repurposed wire hoop, old fruit basket, or milk crate; and a small patch of dirt. Just as boarding school students fabricated their own hoops in school shops and outlined their courts on dairy barn floors, so did they fabricate their own playing equipment and courts back at home.[12]

Taking Root

Basketball nonetheless had humble beginnings in Native communities. There was usually a lag period of a decade or two between the time boarding school students first introduced the game and it becoming widely popular in a given community. There were a few places, though, where it happened more quickly. Basketball was embraced by many reservation residents in Wisconsin and upstate New York prior to World War I, judging from all the adult independent and barnstorming teams these communities spawned. Although the members of these teams were mostly former Indian school students, they received broad support from tribespeople who had not attended those institutions or previously seen the sport played.

Returning to the Tuscarora Indians team's story illustrates the point. Tribal leaders allowed these barnstormers to practice in the council house during the 1910s, which is particularly telling because the building was the heart of community life, and the arrangement required the leaders to make personal sacrifices. As Chief Clinton Rickard later recalled, some of the councilmen grumbled about sharing the building with young tribesmen bouncing basketballs on its floors. They feared that, in their exuberance, these youths would knock over one of the wood stoves at either end of the structure and burn it down. When one of the players proposed a gymnasium be built as a solution, around 1921, the "whole nation" lent their support, said Rickard. "It united our people as nothing else had in many years," he recalled. "Many people donated their labor to make the project a success." No activity regarded as an outside imposition, or trifle, could have compelled tribal leaders to tolerate such intrusions or so galvanized a community to action.[13]

If there was any doubt about the geographic breadth of basketball's appeal to Native communities, one could look to Alaska's southeastern panhandle, three thousand miles from where the Tuscarora Indians competed. The temperate coastal climate and relative ease of seaborne transportation facilitated the sport's early spread to this remote region. Natives attending the Sitka Industrial Training School began playing varsity basketball in 1905 and, during the 1910s, other Natives in the area joined them in forming Sitka city league teams. One of the perennial league favorites was the team representing the Alaska Native Brotherhood, a prominent civil rights advocacy organization. By the end of World War I, basketball was also popular in the Metlakatla Indian Community on Annette Island. A men's town team there gained regional notoriety for going undefeated at home over a ten-year stretch from 1918 until 1928, when they finally lost a game to the Agricultural College/School of Mines (future University of Alaska, Fairbanks).[14] By contrast, basketball was slower to spread to Natives in the Alaskan interior and the Arctic than most parts of the continent. A shortage of indoor facilities and difficulties transporting teams over great distances under harsh conditions stunted the sport's popularity there until the 1970s.[15]

Basketball achieved popularity in Native American communities elsewhere in the United States more so during the 1920s. A variety of developments explain this timing. Most important, basketball achieved status as the most played boarding school sport in this period, and so the volume of sports reporting on it reaching the home communities increased. More students were also returning home wanting to keep at the game and eager to teach it to friends and family. World War I veterans who had learned to play in the training camps or nurtured existing interests there had also returned recently and were personally invested in the game. This was also when barnstorming teams composed of former Indian schoolers were flourishing and a small uptick in the number of college players occurred, demonstrating that basketball could be an avenue to social recognition and economic success beyond the boarding schools.

Other groups also began supporting the game in Native communities during the 1920s. Churches were especially active basketball promoters at the time. Besides Catholic- and Protestant-operated boarding schools that sponsored basketball programs, some reservation-based YMCA associations organized member games. So did reservation-based churches that used basketball as a fellowship activity and form of outreach. In this spirit, Episcopalians placed a basketball court inside their community house, built in 1929 at Irving, on New York's Cattaraugus Reservation. It was available free-of-charge to the adult independent teams springing up in

Figure 30. A men's team from Solen, on the Standing Rock Reservation, in 1940. Courtesy of NARA, Kansas City, Missouri, identifier 285801.

the area. Around this time, Mormon missionaries also constructed courts for their converts on the Navajo Nation and elsewhere in Indian country, believing the sport uplifted them physically and morally and socialized them within the LDS Church.[16]

This combined activity following World War I had a noticeable effect on local sporting cultures. Basketball's maturation as a broadly participatory community sport was especially apparent in Sioux country, in the Dakotas, where numerous adult town teams were active during the 1920s. These teams competed against each other, as well as boarding schools and American Legion squads. Most of these teams comprised returned Indian school students, but they also included members who had attended day schools or had no formal education.[17]

An article in *Indians at Work* revealed that basketball permeated the Rosebud Reservation's sporting culture by the early 1930s. In addition to being a staple offering at St. Francis and the government schools, the sport was played "at Church and YMCA meetings" across the reservation. Signs of unstructured play were also readily apparent. "It is not uncommon to see a basket fastened on the side of a house or barn or pole and used for practice," the article reported. Anthropologist Fred Voget saw similar sights on the Crow Reservation, in Montana, in the 1930s, noting that "Crow boys constantly practiced at shooting baskets through barrel hoops raised on poles" in and around Lodge Grass. This was not a recent phenomenon, he was told, as basketball had been a local obsession since the end of World War I.[18]

By the early 1930s, basketball's popularity was also evident among Native communities in the American Southwest, including the Akimel O'odham (Pima) on Arizona's Gila River Reservation. People were "devoted to basketball, football and baseball," Superintendent Albert H. Kneale later recalled of his time spent in that community during the early 1930s. "Every community had its football team, its basketball team," he added. Basketball also had a firm hold on the New Mexico portion of the Navajo Nation by mid-decade. Numerous adult town teams represented communities there from places like Tohatchi and Crown Point. They played each other and competed against non-Natives in independent tournaments each year in Gallup.[19]

During the mid-1930s and early 1940s, basketball received a further boost in Indian country from New Deal public works programs that sponsored teams and constructed playing facilities on numerous reservations. This was done as part of broader government efforts to promote tribal community development. The main beneficiaries were men in their late teens and twenties who played basketball while employed by the Civilian Conservation Corps' Indian Division (CCC-ID), a works program charged with conserving and managing natural resources on the reservations. About eighty-five thousand Native men participated in the CCC-ID during its years of operation from 1933 to 1942, many of whom spent portions of the year in boarding camps near work sites. During off-hours, after long days of laboring, camp managers encouraged the young men to play basketball and other sports for some of the same reasons the Indian schools and the military did—to keep them in good health and spirts and to avoid disciplinary problems arising from boredom.[20]

Workers at CCC-ID camps competed in basketball, baseball, boxing, and, to a lesser degree, football. Playing cards and pitching horseshoes were also ways to pass the time. Team sports were played both informally and as organized activities, the latter pitting CCC-ID teams against independent teams from nearby towns or against other Native and non-Native camp teams arranged into leagues. Most CCC-ID basketball teams played on dirt courts or inside recreation halls constructed specifically for the workers, but a few played home games in nearby boarding school gymnasiums by permission of the Indian Service superintendents—another way Indian school administers facilitated basketball's dissemination to non-student Natives. Many CCC-ID players were former Indian school students, and large numbers later enlisted in the Armed Forces. These teams thus comprised a middle link in a chain of basketball experiences, extending from the late 1920s through the mid-1940s, as hundreds of Native men went from playing in the boarding schools during the 1920s to playing on

Figure 31. CCC-ID workers practice shooting hoops on the Standing Rock Reservation in 1938. 75-SR-5669. Courtesy of NARA, Kansas City, Missouri.

CCC-ID teams in the 1930s to playing on military service teams during World War II. Basketball thus engaged and comforted them through turbulent years marked by family dislocation, economic strife, and war.[21]

CCC-ID basketball was more than a casual diversion for the hundreds of Native players who took pride in their teams and competed fiercely to win. The most dedicated and talented CCC-ID team was a group from the Crow Reservation called the Crow All-Americans. Respected by opponents for their effective fast-breaking offense, which they played in the Indian basketball style, they were the only CCC-ID team that ever received invitations to compete in the AAU's national tournament in Denver. In 1938, they lost there to the Studebaker Athletic Club of South Bend, Indiana, in the first round despite center Ed Old Crow scoring an impressive twenty-three points. They returned in 1939 to beat a team from Mount Harris, Colorado, in the first round 39–24 behind strong play from Ben Bird, Leonard Pretty Weasel, and Clifford Singer. They faltered in the second round, however, when valiant offensive efforts by Singer and Arlis Whiteman failed to prevent a 59–27 loss to the Antlers Hotel team of Colorado Springs.[22]

In addition to sponsoring camp teams, the CCC-ID also cooperated with other works programs and Indian Service personnel to expand recreational opportunities for Native community members, young and old. On South Dakota's Pine Ridge Reservation, these joint efforts were merged in

Figure 32. A CCC-ID league team (players unidentified) from Bullhead, on the South Dakota portion of the Standing Rock Reservation, in 1939. Courtesy of NARA, Kansas City, Missouri, identifier 57274906.

the late 1930s to form a Recreation Committee. Among its other functions, the body maintained and scheduled the local Legion Hall for the free use of adult independent basketball teams and directly sponsored youth teams. These initiatives were less a matter of federal employees pushing basketball on the local population than of them responding to existing demand. In fact, some committee members only grudgingly supported basketball. They expressed concerns during a 1939 meeting that the time people spent playing the sport took away from other activities they wished to promote, like square-dancing and "local theatricals," but they yielded to popular demand. According to a summary meeting report, the committee members all admitted the impracticality of trying to "turn the people from basketball when it was so evident that this was their prime interest and what they wanted most."[23]

New Deal works programs, with assistance from Indian Service personnel, also helped tribal communities across Montana construct a series of community halls that were usable for indoor basketball. These halls provided the infrastructure necessary to support the sport's development as a widely participatory activity. The log-sided octagonal structures were meant primarily for dances and other local gatherings—not basketball specifically—but a few were fitted with lined floors, backboards, and hoops. These were community endeavors with the federal agencies acting in support. Local residents donated many of the logs for these structures and did most of the labor, either on a volunteer basis or as paid workers for the CCC-ID or Works Progress Administration. The Indian Office provided supplemental funding and some finishing materials, like windows, shingles, and doors. By making space for small courts in the same structures where dances, celebrations, and traditional craft work took place, these halls helped reposition basketball away from the Indian schools and toward the center of community life.[24]

The small Blackfeet Reservation community of Starr School, Montana, became home to one of these Depression-era log halls in December 1934. The court inside was tight quarters but was grand enough to satisfy generations of athletes who would play there, sheltered from the winter cold. Rather than relying on vertically standing support columns, the building's roof was braced by cross-poles attached to the outer wall, which afforded an open space ideally suited for both dancing and shooting baskets. Hoops and backboards were installed, ready for use the first day the hall's doors opened. James Naismith could never have predicted this—the Springfield gymnasium that inspired basketball's invention recast in logs and situated in the Cut Bank River valley, the northern Rockies as a backdrop.[25] What a venue this was for Blackfeet people to hone their skills playing hoops.

These Depression-era construction projects influenced the community basketball scene for decades. Blackfeet tribal member Kevin Kickingwoman has fond memories of growing up in the 1970s and 1980s playing basketball in the Starr School hall. By the time he and his friends got their turn to play there, it was showing signs of age, but it remained the center of community activity and housed a vibrant basketball culture. The young men who played inside had "basketball in their blood," Kickingwoman remembers. The space was consistently available for them to practice, which they did often, determined as they were never to lose a game to rival teams from bigger reservation towns like Heart Butte and Browning. "We had that pride about Starr School," says Kickingwoman.[26]

Day and Public Schools

The 1930s were also years when growing numbers of Native youths played basketball in federally operated reservation day schools and state public schools that often afforded them the opportunity to return to their family homes in the evenings.[27] On many reservations, Indian Service–operated day schools were the first institutions to impart a local flavor to the game.

They existed on reservations through the early decades of the century but rarely sponsored team sports. That changed during the New Deal with the construction of dozens of new community day schools designed both for educating youths and for providing adult meeting spaces and services.[28] Although they often lacked gymnasiums, many of these schools sponsored boys' intramural and interscholastic basketball teams, and some also had girls' teams. These teams practiced and played home games outdoors, weather permitting, and when indoor accommodations were needed, the schools rented space at mission boarding schools or borrowed the use of nearby government boarding school gymnasiums.[29]

Day schools on the Pine Ridge Reservation were among the most active anywhere at sponsoring organized basketball. Boys' teams from these small institutions competed in formal leagues and played approximately ten interscholastic games a year against each other, as well as against the reservation boarding school's teams. Beginning in 1937, they also competed in a twelve-team day school tournament at Wanblee each March. The single-elimination event was an opportunity for reservation residents to gather, and for the student athletes, aged seventeen and younger, to do their home communities proud. The tournament continued into the 1940s even though tire shortages during World War II compelled Indian Service administrators to scale back regular season schedules.[30]

By the 1930s, public schools were important sponsors of youth basketball in Native communities throughout the country. Slightly more than half of all Native students now attended these institutions, rather than federal or parochial schools. The proportion of Native k-12 students in public schools continued to increase thereafter, reaching 60 percent by 1964 and 65 percent by 1970. This trend toward public education was aided by congressional legislation in the 1930s and again in the early 1950s that provided federal funding to public school districts serving Native students living on non-taxable reservation lands.[31]

The shift to public schooling had complex effects on the ways Native youths and communities related to basketball. For one, playing in public school meant Native pupils were less likely to be part of an all-Indian team than were their Indian school or day school counterparts. This was especially true if they attended school off tribal lands but could also be the case on reservations. Many reservation towns had sizeable non-Native populations by the 1930s as a legacy of federal land allotment policy, which decades before had opened portions of the tribal land base to outside settlement. As a result, public schools in the middle of reservations often had a large number of non-Native pupils, sometimes outnumbering tribal members.

Basketball helped many Native youths cope in these integrated public school settings, thus performing a similar function for them as it had for their Indian school predecessors, but under different circumstances. Agnes Yellowtail Deernose, for one, recalled the sport's importance to her and other Crow students who attended elementary school during the 1920s in the town of Lodge Grass, Montana. Although the school was located near the geographic center of their own reservation, the Crow students were in the minority. They and the white students kept to themselves, and the Crows were made to feel unwelcome and alienated. Those who did not quit usually withdrew emotionally and thus struggled in their schoolwork. "In class boys and girls retreated behind the safety of their reading books and often drew pictures of camping, horses, deer, buffalo, and tipis," Deernose recalled. "They knew they were different from White kids, who could beat them at reading, spelling, and arithmetic." Things improved for them whenever time came to play basketball at recess or in after-school intramurals. This was something Crow kids knew they could do and be given a fair chance of success at. The sport enlivened their spirits and took their minds off classroom struggles. "Basketball was one thing about school that we all liked," said Deernose. "I think that is why a lot of Crow boys kept going until high school."[32]

Basketball also helped bridge the social divide separating Native youths in the public schools from children of other races. It was a way for them to find common ground and pursue common goals. They learned to work together as teammates and often became friends.[33] This was partly why Agnes Yellowtail Deernose was fond of the game as a schoolgirl. Although she was initially reluctant to join white girls in intramural basketball at the Lodge Grass elementary school, it turned out to be a positive experience. "At first it wasn't too good, but every year we got better acquainted," she recalled. "I got along pretty well with the White girls and even had some friends."[34]

Later generations of Native and non-Native athletes also bonded while playing on public school teams. Non-Native Steven E. Dyche, for one, recalls getting along well with his Crow teammates at Hardin High School during the mid-1950s. In spite of the town's generally poor race relations, the players worked well enough together to execute a complex five-man weave offense that required impeccable timing and coordination. Navajo and non-Native teammates similarly played well together at the off-reservation Magdalena High School, in New Mexico, during the 1960s. There, too, Native students had difficulty adjusting to life in an integrated setting. The situation was especially complicated, according to David Wallace Adams, because Navajo students found themselves at the bottom of a social hierarchy beneath both white and Hispanic schoolmates. Boys of all three races nevertheless befriended each other on the varsity basketball team. As one of the non-Native members later noted: "The one common denominator was that we loved to play."[35]

Public school basketball also influenced internal relations within tribal communities, helping bond and enliven them during hard times. As Native residents adopted public high school teams as their own during the 1930s, new community versus community rivalries formed that engaged entire populations. Various towns within a tribal land base, or from different reservations, regularly competed against each other, facilitating expressions of local pride and forging a shared social and cultural experience among diverse Native peoples.

Few things uplifted community spirits like state championships brought home by local high school teams. Unfortunately, these were few in number before World War II. Reservation public high schools rarely made it to championship games. They struggled because many top Native athletes still competed for non-public schools (boarding, government day, mission, etc.) during much of the century; and they were disadvantaged against big city opponents in some western states where high school associations had yet to employ class divisions for schools of varying size.

Before the Great Depression, the only public high school champions that likely included more than one or two Native players were Oklahoma teams from towns with sizeable Indian populations, like the Anadarko boys' champions of 1919 and Wewoka girls' of 1920 and 1921.[36] Two of the first (or maybe *the* two first) reservation public high schools to win state championships did so in the 1930s and early 1940s. Both represented mixed-race towns on the southern edge of the Fort Peck Reservation (Assiniboine and Sioux) in Montana. Of the two schools, Wolf Point High School was the first to send one of its boys' teams to the state title game. It did so in 1930 and again in 1936, losing both times. Thereafter, the school's program established a dynasty, winning six Class B boys' titles and one Class A boys' title from 1941 to 1968. Poplar meanwhile, located along the same highway, twenty miles to the east of Wolf Point, won back-to-back Class B boys' championships in 1934 and 1935. The second of these was an upset victory over their rival from Lodge Grass, which was reputed to be the best predominantly Indian team Montana had ever produced.[37]

The 1935 Poplar versus Lodge Grass state tournament matchup was likely the first time two reservation public school teams competed against each other for a state championship anywhere in the country. Both squads had interracial lineups dominated by Native players, which caused a controversy in Lodge Grass. Although the Crow players had used basketball to make friends with non-Native schoolmates in elementary school, they had also bonded tightly as tribesmen in the process. By the time they entered high school, they had developed such interpersonal synergy that their white teammates struggled to find their place on the team. The Crow players simply outclassed them in all aspects of play. Coach David Murray thus saw the value in deploying his Crow players as a coherent unit and so relegated his white players to the bench. For him, it was about finding a winning formula, but the decision so upset some white parents that they called for the firing of school superintendent Bess R. Stevens, who had hired Murray. Although Stevens was white and was backed by Crow agency Superintendent Robert Yellowtail, and most Crow families in the district, the school board sided with the objectors and fired her.[38]

Unshaken by this controversy, Lodge Grass's all-Crow starting lineup won game after game through the 1934–35 season. They deployed the Indian basketball style in exhilarating fashion, displaying such passing precision and ball handling dexterity that reporters likened them to the Harlem Globetrotters (similar to some Lakota teams in neighboring South Dakota). After seeing Lodge Grass in action, Montana State University's Coach Shubert Dyche (Steven E. Dyche's uncle) described their teamwork as otherworldly. "They never look where they are going to pass and they use a system of sotto-voce whoops, barely audible to the spectators to let each other know their whereabouts," he said. This dynamic baffled their opponents, who so often crumbled under the pressure that Lodge Grass achieved a 16–2 season record.[39]

Potent as Lodge Grass was, nobody expected the Poplar boys to be pushovers in the final. They were a veteran team with one title under their belts, were taller, and always shot straight. They were also well-coached by Carl Hansen, who always made sure they kept enough reserve in their tanks to mount a late game surge if they trailed. Lodge Grass was nevertheless favored because they had the stylistic flair, the audacity, and the tight teamwork; and they had Ed Old Crow. Later to be the leader of the Crow All-Americans CCC-ID team, he was at this point Lodge Grass's center—or "pivot man" as these position players were commonly known in that day, because their primary role was to stand atop the key and feed forwards on opposite wings. Old Crow, however, was just as deadly shooting the ball as he was dishing it off, and he sank his fair share. He was "about the sweetest center seen in the state tournament for many a season," one reporter said of him. "He has the height to control the tip when it is necessary and his one hand passes and shots make guarding almost impossible."[40]

A crowd of three thousand was on hand in Havre, Montana, for the highly anticipated state final between the two reservation teams. The action flowed as expected, but the result was a surprise. Poplar trailed most of the way under a steady assault from Old Crow, who "swished the ball through the nets from all angles of the court," and tallied eighteen points on the night. Lodge Grass led by eight at the start of the final quarter when Poplar, true to form, tapped their energy reserve. They surged back, taking a one-point lead with moments to go. Captain Louis Longee sank a final shot as the timer's pistol fired, capping the 37–34 upset victory for Poplar. The now two-time champs received a hero's welcome back home, including a dance thrown in their honor, organized by Native women belonging to the local Home Demonstration Club.[41] Even in defeat, the people of Lodge Grass also had reason to celebrate, as their boys had fought hard and injected style and class into Montana basketball in a manner never to be forgotten by those who witnessed them play.

Outside of Fort Peck, public high schools on western reservations continued to experience a drought through the 1940s and 1950s—unable to match the championship success of some earlier boarding school teams. A noteworthy exception was the 1956 Fort Yates Warriors team from the Standing Rock Sioux Reservation, which captured North Dakota's Class B championship in a thrilling come-from-behind victory over St. Thomas High School. They pulled off the narrow 54–52 win thanks to two late jumpers by Arnold Kills Crow and some clutch free throws by Larry Hayes.[42]

The only surprising thing about Fort Yates's victory was how close it had been. They had been a tough team all season, scoring one hundred points or more five times on their way to a 28–2 season record. They too displayed the Indian basketball style on offense—fast-breaking, sharp passing, and untiring. Teams that tried to stymie them with zone defense were quickly frustrated. A humorous tidbit in the *Sioux County Pioneer-Arrow* told of one non-Indian North Dakotan asking another what defense Washburn High School used against Fort Yates in the tournament opener. The second man responded: "They used a zone defense but before they could set it up, it was full of Indians." Fort Yates was yet another Native team that was commonly likened to the Harlem Globetrotters, as they occasionally resorted to difficult passing and dribbling maneuvers to stall the game and hold a lead. On defense, they more closely resembled some present-day Native teams than they did the Flandreau or Haskell squads of old, because they pressed opponents relentlessly. "We used a kamikaze full-court press from the opening whistle," team member Leonard Villagecenter later recalled. "We forced a lot of turnovers and got to shoot a lot of layups." While the players did their magic, Coach Wallace Galluzzi was content to offer a steady stream of encouragement from the sidelines.[43]

The 1956 Fort Yates Warriors won the hearts of many non-Indian North

Dakotans on their way to that championship. While advancing through the tournament, they received expressions of support from some unexpected places, including a telegram from the Davis Chevrolet Co. car lot in Bismarck, reading "Galluzzi Warriors, Kute-Owotanna, Woakita Waste," which was a rendering of the phrase "Shoot Straight, Look Good" into Lakota. Most of the 6,700 spectators attending the final game in the University of North Dakota fieldhouse were behind them, judging from the cheering. And after their triumph, the *Bismarck Tribune* received a letter from a local reader saying: "I think the entire Slope Area is just as happy as the residents of Fort Yates that the Warriors brought home the State Class B Basket Ball title. Not only is it the first time Fort Yates won the title, it is the first time ANY team from this area can wear the championship crown. . . . It is one of the classiest ball teams I have ever seen."[44]

It was even more gratifying for the Fort Yates boys to return home, where they shared this victory with their tribespeople like warrior ancestors sharing triumphs in battle. A jubilant celebration awaited them. A parade of cars five miles long met them along the highway to guide them on their last leg home, where they were welcomed by a delegation of traditional dancers and singers performing in their honor and a whistle blowing ceaselessly from the heating plant to herald their triumph. This was followed by a feed at the grade school for the team and entire community. In between music selections from the high school band and passing the food, community leaders took turns praising the boys. It was an outpouring of pride and a thanksgiving. This scene would be replayed dozens of times on other reservations in following decades as state high school championships began flowing steadily to Indian country. By the 1990s and early 2000s, a number of dynastic programs would emerge, including the Shiprock High School Lady Chieftains (Navajo Nation—six titles to date) and the Wyoming Indian High School Chiefs (Wind River Reservation—eleven titles).[45]

Robeson County

There were other parts of Native America where public schools were even more crucial to basketball's rise as a community sport than out west. Nowhere was this more the case than in Robeson County, North Carolina, home to the Lumbee people. Their basketball story differs from that of many other Natives in some fundamental ways, but the love they developed for the game was no less profound.

Although North Carolina had officially acknowledged the Lumbee as an Indian tribe in 1885, they lacked the full federal recognition many tribes received, and thus neither had a reservation nor federal affirmation of their sovereign rights; and they were not compelled to send their children to government boarding schools. Because the state had instituted a system of trilateral segregation—providing separate facilities for white, Native, and African American residents—the Lumbee were subjected to countless indignities, but they also acquired their own public school system, which afforded them autonomy in academic and athletic affairs. Forbidden by the white-run county school board from competing in the same athletic associations with either the white or the African American schools, they instead operated their own. The Robeson County Indian High School Athletic Conference, or "Indian Conference," formed during the 1920s, oversaw all high school basketball competition. With help from local principals, it began sponsoring championship tournaments in the sport for boys in 1940 and girls in 1946.[46]

Despite the fact that the Lumbee people lived in a racially mixed county, with no legal boundaries demarcating tribal lands from those owned by non-Natives, prescribed segregation ensured that their basketball culture developed in greater seclusion than among Native peoples residing on reservations. Apart from a few non-conference contests against white high schools outside their county, their regular high school season and postseason games were all-Native affairs. They exercised control over the game at all levels, with Native residents of the county constituting all the players, coaches, officials, and conference administrators.[47]

It is unknown how basketball began among the Lumbee people. All that is for certain is that, as opposed to Natives elsewhere, they did not learn to play the sport in the boarding schools, and no outsiders introduced it to them with the intent of assimilating and integrating them. Perhaps people acquired an interest by reading about the college game in newspapers, seeing barnstormers pass through, or conversing with their white and African American neighbors. All that is certain is that basketball became one of the two favored Lumbee community sports by the 1930s—the other being baseball, which equaled or surpassed basketball in overall popularity. No traditional field sports the ancients may have played lasted the two centuries of migrations and cultural amalgamation that led to the founding of Lumbee settlements in Robeson and adjacent counties, and football would take hold only after the public schools were integrated and consolidated in 1968. Before that, the Indian high schools were too small to support it.[48]

Basketball, in contrast to football, was a humble game for hardworking Lumbee farmers who took advantage of every opportunity to play it when not busy with their tobacco, cotton, and corn fields. This was a sport for all the people in Robeson County, male and female. Free from the limits placed on female competition by state athletic associations, Lumbee educators condoned basketball as a girls' interscholastic game throughout the post–World War II era. Although schools restricted girls to women's divided-court rules, they maintained varsity programs for them and allowed them to play as many games per year as the boys.[49]

Thus no one discouraged Lumbee girls like Rose Oxendine Hill from becoming as devoted to basketball as most boys were. For Hill, the privilege of playing this game was the reward for a hard days' work. Like most youths in her time, during the late 1940s and early 1950s, she kept busy at chores when not in school. She fed the livestock and brought in the wood for the stoves to heat the home—a daily necessity at a time when few Lumbee homes had electricity or indoor plumbing. When her chores were complete, she went to the backyard, where her father had erected a homemade pole and backboard and affixed to it a store-bought hoop. "I practiced basketball every chance I got all by myself," Hill recalls. On evenings, when it was not too cold, she played into the night using a lantern her father hung up by the pole for her.[50]

Like Rose Hill, most Lumbee youths knew basketball as a mainly outdoor activity, whether played informally or interscholastically. Hill's contemporary, Tim Brayboy, also practiced outside, shooting at a hoop on the side of a barn. Most interscholastic games were also played outside on school playgrounds. The only indoor facility available to the public school teams until the 1950s, when the high schools began building their own gymnasiums, was at the college in Pembroke. As part of a New Deal effort to expand athletic facilities for towns across America, the Public Works Administration (PWA) helped the state construct the facility in 1940. There was a college regulation size 94-by-50-foot court and seating for one thousand spectators. While Lumbee high school teams still practiced and played most regular-season games outdoors, the college gym permitted them to play a few regular season games each year and began hosting the championship high school tournaments for both the boys and the girls.[51]

Access to this fine facility stoked Lumbee passions for basketball, inspiring new excitement in players like Ray Oxendine, who had rarely competed on any surface other than dirt or asphalt. "I remember going into that gym . . . and I sort of thought I was at Madison Square Garden," says Oxendine. Pembroke's gymnasium and the high school tournament it hosted became the focal point of a tribal basketball culture, as Lumbee people rooted for competing local high schools gathered under one roof. All other activities in Robeson County came to a halt as people flocked to the facility at tournament time. The place was packed every time, and the memory of hundreds of people "hanging from the rafters" to catch the action later inspired Brayboy and Bruce Barton to title their history of Native basketball in Robeson County, *Playing Before an Overflow Crowd*.[52]

Holding their own high school basketball championships in their own arena both accented town identities within Robeson County and was a shared experience that helped bond Lumbees as a tribe. The rivalries that developed between the various high schools from different towns were intense—especially when teams from Pembroke played teams from Prospect. Things were "fiercely competitive" between those schools during the 1950s, says Brayboy, but players followed the rules and left any hard feelings on the floor. As much as they craved victory, they respected each other and the game they played.[53]

Ronnie Chavis, who competed for Prospect during the 1960s, recalls the rivalry with Pembroke in his day being about the pride players took in defeating worthy opponents. This shared experience bonded Lumbee players not only with their teammates but also with competitors from other Lumbee towns. "A lot of those guys, as we grew older and got out of high school, we became friends," Chavis recalls. As it was for tribes on western reservations, basketball was thus a way for Lumbee people to express the passionate local-level identities that distinguish peoples within the tribe, but at the same time, it was an attractive force, pulling tribespeople together as a nation. It was a collective activity that mattered deeply to nearly all Lumbee people, regardless of their town, church, or political persuasion.[54]

Come tournament time, though, it was every team for itself. Winning mattered and players did everything they could to prove their team was the best. Pembroke's boys and girls fared better at this than did Prospect most years, the Pembroke boys winning eleven championships to Prospect's five from 1940 to 1967, and the Pembroke girls winning seven to Prospect's one. Ray Oxendine and Rose Hill both played key roles in securing these Pembroke honors while playing varsity in the 1950s. On the six occasions when the Pembroke and Prospect boys met each other in the championship final, Prospect nevertheless performed equally as well as their rivals, winning half the contests.[55]

Until the late twentieth century, the Lumbee game of basketball was very different from the up-tempo game played on western reservations. As Ronnie Chavis recalls, most teams in the Indian Conference played a "slow-down game" that was "under control," relying on designed plays and zone defense. Perhaps being separate from the stylistic evolutions of the game occurring in the boarding schools led Lumbee basketball down a distinct path, but Chavis offers a more straight-forward explanation for Lumbee teams preferring the deliberate approach. "Well to be honest with you," he says, "we were not blessed with an awful lot of speed." Times have changed though, as later generations of Robeson County youths have adopted the faster NBA and college style they have seen on television. In contrasting the "up and down" twenty-first-century Lumbee game with that of his day, Chavis says "these kids" would "run us off the court today."[56]

Another reason for the style change is that Robeson County athletics are no longer racially segregated, and so Natives players have modified their styles along with everyone else. In 1968, the federal government compelled North Carolina public schools to integrate, and so the Indian Conference dissolved. As Robeson County's schools integrated, Native athletes competed alongside and against non-Natives for the same championships under the governance of the North Carolina High School Athletic Association (NCHSAA). Not all Lumbee people supported the change. Playing their game, by their own rules, was something they had grown accustomed to, and they balked at the prospect of white officials in the state association directing their affairs. Ronnie Chavis remembers hearing people say: "We don't like the idea of the white man telling Indians how to play." Chavis and many others, however, welcomed the change, not just as a step toward justice and equality but also as a chance for Lumbee athletes to test their skills against non-Natives. Ray Oxendine remembers how he and other players, before integration, had longed for interracial competition: "Back then we thought we were better than some of the other [non-Native] schools that got publicity and we were just dying to get a chance to play them."[57]

After their playing days ended, Oxendine, Brayboy, and Chavis worked to ensure that younger Native generations had the chances they deserved to excel in the classroom and on the court. All three did so by serving as coaches or athletic officials. Oxendine also did so as a high school principal, Brayboy as a teacher and employee of the state Department of Public Instruction, and Chavis as the county schools' athletic director. They guided communities through the process of integration and were pleased to see Native youngsters work in harmony with non-Native teammates. "They don't look at race like adults do," Chavis says. "Our kids get along fine. . . . It makes me proud to know my kids won't have to worry about the stuff I had to as a young man."[58]

By the late 1990s, after thirty years of integrated play, memories of the days when the Native residents of Robeson County competed primarily among themselves had faded. Understanding that more ex-Indian Conference players were passing away each year, Tim Brayboy and Bruce Barton set out to record their stories for posterity. With support from the NCHSAA's executive director, Charlie Adams, they also spearheaded an effort to get the association to officially recognize the Indian Conference's past contributions. These efforts led to the NCHSAA erecting a commemorative plaque in 1999 honoring the legacy of the Indian Conference and its former players. At the unveiling, Brayboy acknowledged the "bitter feelings" many people still had about the segregated past while lauding North Carolinians for progress made. And he praised the Native boys and girls who had once given their all to do their families, communities, and tribespeople proud, playing before packed houses in Pembroke: "Being here today for this historic event brings back fond memories of a simple time and place—a time when ordinary people had the pleasure to show their skills in sports activities before a cheering crowd. We were ordinary people doing extra ordinary things."[59]

City Hoops

It was not just on the reservations or in rural nonreservation areas that Native communities embraced basketball. They also did in large numbers in America's cities during the second half of the twentieth century. As Indian country's demographics shifted toward urban areas, Native peoples turned to basketball to further enrich their lives while adjusting to city life.

Although Natives had been moving back and forth between rural homelands and American cities throughout the early twentieth century, Indian country remained predominantly rural prior to World War II. Less than 10 percent of the Native population resided in cities as late as 1940. The war then initiated a mass migration of thousands of Native people to cities for military service and to work in defense industries. Tens of thousands followed during the 1950s and 1960s, drawn by the promise of a better postwar standard of living. Through these migrations, the proportion of Natives living in urban areas swelled to 28 percent in 1960 and 45 percent in 1970. This trend continued so that, by the twenty-first century, more than two-thirds of all American Indians were urbanites.[60]

Some Natives adapted quickly to city life, while others struggled to find their way. Many had difficulty securing adequate housing and steady employment—especially after World War II—and were discouraged by the impersonal, materialistic, and often racist urban environment. Some abandoned the cities during the 1950s and 1960s and returned to rural areas, but hundreds of thousands remained. To make the cities more livable, they sought out other Natives by settling in the same areas, praying together in churches, dancing together at urban powwows, and standing shoulder to shoulder as political reformers and activists. They also played sports together—especially basketball.[61]

Indian basketball teams were not new to the cities in the postwar era.

Natives had, of course, been playing for decades at urban off-reservation Indian schools. Seeking to find jobs or further their educations, some student athletes remained in the host cities after leaving school or moved to other urban areas. Once there, they found other Indians to play amateur ball with and so regained the intertribal camaraderie they had enjoyed in school. Initially, though, there were not large enough Native populations to make all-Indian teams easy to organize in every city. One who tried to assemble one in Chicago before World War II was Albert Cobe, from Lac du Flambeau, who had played varsity basketball at Haskell during the 1920s. Upon returning home, he became disillusioned with the Indian Office for failing to uplift Native peoples as promised, moved to Chicago in 1930, and there became a community advocate who encouraged urban Indians to pull themselves up by their own bootstraps. Knowing from his Haskell days how sports could bond and inspire Native peoples, one of Cobe's first orders of business in the city was to assemble an all-Indian basketball team to play city league competition. He did this, said Cobe, to feed peoples' hunger for the "companionship of other Indians." This proved difficult with the small prewar population, however, and so, to fill out his "all-Indian" roster, he recruited a few Cuban American and Italian American teammates and opted, he said, to "make Indians out of them."[62]

It became easier to organize all-Indian teams from the swelling urban populations immediately following the war, and so a burgeoning Native basketball scene began to develop in cities across the Midwest and West. The Bureau of Indian Affairs (BIA—formerly Indian Office) capitalized on this activity in the early 1950s, by printing photographs of urban Natives enjoying basketball and other recreational activities.[63] This was done to promote the federal government's voluntary urban relocation program, which in the conservative postwar environment aimed to advance Native social and political integration by immersing them in urban settings. The ample opportunities to play and watch sports in big cities indeed appealed to many American Indians and was part of the urban allure.[64] Those who eagerly took up city sports in the 1950s and 1960s, however, did so more to maintain associations with other Natives and express indigenous identities than blend into a broad populace. One way they did this was by forming all-Indian independent basketball teams within city leagues.

The accessibility of city league basketball to urban Natives helps explain the sport's rise to new heights of popularity in American Indian communities after the war. Naismith had of course designed basketball in an urban environment, and its ability to be played inexpensively, indoors and out, in tight spaces made it the ideal city league activity. All ethnicities played hoops in the cities regardless of their financial means. As Indian country became more urban, basketball thus remained accessible to Native athletes. It was one of a handful of sports that Native adults of all income levels could stay active in after transitioning to a city, the others being softball (and to a lesser degree baseball) and the quintessentially urban game of bowling.[65] By contrast, football, the king of the Indian school spectator sports, was more difficult to organize in urban environments. Whether on a rural reservation, in the farm country of Robeson County, or in the midst of a metropolis, basketball was the more adaptable sport, easily accessible to any American Indian community.

The cities and outlying areas witnessed a stunning proliferation of Native youth and adult city league basketball teams during the 1950s and 1960s. These were both male and female squads, some of which were multitribal, reflecting the diverse character of urban Indian populations, while others teamed fellow tribespeople who stayed connected amid the city sprawl. Every conceivable Native-centric work environment, organization, and club arising in the cities spawned basketball teams. A common source for postwar urban Indian basketball teams (as well as softball and bowling teams) were military ordnance depots where Native men and women worked during the war years and stayed on thereafter. Such teams were organized among Native employees at the Navajo Ordnance Depot, located near Flagstaff, Arizona, and the Tooele Ordnance Depot next to the town of Tooele, Utah, near Salt Lake City.[66] Other team sponsors included urban churches serving Native congregations and urban Indian centers, which were facilities, often administered by Natives, that provided social services and meeting places for Indians from all tribes. The American Indian Center in Chicago, for example, began sponsoring all-Native basketball teams for male and female athletes within a year of opening in 1953. By the mid-1960s, other Indian center teams were being organized throughout the country, including in California's Bay area, Los Angeles, Minneapolis, Sioux City, Iowa, and Gallup, New Mexico.[67]

There were so many all-Indian teams playing integrated league basketball in cities by the 1960s that Native community members began forming amateur leagues of their own. These leagues allowed Native amateur athletes from diverse tribes to enjoy each other's camaraderie and mutual support as people dealing with similar life circumstances. In 1961, the Inter-Tribal Indian Basketball League was established in Los Angeles. Later renamed the American Indian Athletic Association (AIAA), it expanded its offerings to other sports as well, including softball and bowling. In 1963, All-Indian city leagues were also established for Bay Area residents in both basketball and softball.[68]

Meanwhile, in Arizona, a vibrant multitribal basketball scene gave rise

Figure 33. The Phoenix Chiefs (players unidentified), sponsored by Fred Wilson's Indian Trading Post, with their most recent championship trophy in 1957. NAU.ARC.1957-8-54. Courtesy of Northern Arizona University, Cline Library.

to the most successful all-Indian city league team anywhere in the country, the Phoenix Chiefs. Operating continuously from 1949 through the early 1970s, they were organized and managed by Julian Dinehdeal, a Navajo graduate of Phoenix Indian School who returned to the city after his intervening military service to work as a newspaper printer. The Chiefs remained at or near the top of the Phoenix Metropolitan League standings every year by attracting the best Native athletes the city had to offer. At the start of each season, they issued open calls through the *Arizona Republic*, inviting men to bring their own "shoes and trunks" to a city park to try out for the team and attend an organizational meeting. Enthusiastic turnouts ensured the Chiefs always had a diverse group of urban talents. Playing together were former and current students from Phoenix Indian School, public high school students, students attending Arizona State University, and other urban residents. These young men came from throughout the West, representing dozens of tribes. Over the years, Chiefs stars included Pete Homer Jr. (Mohave), Hiram Olney (Yakima), and Adam Singer (Crow). For many players, time spent with the Chiefs was an enjoyable interlude on the way to a distinguished life station, as it was for future Navajo Nation president Peterson Zah (joined in 1959) and American Indian

Movement national coordinator (and Hollywood actor) Russell Means (Lakota; joined in 1967).[69]

The Phoenix Chiefs were more than just a basketball team. They were also dedicated public servants who played fundraising games to provide athletic opportunities to urban Natives in other sports. Among other initiatives, they sponsored Phoenix Indian School's annual football banquet during the 1950s and municipal Little League baseball teams for Native youths during the 1960s and early 1970s.[70]

All-Indian Tournaments

The Phoenix Chiefs also served as the leading attraction at a number of all-Indian tournaments that sprang up across the West during the 1950s and 1960s. In the past, Native teams had played each other from time to time in Indian school tournaments, invitational integrated tournaments and, more recently, state high school tournaments, but these newer affairs fundamentally differed from the others in that they were organized exclusively for Natives by Natives. They were grand events designed to cut the distance between Indian people, town from town, tribe from tribe, and city from countryside. These events were about Natives sharing a common love for the game and fostering a spirit of community service on both the tribal and pan-tribal levels.

Three types of Native-run tournaments, exclusively for Native teams, proliferated after 1950. There were closed reservation tournaments where all competition was local, often within a single tribe, reservation-based affairs that invited local teams and outside visitors from all tribes, and urban-based ones that invited diverse Native teams from within and without a host city. Indian tournaments bred Indian tournaments. Any event that visitors judged to be successful spun off imitators, so that by the early 1960s, dozens of these tournaments, of varying type and size, were operating.

The Southwest All-Indian Basketball Tournament in Phoenix began in 1952 as a pioneering event. Small Native-run tournaments had existed on some Arizona reservations in prior years, like one organized by the Colorado River Indian Tribes in the west of the state, but Phoenix was the first high-profile intertribal affair to draw teams from great distances. Organized by the Phoenix Indian Center's director Leon Grant (Omaha) and others, it took place in the North Phoenix High School gymnasium. The first year, sixteen Native men's teams from Phoenix and throughout Arizona took part, including one entrant from Ganado, 270 miles north of the city on the Navajo Nation. The Parker "Vets" from Colorado River won the first title by defeating a team from the White Mountain Apache Reservation 69–50. In subsequent years, the host Phoenix Chiefs dominated, winning seven of ten championships through 1961.[71]

In addition to serving as a successful organizational model for others interested in starting their own tournaments, the Southwest tournament set an example by privileging community values over financial profit. This emphasis on basketball as a form of community service would characterize many Native-run tournaments to follow. Despite high operational costs, the tournament used a portion of its proceeds to fund scholarships for Native men and women attending college in the local metropolitan area. Multiple scholarships were awarded each year for modest sums of one hundred dollars or more. Believers in the importance of providing athletic opportunities for all Native Americans, the tournament organizers also began welcoming women's competitors in 1954—this at a time when most tournaments in the United States, at any level, still regarded female competition as inappropriate and unprofitable. The 1954 event included four women's squads, which expanded to eight in 1955, with teams from the San Carlos, Colorado River, and Gila River reservations occupying the bracket alongside host city competitors. The Phoenix BIA Arrows, presumably composed of Native women working for the Bureau, won back-to-back titles the first two years of women's competition.[72]

In 1954, an even more ambitious tournament began at Chiloquin, Oregon, on the Klamath Reservation. It ran amid the turmoil of termination, a federal policy born of 1950s conservatism. Termination policy promoted Native socioeconomic integration by extinguishing tribes' federally recognized status, which circumscribed their sovereign powers and ended access to specific federally provided social services. The Klamath Reservation tribes (Klamath, Modoc, and Yahooskin Paiute) were among the first targeted by the policy (most tribes, elsewhere, eventually escaped this fate). In August 1954, Congress passed legislation officially terminating them. Just a few months before this fateful act, in the winter and spring of 1954, community members determined to persevere as a distinct identifiable group conceived and carried out their first multitribal tournament. A committee of local team managers, with funding from the tribal council, organized the tournament as an invitational affair to be held in Chiloquin every March. They were more successful in this endeavor than they could have hoped. On the brink of their political dissolution, they made their reservation a focal point for hoops in Indian country.[73]

The Klamath Invitational All-Indian tournament, as it was called, capitalized on a preexisting local tournament for men's independent teams. When the tournament expanded to include men's teams from other tribes, the local event was rebranded as a preliminary playoff to determine which teams would represent the Klamath tribes. Four outside teams were invited the first year, which doubled to eight in 1955, coming from six western states. The Northern Cheyenne All-Stars from Busby, Montana, traveled the farthest in 1955, trekking more than a thousand miles, one-way. The journey was worth it, as Busby captured the title by beating the defending champions and favored hosts, the Chiloquin Townies, 78–67.[74]

Thereafter, the Klamath tournament increased in profile and geographic reach so that, by the end of its first decade, it had been renamed the National Invitational All-Indian Basketball Tournament. Attracting the best Native independent men's teams in the West, its winners were widely recognized as national Indian champions. Never was the event's supreme status more apparent than in 1959, when the two most nationally renowned all-Indian teams met in the final game: the Crow Saints, from Lodge Grass, and the Phoenix Chiefs. The Saints had been to Chiloquin before, having won the championship in 1958, and they were determined to do it again. They were playing for all Crows and they knew it. Back in 1957, reservation residents were so emotionally invested in them and their performance in Chiloquin that the tribal council provided $250 in tribal funds to cover their travel costs. The Phoenix Chiefs were also driven to succeed. Having just won the Southwest tournament title, they sought a national title to go with it. All of Indian country converged, figuratively speaking, when these teams clashed—reservation Natives versus urban Natives, a tribal team against a multitribal one, the Northern Plains against the desert Southwest. As expected, the game was close most of the way. At the end of the third quarter, the Chiefs held a slim lead, but then game high-scorer Larry Pretty Weasel and his Saints teammates went on a run to score the 71–63 win and carry home the prize to their Crow people.[75]

Like the Southwest tournament, the Klamath event was also about sports as community enrichment. It was an opportunity for the host tribes to demonstrate hospitality to outsiders and generous care for their own community members while proving they could operate a large-scale self-sustaining event. This dual focus on community service and sound business management prompted the original planning committee to turn the tournament's operation over to their tribespeople in the Junior Chamber of Commerce (Jaycees) in the fall of 1955.[76]

The Klamath tournament organizers did all they could to make their far-flung tribal visitors feel welcomed and cared for. This was a tall order the first year, when the tournament had yet to be established as a viable event and operated on a meager budget. To get by, the Klamath community opened the general council hall as temporary living quarters for the visitors. They also fed them venison donated by local hunters. In subsequent years, the Jaycees coordinated with local church groups to provide free meals for all the teams and low-cost meals for all spectators. The various churches also sponsored "get acquainted" social dances to encourage a spirit of intertribal community. At the tournament's peak, in 1961, the Jaycees had sufficient cash flow to offer all participating players five-dollar-per-day stipends to help offset their expenses. The tournament champions were also awarded handsome, green felt sport jackets with gold insignia to herald their triumph. Other all-Indian tournaments were soon offering similar jackets to winners, which became highly sought after prizes, worn as markers of earned respect and status in Indian country.[77]

While focusing their efforts on being gracious hosts to outsiders, the Klamath Jaycees also gave back to their community. Portions of tournament proceeds were dedicated to local athletics-themed causes, such as sponsoring reservation Little League baseball teams in 1958, donating $500 toward a Chiloquin community swimming pool in 1959, and adding lights to the local high school athletic fields in 1963.[78]

Reminiscent of the Indian school and barnstorming days, the Klamath event also featured powwow-style dancing between halves, often performed by players from local and visiting teams. These were celebrations of indigenous cultural expression more so than performances meant to satisfy non-Native spectators. By 1960, the dancing had evolved into a competition, with cash prizes for the top three performers ranging from twenty-five to seventy-five dollars. The organizers also sponsored a Tournament Queen competition, open to Native women from the area who were twenty-one and under. The winner, and her court, represented the Klamath tribes during the games. In 1959, the crown went to Viola James, daughter of legendary Modoc player, Clyde LeClair James.[79]

The Klamath tournament declined in stature during the early 1960s, likely due to the socioeconomic turmoil that termination caused, as well as increased competition from other all-Indian tournaments, but event organizers kept things going. In 1986, tribal member Clayton Shultz, while speaking in favor of tribal restoration before a congressional committee, touted the tournament, as well as other community-organized events and cultural practices, as evidence that the Klamath people were "in many ways the People we have always been, the People our Creator meant us to be." The Klamath tribes won their fight for federal recognition the same year, and thereafter their tournament regained much of its former luster. The year 2019 marked its sixty-sixth annual running.[80]

Inspired by the successful Phoenix and Klamath events, all-Indian tournaments soon abounded in other communities. They were operated by

Figure 34. Arizona State College's (NAU) All-Indian Tournament organizers Wesley Bonito, Buster Madriaga, and John Salter arrange the tournament brackets in the winter of 1956. NAU.ARC.1956/57-8-60. Courtesy of Northern Arizona University, Cline Library.

urban Indian centers, reservation-based service organizations (like the Jaycees), and tribal recreation departments and were invariably dedicated to serving tribal and multitribal communities beyond providing entertainments. In all cases, playing basketball for its own sake was prized, but people also understood greater things could be accomplished by bringing diverse Native cultures together in common celebration, providing local youths with positive avenues to channel their energy, and raising money for good causes.

During the mid- to late 1950s, major multitribal tournaments began on the Uintah and Ouray Ute Reservation, in Utah, on the Yakima Reservation in Washington State, in the town of Okmulgee in Oklahoma, and on the San Carlos Apache Reservation in Arizona. Arizona also held another tournament, hosted in 1957 by Native students attending Arizona State College (future Northern Arizona University) in Flagstaff. Open by invitation to independent teams throughout the state, the tournament donated all its proceeds to scholarship funds for Native collegians.[81]

Arizona's Indian basketball calendar became fuller still in 1959 when the Navajo Nation hosted its Holiday Tournament, which was later renamed the Navajo Invitational Tournament (NIT). Staged in Window Rock's three-thousand-seat Civic Center, it involved twenty-three teams from three states its first year, including the local favorite, and ultimate champion, Window Rock Lodgers. The tournament committee added a women's division in the early 1960s to stimulate the proliferation of female teams on the reservation, which were at that time few in number. This disparity in male versus female Navajo basketball was largely the consequence of the public schools deemphasizing girls' basketball for many years rather than a lack of female interest. Demonstrating their enthusiasm, Navajo women's teams competed fiercely in the NIT, especially the Shiprock, New Mexico, Bankers, who were top competitors, year after year. Their team name recognized their hometown sponsor, the First National Bank, but much to their chagrin, male reporters insisted on calling them the "Bankerettes." In the mid-1960s, they traded in that name for a new one, the Shiprock Cardinals, and continued playing and winning Southwestern tournaments through the mid-1980s.[82]

The 1960s witnessed the proliferation of dozens more all-Indian tournaments for both Native men's and women's teams. It seemed by mid-decade that every Indian reservation in the country was running at least one, if not more, as were many universities and urban Native communities across the country from San Francisco to Chicago. The Fort Hall Shoshone-Bannock's Recreation Department in Idaho began operating one of the largest, and ultimately longest-running, of these events in 1965. It started small and grew quickly, tapping into Indian country's broad obsession with basketball. What began with four local and three outsider teams competing in Fort Hall's Timbee Hall gymnasium the first year swelled to sixteen teams the second year, with entries from seven western states and with players representing twenty-six different tribal nations. A women's category was added in 1970, securing the tournament's status as one of the most prestigious and inclusive Native basketball events in the country.[83]

The emergence of these Native-run, all-Indian tournaments marked a climatic stage in basketball's long rise to prominence in Indian country. Through these events, American Indians seized full stewardship of the sport and turned it toward promoting a spirit of tribal and pan-tribal community. Competing in them was not about adapting to Native-controlled environments or proving to whites what Indians could achieve. Native athletes had done that before and continued to do so in the high school ranks, and elsewhere, but not here. These tournaments were about Native people relating to each other—making new friends, getting reacquainted with old ones, and playing out rivalries on level ground, just as their ancestors had bonded and battled for centuries on lacrosse and shinny fields. At the same time, the tournaments brought things full circle to the early Indian school days, in that many of these events conceived of basketball as a sport for everyone, girls and women included. They offered young Native women, such as the members of the Shiprock Cardinals, chances to compete at high levels and do their people proud, as their ancestors had many decades before in places like Chemawa and Fort Shaw.

Conclusion: An Enduring Tradition

By the late 1960s, basketball was for many Native peoples an established community tradition. What had begun as a boarding school activity seventy-five years before had been widely adopted throughout Indian country. This happened because former students carried the activity forward wherever life took them. Those who returned home planted the basketball seed and, with help from other historical actors, cultivated it until it became the most widely played and followed team sport of all. In some parts of Indian country, like Robeson County, North Carolina, or the Alaskan interior, the story differs in basketball's modes of transmission and historical timing, but in these places, too, it became a community tradition. This sport was handed down through the generations and accepted by people of all genders, cultural practices, and political outlooks to enliven and enrich their lives.

This all had occurred by 1970 in most Native communities, which serves as the terminus of this story, as told in detail. Basketball, however, had yet to plateau in popularity at that point, and so an epilogue is in order. Unfolding developments ensured that the sport's star kept ascending in Indian country through the end of the century and beyond. Chief among these developments were revolutions in transportation and broadcast technology that made it progressively easier for people living in rural areas to follow the game at all levels of competition.[1] The 27,000-square-mile Navajo Nation is a prime example. Between 1945 and 1980, the farming and shepherding way of life that people had lived for centuries on this expansive landscape underwent significant change. People by the thousands took jobs in reservation towns, traveled hundreds of miles of newly constructed highways in cars and pickups, and purchased radios. By the mid-1970s, many Navajo families owned television sets as well. All this made it easier for them to watch and listen to basketball games in person and over the airwaves.[2]

Increased consumer access allowed Native people everywhere to become more enthusiastic and better informed hoops fans, but in the 1990s, Navajos also gained the added advantage of hearing NBA (specifically Phoenix Suns) and high school games broadcast in their own language.

These Navajo (Diné)-language services, provided by the KTNN Window Rock and KGAK Gallup radio stations made basketball fully accessible to fans who spoke Navajo as their first language. A pioneer in this effort, Harrison Dehiya became a regional celebrity for his spirited play-by-play coverage of both high school basketball and football games. The response he and other Navajo-language sportscasters received for their efforts was overwhelming, said Dehiya: "It's amazing when you go out in public and an elderly grandpa comes up to you, and says 'I really like your broadcasting. I can understand it. It's just like being at courtside or the 50-yard line, and I get so excited I start yelling at my own place.'"[3]

Female Native athletes also gained greater access to organized basketball in the last third of the twentieth century. This happened because all-Indian tournaments added women's competitive categories and because societal changes during the 1970s opened doors wider for female athletes of all races. Title IX of the Education Amendments Act of 1972 revolutionized women's basketball in the United States by mandating that educational institutions receiving federal funding provide female students with gender-equitable access to organized sports. Despite continued resistance from conservative politicians and much of the male-dominated sports world, the mandate prompted major changes in high school and college athletics—particularly in basketball. During the 1970s, the number of young women of all races playing college basketball doubled, and by 1981, the number of American girls playing high school basketball had reached 4.5 million—more than ten times the number in 1972.[4]

Female players throughout the United States also set their sights on lofty goals that were unattainable in decades past. During the 1970s, the number of state high school athletic associations hosting girls' championship tournaments increased from eight to forty-nine (New York was the final hold out). Meanwhile, the addition of a short-lived women's professional league in 1978 and the more stable Women's National Basketball Association (WNBA) in 1997 provided top players with opportunities to achieve celebrity status and make a living in the game.[5]

These broad developments profoundly impacted Indian country as the public spotlight fell on female athletes and teams with an intensity unseen since the early twentieth century. Communities began to rally around their girls' high school teams as they had in prior years around their boys' teams. Girls' teams rarely exceeded their male counterparts in public popularity, but some did, like the Shiprock Lady Chieftains, who unified and electrified their Navajo community during repeated runs at the New Mexico state championship beginning in the late 1980s.[6] Young Native women also achieved revered status as individual players in many places, none more so than SuAnne Big Crow (Lakota), who played for the Pine Ridge High School Lady Thorpes in the late 1980s and early 1990s. A supremely skilled player, she set a state scoring record and helped her team win the championship in 1989. She also earned her community's respect through her academic achievements and selfless social activism against substance abuse. After she died in a car accident in 1992, people memorialized Big Crow in many ways, including through a namesake "Spirit of Su Award," which the South Dakota High School Activities Association bestowed each year on an exemplary student athlete from the state.[7]

American Indian women in recent decades have made important strides in college basketball as well, even as their numbers have remained small relative to their non-Native counterparts. The number playing for Division I teams rose to twenty-three in 2004—not a big figure to be sure but significantly larger than in decades past and only five fewer than the number of Native men playing at that level. Among the many Native women who excelled in college after 1970, a few even made it to the WNBA, most recently Shoni Schimmel. But the first to get there was Arizona State University point guard, and pride of the Navajo Nation, Ryneldi Becenti, who was signed by the Phoenix Mercury in 1997. She left the league after her inaugural season but remains today a role model for budding Native players everywhere, girls and boys alike.[8]

Basketball's popularity in Indian country also intensified because of broad rules and tactical changes that made the sport progressively faster, freer flowing, and higher scoring, allowing the Indian basketball style of old to blossom into an even more exciting form, commonly known as Rez ball (or, as some prefer, Indian ball). The term "Rez ball" first appeared in newspapers in the mid-1980s as "Reservation ball," before acquiring its shortened label in the late 1990s. Native peoples have not just employed it to describe a playing style. Rez ball can also refer to an Indian team's grit and determination or describe the physical and social reservation environments in which the sport is played. Harrison Dehiya has defined it as the excitement of the game, the atmosphere of it all in Indian country, the families, and the crowd noise.[9] In most cases, though, the term refers to the *way* the game is played in the modern era: a fast-breaking, quick-firing style of play characterized as "run and gun" or "run and shoot" basketball.

Rez ball exists along a stylistic continuum extending across the twentieth century and should be understood as the product of an incremental evolution induced by changes to the overall sport. In the 1930s and 1940s, and again in the 1970s and 1980s, official rules and widespread tactical changes at all levels sped up the pace at which people of all ethnicities played basketball and increased scoring. First came the ten-second rule in

1932 and the elimination of the center jump after each scoring drive in 1937. Opposing teams thenceforth inbounded the ball from the end line and had ten seconds to advance across the center line, speeding the flow of play. By the late 1940s, players were also shooting one-handed jump shots rather than relying exclusively on two-handed set shots, which allowed for more artistic play, boosted scoring, and increased spectator appeal. The 1970s and 1980s brought another wave of change. First, the NCAA and many high schools discarded the old women's rules in 1971, freeing up female teams to play full-court. Then, in the 1980s, the NCAA and high schools instituted shot clocks for men and women alike, limiting offensive stalling. They also added three-point lines to reward teams that shot accurately from a distance, again making the game more exciting to watch and higher scoring.[10]

All of these changes freed Native teams to accent existing strengths, especially those of girls and women, who could for the first time in many decades deploy their quickness down the length of the court. And so the up-tempo, long-shooting style that Indian school teams exhibited during the first third of the twentieth century evolved into Rez ball. To be sure, not all predominantly Native basketball teams have played this style in recent decades, have played it without tactical variation, or have relied on it at all points in a game, but it has become sufficiently pronounced and widely enough employed to be identified as a distinctly Indian approach to the game.

In recent form, Rez ball is by degree a more exhilarating style than that played by early Indian school teams or the styles many non-Native teams utilize today. As former-high-school-and-college-standout-player-turned-coach Mike Chavez (Crow-Cheyenne) describes it, the style involves "a lot of fast pace up and down the court . . . not a lot of passing, just get up the court, maybe a pass or two and the shot's up." It is also identifiable on the defensive side of the ball, explains Chavez, by the frequent use of the full-court press, wherein defenders challenge the offense the whole length of the court. Other observers vary in assessing how aggressively Native teams defend while employing this style, but they widely concur about its offensive elements.[11]

Although some observers say Rez ball is more about showboating than fundamentals, insiders like Chavez and Ryan Wetzel understand it has strategy and structure undergirding its seemingly chaotic flow. Wetzel was raised with basketball and has spent his life playing, studying, and teaching the game. A gifted athlete himself, he is the son of Blackfeet legend Don Wetzel, Sr., one of the best basketball players and coaches Montana has ever produced. Don, Sr., was a star player for Cut Bank High School in the 1960s and later the University of Montana, in Missoula. Ryan followed in his footsteps during the 1990s by becoming a top player in high school, and he went on to play college ball, professionally in Europe, and on all-Native independent teams. Along the way, he encountered many styles of play, including Rez ball, or "Native ball" as he also refers to it.[12] Rez ball, he explains, is a well-defined approach that is highly effective when properly executed. It keeps a defense back on its heels, not giving them time to set up. There is a science behind it. A planned counter attack is put in motion as soon as the opposing team attempts a shot, says Wetzel. Whether they miss or make it, a defender under the basket is ready to send the ball to teammates streaking the other way in set patterns.

> Right when he gets that ball. Right when it comes through that net, he grabs it, steps his one foot out of bounds, and throws it to the key person that can handle that ball. They immediately turn and you have those three other teammates running the sidelines and the middle, filling the lanes . . . and they do it instantly. It's instant! They get that ball to the one that they think will score the quickest. It's a matter of two passes, and the ball's already in.[13]

For the scheme to work, the players must execute as a unit and always know where to position themselves on the floor. Native teams can do these things, says Wetzel, because they "read each other well," and because "by the time they are fifteen years old, they have been playing this way since they were five."[14] As Wetzel, Chavez, and others describe Rez ball, it is evident that this is the game Natives played in the boarding schools and have played continuously since, but it has been made quicker by the ability to fast-break immediately following a basket, higher scoring through the addition of the jump shot and three-pointer, and, since the early 1970s, fully playable by female teams.

As more American Indians watched and listened to basketball, and as they played it in an increasingly exhilarating manner, an established athletic tradition gained increased popularity. This is illustrated by the contemporary examples presented in this book's introduction, as well as the continued proliferation of all-Indian tournaments. Some far exceed their earlier predecessors in participatory size, like the Lakota Nation Invitational, established in 1977, and the Native American Basketball Invitational (NABI), established in 2003. The latter event has become especially big. Played in Phoenix, and sponsored in part by the Phoenix Suns and the Nike Corporation, the NABI has followed in the long-standing tradition of multitribal, socially conscious tournaments—a tradition begun in the same city fifty years earlier—but everything is supersized: larger crowds, more teams, increased publicity. More than just a celebration of American Indian basketball, the NABI has endeavored to help Native athletes get to college by offering them increased public exposure, access to instructional clinics, and scholarship support (amounting to $250,000 by 2018). The NCAA's decision to sanction the event in 2007 aided the effort by permitting university basketball recruiters to attend. The tournament has been a testament to basketball's lofty status in Indian country. What began with twenty-six teams in the NABI's inaugural year had grown to 128 by 2017, equally split between male and female squads, representing about 1,500 athletes and making it the largest all-Indian tournament ever staged.[15]

That basketball has become a peoples' sport in Indian country is clear from sheer participatory numbers. As athletes have passed on their love of basketball to successive generations, while continuing to play recreationally themselves, the overall percentage of people playing the sport at any given time, in any given community, has been increasing since 1970. Mike Sakelaris has witnessed this accumulative multigenerational dynamic on the Fort Hall Reservation. A graduate of Idaho State University, Sakelaris was hired by the Shoshone-Bannock to serve as their recreation director in 1968, and in that capacity he has helped administer a wide variety of basketball activities, including their continuously running multitribal tournament. Still at his post in 2016, Sakelaris could state unequivocally that basketball had become the "number one" sport on Fort Hall. "Basketball is king," he said. It seemed like nearly everyone was playing, young and old. The recreational leagues and tournaments operating on the reservation in 2016, Sakelaris estimated, encompassed at least ninety teams, representing male and female players of all ages. "That's hundreds and hundreds of people," he said. People's passion for the game was undying. As aging players kept at it, new recreational league age categories were added to accommodate them. Separate categories became necessary for women forty and over, as well as men sixty and over, and sixty-five and over. "The competition in that [men's] sixty and sixty-five—you just can't believe it. It's really neat to see," said Sakelaris. "Our oldest player, he was about seventy-four or seventy-five."[16]

To say that organized basketball has become intensely popular across Indian country is not to say that no one worries it can become too much of a good thing—or that in the minority opinion, too much of a not so good thing. As in any American community, there are people who worry that spending too much human energy and money on high school sports detracts from academics and other extracurricular activities.[17]

More than that, people worry about the harms that befall groups and individuals when they lean on this one thing too heavily or see it as a solution to all life's problems. Stories abound within American Indian communities, and have been featured prominently in documentary writing and film, of high school stars whose athletic dreams were dashed and who were left, for a time, with little direction in life. Whether they suffered career-ending injuries, succumbed to self-destructive behaviors under pressure, or were overlooked by college recruiters, they fell short and paid a price for their lofty ambitions. In some cases, they also fell short because they felt pressure from relatives and peers to remain at home or to not overachieve and thus shame their peers and break a communal dynamic. Players have sometimes been placed in paradoxical situations where they feel caught between fears of failing, on the one hand, and being too successful, on the other. No matter the cause, in societies where family and community bonds are water tight, and people identify strongly with local players and teams, the pangs of personal failure have reverberated through the larger group and been reflected back more intensely on the athletes. Sherman Alexie's short story "The Only Traffic Signal on the Reservation Doesn't Flash Red Anymore," speaks to the cycle of hope and disappointment whole communities have gone through predicting which high school stars will "make it all the way" and mourning those who have failed to live up to expectations.[18]

As sobering as accounts of personal failure and distress are, it is also true that, since the 1960s, college-bound Native players have had more successful role models to look up to than ever before. Scores of young women and men have proven that Natives can excel in college basketball if they work hard and strike the right balance in their academic and athletic endeavors. Youths benefit from the sage advice these veteran players offer. They learn going in how uncertain and difficult the road ahead will be: difficult to get a fair shake from college recruiters who might prejudge them based on their race; difficult to adjust to the aggressive coaching and regimented playing styles employed by university programs; and difficult to resist the socioeconomic and cultural pressures beckoning them home. Those who take to heart their role model's counsel know they can succeed if they persevere through the initial shock of entering university environments where academic and athletic pressures are more intense and kin support networks less immediate. As Mike Chavez advises, based on his experiences playing for the University of Montana, "it's just being able to bounce back from that . . . coming in humble and being ready to work your behind off."[19]

For male players, to *make it all the way* means progressing beyond college to sign an NBA contract, which is an ambition that, as of yet, few have realized. Only a handful of players with Native heritage have ever competed in the NBA; these include Gary Gray (Delaware, 1967–1968), John Starks (Muscogee, 1988–2002), and Cherokee Parks (Cherokee, 1995–2003).[20] More recently, Citizen Band Potawatomi tribal member Ron Baker made the league after completing his college career at Wichita State. He signed with the New York Knicks as a walk-on in 2016 and competed there until moving to the Washington Wizards in December 2018. The Wizards then waived him in January 2019. Meanwhile, six-foot-four Ho-Chunk tribal member Bronson Koenig narrowly missed out on his own NBA dreams. After a stellar college career playing for the University of Wisconsin, both the Milwaukee Bucks and Chicago Bulls organizations signed him. Both then waived Koenig prior to his making a regular season roster. As more Native men excel at the college level, the hope in Indian country is that more young men like Baker and Koenig will have their chances to succeed at basketball's highest level.[21]

The majority of people in Indian country, judging from widespread enthusiasm, believe that basketball's benefits outweigh its potential costs and could scarcely imagine life without it. A question remains, though, whether the sport's rise to athletic centrality has contributed to the decline of the indigenous sports and thus claimed a cultural cost that people might overlook. Logic dictates that the extensive time, money, and human energy expended on basketball over many decades must have diverted some resources and focus from the traditional field sports. Surely this is the case to some extent, but it must be kept in mind that it was not initially a matter of Indian people choosing basketball *over* the indigenous sports. Native youths first encountered basketball in places—namely, boarding schools—where indigenous sports were inaccessible. The alternative to playing introduced sports like basketball, baseball, and football was to play no sports at all. In this context, basketball's rise did less to detract from the traditional athletic ways than to perpetuate them in modified form. This is the perspective shared by other scholars who have documented the rise of other introduced sports in Indian country during the late nineteenth and twentieth centuries. The new sports, while not fully replicating the old, structurally paralleled them, performed similar functions, and to an extent facilitated the expression of accepted social values. They enabled people to carry on important aspects of traditions that were under assault. The old survived, to a degree, in the new.[22]

As the twentieth century drew to a close, it also became clear that the old and new sports could coexist. Where there was a will, there was a way. Many American Indians stepped forward to support the new sports while, at the same time, insisting that their communities retain what George W. Bent, Jr., once referred to as "the games that we used to love to play by the full moon."[23] They understood that for all the benefits the new sports provided, they could not duplicate every function the old ones had, such as reenacting timeless connections to the creation stories. And so these people worked hard to keep their indigenous sports alive while still cheering passionately for their basketballers, boxers, and bronc riders. They expanded the garden to make room for all good things.[24]

A case in point are the Six Nations of the Iroquois Confederacy (Haudenosaunee), who, despite past efforts by non-Natives to muscle them out of their own sport, have kept lacrosse near their hearts. The Iroquois were some of the first tribes to adopt basketball into their homelands (e.g., the Tuscarora Indians) and yet they remained avid lacrosse players. In 1983, players representing the Six Nations formed a collective lacrosse team, called the Iroquois Nationals, to represent the Confederacy in international competition. They played the world under the Confederacy flag, gaining widespread recognition for their talents. A source of great pride for their tribespeople, the Nationals have continued to inspire new generations of players to become active in the timeless sport of their people.[25]

In other places, too, some indigenous guessing games and team sports have endured alongside basketball, most notably, the hand game (also known as stick game), which scores of tribal communities play throughout the West. The Mississippi Choctaws's present-day comaintenance of basketball and baseball alongside stickball serves as another example. After 1950, traditional stickball resurged in popularity among the Choctaws just as basketball was gaining traction, proving that the rise of one need not spell the demise of the other.[26] Since the 1970s, basketball has also penetrated the Alaskan interior north of the Arctic Circle, gaining popularity among Native people who were, at the same time, renewing their emphasis on traditional contests. These contests, including the one-foot high kick, scissor broad jump, and knuckle hop, were activities that Alaska Natives had long relied upon to increase their strength, agility, and mental fortitude so to survive and thrive in a forbidding climate. During the 1960s and early 1970s, these old ways were organized into elaborate multitribal and international competitions such as the World Eskimo-Indian Olympics, first hosted in Fairbanks in 1961. These traditional competitions not only coexisted with basketball but also benefited from the construction of gymnasiums that were built to suit basketball, which served as ideal indoor practice and competition spaces for the old games. And so, while the rise of basketball might distract from some indigenous competitions, the facilities it produced could also physically aid their maintenance. The same is true anywhere in Indian country where traditional sports, games, and powwow dances take place inside hoops-centric arenas.[27]

For most Native basketball lovers, any distinction made between it and the ancient indigenous sports is hardly the point. Many view it as essentially indigenous to begin with, either believing that Naismith adapted it from an ancient Native sport (e.g., the Mesoamerican ballgame) or was heavily inspired by one (e.g., lacrosse, as has been argued here). Others may perceive basketball as an introduced activity but nevertheless regard it as largely indigenous in character because it structurally parallels the old sports and serves common functions. Most Native basketball fans and players, though, do not dwell on such things. They just know basketball matters. They know it is fun to play and entertaining to watch, and it is more than that.

Native hoops lovers know it is about bringing people together as a community, as the traditional sports always have. In the boarding school days, playing basketball was about forming the surrogate family of team and the solidarity of schoolmates, which many students sorely needed to endure the experience. In later years, it was more about bonding with one's kin, townsfolk, tribespeople, and a broader pan-tribal community. No theme emerges so clearly from conversing with American Indian players, coaches, and fans than that of togetherness. In addition to bonding with teammates and coaches, basketball is about people of all ages socializing in the stands and corridors. As Iva Croff has said of her experiences on the Blackfeet Reservation, basketball's popularity rests in large part on the fact that, on cold winter nights, "this is where we come together." It is reason enough for people to get out of their homes and brave the dark and snow, to get to a place where they can visit old friends, trade stories, and enjoy being part of it all. Croff has felt the pure joy of saying on such nights: "I made it out of my house! I'm going to the basketball game!"[28]

Teacher, professor, and former coach George Price (Assonet Wampanoag) has also experienced the wondrous ways this game brings people together. After the Price family lost their twenty-four-year-old son, Lem, in a 2002 automobile accident, friends rallied to their side on Montana's Flathead Reservation, where the family had lived since the mid-1980s. Among other forms of support, these friends helped the Price's organize a memorial basketball tournament to honor Lem, who had been a talented basketball player and photojournalist, as well as a devoted father. Memorial tournaments, by that time, were common throughout Indian country as means for well-wishers to honor and celebrate extraordinary lives like Lem's. This particular event also drew together independent teams from multiple tribes to raise money for a photojournalism scholarship in Lem's name. The togetherness of that tournament was healing and, for George Price, unforgettable. It was, he says, "one of those [experiences] where

Figure 35. The community gathers at Wakpala, on the Standing Rock Reservation, to see adult league teams compete in 1941. Courtesy of NARA, Kansas City, Missouri, identifier 57275402.

you learn something much better than just hearing it through words; when you actually see community in action and see generosity and all those community values acted out around you."[29]

People also know that basketball meets individual needs, especially for young people. It has provided generations of Native youths with a positive outlet for their energies and has inspired them to work hard at something and toughened them physically and mentally in the process. Although Native youths in recent decades have come of age in diverse physical and financial environments, it is true that, in many cases, basketball has been one of the few positive outlets for them to expend their energy. As Jesse DesRosier has heard people say in Blackfeet country: "There's only three things to do on a reservation. You can ride horses, get into trouble, or you can play basketball." Yes this saying is an exaggeration, but it underscores how accessible basketball has been to generations of Native youths, and how important a part of growing up it has been for many of them.[30]

Basketball has offered young players valuable experiences and life lessons they have carried into their adult lives. It has enabled them to explore the world around them, largely on their own terms. This was true for the Indian school players of old and for the barnstormers who came after, and it still holds for contemporary Native athletes, like Mike Chavez. "For me, it's huge," Chavez says of the game's influence on him. "Because of basketball I was able to go places and see things and experience things I wouldn't have been able to experience, because I don't come from a lot of money."[31] Like the old sports, basketball has also imparted a self-confidence that has allowed young athletes to persevere in life and better serve their communities as adults. That is what Tim Brayboy most took from his playing years. The confidence that "you could do it" and achieve something seemingly unachievable helped make him the man he is as an educator, author, and public servant. So too for Kevin Kickingwoman. "For me, basketball gave me hope," he says. "It made me want to be better. . . . It made me competitive. It made you realize, when you love the game, it will love you back. I always tell my kids this. Love the game and it will love you back."[32]

Native lovers of the game also know it is part of their spiritual lives—not in every way that lacrosse and other sports bequeathed them by immortal ancestors are but a part nonetheless. Occasionally one hears stories of spiritual ways, of *medicine*, being used to influence the flow of a game or individual performances, but just how widespread such things are is uncertain. For many Native athletes, this is not part of their reality, and for others it is not something to be openly discussed.[33] The spiritual connection is more evident in all the blessings people give to protect players and teams in their travels along winter roads and from physical injuries on the court. It is in the sweats teams take prior to a tournament, the smudging players do before a game, or a sprinkle of sage put in the insole of a sneaker. It is in all the prayers Native people offer on behalf of their athletes, in all the diverse ways Native people pray.[34]

In the end, lovers of this game know basketball is a part of who they are as Indian people. They exclaim this as fact by stating that basketball is "in our blood" or "a part of our system."[35] They display it through the style they often employ on the court and the "Rez ball" label they use to identify it. They celebrate it by organizing their own teams and tournaments and inviting other Natives to join in. They live it by erecting hoops in dairy barns and outside their family homes, crafting their own if need be. And they claim it as their history through the stories they tell of all the great teams and players of the past. Basketball is a tradition that Native peoples made for themselves and is a story that is ongoing. Jesse DesRosier says it well: "We're nowhere near the beginning stages of it, and we're far from the end of that basketball experience. . . . It's something that we consider our own. We'll never accept it being introduced as foreign. We'll never accept not being treated as equal players in the game of basketball. We definitely feel just as much a part of it as it is a part of us. It's ingrained in us."[36]

Notes

List of Abbreviations for Citations

AIS	Albuquerque Indian School Records, RG75, DEN
BCIM	Bureau of Catholic Indian Missions Records, microfilm, Special Collections and Archives, Marquette University, Milwaukee, WI
BIS	Bismarck Indian School Records, RG75, KC
CCF	Central Classified Files, RG75
CDRC	Carlisle Indian School Digital Resource Center, Dickinson College, Carlisle, PA
CHEM	Chemawa Indian School Records, RG75, SEA
CHIL	Chilocco Indian School Records, RG75, FW
CIA	Commissioner of Indian Affairs
CISC	Chilocco Indian School Collection, 1884–2005, OKHS
DC	National Archives at Washington, DC
DCF	Decimal Correspondence Files, RG75
DEN	National Archives at Denver, CO
DOI	Department of the Interior
FIS	Flandreau Indian School Records, RG75, KC
FSIS	Fort Shaw Indian School Records, RG75, DEN
FW	National Archives at Fort Worth, TX
GCF	General Correspondence Files, RG75
KC	National Archives at Kansas City, MO
HI	Haskell Indian Nations University (Haskell Institute) Records, RG75, KC
JNM	James Naismith Morgue Files, KSL
KSL	Kenneth Spencer Research Library, University of Kansas, Lawrence
LA	National Archives at Los Angeles (Riverside), CA
LUC	University Archives, Loyola University of Chicago, IL
NARA	National Archives and Records Administration
NCIBT	National Catholic Interscholastic Basketball Tournament Records, LUC
RG75	Record Group 75, Records of the Bureau of Indian Affairs
OIA	Office of Indian Affairs (later the Bureau of Indian Affairs)
OKHS	Oklahoma Historical Society, Oklahoma City
RCIS	Rapid City Indian School Records, RG75, KC
SANSR	*Superintendents' Annual Narrative and Statistical Reports from Field Jurisdictions of the Bureau of Indian Affairs, 1907–1938*, microfilm
SCF	Subject Correspondence Files, RG75
SEA	National Archives at Seattle, WA

Acknowledgments

1. Maria Allison, "Sport, Culture and Socialization," *International Review for the Sociology of Sport* 17, no. 4 (1982): 11–37; Maria T. Allison and Gunther Lueschen, "A Comparative Analysis of Navaho Indian and Anglo Basketball Sport Systems," *International Review for the Sociology of Sport* 14, nos. 3–4 (1979): 75–86; Eric D. Anderson, "Using the Master's Tools," *International Journal of the History of Sport* 23 (Mar. 2006): 247–66; Kendall Blanchard, "Basketball and the Culture-Change Process," *Council on Anthropology and Education Quarterly* 5 (Nov. 1974): 8–13; Peter Donahue, "New Warriors, New Legends," *American Indian Culture and Research Journal* 21, no. 2 (1997): 43–60.

2. Larry Colton, *Counting Coup* (New York: Warner, 2000). For a similar account of basketball in contemporary Alaska Native communities, see Michael D'Orso, *Eagle Blue* (New York: Bloomsbury, 2006).

3. Tim Brayboy and Bruce Barton, *Playing Before an Overflow Crowd* (Chapel Hill, NC: Chapel Hill, 2003); Linda Peavy and Ursula Smith, *Full-Court Quest* (Norman: University of Oklahoma Press, 2008).

4. Stewart Culin, *Games of the North American Indians* (New York: Dover, 1975); Kendall Blanchard, *The Mississippi Choctaws at Play* (Urbana: University of Illinois Press, 1981); Peter Nabokov, *Indian Running* (Santa Fe: Ancient City, 1987; Santa Barbara: Capra, 1981); Joseph B. Oxendine, *American Indian Sports Heritage* (Lincoln: University of Nebraska Press, 1995), 3–33; Thomas Vennum, Jr., *American Indian Lacrosse* (Washington, DC: Smithsonian Institution, 1994); Gregory Cajete, *Spirit of the Game* (Skyland, NC: Kivaki, 2005); Matthew Sakiestewa Gilbert, *Hopi Runners* (Lawrence: University of Kansas Press, 2018).

5. Peter Iverson, *Riders of the West* (Seattle: University of Washington Press, 1999); Jeffrey Powers-Beck, *The American Indian Integration of Baseball* (Lincoln: University of Nebraska Press, 2004); Lars Anderson, *Carlisle vs. Army* (New York: Random House, 2007); Sally Jenkins, *The Real All Americans* (New York: Doubleday, 2007).

6. David Wallace Adams, *Education for Extinction* (Lawrence: University Press of Kansas, 1995); C. Richard King, ed. *Native Athletes in Sport and Society* (Lincoln: University of Nebraska Press, 2005); Frank A. Salamone, ed., *The Native American Identity in Sports* (Lanham, MD: Scarecrow, 2013); C. Richard King, ed., *Native Americans in Sports*, 2 vols. (Armonk, NY: Sharp Reference, 2004).

7. Robert W. Peterson, *Cages to Jump Shots* (Lincoln: University of Nebraska Press, 2002; first published in 1990); Kathleen S. Yep, *Outside the Paint* (Philadelphia: Temple University Press, 2009); Ignacio M. Garcia, *When Mexicans Could Play Ball* (Austin: University of Texas Press, 2013).

Introduction

1. *HBO: Real Sports with Bryant Gumbel*, episode 204, Mar. 25, 2014.
2. *Off the Rez*, directed by Jonathan Hock (New York: Cinema Guild, 2014).
3. *Off the Rez.*
4. Abe Streep, "What the Arlee Warriors Were Playing For," *New York Times*

Magazine, Apr. 4, 2018: https://www.nytimes.com/2018/04/04/magazine/arlee-warriors-montana-basketball-flathead-indian-reservation.html.

5. *Beyond the Paint*, "Arlee Warriors," parts 1 and 2, directed by Matt Winer, NBA-TV, Feb. 10, 2019: http://www.nba.com/video/2019/02/10/20190210-beyond-paint-arlee-warriors-part-one?collection=video/beyond-the-paint; http://www.nba.com/video/2019/02/10/20190210-beyond-paint-arlee-warriors-part-two?collection=video/beyond-the-paint; "Arlee Warriors State Dedication," https://www.facebook.com/watch/?v=963987443764499; *Great Falls Tribune* (MT), Mar. 4, 2018, S1 and S5; *Missoulian* (MT), Feb. 9, 2019, D1 and D4.

6. Kim Elise Taylor, "The Fabrication and Function of Star Quilts on Fort Peck Reservation in Northeastern Montana," master's thesis, University of Montana, Missoula, 1994, 87–88.

7. Helen Boyd interviewed by Kim Taylor, July 14, 1992, OH 285-4, Archives and Special Collections, Mansfield Library, University of Montana, Missoula.

8. Richard Peterson, "A Treasured Tradition, Star Quilt Giveaways Teach Generosity and Ease Racial Tensions," *Great Falls Tribune*, Feb. 23, 2014, L1 and L3.

9. Taylor, "The Fabrication and Function of Star Quilts on Fort Peck Reservation in Northeastern Montana," 1 and 30–44; Sybil and Barney Lambert interviewed by Kim Taylor, July 13, 1992, OH 285-1, Archives and Special Collections, Mansfield Library, University of Montana, Missoula. Brenda J. Child also views the star quilts as symbolic of Native American's interaction with the boarding schools, given that some quilters learned about them during their time as students. Brenda J. Child, *Boarding School Seasons* (Lincoln: University of Nebraska Press, 1998), 4.

10. On ways Euro-Americans also used basketball and other sports as colonial tools elsewhere in the world, see Allen Guttmann, *Games and Empires* (New York: Columbia University Press, 1994), 97–110, and Gerald R. Gems, *The Athletic Crusade* (Lincoln: University of Nebraska Press, 2006), 20–26.

11. Peter Iverson argues that rodeo became a traditional sport for Native people as well, allowing them to gather, nurture family connections, tell stories, and make statements about their "present well-being;" Iverson, *Riders of the West*, 17.

12. For basketball's influence on Native novelists, see Donahue, "New Warriors, New Legends," 43–60. For an example in poetry, see Natalie Diaz, "Top Ten Reasons Why Indians Are Good at Basketball," *Indian Country Today,* June 7, 2013: https://newsmaven.io/indiancountrytoday/archive/top-ten-reasons-why-indians-are-good-at-basketball-a-poem-by-natalie-diaz-9efjNo_3cEOuGVHio8X2cQ/. In feature film *Smoke Signals*, VHS, directed by Chris Eyre (screenplay by Sherman Alexie) (Miramax, 1998).

13. Iva Croff, interview by author, Missoula, Montana, Jan. 19, 2016.

Chapter 1. Origins

1. Sherman Alexie, *The Lone Ranger and Tonto Fist Fight in Heaven* (New York: Harper Collins, 1994), 45; Nancy J. Peterson, *Conversations with Sherman Alexie* (Jackson: University Press of Mississippi, 2009), 8.

2. On Native American antecedents: King, "Basketball," in King, *Native*

Americans in Sports, 1:34–35. Frank J. Basloe claimed Will invented basketball in 1890; Frank J. Basloe, *I Grew Up with Basketball* (Lincoln: University of Nebraska Press, 2012), 3–35. Basloe's claims were later refuted by Alexander M. Weyand, who noted that he had his dates wrong; Alexander M. Weyand, *The Cavalcade of Basketball* (New York: Macmillan, 1960), 1–2.

3. Wagering was listed by Wilma J. Pesavento as the primary motive for playing Native sports: "Motivations of North American Indians in Athletic Games," US Department of Health Education and Welfare, National Institute of Education, *Annual Reports of the Bureau of American Ethnology*, 1974.

4. Davies, "American Indian Sports," in *American Indians and Popular Culture*: vol. 1, *Media, Sports, and Politics*, ed. Elizabeth DeLaney, Hoffman, 243–50 (Santa Barbara, CA: Praeger, 2012); Oxendine, *American Indian Sports Heritage*, 3–33; Cajete, *Spirit of the Game*, 23.

5. Nabokov, *Indian Running*, 9, 47–50; Vennum, *American Indian Lacrosse*, 28–30; Cajete, *Spirit of the Game*, 24, and 49–51; Culin, *Games of the North American Indians*, 32–33.

6. Davies, "American Indian Sports," 246–47; Nabokov, *Indian Running*, 27 and 67–68; Vennum, *American Indian Lacrosse*, xv, 7, and 11–22.

7. Davies, "American Indian Sports," 247; Oxendine, *American Indian Sports Heritage*, 10–14; Blanchard, *The Mississippi Choctaws at Play*, 36; *Hand Game*, VHS, directed by Lawrence Johnson (Portland, OR: Lawrence Johnson, 2000); Richard Sattler, interview by author, Missoula, Montana, May 24, 2016.

8. Charles A. Eastman, *Indian Boyhood* (New York: McClure, Phillips, 1902), 64.

9. Cajete, *Spirit of the Game*, 144; Oxendine, *American Indian Sports Heritage*, 122–23 and 149–51.

10. Vennum, *American Indian Lacrosse*, 120; On pelota's rough play, see Bushnell, "That Demonic Game," *Americas* 35 (July 1978): 7.

11. Vennum, *American Indian Lacrosse*, 112 and 213–35; Blanchard, *The Mississippi Choctaws at Play*, 28–29; Taladoire and Colsenet, "'Bois Ton Sang, Beaumanoir,'" in *The Mesoamerican Ballgame*, ed. Scarborough and Wilcox, 174; S. Wilkerson, "And Then They Were Sacrificed," in *The Mesoamerican Ballgame*, ed. Vernon L. Scarborough and David R. Wilcox, 45–71 (Tucson: University of Arizona Press, 1991), 52–55 and 63–67; Oxendine, *American Indian Sports Heritage*, 59.

12. Oxendine, *American Indian Sports Heritage*, 22–26 and 50–58; Culin, *Games of the North American Indians*, 647; Cheska, "Ball Game Participation of North American Indian Women," in *Her Story in Sport*, ed. Reet Howell, 19–34 (West Point, NY: Leisure, 1982).

13. Stacy Sewell similarly argues that white-introduced sports shared a "similar skill set and common goals" with traditional Arapaho and Shoshone sports in "Asserting Native American Agency in an Assimilationist Institution," in Salamone, ed., *The Native American Identity in Sports*, 31–32.

14. Culin, *Games of the North American Indians*, 420–527; International Traditional Games Society, *Indian Education for All*, 45–49 and 57–65. Donahue also

identifies the parallels between basketball and hoop and pole in "New Warriors, New Legends," 46.

15. A similar game was played by the Tarahumare across the Mexican border: Culin, *Games of the North American Indians*, 722–28.

16. Bushnell, *Drawing by Jacques Lemoyne de Morgues of Saturioua, A Timucua Chief in Florida, 1564*; Hulton, "Images of the New World," in *The Westward Enterprise*, ed. K. R. Andrews, N. P. Canny and P. E. H. Hair, 195–214 (Detroit: Wayne State University Press, 1979); Milanich, "The Devil in the Details," *Archaeology* 58 (May/June 2005): 26–31; Richard Sattler, interview; Sattler and William Sturtevant both point out that the sticks may have been omitted from the picture; Hulton et al. (including Sturtevant), *The Work of Jacques Le Moyne De Morgues* (London, UK: Trustees of the British Museum by British Museum Publications Limited, 1977), 213.

17. Culin, *Games of the North American Indians*, 573; Sattler interview. This sport is also very similar to a game called community lacrosse that was described by Robert Upham (Gros Ventre) in 1999: The International Traditional Games Society, *Indian Education for All* (Helena, MT: Montana Office of Public Instruction, 2013), 52.

18. J. C. McCaskill, "Indian Sports," *Indian Leader* (Haskell), July 1, 1936, 29; de Borhegyi, "America's Ballgame," *Natural History* 69 (Jan. 1960): 48–59. Other scholars who have suggested either a coincidental parallel or a possible direct connection include: R. Brasch, *How Did Sports Begin?* (New York: David McKay, 1970), 44–45, and Emory Dean Keoke and Kay Marie Porterfield, *American Indian Contributions to the World* (New York: Checkmark, 2003), 28–29. In an endnote, June Nash goes even further, suggesting that Naismith learned about the Mesoamerican game from a missionary who had visited Chichen Itza and created a modified version of the game upon her return to Massachusetts: June C. Nash, *Mayan Visions* (New York: Routledge, 2001), 268.

19. "The Sport of Life and Death: The Mesoamerican Ballgame," www.mesoballgame.org.

20. Cajete refers to "Mayan handball" where he says players threw the ball on a much larger field; *Spirit of the Game*, 187–88; Ted J. J. Leyenaar, "Ulama," *Kiva* 58, no. 2 (1992): 132–45.

21. Culin, *Games of the North American Indians*, 29–32; Erika Marie Bsumek, "The Navajos as Borrowers," *New Mexico Historical Review* 79 (Summer 2004): 326.

22. These conclusions are based on my analysis of his entries for specific tribal variants of archery, snowsnake, hoop and pole, shinny, and double ball. Of those entries where the informant says directly whether, or suggests, these sports were still played, more than three-quarters indicate that the described sport was still active. More than half of the sports mentioned in these sections are written in language that provides no sense of time, are ambiguously written in that regard, are written based on origin stories, or are from informant accounts that predate 1880, making it impossible to tell from Culin's volume whether they were still being played in the late nineteenth century. Nevertheless, it is clear from this source that

multiple variants of these sports endured in multiple locations throughout North America. On the persistence of Lakota games in the early 1900s and studies of them, see Raymond A. Bucko, "When Does a Cactus Become an Angry Buffalo?" *Montana* 57 (Spring 2007): 14–31.

23. Blanchard, *The Mississippi Choctaws at Play*, 26.

24. Oxendine, *American Indian Sports Heritage*, 59; indigenous peoples in the region nonetheless proved their ability to respond and adapt, as they still play today what is likely a modified version of these games, known as ulama, played without the stone courts; Leyenaar, "Ulama," 117–18.

25. This was one of the many team sports the Spanish called "el juego de la pelota" ("the ballgame") and involved kicking a small ball toward a goal post; Bushnell, "That Demonic Game," 1–19.

26. See for example E. M. Yearian report on Lemhi Shoshone, Department of the Interior (hereafter DOI), *Annual Report of the Secretary of the Interior, Volume 2, 1897* (Washington, DC: Government Printing Office, 1898), 145; on middle-class Victorians expressing similar concerns about the ills of sports in white America, see Benjamin G. Rader, *American Sports* (Upper Saddle River, NH: Pearson, Prentice Hall, 2009), 23–25.

27. Kendall Blanchard, "Stick Ball and the American Southeast," in *Forms of Play of Native North Americans*, ed. Edward Norbeck and Claire R. Farrer, 189–207 (St. Paul, MN: West, 1979), 190; Blanchard, *The Mississippi Choctaws at Play*, 41–42; John Finger, *Cherokee Americans* (Lincoln: University of Nebraska Press, 1992), 15; Vennum, *American Indian Lacrosse*, 117.

28. Culin downplayed the frequency of Native-European athletic interactions since 1492: Culin, *Games of the North American Indians*, 31–32, 789–801, and 809. Joseph Oxendine has similarly concluded that Natives and whites did not extensively adopt each other's sports before the twentieth-century: *American Indian Sports Heritage*, 160 and 165.

29. Vennum, *American Indian Lacrosse*, 253–78; W. G. Beers, *Lacrosse* (Montreal: Dawson Brothers, 1869), 33 and 254.

30. Oxendine argues, to the contrary, that school officials may have intentionally aimed to extinguish the traditional sports, *American Indian Sports Heritage*, 178. On the role new sports in boarding schools played in extinguishing traditional sports, see Sean Sullivan, "Federal Indian Boarding Schools in New Mexico," in Salamone, *The Native American Identity in Sports*, 67–68. Lacrosse began under Superintendent Hervey Peairs at Haskell in 1908. *Indian Leader* (Haskell), Oct. 30, 1908, 2; and Dec. 18, 1908, 1; *The Red Man* (Carlisle), Feb. 1911, 263.

31. Rader, *American Sports*, 39; Nabokov, *Indian Running*, 178. On Hopi and other Native racers competing independently or for Indian schools in distance footraces, including during the 1908 and 1912 Olympics, see Gilbert, *Hopi Runners*, 67–72, and 88–151.

32. Powers-Beck, *The American Indian Integration of Baseball*, 6–7; Blanchard, *Mississippi Choctaws at Play*, 43; Finger, *Cherokee Americans*, 28.

33. For nuanced accounts arguing that individualistic competition was alien to

Native traditions, see Cajete, *Spirit of the Game*, 138–39, and Anderson, "Using the Master's Tools," 248.

34. Iverson, *Riders of the West*, 74.

35. *Oregon Statesman* (Salem) (obituary), Dec. 26, 1943, 2; *The Indian Leader* (Haskell) 18, no. 29 (Mar. 1915): 20; Richard G. Hardorff, ed., *Washita Memories* (Norman: University of Oklahoma Press, 2006), 354.

36. James Naismith, *Basketball* (Lincoln: University of Nebraska Press, 1996), 33; James Naismith, "Basket Ball," *American Physical Education Review* 19 (May 1914): 339–51; Peterson, *Cages to Jump Shots*, 15.

37. Muscular Christianity had originated in England in the mid-nineteenth century; Rader, *American Sports*, 26; Steven A. Riess, *Sport in Industrial America, 1850–1920* (Wheeling, IL: Harlan Davidson, 1995), 18–19; Bernice Larson Webb, *The Basketball Man* (Lawrence: University Press of Kansas, 1973), 1–65; Rob Rains, with Hellen Carpenter, *James Naismith* (Philadelphia: Temple University Press, 2009), 3–27.

38. Naismith, *Basketball*, 29–60; Naismith, "Basket Ball," 339–51.

39. Albert Gammon Applin, II, "From Muscular Christianity to the Market Place," PhD diss., University of Massachusetts, Amherst, 1982, 31; Naismith, *Basketball*, 41.

40. Naismith, *Basketball*, 63–65.

41. Naismith, *Basketball*, 42–60.

42. Naismith, *Basketball*, 42–60.

43. "Father of Basketball, 74, Retains Zest for Cage Game," Folder 1935, Box 1, James Naismith Morgue Files (JNM), Kenneth Spencer Research Library, University of Kansas, Lawrence (KSL).

44. Webb and Rains both present him as a generally mild-mannered man, although he was somewhat protective of his sport in its original form and was displeased by some of the later rules changes.

45. The YMCA had been founded in England in 1851 and come to the United States prior to the Civil War: Rader, *American Sports*, 105.

46. Naismith, *Basketball*, 102–3 and 112–13; Peterson, *Cages to Jump Shots*, 22–24; Weyand, *The Cavalcade of Basketball*, 27; Guttmann, *Games and Empires*, 101–10; Webb, *The Basketball Man*, 73–76; Rader, *American Sports*, 107–8; Applin, "From Muscular Christianity to the Market Place," 44–49; Gulick, "Biennial Report of Luther Gulick," *Young Men's Christian Association, Year Book, 1897* (New York: International Committee, 1897), 33.

47. Naismith, *Basketball*, 129–42; Webb, *The Basketball Man*, 74; Guttmann, *Games and Empires*, 105–6; Weyand, *The Cavalcade of Basketball*, 224; Riess, *Sport in Industrial America*, 141–42.

48. Rader, *American Sports*, 109–17; Henry S. Curtis, *Education through Play* (New York: Macmillan, 1915), 202–5; Naismith, *Basketball*, 124–29.

49. Weyand, *The Cavalcade of Basketball*, 28–40; Naismith, *Basketball*, 120–21; Peterson, *Cages to Jump Shots*, 32–38 and 46–48.

50. Pamela Grundy and Susan Shackelford, *Shattering the Glass* (New York: New Press, 2005), 9–33; Naismith, *Basketball*, 161–70; Webb, *The Basketball Man*, 71–72; Powell, "'Playing Fairly and Fiercely,'" *Register of the Kentucky Historical*

Society 109 (Spring 2011): 156–57; Peavy and Smith, *Full-Court Quest*, 59–61; Robert Pruter, *The Rise of American High School Sports and the Search for Control, 1880–1930* (Syracuse, NY: Syracuse University Press, 2013), 148–56.

51. Gerald R. Gems, "Blocked Shot," *Journal of Sport History* 22 (Summer 1995): 135–48; McKissack, *Black Hoops* (New York: Scholastic, 1999), 25–30; Yep, *Outside the Paint*; Yep, "Peddling Sport," *Ethnic and Racial Studies* 35 (June 2012): 971–87; Peterson, *Cages to Jump Shots*, 95–97 and 116–23; Garcia, *When Mexicans Could Play Ball*, 30 and 40; Levine, "Basketball and the Jewish-American Community, 1920s–1930s," in Riess, ed., *Major Problems in American Sport History* (Boston: Houghton Mifflin Company, 1997), 299–308.

52. Marie Helen Witkay, "Henry Franklin Kallenberg: Pioneer Physical Educator," master's thesis, George Williams College, Chicago, June 1958, 4–8; Naismith, *Basketball*, 138.

53. Historians, including myself, have previously accepted the 1892 date based on Naismith's account, and the *Argus-Leader* of Sioux Falls enthusiastically did as well soon after Naismith's book was published, *Argus-Leader*, Mar. 31, 1941, 9. Further confusing things, Naismith told a reporter in 1936 that the conference at Big Stone Lake took place in 1893 rather than "in the summer of 1892," as he said in the 1941 book: Typed manuscript, n.a. "from *Esquire,* 2–36," 7–8, Folder 1936, Box 1, JNM, KSL.

54. "Radio Interview, Dec. 15, '32," Folder 1932, Box 1, JNM, KSL.

55. Hazel W. Hertzberg, *The Search for an American Indian Identity* (Syracuse: Syracuse University Press, 1971), 38–42; Raymond Wilson, *Ohiyesa* (Urbana: University of Illinois Press, 1999), 83–89; Tom Holm, *The Great Confusion in Indian Affairs* (Austin: University of Texas Press, 2005), 56–64.

56. Wilson, *Ohiyesa*, 83–84; "Report of Francis E. Leupp," Aug. 15, 1896, in United States Board of Indian Commissioners, *Twenty-Eighth Annual Report of the Board of Indian Commissioners, 1896* (Washington, DC: Government Printing Office, 1897), 14–21; Witkay adds that this outdoor basketball game was played using a soccer ball: "Henry Franklin Kallenberg," 8–9. Leupp made it clear that this was the first of these conferences ever to take place. I have been unable to locate any sources confirming a date for any conference that Naismith said occurred the following year in Pierre.

57. Kallenberg later told Naismith that he did not know whether the enthusiastic response the sport received at Big Stone Lake had a lasting effect, nor have I come across evidence confirming whether basketball's later popularity among Dakotas and Lakotas stemmed from this event: "from *Esquire,* 2–36," 8, Folder 1936, Box 1 JNM, KSL. On the use of willow, see Culin, *Games of the North American Indians*, 418–19, 441, 454, 460, 520, 523, 663, 706.

Chapter 2. Emergence

1. Adams, *Education for Extinction*, 58; Joshua Jerome Meisel, "Historical Demographics, Student Origins, and Recruitment at Off-Reservation Indian Boarding Schools, 1900," master's thesis, University of Kansas, Lawrence, 2014, 18; Francis

Paul Prucha, *The Great Father*, unabridged edition (Lincoln: University of Nebraska Press, 1995), 815–16.

2. Adams, *Education for Extinction*, 28 and 181–82; Bloom, *To Show What an Indian Can Do*, xvii, 4 and 10; Oxendine, *American Indian Sports Heritage*, 186–92; Jenkins, *The Real All Americans;* Anderson, *Carlisle vs. Army.*

3. Adams, *Education for Extinction*, 184–85; David Wallace Adams, "More than a Game," *Western Historical Quarterly* 32 (Spring 2001): 26–27; Bloom, *To Show What an Indian Can Do*, 13–17.

4. Adams, *Education for Extinction*, 321–25; Adams, "More than a Game," 25–53; John Bloom also argues that the schools failed to employ a "coherent or seamless ideology" administering athletics: *To Show What an Indian Can Do*, xx and 8–20.

5. Keith A. Sculle, "'The New Carlisle of the West,'" *Kansas History* 17 (Autumn, 1994): 192–208; Oxendine, *American Indian Sports Heritage*, 195–98; *Haskell Institute Information Bulletin of Information, 1941*, Folder 22, Box 2, Wallace Galluzzi Papers, 1926–1984, KSL.

6. School papers like Carlisle's *Indian Helper* and *Red Man*, Haskell's *Indian Leader*, Chemawa's *American*, and Phoenix Indian School's *Native American*, devoted significant coverage to athletics.

7. Bloom, *To Show What an Indian Can Do*, xvi; Clyde Ellis, *To Change Them Forever* (Norman: University of Oklahoma Press, 1996), 131–52.

8. DOI, Bureau of Education, *Course of Study for the Indian Schools of the United States, Industrial and Literary* (Washington, DC: Government Printing Office, 1901) 197–99; Bloom, *To Show What an Indian Can Do*, xvi; Adams, *Education for Extinction*, 153–54; Scott Riney, *The Rapid City Indian School, 1898–1933* (Norman: University of Oklahoma Press, 1999), 81–82. Estelle Reel to Agents and Superintendents, Circular No. 91, Feb. 5, 1908, Folder "1908," Box 146, Circulars Received from the Office of Indian Affairs (hereafter OIA), 1890–1911, Records of Haskell Indian Nations University (hereafter HI), Records of the Bureau of Indian Affairs, Record Group 75 (hereafter RG 75), National Archives and Records Administration (hereafter NARA), Kansas City, MO (hereafter KC).

9. DOI, OIA, *Tentative Course of Study for United States Indian Schools* (Washington, DC: Government Printing Office, 1915), 117–23; Keith A. Sculle argues that Peairs resisted the trending cynicism: "The New Carlisle," 196–97. On nationwide efforts to bring sports under institutional control, see Pruter, *The Rise of American High School Sports*, 45–50.

10. DOI, *Tentative Course of Study*, 117–23.

11. What Indian Office oversight there was of athletics came in the form of mailing circulars, issuing handbooks, and fielding questions from superintendents. Indian Office audits and criticisms of athletic activities targeted Haskell in 1909 and 1928, Carlisle in 1914, and Albuquerque Indian School in 1931: Sculle, "The New Carlisle," 197; Oxendine, *American Indian Sports Heritage*, 192–193; J. Henry Scattergood to Rueben Perry, July 15, 1931, Folder 750, "Amusements and Athletics, 1929–1934," Box 34, General Correspondence Files, 1917–1936, Albuquerque Indian School, (hereafter AIS), RG75, NARA, Denver, CO (hereafter DEN).

12. Carlisle played Y teams from Germantown and York and Haskell commonly played against Y teams from Kansas City, Lawrence, Topeka, and various Nebraska towns: *Indian Helper*, Mar. 26, 1997, 3; *York Daily* (PA), Feb. 14, 1906, 3; *Lawrence Daily World*, Jan. 25, 1899, 3; Mar. 21, 1900, 3; *Lawrence Journal World*, Mar. 5, 1900, 3; *Indian Leader*, Jan. 23, 1903, 3.

13. Alexander Weyand claims that basketball appeared at Carlisle in February 1894 but provides no supporting evidence. I have not been able to confirm this date with available sources: Weyand, *Cavalcade of Basketball*, 18–24.

14. Pearl Lee Walker-McNeil, "The Carlisle Indian School," PhD diss., American University, Washington, DC, 1979, 236; Carlisle Indian School, *United States Indian School, Carlisle, Pa.*, ca. 1895, CIS-I-0037, Carlisle Indian School Digital Resource Center, Dickinson College Archives and Special Collections, Carlisle, PA, (hereafter CDRC), http://carlisleindian.dickinson.edu/publications/united-states-indian-school-carlisle-penna, 52; *Pittsburgh Press*, Sept. 11, 1892, 7; *Wilkes-Barre Evening Leader*, Sept. 19, 1892, 4; *The Scranton Republican*, Dec. 1, 1892, 3; *Philadelphia Inquirer*, Dec. 6, 1892, 3; Weyand, *Cavalcade of Basketball*, 18–24.

15. Naismith, "Basketball" in Andrew Sloan Draper, ed., *Self Culture for Young People* (Saint Louis: Twentieth Century Self Culture Association, 1906), 56; Naismith, *Basketball*, 138.

16. *Ames Intelligencer* (IA), Apr. 6, 1895, 14.

17. *Indian Helper* (Carlisle), Apr. 8, 1892, 3.

18. *Indian Helper*, Dec. 13, 1895, 3; Feb. 7, 1896, 2; and Feb. 26, 1897, 3.

19. *Indian Helper*, Apr. 3, 1896, 2.

20. "Basket Ball Boys," photograph reproduction from *The Indian Industrial School, Carlisle, Pa.: 23rd Year* (Carlisle, PA: The School, 1902), CDRC, http://carlisleindian.dickinson.edu/images/boys-basketball-game; Weyand, *Cavalcade of Basketball*, 11 and 15; Peterson, *Cages to Jump Shots*, 26.

21. DOI, OIA, *Annual Report of the Commissioner of Indian Affairs* (Washington, DC: Government Printing Office, 1896), 494–95 and 500–501.

22. Peavy and Smith, *Full-Court Quest*, 62–65 and 390–91.

23. Peavy and Smith, "World Champions," *Montana* 51 (Winter 2001): 9. Peavy and Smith surmise that Langley also served as team coach and girls' physical culture director: *Full-Court Quest*, 70–71 and 391.

24. Acting Commissioner of Indian Affairs to W. H. Winslow, Nov. 19, 1897, Box 1, Letters Received, 1897–1898, Fort Shaw Indian School, RG 75, NARA, DEN; Roster of Employees, 1892–1910, Fort Shaw Indian School, RG 75, NARA, DEN; *Lead Daily Call* (SD), Apr. 7, 1926, 1.

25. Peavy and Smith, *Full-Court Quest*, 66.

26. Chauncey Yellow Robe Student File, reproduction of Folder 5297, Box 135, Series 1327, RG75, NARA, CDRC, http://carlisleindian.dickinson.edu/student_files/chauncey-yellow-robe-killed-timber-student-file.

27. *Montanian* (Choteau), July 2, 1897, 3.

28. Jones to Winslow, Aug. 13, 1898, Box 1, Letters Received, Fort Shaw Indian School, RG75, NARA, DEN; Peavy and Smith, *Full-Court Quest*, 103–5 and 149;

Indian Leader, Feb. 14, 1902, 3 and Nov. 22, 1907, 3; *Montana Daily Record* (Helena), Feb. 2, 1904, 2; Feb. 26, 1904, 7; and Feb. 29, 1904, 4; *Weekly Oregon Statesman*, Aug. 29, 1905, 6; Retirement announcement: *Great Falls Tribune*, June 30, 1932, 5.

29. *Daily Capital Journal* (Salem) Jan. 16, 1893, 3.

30. *Weekly Oregon Statesman*, Oct. 25, 1895, 2.

31. *Daily Capital Journal*, Oct. 19, 1895, 1, and Mar. 20, 1897, 1; Chemawa began its athletic program in 1894–1895: David Lewis, "Chemawa Indian School Athletics Program," *Oregon Encyclopedia*, https://oregonencyclopedia.org/articles/chemawa_indian_school_athletics_program/#.VzIm.

32. Historical sources variously referred to Indian school varsity teams as "boys" or "men," and female varsity teams invariably as "girls." In fact, player ages ranged widely on some teams from the early teenage years to athletes in their early to mid-twenties. I have opted to refer to varsity teams form Carlisle and Haskell (which often had older players) as men's and women's teams, and teams from other Indian schools as boys and girls teams. *Daily Capital Journal*, Mar. 30, 1897, 3; "Basketball in Salem," Salem Online History, www.salemhistory.net/culture/basketball.htm; on the boys' team, see *Daily Capital Journal*, Dec. 17, 1897, 4.

33. *Daily Capital Journal*, Apr. 27, 1897, 4; Superintendent Thomas W. Potter of Chemawa report in DOI, OIA, *Annual Report of the Commissioner of Indian Affairs* (Washington, DC: Government Printing Office, 1898), 387.

34. Myriam Vučković, *Voices from Haskell* (Lawrence: University of Kansas Press, 2008), 130; *Indian Leader*, May 1897, 2.

35. Naismith, *Basketball*, 126 and 138; Webb, *The Basketball Man*, 114–16.

36. DOI, *Annual Report* (1898), 316; DOI, OIA, *Annual Report of the Commissioner of Indian Affairs* (Washington, DC: Government Printing Office, 1899), 633; *Lawrence Daily Journal-World* (obituary) Apr. 5, 1937, 1.

37. *Lawrence Daily Journal-World* (obituary) Apr. 5, 1937, 1; James Naismith to Maude Naismith, Aug. 5, 1900, and Aug. 12 1900, excerpted, N.A. "The Naismith Chronicles, Being Letters by, to, and about James Naismith, Father of Basketball and Other Creations Even more Beguiling," Box 3, JNM, KSL; *Indian Leader*, Jan. 19, 1900, 3; Oct. 19, 1900, 2; and Mar. 6, 1903, 2.

38. *Indian Leader*, Dec. 1, 1898, 3, and Feb. 27, 1903, 2; "Edward Valley," Record of Students, 1890–1897, one ledger, HI, RG 75, NARA, KC.

39. "Rough" likely meant disorderly rather than suggesting physical aggression: *Lawrence Daily World*, Jan. 25, 1899, 3; *Indian Leader*, Feb. 1, 1899, 2.

40. "Frank O. Jones" bio-sketch, in *Haskell Annual, 1924*, no page listing, reprinted in Haskell Institute, Reel 60, *Superintendents' Annual Narrative and Statistical Reports from Field Jurisdictions of the Bureau of Indian Affairs, 1907–1938*, M1011, microfilm (Washington, DC: National Archives and Records Services, 1975) (hereafter SANSR); *Indian Leader*, Aug. issue, 1898, 3; *Indian Leader*, Feb. 1, 1899, 2, and June 15, 1900, 2; Frank O. Jones Student File, reproduction of Folder 5323, Box 135, Series 1327, RG75, NARA, CDRC, http://carlisleindian.dickinson.edu/sites/all/files/docs-ephemera/NARA_1327_b135_f5323.pdf.

41. *Indian Leader*, Mar. 9, 1900, 3.

42. *Indian Leader*, Jan. 19, 1900, 3.

43. *Lawrence Journal World*, Jan. 29, 1900, 4.

44. *Indian Leader*, Mar. 30, 1900, 3; Dec. 24, 1900, 2; Feb. 1, 1901, 3; and Mar. 15, 1901, 2.

45. *Indian Leader*, Mar. 9, 1900, 2–3.

46. *Indian Leader*, Mar. 8, 1901, 2; *Topeka State Journal*, Mar. 5, 1901, 2.

47. *The Native American*, Apr. 13, 1901, Card 6, microfiche, American Indian Periodicals in the Princeton University Library (New York: Clearwater, 1981) (hereafter *Native American*).

48. *Indian Leader*, Apr. 5, 1901, 3.

49. *Native American*, June 8, 1901, Card 8.

50. *Native American*, Feb. 2, 1901, Card 4, and Oct. 12, 1901, Card 9.

51. Dozens of sources were compiled to determine this information, including school and municipal newspapers, Indian Office superintendent's reports, archival records, and photographs.

52. This willingness to respond to initiatives from student athletes was not the case only with basketball. Pratt had been persuaded by students to overturn his 1893 ban on football: Adams, *Education for Extinction*, 181–82.

53. Pruter, *The Rise of American High School Sports*, 21–49.

54. Official school rosters did not list athletic position titles next to employee names, making it difficult to know who had those duties at any given time; nor were athletic staff positions described in Indian Service duty descriptions: OIA, *Rules for the Indian School Service, 1900* (Washington, DC: Government Printing Office, 1900); conclusions here are also based on employee rosters for multiple schools during the 1890s and early 1900s (including Chemawa, Chilocco, Fort Shaw, and Haskell), as found in RG 75 collections at NARA branches. On high employee turnover rates in the Indian Service, see Cathleen D. Cahill, *Federal Fathers and Mothers* (Chapel Hill: University of North Carolina Press, 2011), 89.

Chapter 3. An Indian School Sport

1. Adopting as a winter sport: Arnold of Klamath Agency to the Commissioner of Indian Affairs (hereafter CIA) Apr. 13, 1926, Folder "Physical Training, 1926," Box 125, Decimal Correspondence Files (hereafter DCF), 1916–1960, Klamath Indian Agency, RG75, NARA at Seattle, WA (hereafter SEA); Peavy and Smith, "World Champions," 9; *The Southern Workman*, 41 (Jan.–Dec. 1912): 57 and 189; Vučković, *Voices from Haskell*, 146. "Great Indoor Game" references: *Spalding's Official Basket Ball Rules* (New York: American Sports Publishing Company, 1909), 17; *Indian Leader*, Feb. 18, 1916, 1.

2. Haskell indoor track meets and indoor volleyball: *Indian Leader*, Mar. 8, 1918, 4, Mar. 22, 1918, 2, Mar. 4, 1921, 4, and May 27, 1921, 14. Boxing: Bloom, *To Show What an Indian Can Do*, 61–72; Eccleston to CIA, May 14, 1934, Folder 750, Box 27, Central Classified Files (hereafter CCF), Chilocco Indian School (hereafter CHIL), RG75, NARA, Washington, DC.

3. There was an attempt to organize ice hockey at Haskell in 1906, but Indian

Office requisition forms for Haskell and other schools commonly showed they purchased no hockey gear (either field or ice): *Indian Leader*, Jan. 19, 1906, 5; Chemawa Annual Report, 1916, Folder "Annual Report 1916," Box 1, Annual Reports, 1916–1940, Chemawa Indian School (hereafter CHEM), RG75, NARA, SEA; Haskell, 1920, Reel 60, SANSR; Yakima Indian Agency Annual Report, 1920, Folder "Annual Reports, 1917," Box 204, General Reports Relating to the Yakima Indian School, 1912–1921, Yakima Indian Agency, RG75, NARA, SEA.

4. Naismith, "Basket Ball," 2.

5. According to an article by Heisman in 1905, "any fair sized hall" was considered suitable for the game if it could accommodate a court that was 60 × 40 feet with space for a three-foot perimeter: *Atlanta Constitution*, Jan. 1, 1905, 4.

6. *The Red Man* (Carlisle), September 1909, 41.

7. Fort Shaw: Peavy and Smith, *Full-Court Quest*, 70 and 112–13. Haskell: Blair Kerkhoff, *Phog Allen* (Indianapolis: Masters, 1996), 26; *Indian Leader*, Feb. 1, 1899, 1, Apr. 15, 1904, 3, and Feb. 16, 1906, 2. Other school gymnasiums: DOI, OIA, *Annual Report of the Commissioner of Indian Affairs* (Washington, DC: Government Printing Office, 1900), 487; F. H. Abbott to Dodds, Jan. 12, 1910, folder 750, box 125, General Service CCF, NARA, Washington, DC; *Chilocco School Views* (Chilocco Indian Print Shop, 1906), Folder 96.69, Box 16, Chilocco Indian School Collection, 1884–2005 (hereafter CISC), Oklahoma Historical Society, Oklahoma City, OK (hereafter OKHS); Chilocco School, 1916 and 1921, Reel 18, SANSR.

8. Kerkhoff, *Phog Allen*, 26.

9. Screens: Fort Hall, 1920, Reel 49, SANSR 1920. Fire: Adams, *Education for Extinction*, 229.

10. Sullivan cites the Albuquerque fire as occurring in 1922 in "Education through Sport," PhD diss., University of New Mexico, Albuquerque, 2004, 126. Chilocco: Chilocco School, 1926, Reel 18, SANSR. The fire at Fort Totten in 1923 was attributed to the combustion of "oily rags": W. R. Beyer to O. B. Burtness, Sept. 12, 1923, Folder "Buildings, 1923," Box 28, Subject Correspondence Files (hereafter SCF), 1884–1947, Fort Totten Indian Agency, RG75, NARA, KC. Crow gymnasium: Robert Yellowtail to CIA, Apr. 9, 1937, Folder 419.3, Box 44, DCF, 1926–1958, Crow Indian Agency, 1872–1992, RG75, NARA, DEN. An old gym at Wind River was also cited as a fire hazard because of faulty wiring: Stenberg to Forrest R. Stone, Apr. 23, 1938, Folder 414.3, Box 337, GCF, 1890–1960, Wind River Indian Agency, RG75, NARA, DEN.

11. Sutton, interview, June 25, 1967, volume 8, ID T-67, Doris Duke Collection, Western History Collections, University of Oklahoma Libraries, Norman, OK, https://digital.libraries.ou.edu/cdm/compoundobject/collection/dorisduke/id/17007/show/16971/rec/1; *Indian Leader*, Apr. 21, 1905, 4.

12. Kerkhoff, *Phog Allen*, 26.

13. Naismith's original rules had intentionally avoided specifying a regulation court size: Naismith, *Basketball*, 96–97; Frank J. Basloe describes on-court obstacles in *I Grew Up with Basketball*, 79 and 121.

14. *Lawrence Journal World*, Jan. 1, 1901, 5; Rains, with Carpenter, *James Naismith*, 72.

15. *Indian Leader*, Apr. 12, 1901, 2.

16. Outdoor basketball began to be played at Tulalip in 1905: *Indian Leader*, May 19, 1905, 4; Carolyn J. Marr, "Between Two Worlds," www.hibulbcultural center. org.assets/pdf/Between-Two-Worlds.pdf; Charles H. Burke School (Fort Wingate), 1928, Reel 11, SANSR; Greenville School, 1921, Reel 59, SANSR.

17. *Native American* 5 (Dec. 24, 1904): 358.

18. Peavy and Smith, *Full-Court Quest*, 70; *Indian Leader*, Jan. 12, 1906, 2.

19. Crow Creek (SD), 1914, Reel 31, SANSR; Blackfeet, 1916, Reel 5, SANSR.

20. Some physical educators argued that aggressive basketball could interfere with menstruation or injure reproductive organs; Anonymous, "Basketball for Girls," *Playground* 18 (Jan. 1925): 646; see also Alice W. Frymir, *Basket Ball for Women* (New York: A. S. Barnes, 1930), 23–26; Powell, "'Playing Fairly and Fiercely,'" 156–57.

21. DOI, Bureau of Education, *Course of Study for The Indian Schools*, (1901) 197–99; Bloom, *To Show What an Indian Can Do*, 82–83. K. Tsianina Lomawaima also stresses the racist logic the schools used to restrict and direct female physical activity in *They Called It Prairie Light* (Lincoln: University of Nebraska Press, 1995), 82.

22. Bloom, *To Show What an Indian Can Do*, 88–89.

23. On soccer, see Albuquerque Training School, 1934, Reel 2, SANSR; *Chiloccoan, 1935* (yearbook), Folder 2, Box 9, CISC, OKHS; Sally Hyer, *One House, One Voice, One Heart* (Santa Fe: Museum of New Mexico Press, 1990), 51. Chilocco did allow girls' interscholastic tennis during the 1930s, *Chiloccoan, 1931*, Folder 8, Box 8, CISC, OKHS. Bat and ball sports: Powers-Beck, *The American Integration of Baseball*, 33–34. Concho softball: *Oklahoma Indian School Magazine: Cheyenne—Arapaho Indian Boarding School, Concho Oklahoma* 2 (Feb. 1933): 18.

24. On track, *Arizona Republic*, Mar. 21, 1914, 2 (Phoenix); Fort Peck (MT), 1933, Reel 53, SANSR; Mote to Peters, Feb. 24, 1931, Folder 750, Amusements and Athletics, 1931–1937, Box 465, DCF, Bismarck Indian School (hereafter BIS), RG75, NARA, KC; Sarah K. Fields, "Representations of Sport in the Indian School Journal, 1906–1913," *Journal of Sports History* 35 (Summer 2008), 248; Hyer, *One House, One Voice, One Heart*, 51.

25. In their annual reports (SANSR) during the 1910 and 1920s, superintendents were far more likely to comment positively on basketball than on any other sports female students played.

26. Grundy and Shackelford, *Shattering the Glass*, 25–28.

27. Hough, "Physiological Effects of Basket Ball," in *Spalding's Official Basket Ball Guide for Women, 1916–17*, Abbott (New York: American Sports, 1916), 61–65.

28. *Indian Leader*, Jan. 3, 1903; McGregor to Rudolf Hertz, Apr. 22, 1927, Folder "Allison Grinnell," Box 109, Chemawa Indian School Individual Student Case Files, 1894–1957, CHEM, RG75, NARA, SEA; Hyer, *One House, One Voice, One Heart*, 51.

29. Santa Clara student quoted from Hyer, *One House, One Voice, One Heart*, 52; Bloom, *To Show What an Indian Can Do*, 86–87.

30. From Hyer, *First One Hundred Years*, May 28, 1986 as reprinted in Bloom, *To Show What an Indian Can Do*, 87.

31. *Indian Leader*, Mar. 14, 1919, 2, Dec. 26, 1919, 22, Mar. 11, 1921, 3. Also see *Indian Leader* Jan. 21, 1927, 6.

32. *Yankton Daily Dakotan*, Feb. 20, 1925, n.p.

33. Peavy and Smith, *Full-Court Quest*, 61 and 103; Grundy and Shackelford, *Shattering the Glass*, 22; Pruter, *The Rise of American High School Sports*, 148–56.

34. *Arizona Republic*, Apr. 16, 1906, 3; Peairs to Louise Pound, Feb. 19, 1903, bound ledger, Letters Sent by the Athletic Program, 1903–1912, HI, RG75, NARA, KC; Pruter, *The Rise of American High School Sports*, 149.

35. *Native American*, Feb. 1, 1908, 34; Fields, "Representations of Sport in the Indian School Journal," 248.

36. *Spalding's Official Basket Ball Guide for Women, 1916–17*, Abbott (New York: American Sports, 1916), 12–39.

37. Mote to Balmer, Feb. 13, 1931, Folder 754 "Basketball, 1932–37," Box 465, DCF, BIS, RG75, NARA, KC.

38. George interviewed by Whitesell, Dec. 1971, Southeastern Indian Oral History Project, Samuel Proctor Oral History Program, University of Florida, Digital Collections, http://ufdc.ufl.edu/UF00007219/00001?search=elsie+%3dblue+%3dgeorge.

39. Plank to Pond, Feb. 26, 1903, Letters Sent by the Athletic Program, HI, RG75, NARA, KC; Many male administrators at non-Indian schools also deemphasized women's basketball after 1900 to divert resources to the men: Cahn, *Coming on Strong* (Urbana: University of Illinois Press, 2015), 90.

40. Peters to Mote, Feb. 11, 1931, and Mote to Calhoun, Jan. 20, 1938, Folder 754 "Basketball, 1932–37," Box 465, DCF, BIS, RG75, NARA, KC; Mote to Peters, Feb. 24, 1931, Folder 750 "Amusements and Athletics, 1931–37," Box 465, DCF, BIS, RG75, NARA, KC; Report of Attendance, 1922, Box 467, DCF, BIS, RG75, NARA, KC. On Haskell girls' sports being less lucrative than boys', see Israelson, "The Haskell Indians," master's thesis, University of Nebraska, Lincoln, 1995, 58.

41. Makescry interviewed by Maker, May 10, 1969, Doris Duke Collection, Western History Collections, University of Oklahoma Libraries, Norman, OK, https://digital.libraries.ou.edu/cdm/compoundobject/collection/dorisduke/id/15054/rec/81.

42. Makescry interview.

43. Makescry interview.

44. *Chemawa American*, March 1914, 1.

45. Oxendine, *American Indian Sports Heritage*, 192–93 (Carlisle); Haskell athletics were also investigated by the Indian Office in 1909 and along with Albuquerque Indian School's program in 1931: Sculle, "The New Carlisle of the West," 197; Scattergood to Perry, Superintendent, July 15, 1931, Folder 750, "Amusements and Athletics, 1929–34," Box 34, GCF, 1917–36, AIS, RG75, NARA, DEN; Meriam et al., *The Problem of Indian Administration* (Washington, DC: Brookings Institution, 1928), 27.

46. Bloom, *To Show What an Indian Can Do*, 49–50 and 55–58.

47. *Indian Leader*, Mar. 26, 1915, 23; DOI, OIA, *Annual Report of the Commissioner of Indian Affairs, 1914* (Washington, DC: Government Printing Office, 1915), 189.

48. Haskell Institute, *Catalogue and Calendar of Haskell Institute, For the School September 4, 1923 to June 7, 1924* (Haskell Institute: Lawrence, 1924), 25 in Haskell, 1924, Reel 60, SANSR.

49. Schools with midget teams included Chemawa, Concho, Flandreau, Haskell, Rapid City, and Phoenix, *Chemawa American*, March 1916, 29, and April 1916, 4; *Native American*, July 1929, 202, Card 141, microfiche; Cheyenne and Arapahoe (Concho), 1932, Reel 15, SANSR; "Basket Ball Schedule for season of 1925–26," Folder 754 "Basketball," Box 26, DCF, 1903–1933, Rapid City Indian School (hereafter RCIS), RG75, NARA, KC.

50. *Topeka Daily Capital*, Mar. 18, 1902, 2 (Haskell); *Indian Leader*, Apr. 4, 1902, 3, Jan. 16, 1903, 2, Feb. 27, 1903, 2, Jan. 27, 1905, 3, Mar. 2, 1917, 1, Dec. 26, 1919, 22, and Feb. 27, 1920, 23.

51. *Indian Leader*, Mar. 7, 1930, 5; Charlotte Cooke to Girl's coach, Fulda, MI, Oct. 29, 1934, Folder 754, Box 123, DCF, 1916–1954, Flandreau Indian School (hereafter FIS), RG75, NARA, KC.

52. *Indian Leader*, Jan. 27, 1905, 3, and Feb. 27, 1920, 23.

53. *Indian Leader*, Jan. 21, 1916, 1.

54. Concho intramural team rosters and tournament brackets, 1928 (hereafter Concho intramural, 1928), Folder 750, "Athletics 1928–1932," Box 73, Central Files, 1926–1984, Cheyenne and Arapaho Indian Agency, RG75, NARA, Fort Worth, TX (hereafter FW); *Indian Leader*, Feb. 26, 1904, 3, and Apr. 2, 1920, 2; *Daily Capital Journal*, Dec. 17, 1897, 4; *Carlisle Arrow*, Jan. 19, 1912, 5, and Mar. 15, 1912, 3; *Native American* (Phoenix), Dec. 12, 1914, 561.

55. *Indian Leader*, Mar. 5, 1915, 1, and Mar. 12, 1915, 2.

56. Lomawaima discusses the importance and complexity of this student-driven social process in *They Called It Prairie Light*, 129–59.

57. On vocational identities, see Lomawaima, *They Called It Prairie Light*, 71 and 158; Vučković, *Voices from Haskell*, 119–21; Ellis, *To Change Them Forever*, 119 and 196.

58. *Indian Leader*, Jan. 14, 1910, 3.

59. *Indian Leader*, Nov. 13, 1903, 3, Dec. 23, 1903, 2, Dec. 1, 1905, 2 ("Wake up"), Apr. 6, 1906, 2. On students organizing shop baseball teams, Powers-Beck, *The American Indian Integration of Baseball*, 32.

60. *Native American*, Mar. 23, 1929, 100, Card 140, microfiche.

61. *Indian Leader*, Dec. 23, 1903, 2, Jan. 1, 1904, 2.

62. *Carlisle Arrow*, Mar. 8, 1912, 3; *Indian Leader*, Jan. 26, 1923, 8; Concho intramural, 1928.

63. *Red Man* (Carlisle), 2 (Jan. 1910): 31; *Chilocco Annual Senior Class Annual, 1924*, n.p., Folder 4, Box 8, CISC, OKHS; *Indian Leader*, Feb. 12, 1915, 1, Jan. 19, 1923, 4, Jan. 6, 1928, 6 (regarding Mt. Pleasant), and Mar. 6, 1931, 8; Concho intramural,

1928; Perry to CIA, Oct. 18, 1932, Folder 775 "Amusements and Athletics, Other Sports, 1928–1932," Box 34, GCF, AIS, RG75, NARA, DEN.

64. Ellis, *To Change Them Forever*, 116; Report of Attendance, 1928, Box 467, DCF, BIS, RG75, NARA, KC; Boys' team roster, Feb. 1, 1929, Folder 750, "Athletics 1928–1932," Box 73, Central Files, Cheyenne and Arapaho Indian Agency, RG75, NARA, FW (Concho); Record of Pupil, Ignacio Rocha File, Student Case Files, 1912–1980, CHIL, RG75, NARA, FW; *Wichita Beacon*, Jan. 11, 1913, 7.

65. *Indian Leader*, Feb. 2, 1923, 7, and Feb. 9, 1923, 8.

66. Haskell, 1924, Reel 60, SANSR; *Indian Leader*, Feb. 9, 1923, 8.

67. Bloom, *To Show What an Indian Can Do*, 91; Fields, "Representations of Sport," 248; *Indian Leader*, Dec. 31, 1915, 23.

68. *Chemawa American*, Dec. 1, 1926, 3, Mar. 9, 1927, 2, and Dec. 14, 1927, 2.

69. Bloom, *To Show What an Indian Can Do*, 91; Mote to Lawrence Zacharies, Nov. 26, 1932, Folder 754, "Basketball, 1932–1937," Box 465, DCF, BIS, RG75, NARA, KC.

70. *Chemawa American*, Dec. 23, 1910, 2; *Bismarck Tribune*, Feb. 7, 1935, 3.

71. Becker to Perry, Oct. 17, 1930, and Perry to Becker, Oct. 20, 1930, Folder 753, "Baseball, 1926–1930," Box 34, GCF, AIS, RG75, NARA, DEN.

72. *Chemawa American*, Dec. 15, 1926, 2; Concho intramural, 1928; *Oklahoma Indian School Magazine: Cheyenne—Arapaho Indian Boarding School, Concho Oklahoma* 2 (Feb. 1933): 18; Chilocco, 1932, Reel 18, SANSR; Carmody to R. M. Kelley, Feb. 8, 1938, Folder "Correspondence, 1939–1943," Box 113, DCF, 1917–1959, HI RG75, NARA, KC.

73. *Haskell Annual, 1924*, Haskell, Reel 60, SANSR; *Chiloccoan, 1932*, Folder 8, Box 8, CISC, OKHS.

74. 127 applications were surveyed from multiple folders, Boxes 1–2, Subject Files (education), 1928–32, Pawnee Indian Agency, RG75, NARA, FW.

75. Johnson to Kelley, Mar. 11, 1937, re: Haskell Questionnaire, 1936 (hereafter Haskell Questionnaire, 1936), Folder 820.5, Box 125, DCF, HI, RG75, NARA, KC; Israelson, "The Haskell Indians," 53–60.

76. Haskell Questionnaire, 1936; Schmidt, "Lords of the Prairie," *Journal of Sport History* 28 (Fall 2001): 420.

77. Ryan to Barnett, Sept. 17, 1934, Folder 750, "Athletics, 1928–1939," Box 25, DCF, 1924–1955, CHEM, RG75, NARA, SEA; Israelson, "The Haskell Indians," 22–23.

78. Albuquerque's superintendents served only in advisory capacities to the association: Athletic Association for the U.S. Indian Vocational School of Albuquerque, NM," Folder 758, Box, 34, GCF, AIS, RG75, NARA, DEN. By the early 1930s, the Indian Office was urging all Indian schools that did not have them to adopt the student activities association model: Indian Office Traveling Auditor O'Hara to Baumgarten, Jan. 5, 1932, Folder 754.5 (digital files courtesy of archives), DCF, 1926–1946, Mount Pleasant Indian School, RG75, NARA, Chicago. On other associations: Riney, *The Rapid City Indian School*, 121; *Indian Helper* (Carlisle), Apr. 8, 1892, 3; *Native American* (Phoenix) Sept. 9, 1900, Card 2, microfiche and Apr. 27, 1900, 3 (for Genoa); *Chemawa American*, November, 1912, 25; Concho Indian School

Athletic and Intellectual Association governing documents, 1928–1929, Folder 750, "Athletics 1928–1932," Box 73, DCF, Cheyenne and Arapaho Indian Agency, RG75, NARA, FW; Treasurer of Athletic Association to Lowe and Campbell Athletic Goods, Jan. 31, 1928, Folder 595, Box 71, DCF, 1926–1956, Pierre Indian School, RG75, NARA, KC.

79. Warner, "Athletics at the Carlisle Indian School," 11; Carlisle Indian Industrial School, *Catalogue and Synopsis of Courses, 1915* (Carlisle, PA: Carlisle Indian, 1915), 19.

80. Israelson, "The Haskell Indians," 22–23; Haskell Athletic Association Ledger, 1932, Folder "Student Activities Association," Box 219, Student Activities Association Ledger and Related Records, 1931–1934, HI, RG75, NARA, KC.

81. *Indian Leader*, Apr. 19, 1901, 3; *Spalding Trade Price List* catalog pages (basketball equipment) in Folder 232, A.G. Spaulding Co., 1917–22, Box 7, DCF, Pierre Indian School, RG75, NARA, KC; Farrell to Neddeau, Jan. 29, 1929 (officiating fees), Folder 750, "Athletics 1928–1932," Box 73, DCF, Cheyenne and Arapaho Indian Agency, RG75, NARA, FW; Allen to Peairs, Dec. 20, 1918, and Peairs to Speer, Dec. 24, 1918 (guarantees), Folder "Basketball, 1919," Box 2, SCF, 1904–1941, HI, RG75, NARA, KC; Upchurch to Severson, Feb. 10, 1927, and Stevens to McGregor, Oct. 22, 1928 (guarantees), Folder 754, Box 123, DCF, FIS, RG75, NARA, KC (guarantees); Flandreau, 1920 (equipment costs), Reel 41, SANSR; *Spalding's Official Baseball Guide, 1919* (New York: American Sports, 1919), catalog back matter (equipment costs).

82. Correll to CIA, July 16, 1934, Folder 750, Box 27, CCF, Chilocco, RG75, NARA, DC.

83. Birmingham to Bart (Quinn), Mar. 11, 1928, Folder 13, Box 15, National Catholic Interscholastic Basketball Tournament (hereafter NCIBT), University Archives, Loyola University of Chicago, IL (hereafter LUC); Haskell Athletic Association Ledger, 1932, Folder "Student Activities Association," Box 219, Student Activities Association Ledger and Related Records, HI, RG75, NARA, KC.

84. *Indian Leader*, Dec. 22, 1905, 2; Kirk to Bonnin, Jan. 8, 1930, in Cheyenne and Arapahoe, 1930, Reel 15, SANSR.

85. Downie to Jackson, July 17, 1937, Folder 754, "Basketball," Box 26, DCF, CHEM, RG75, NARA, SEA; bids for girls' basketball shoes, Folder 754, Box 123, DCF, FIS, RG75, NARA, KC; Mossman to Marshall-Wells, Aug. 5, 1931, Folder 750, Box 291, DCF, 1906–1959, Standing Rock Indian Agency, RG75, NARA KC; Perry to Jones, Oct. 5, 1932, Folder 752, Box 34, GCF, AIS, RG75, NARA, DEN (on athletic fund shortages).

86. Lomawaima, *They Called It Prairie Light*, 65–69; Child, *Boarding School Seasons*, 69–76.

87. *Native American*, Oct. 19, 1901, Card 9, microfiche and Dec. 8, 1906, 340; *Indian Leader*, Dec. 9, 1910, 5; *Chemawa American*, April, 1915, 29, and Jan. 19, 1927, 2.

88. *Chemawa American*, Oct. 1915, 20, and Jan. 1916, 25; Haskell, 1924, Reel 60, SANSR; *Indian Leader*, Dec. 17, 1915, 3, and Dec. 31, 1915, 23.

89. *Chemawa American*, Dec. 9, 1910, 5.

90. *Indian Leader*, Dec. 15, 1916, 3.

91. Peavy and Smith, *Full-Court Quest*, 237–41.

92. Entry for Feb. 8, 1910, Superintendent's Diary, 1909–1913, Tulalip Indian Agency, RG75, NARA, SEA; Memo to "All Employees," Dec. 23, 1927, Folder 758, Box 26, DCF, RCIS, RG75, NARA, KC.

93. Metoxen to CIA, Jan. 27, 1911, and Abbott to Metoxen, Feb. 11, 1911, Folder 750, Box 1, CCF, 1907–1939, Hampton Institute, RG75, NARA, DC.

94. Carlisle Indian Industrial School, *Catalogue and Synopsis of Courses, 1915*, 19; Metoxen to CIA; Dial to Leonard, Jan. 30, 1928, Folder 754, Box 121, DCF, 1917–1958, Fort Belknap Indian Agency, RG75, NARA, DEN.

95. *Indian Leader*, Mar. 26, 1915, 23; Jas. Ryan to "Persons in Charge," Dec. 7, 1931, Folder "Personnel, 1930–1932," Box 3, Correspondence of the Superintendent, 1909–1932, CHEM, RG75, NARA, SEA; *Chemawa American*, Mar. 6, 1914, 1, and Jan. 1916, 2–4 and 25.

96. Brophy to "Dear Students," Aug. 11, 1933, Folder 821, Box 123, DCF, FIS, RG75, NARA, KC.

97. Example of seeking congressional assistance: Beyer to Congressman Young, Dec. 18, 1923, Folder "Buildings, 1923," Box 28, SCF, Fort Totten Indian Agency, RG75, NARA, KC. In addition to student excavations for the Hiawatha Hall gymnasium cited below, Mount Pleasant student workers helped build athletic fields (though not a gymnasium) in 1930: Woodruff to Baumgarten, Nov. 25, 1930, and Baumgarten to Woodruff, Nov. 27, 1930, Folder 752.6 (digital files courtesy of archives), DCF, Mount Pleasant Indian School, RG75, NARA, Chicago.

98. Crow, 1916 and 1919, Reel 30, SANSR; Flandreau, 1914, Reel 41, SANSR; *Haskell Institute, U.S.A., 1884–1915*, 66–68, Folder 13, Box 2, Wallace Galluzzi Papers, 1926–1984, KSL; Haskell, 1915, Reel 59, SANSR; *Indian Leader*, Jan. 14, 1916, 3; Albuquerque's 1916 gymnasium cost just over $25,000: Albuquerque Indian School, 1916, Reel 2 SANSR; DOI, OIA, *Annual Report of the Commissioner of Indian Affairs, 1915*, 191 (Mount Pleasant).

99. Sullivan, "Education Through Sport," 126; Bellanger to Elliot, Nov. 10, 1939, Folder 750, "Athletics, FY 1939–1940," Box 129, CCF, 1891–1951, Phoenix Indian School, RG75, NARA, Los Angeles (Riverside), CA (hereafter LA); Lipps to CIA, May 31, 1930, and Rhodes to Lipps, Aug. 14, 1930, Folder 414.3, Box 15, DCF, CHEM, RG75, NARA, SEA; Fort Peck, 1928, Reel, 53, SANSR; "New Gymnasium," 1926, Cost Ledger, 1918–1933, CHIL, RG75, NARA, FW; Kappler, United States Senate, *Indian Affairs, Laws and Treaties, vol. 5* (Washington, DC: Government Printing Office, 1941), 159 (Pipestone); Thompson, "The Student Body," PhD diss., Arizona State University, Tempe, 2013, 222.

100. Lipps to CIA, May 31, 1930, Lipps to CIA, July 18, 1930, and Rhodes to Lipps, Aug. 14, 1930, Folder 414.3, Box 15, DCF, CHEM, RG75, NARA, SEA.

101. Rhodes to Lipps, Aug. 14, 1930, and photographs of gymnasium interior, Folder 414.3, Box 15, DCF, CHEM, RG75, NARA, SEA; Sheets 0327–0331, Folder "Sports," Box 3, Photographs, 1907–1971, CHEM, RG75, NARA, SEA.

Chapter 4. Bonding with Basketball

1. Rader, *American Sports*, 115; Pruter, *The Rise of American High School Sports*, 56–59.

2. *Indian Leader*, June 25, 1902, 22; 1937 tournament program, Folder 2, Box 6, NCIBT, LUC; Melissa D. Parkhurst, *To Win the Indian Heart* (Corvallis: Oregon State University Press, 2014), 12 and 71–76; *Chemawa American*, Mar. 1914, 1.

3. Entries for Dec. 17, 1910, and Feb. 10, 1912, Superintendent's Diary, 1909–1913, Tulalip Indian Agency, RG75, NARA, SEA; *Native American*, Jan. 31, 1914, 62 (Leupp).

4. Parkhurst, *To Win the Indian Heart*, 74–75; Plank to Philip Eastman, Feb. 9, 1903, bound volume, Letters Sent by the Athletic Program, HI, RG75, NARA, KC.

5. *Chemawa American*, Feb. 9, 1927, 2 ("yelling"); *Sandusky Star-Journal*, Mar. 23, 1904, 7 ("sea of faces"); *Indian Leader*, Feb. 16, 1906, 2 (report from Chilocco); Jan. 5, 1923, 4 ("like fiends"); Jan. 22, 1926, 130 ("frenzy"); and Jan. 14, 1927, 6 ("rafters").

6. Picotte, interview by author, Chamberlain, SD, July 17, 2016.

7. Bloom, *To Show What an Indian Can Do*, 58–59; Sullivan, "Federal Indian Boarding Schools in New Mexico," in Salamone, ed., *The Native American Identity in Sports*, 68–70; *Indian Leader*, Mar. 13, 1908, 3, and Jan. 11, 1924, 2; Perry, Chilocco Indian School Questionnaire, Folder 4, Box 18, CISC, OKHS; Knight to Allen, Oct. 1, 1914, Frank Knight File, Student Case Files, CHIL, RG75, NARA, FW; Perry to Kyceroa, Nov. 9, 1931, Folder 752.2, Box 34, GCF, AIS, RG75, NARA, DEN.

8. Setter to Peairs, May 17, 1917, Mamie Setter File, Box 106, Student Case Files, 1884–1980, HI, RG75, NARA, KC; *Indian Leader*, Jan. 9, 1903, 3.

9. Myriam Vučković, *Voices from Haskell*, 84; Lomawaima, *They Called It Prairie Light*, 167.

10. On solidarity and school loyalty, see Sullivan, "Federal Indian Boarding Schools in New Mexico," 65–67. Shows of school spirit surrounding athletics were not confined to the off-reservation schools. See, for example, Ellis, *To Change Them Forever*, 125–26.

11. *Indian Leader*, Mar. 2, 1900, 2.

12. Wilson's report in DOI, OIA, *Annual Report of the Commissioner of Indian Affairs, Part I* (Washington, DC: Government Printing Office, 1904), 236; Adams, *Education for Extinction*, 66 (funding).

13. Frachtenberg, "The Value of School Athletics," *Chemawa American*, April, 1916, 1–3.

14. Digmann to Lusk, Jan. 21, 1924, frame 706, correspondence roll 118, series 1, Bureau of Catholic Indian Missions Records, microfilm, Special Collections and Archives, Marquette University, Milwaukee, WI (hereafter BCIM).

15. Stevens to Arnold Homes, Dec. 27, 1932, and Stevens to B.C. Tighe, Nov. 19, 1932, Folder 754, Box 8, DCF, 1923–1967, Wahpeton Indian School, RG75, NARA, KC.

16. Cahill, *Federal Fathers and Mothers*, 138–42; *Indian Leader*, Jan. 13, 1928, 6–7 (regarding Rapid City Indian School); *Lawrence Journal World*, Mar. 1, 1900, 4; *Indian School Journal* (Chilocco) 15 (December 1914): 218; *Albuquerque Journal*, Feb. 12, 1928, 2 (regarding Albuquerque Indian School).

17. James Arentson of Charles H. Burke School to C. M. Blair, Feb. 13, 1934, Folder 752, Box 34, GCF, AIS, RG75, NARA, DEN; R. L. Spalsbury of Pierre Indian School to Mote, Feb. 9, 1931, Folder 754, Box 465, DCF, BIS, RG75, NARA, KC.

18. Peairs to Wells, Jan. 3, 1918, and other letters scheduling games, Folder "Basketball," Box 2, SCF, HI, RG75, NARA, KC; *Indian Leader*, Mar. 25, 1921, 23; Israelson, "The Haskell Indians," 55–58.

19. Mossman to "Dear Friends in Crime," Apr. 21, 1932, Standing Rock Indian Agency, in author's possession courtesy of Richmond Clow.

20. Bloom, *To Show What an Indian Can Do*, 98; Coleman, *American Indian Children at School, 1850–1930* (Jackson: University Press of Mississippi, 1993), 91–92; Ellis, *To Change Them Forever*, 125; Littlefield, "The BIA Boarding School," *Humanity and Society* 13, no. 4 (1989): 438; Oxendine, *American Indian Sports Heritage*, 178; Riney, *The Rapid City Indian School*, 113; Sullivan, "Education Through Sport," 103; Robert A. Trennert, Jr., *The Phoenix Indian School, 1891–1935* (Norman: University of Oklahoma Press, 1988), 131.

21. Cheadle, Chilocco Indian School Questionnaire, Folder 3, Box 18, CISC, OKHS; Resume and "summary of accomplishments," Folder "Biography of Buck Cheadle," Box 19, CISC, OKHS.

22. Lucille Winnie, *Sah-Gan-De-Oh* (New York: Vantage, 1969), 13–20, 44, 53, and 57.

23. Irene Stewart, edited by Doris Ostrander Dawdy, *A Voice in Her Tribe* (Socorro, NM: Ballena, 1980), 11–30.

24. Peterson Zah and Peter Iverson, *We Will Secure Our Future* (Tucson: University of Arizona Press, 2012), 38–39.

25. Beane, telephone interview by author, Jan. 4, 2018.

26. Beane interview.

27. Bloom, *To Show What an Indian Can Do*, xxi.

28. Beane interview.

29. Keeley, "Basket Ball in Indian Schools," in *Spalding's Official Basket Ball Guide, 1916–17* (New York: American Sports, 1916), 111–13.

30. Gibney, Supervisor of Playgrounds NYC, "Basketball in Recreation Centers," in *Spalding's Official Basket Ball Guide, 1916–17*, 55; Peairs' report, *Annual Report*, 1904, 419; Bentley, "Report of An Enquiry Into the Status of Athletics and Physical Education At Haskell Institute," July 16–18, 1931, Folder 750, Box 45, CCF, HI, RG75, NARA, DC. Peairs and Wilson also stressed sports as tools of discipline: Peairs report, in DOI, OIA, *Annual Report of the Commissioner of Indian Affairs, Part I* (Washington, DC: Government Printing Office, 1902), 539; Wilson, *Annual Report*, 1904, 236; Kirk to Bonnin, July 20, 1931, in Cheyenne and Arapahoe, Reel 15, SANSR.

31. Haskell, 1914 and 1915, Reel 59, SANSR 1914 and 1915; Howard, Associate Supervisor of Education, DOI, address to Seneca Indian School, 1943, 49–50, Folder 4, Box 1, Seneca Indian School Collection, 1931–2005, OKHS.

32. *Indian Leader*, Feb. 2, 1900, 3; Wilson, *Annual Report*, 1904, 236; Cantonment

School (Cheyenne and Arapaho), 1920, Reel 8, SANSR; Perry to CIA, Oct. 18, 1932, Folder 775, "Amusements and Athletics, Other Sports, 1928–1932," Box 34, GCF, AIS, RG75, NARA, DEN.

33. Bonnin to Dias, Jan. 10, 1929, Folder 750, Box 73, Central Files, Cheyenne and Arapaho Agency, RG75, NARA, FW. See also Haskell, 1915, Reel 59, SANSR and Kirk report in Cheyenne and Arapaho, 1932, Reel 15, SANSR; and "Report of the Superintendent of Oglala Boarding School," *Annual Report*, 1904, 311.

34. *Indian Leader*, Aug. 23, 1901, 4.

35. Wright, "Athletics," *The Chilocco Senior Class Annual, 1919*, 39–40, Folder 2, Box 8, CISC, OKHS.

36. Holm, *The Great Confusion in Indian Affairs*, 50–84; LaPier and Beck, *City Indian* (Lincoln: University of Nebraska Press, 2015), 43.

37. Specific student names are intentionally omitted in this section. These broad conclusions are based on a select survey of 150 student files (found in NARA regional branches and online from Dickinson College) for varsity basketball players at the Albuquerque, Carlisle, Chemawa, Chilocco, Flandreau, and Haskell Indian schools. Their academic performance was tracked using annual grade cards and instances of disciplinary action noted in their files. Athletes ranged in academic performance from well above to well below average (with a C grade as average) and made up no consistent groupings along this grade spectrum. Separate disciplinary records from Albuquerque, Chemawa, and Haskell were also consulted. Instances of disciplinary action against students were cross-checked with basketball team rosters. Players were as well represented there as they were in the student population overall.

38. Crow, 1914, Reel 30, SANSR; Fort Apache, 1914, Reel 43, SANSR; Crow Creek (SD), 1916, Reel 31, SANSR; Greenville School, 1921, Reel 59, SANSR; Chilocco School, 1921, Reel 18, SANSR; Fort Peck, 1928, Reel 53, SANSR; Cheyenne and Arapahoe, 1929, Reel, 15, SANSR; Charles H. Burke School (Fort Wingate), 1930, Reel 11, SANSR; E.E. Morris to Correll, Mar. 6, 1939, Folder "Minutes of Employees Meetings, 1937–1939," Box 1, Records Relating to Personnel, CHIL, RG75, NARA, FW. Riney notes the problem that schools had supervising school grounds because of imbalanced student-to-staff ratios in *The Rapid City Indian School*, 145.

39. Adam Fortunate Eagle, *Pipestone* (Norman: University of Oklahoma Press, 2010), 15; Lomawaima, *They Called It Prairie Light*, 130–32. Also see Curtis A. Kachur, "The Freedom and Privacy of an Indian Boarding School's Sports Field and Student Athletes' Resistance to Assimilation," master's thesis, Bowling Green State University, OH, 2017.

40. *Chemawa American*, Feb. 1915, 36–38.

41. Dial to Clark, Nov. 26, 1930, Folder 754, Box 121, DCF, Fort Belknap Agency, RG75, NARA, DEN.

42. Moss, interviewed by Kahin and Wiles, spring 1992, Warm Valley Historical Project, University of Wyoming, American Heritage Center.

43. Lomawaima, *They Called It Prairie Light*, 52–56; Stella Carter, Chilocco Indian School Questionnaire, Folder 3, Box 18, CISC, OKHS.

44. Report of Staff Meeting, Nov. 3, 1937, Folder "Minutes of Employees

Meetings, 1937–1939," Box 1, Records Relating to Personnel, CHIL, RG75, NARA, FW.

45. "Note's on Employees' Meeting," Jan. 17, 1940, Folder "Employees Meetings, 1939–1941," Box 1, Records Relating to Personnel, CHIL, RG75, NARA, FW.

46. See McGregor to Bent, Sept. 21, 1926 (student file left anonymous), Box 10, Graduated Student Case Files, 1900–1962, CHEM, RG75, NARA, SEA; Principal to Bonnin, Feb. 23, 1928, Folder 754, Box 73, Central Files, Cheyenne and Arapaho Agency, RG75, NARA, FW; Perry to Harrington, Sept. 12, 1927, (student file left anonymous), Box 172, Student Case Files, 1886–1964, AIS, RG75, NARA, DEN (concrete mixer).

47. Not only did I come across no examples of desertion and scant examples of disciplinary actions in the female athletes' student files, but their names also did not appear on lists of expelled students including other female students, such as Jas. T. Ryan to CIA, July 15, 1932, Folder 824, "Incorrigible Students, 1931–1947," Box 38, DCF, CHEM, RG75, NARA, SEA.

48. Correll response to report on student, Oct. 9, 1908, (student file left anonymous), Student Case Files, CHIL, RG75, NARA, FW.

49. See, for example, Allen for Knight, Sept. 10, 1914, Frank Knight File, Student Case Files, CHIL, RG75, NARA, FW; Correll to Wilson, Mar. 17, 1930, Wilson File, Student Case Files, CHIL, RG75, NARA, FW; and Jackson for Van Pelt, Oct. 31, 1942, Van Pelt File, Box 35, Graduated Student Case Files, RG75, CHEM, NARA, SEA.

50. Scott Morro Johnson, *Phog* (Lincoln: University of Nebraska Press, 2016), 40–42.

51. DOI, OIA, *Rules for the Indian Service, 1900*, heading 89; Riney, *The Rapid City Indian School*, 176; Peairs to CIA, Sept. 6, 1902, v. 2 May 1902–July 1903, Box 144, Correspondence of the Superintendents, 1890–1942, HI, RG75, NARA, KC; Peairs letter of reference for Bent, Oct. 26, 1918, Bent File 3 of 3, Box 10, Student Case Files, HI, RG75, NARA, KC; "Report of the Superintendent of Oglala Boarding School," *Annual Report*, 1904, 311; Flandreau, 1915, Reel 41, SANSR; Davis of Genoa to Mote, Mar. 1, 1928, Folder 754.6, Box 26, DCF, RCIS, RG75, NARA, KC; "Boy's Adviser Pierre Indian School, Conception of Duties" and "Activity List-Boys Advisers Duties, Compiled at Santa Fe and Haskell Institutes," Folder 162.8, Box 48, DCF, Pierre Indian School, RG75, NARA, KC; "Constitution of the Athletic Association," *Chemawa American*, Jan. 1916, 3.

52. Cahill's figures for 1905 show that a little over one-third of Indian Service disciplinarians were American Indian; Cahill, *Federal Fathers and Mothers*, 110. The large number of Native athletic staff members who were also disciplinarians suggests this percentage may have increased after 1905: *Indian Leader*, Dec. 24, 1926, 14 (regarding Levi at Chilocco); Charles to Whitlock, Apr. 8, 1927, Folder 750, Box 74, DCF, Pierre Indian School, RG75, NARA, KC; McClean to Peairs, Feb. 25, 1925, Samuel McLean File, Box 75, Student Case Files, HI, RG75, NARA, KC; other examples see: *Indian Leader*, June 6, 1919, 41; Yellowrobe to Crandall, Feb. 28, 1922, Folder, "Chauncey Yellow Robe, 1921–1922," Box 20, Superintendent's Correspondence, 1917–1926, Pierre Indian School, RG75, NARA, KC.

53. Other reasons for hiring former students, see: Cahill, *Federal Fathers and Mothers*, 2, 7, 51–52, and 105–6; Ellis, *To Change Them Forever*, 47.

54. Blair to Perry, Feb. 2, 1928, Richard Milda Student File, Box 123, Student Case Files, AIS, RG75, NARA, DEN.

55. Cahill, *Federal Fathers and Mothers*, 104–35.

56. Record of Employees, 1883–1924, v. 1, 34, CHEM, RG75, NARA, SEA; May, 1901 roster, Folder, "List of Positions and Salaries," Box 1, Records Relating to Personnel, CHIL, RG75, NARA, FW; Bent to Peairs, Feb. 20, 1909, and Bent to Peairs, Aug. 31, 1920, Bent File 3 of 3, Student Case Files, HI, RG75, NARA, KC; *Lawrence Daily Journal*, June 17, 1897, 4; *Indian Leader*, Dec. 6, 1907, 3; *Topeka Daily Capital*, Mar. 27, 1910, 5; *Oregon Statesman*, Jan. 3, 1919, 8; Jan. 4, 1919, 10; Aug. 7, 1921, 7; and Dec. 26, 1943, 2 (obit).

57. *Lawrence Daily Journal*, June 28, 1899, 4; Bent to Hall, n.d., 1925, and Bent to Ryan, Dec. 15, no year, and Hall to Coe, Aug. 21, 1925 (student file left anonymous), Box 60, Individual Student Case Files, CHEM, RG75, NARA, SEA; Bent to McGregor, Jan. 26, 1927, (student file left anonymous), Box 1, Graduated Student Case Files, CHEM, RG75, NARA, SEA; Bent to Lipps, July 5, 1928, Folder 824, Box 38, DCF, CHEM, RG75, NARA, SEA.

58. Nelson to Hall, Mar. 22, 1922, and Bent to Nelson, Mar. 24, 1922, Folder "Athletics 1922," Box 3, Corr. of the Superintendent, CHEM, RG75, NARA, SEA.

59. *Chemawa American*, March, 1914, 8, and June, 1914, 6–7; Bent to Downie, n.d. Folder, "Games—Mount Angel, 1920," Box 2, Corr. of the Superintendent, CHEM, RG75, NARA, SEA; White to Bent, n.d., Folder 750, "Athletics, 1928–1939," Box 25, DCF, CHEM, RG75, NARA, SEA; Susan Applegate Krouse, *North American Indians in the Great War* (Lincoln: University of Nebraska Press, 2007), 103 and 195; *Daily Capital Journal*, June 21, 1943, 5.

60. Downie to B. J. Brophy, Dec. 18, 1934, (student file left anonymous), Student Case Files, 1924–1957, FIS, RG75, NARA, KC.

61. McGregor to Bent, Sept. 21, 1926 (student file left anonymous), Box 10, Graduated Student Case Files, CHEM, RG75, NARA, SEA.

62. Anonymous, "Why the Boarding School Fails," *Indian Education* 3 (October 15, 1936): 6–8; Letter to the editor by Reginald G. Downie, *Indian Education* 8 (February 15, 1937): 4. David J. Laliberte has also emphasized the role Native baseball coaches may have played in insulating Pipestone's athletes from assimilation policy in "Natives, Neighbors, and the National Game," *Minnesota History* 62 (Summer 2010): 65–66.

63. Riney, *Rapid City Indian School*, 143; Beane interview.

64. I arrived at this figure by consulting scores of newspaper and archival sources, including cross-checking athletic staff names with student and employee records.

65. Cahill cautions, however, that few students accepted Indian Service employees as being actual surrogate parents in *Federal Fathers and Mothers*, 79–80.

66. Picotte interview; "Bob Clifford," South Dakota Sports Hall of Fame site http://www.sdshof.com/inductees/clifford-bob/.

67. Oxendine, *American Indian Sports Heritage*, 214; Adams, *Education for Extinction*, 114–15 and 324; Powers-Beck, *The American Indian Integration of Baseball*, 42.

68. Plank to Herrnstein, Mar. 7, 1903, bound volume, Letters Sent by the Athletic Program, HI, RG75, NARA, KC.

69. Winnie, *Sah-Gan-De-Oh*, 50; *Lawrence Daily World*, Dec. 10, 1901, 3.

70. Hall to Thayer, March 6, 1905, Book 3, Box 57, Records of the Superintendent, Letters Sent, 1902–1948, Sherman Institute, NARA, LA; on Hall's role at Sherman, see various articles in Clifford E. Trafzer et al., eds., *The Indian School on Magnolia Avenue*.

71. *Indian Helper*, Jan. 15, 1897, 2; *Indian Leader*, March 1898, 2; Mar. 23, 1900, 3; Oct. 19, 1900, 2; Mar. 8, 1901, 3; and Feb. 6, 1903, 3; *Chemawa American*, Mar. 1916, 33, and Mar. 23, 1927, 2; Chemawa menu, 1927, Folder 752, Box 74, DCF, Pierre Indian School, RG75, NARA, KC.

72. *Indian Leader*, Mar. 29, 1901, 2, Jan. 12, 1906, 2, Mar. 1, 1918, 2, and June 3–17, 1921, 16. *Indian Leader*, Mar. 15, 1929, 7 (regarding Concho and Fort Sill).

73. Ellis, *To Change Them Forever*, 103–4; Lomawaima, *They Called It Prairie Light*, 131–33; Vučković, *Voices from Haskell*, 143–45.

74. Bloom's interviews with former Flandreau students provide exceptions to the rule that the genders sat separately, *To Show What an Indian Can Do*, 95; Chemawa student guidelines, 1937, Nellie Walters File, Individual Student Case Files, CHEM, RG75, NARA, SEA.

75. Bloom, *To Show What an Indian Can Do*, 94; Eve Ball et al., *Indeh* (Norman: University of Oklahoma Press, 1988), 147.

76. Girls' Adviser, L. Bissel report, n.d., Folder 824, Box 38, DCF, CHEM, RG75, NARA, SEA.

77. On the commonly held notion in physical education that sports relieved sexual energy, see Rader, *American Sports*, 115. Also see: Morris to Correll, "Some Situations and Conditions," Mar. 6, 1939, Folder "Minutes of Employees Meetings, 1937–1939," Box 1, Records Relating to Personnel, CHIL, RG75, NARA, FW.

78. *Oregon Daily Journal* (Portland), Mar. 12, 1916, sec. 2–4; *Statesman Journal* (Salem), Aug. 10, 1920, 5; *Chemawa American*, Dec. 15, 1926, 2, and Mar. 2, 1927, 2; *Daily Capital Journal*, June 21, 1943, 5.

79. See, for example: Barr, "'Looking Backward': The Life and Legend of Louis Francis Sockalexis," in King, ed., *Native Athletes in Sport and Society*, 27–33; Oxendine, *American Indian Sports Heritage*, 233–34.

80. Powers-Beck points out that the nickname "Chief" was not always meant respectfully, as it could be used to demean Native players and put them "in their place." "'Chief,'" *American Indian Quarterly* 25 (Autumn 2001): 510–11. *Chilocco Senior Class Annual*, 1923, Folder 3, Box 8, CISC, OKHS; *Haskell Annual, 1924*, in Haskell, 1924, Reel, 60, SANSR; Frank W. McDonald, *John Levi of Haskell*, 13 and 87; *Indian Leader*, Mar. 4, 1927, 7.

81. Sullivan, "Education through Sport," PhD dissertation, University of New Mexico, Albuquerque, 2004, 105–8.

82. McDonald, *John Levi of Haskell*, 12–13

83. Lomawaima, *They Called It Prairie Light*, 147. Also on sports and self-esteem, Alice Littlefield, "The BIA Boarding School," *Humanity and Society* 13, no. 4 (1989): 438.

Chapter 5. The World Outside

1. Carlisle Indian Industrial School, *Catalogue and Synopsis of Courses, 1915*, 19.

2. On the difficulties and contradictions involved in using sports to change public perceptions of Native students, also see Bloom, *To Show What an Indian Can Do*, 65.

3. On Fort Shaw's enthusiasm for basketball travel, see Peavy and Smith, "World Champions," 5, and *Full-Court Quest*, 281. On St. Francis's excitement about Chicago, see Davies and Clow, "The St. Francis Mission Indians and the National Interscholastic Catholic Basketball Tournament, 1924–1941," *International Journal of the History of Sport* 23: 219. Arnold Headley (Arapaho) cited travel as the primary perk of playing varsity sports at Haskell in an interview by Kahin, April 14, 1991, Warm Valley Historical Project, University of Wyoming, American Heritage Center. On Wild West show participants seeking adventure, see Moses, *Wild West Shows and the Images of American Indians, 1883–1933* (Albuquerque: University of New Mexico Press, 1996), 44–45.

4. Keeley, "Basket Ball in Indian Schools," 111–13. For examples of other Indian school administrators expressing similar views see Allender to Ziebach, Feb. 7, 1928, Folder 750, Box 26, RCIS, RG75, NARA, KC, and Davies and Clow, "The St. Francis Mission Indians and the National Interscholastic Catholic Basketball Tournament," 214.

5. On lodging, see endnote 9; article from *William Jewell Student* reprinted in *Indian Leader*, Mar. 14, 1902, 4.

6. Warner, "Athletics at the Carlisle Indian School," 11; Bonnin to Dias, Jan. 10, 1929, Folder 750, "Athletics 1928–1932," Box 3, Central Files, Cheyenne and Arapaho Agency, RG75, NARA, FW.

7. Presaging what would occur with interscholastic basketball, however, the outing programs proved less effective at advancing stated aims than they did at catering to outside economic interest. See Adams, *Education for Extinction*, 156–63, and Trennert, *The Phoenix Indian School* 20, 72–73, 92, and 100–101.

8. Mote to CIA, Jan. 15, 1931, Folder 850, Box 468, DCF, BIS, RG75, NARA, KC; Blair to Correll, Dec. 9, 1933, Folder 752, Box 34, GCF, AIS, RG75, NARA, DEN; Entry for Mar. 16, 1910, Superintendent's Diary, Tulalip Indian Agency, RG75, NARA, SEA; *Jeffersonian Gazette* (Lawrence), Feb. 20, 1907, 7.

9. Colleges: *Evening Kansan-Republican* (Newton), Jan. 8, 1913, 5 (regarding Chilocco); Allen to Peairs, Dec. 20, 1918, and Peairs to Schabinger of Ottawa University, Feb. 19, 1919, Folder "Basketball," Box 2, SCF, HI, RG75, NARA, KC; Martindale to Harrington High School, Dec. 31, 1921, and Marr to Martindale, Jan. 31, 1922, Folder 754, Box 116, SCF, HI, RG75, NARA, KC; Faris of Santa Fe Indian School to Blair, Mar. 7, 1934, Folder 752, and Perry to Dale of Charles H. Burke,

Nov. 13, 1931, Folder 752.2, Box 34, GCF, AIS, RG75, NARA, DEN; Stevens to Arnold Strand of Mayville, Oct. 29, 1935, Folder 754, Box 8, DCF, Wahpeton Indian School, RG75, NARA, KC. High Schools: *Indian Leader,* Mar. 4, 1921, 3; Kirk to Bonnin, Jan. 8, 1930, in Cheyenne and Arapahoe, Reel 15, SANSR; Rodewald to Mote, Nov. 30, 1933 and Carter to Rodewald, Jan. 15, 1934, Folder 754, Box 465, DCF, BIS, RG75, NARA, KC.

10. *Albany Democrat* (OR), Feb. 27, 1903, 5; *Indian Leader*, Mar. 15, 1901, 2, Mar. 20, 1903, 2, and Mar. 24, 1905, 2; *Chemawa American* Mar. 2, 1927, 2.

11. *Indian Leader*, Mar. 15, 1901, 2.

12. *Indian Leader*, Mar. 6, 1903, 3, Feb. 21, 1919, 2, and Feb. 25, 1921, 3; Peairs to Pound, Feb. 19, 1903, bound volume, Letters Sent by the Athletic Program, Box 192, HI, RG75, NARA KC; Stevens to Mote, Apr. 10, 1931, and Mote to Livesay, Mar. 7, 1933, Folder 750, Box 465, DCF, BIS, RG75, NARA, KC.

13. See chapter seven on the Fort Shaw players' attitudes about the 1904 St. Louis World's Fair trip.

14. *Indian Leader*, Mar. 29, 1907, 2; *Chemawa American*, Dec. 8, 1926, 2; Arentson to Blair, Mar. 6, 1934, Folder 752, Box 34, GCF, AIS, RG75, NARA, DEN.

15. *Indian Leader*, Mar. 29, 1907, 2.

16. *Statesman Journal*, Jan. 10, 1930, 10; *Indian Leader*, Mar. 2, 1928, 6; McLean to Whitlock, Mar. 14, 1929, Folder 754, Box 74, DCF, Pierre Indian School, RG75, NARA, KC.

17. *Miami Daily News-Record* (OK), Jan. 29, 1937, 1; *Emporia Gazette*, Jan. 29, 1937, 7; *Star Tribune* (Minneapolis), Jan. 30, 1937, 21; *Hutchinson News* (KS), Jan. 8, 1938, 2; *Sedalia Democrat*, Jan. 14, 1938, 6; *Miami Daily News-Record*, Jan. 18, 1938, 5; *Iola Register* (KS), Jan. 19, 1918, 6. Also see Lomawaima, *They Called It Prairie Light*, 55–56.

18. Peairs to Allen, Dec. 28, 1918, Folder "Basketball, 1919," Box 2, SCF, HI, RG75, NARA, KC; Dial to Minnehan, Dec. 19, 1930, Folder "Playground and Athletics," Box 1, Health, Education and Welfare General Correspondence, 1908–1948, Fort Belknap Agency, RG75, NARA, DEN.

19. *Chilocco Weekly Journal*, Dec. 14, 1905, 3; Warner, "Athletics at the Carlisle Indian School," 9–15; Weyand, *The Cavalcade of Basketball*, 51.

20. *Chilocco Weekly Journal*, Dec. 14, 1905, 3. Haskell's 1908 trip included games versus the Kansas City Athletic Club, Chicago University, Indiana University, the New Albany, Indiana YMCA, the independent Krebs and Central High School in Hamilton, Ohio, and the Carlisle Indians in Pennsylvania: *Lawrence Daily World*, Jan. 12, 1906, 1; *Omaha Daily Bee* (NE), Feb. 2, 1908, 27; *Courier-Journal* (Louisville, KY), Mar. 8, 1908, 32 and Mar. 11, 1908, 6; *Journal News* (Hamilton, OH), Jan. 20, 1908, 6, and Mar. 5, 1908, 7.

21. Bonnin to Dias, Jan. 10, 1929; Kirk to Bonnin, Jan. 8, 1930.

22. Peairs to French, Mar. 4, 1921, and Peairs to Mary Rease, Jan. 23, 1924, Folder 754, "Corr. 1921–1924," Box 116, SCF, HI, RG75, NARA, KC; *Lawrence Daily Journal-World*, Jan. 4, 1918, 1; Israelson, "The Haskell Indians," 54–59; Grundy and Shackelford, *Shattering the Glass*, 47; Cahn, *Coming on Strong*, 89–90.

23. There is no centralized source for determining team schedules year to year for every Indian school. These conclusions are based on a compilation of data drawn from such sources as the *Indian Leader*, *Chemawa American*, *Native American* (Phoenix), *Indian School Journal* (Chilocco), *Spalding's* guides, various school yearbooks, superintendents' annual reports, archived correspondence, and municipal newspaper articles.

24. Mote to S.A.M. Young, Feb. 24, 1931, Folder 750, Box 465, DCF, BIS, RG75, NARA, KC.

25. *Indian Leader*, Feb. 9, 1900, 3, Mar. 2, 1900, 2, Mar. 14, 1902, 2, and Mar. 18, 1904, 2; Peavy and Smith, "World Champions," 12; *Great Falls Daily Tribune*, Jan. 30, 1903, 8, and Jan 31, 1903, 8.

26. *Eugene Guard* (OR), Feb. 9, 1907, 2 (regarding Chemawa); *Native American*, Jan. 30, 1904, 29 (Phoenix); *Winfield Daily Free Press* (KS), Dec. 19, 1910, 2 (Chilocco); *Indian Leader*, Jan. 20, 1928, 7 (Haskell); *Albuquerque Journal*, Apr. 1, 1928, 2 (Albuquerque). Many authors have cited non-Natives' interest in Indian school football and baseball teams, including Laliberte, "Natives, Neighbors, and the National Pastime," 60–69, and Raymond Schmidt, "Lords of the Prairie," 403–26.

27. *Great Falls Daily Tribune*, Jan. 31, 1903, 8; *Indian Leader*, Feb. 6, 1903, 2, and Feb. 8, 1907, 2; *Daily Deadwood Pioneer-Times* (SD), Mar. 12, 1905, 6. White fans commonly rooted for Indian school football teams as well: Adams, "More than a Game," 38.

28. Examples of newspaper articles highlighting Indian school teams as local favorites: *Albuquerque Journal*, Feb. 25, 1928, 2 (regarding Albuquerque); *Bismarck Tribune*, Feb. 7, 1935, 3 (Bismarck); *Carlisle Evening Herald* (PA), Dec. 20, 1915, 8 (Carlisle); *Statesman Journal*, Dec. 23, 1916, 2, and Mar. 7, 1933, 6 (Chemawa); *Lawrence Journal World*, Mar. 21, 1901 4 (Haskell); *Arizona Republic*, Oct. 14, 1916, 8, and Jan. 21, 1923, 6 (Phoenix); *Arizona Daily Star* (Tucson), Dec. 11, 1926, 4 (Tucson Indian School).

29. *Albuquerque Citizen*, Dec. 31, 1902, 5, and Jan. 12, 1903, 5.

30. Davies, "'We Are Looking for a Splendid Tournament Here,'" *South Dakota History* 41 (Summer 2001): 215–16 (regarding support from Rapid City); *Albuquerque Journal*, Mar. 15, 1928, 2, and Mar. 29, 1928, 2 (support from Albuquerque).

31. Trennert, *Phoenix Indian School*, 79–81; Parkhurst, *To Win the Indian Heart*, 241–42; John W. Troutman, *Indian Blues* (Norman: University of Oklahoma Press, 2009), 120–21. Early in the century, Chemawa invited Salem residents to stay after games for socials, with refreshments: *Daily Capital Journal*, Mar. 20, 1903, 1.

32. *Indian Leader*, Mar. 15, 1901, 3, Apr. 25, 1902, 4, and Mar. 26, 1915, 23; Haskell 1914 and 1916, Reel 59, SANSR; *Indian Leader*, Apr. 1, 1921, 1 (regarding Flandreau); *Native American*, Feb. 1, 1908, 34 (Phoenix); Reception Committee team reports, 1925, Folder 4, Box 2, NCIBT, LUC (St. Francis); Turner to Paul Jackson, Jan. 12, 1938, Folder 754, Box 26, DCF, CHEM, RG75, NARA SEA (Chemawa).

33. *Indian Leader*, Mar. 24, 1905, 2.

34. *Salina Evening Journal* (KS), Feb. 12, 1915, 7.

35. Sullivan emphasizes Indian school sports' power to facilitate cultural exchange and ease "the Americanization process" in "Education through Sport," 115.

36. Peairs to Olney, Apr. 2, 1919, Folder "Basketball, 1919," Box 2, SCF, HI, RG75, NARA KC; Lawrence High School was still playing home games at Haskell in 1922: Evelyn Pierce to Robert L. Henderson, Mar. 22, 1922, Folder 754, "Corr. 1921–1924," Box 116, SCF, HI, RG75, NARA, KC. On Pipestone, Minnesota, and other towns similarly promoting local Indian school baseball for their own purposes, see Laliberte, "Natives, Neighbors, and the National Pastime," 60–69.

37. On developments in sports journalism more generally, see Michael Oriard, *Reading Football* (Chapel Hill: University of North Carolina Press, 1993), 58–60; Rader, *American Sports*, 23, 97, and 121–22; Riess, *Sport in Industrial America*, 29–33.

38. Examples include, *Chicago Daily Tribune*, Mar. 2, 1907, 6; *Philadelphia Inquirer*, Jan. 30, 1910, 29; *Oshkosh Northwest* (WI), Mar. 7, 1927, 12; *Lincoln Star* (NE), Mar. 13, 1927, 12; *Albany Leader* (MO), Feb. 14, 1935, 1. For an example of a syndicated novelty article spreading to Canada, see *Lethbridge Herald*, Feb. 23, 1938, 4.

39. Oriard, *Reading Football*, 238–39, and 243; Adams, *Education for Extinction*, 186–88; Adams, "More than a Game," 28–36. On Wild West shows emphasizing the "martial spirit" of Native Americans in the public imagination, see Moses, *Wild West Shows*, 5.

40. Adams suggests white spectators may have sympathized with Native football teams because of past injustice: "More than a Game," 39–40. On baseball, see Barr, "Looking Backward," 27–28, and Powers-Beck, *The American Indian Integration of Baseball*, 55–57.

41. Philip J. Deloria notes how Indian athletes could simultaneously represent primitivism and assimilation to white Americans in *Indians in Unexpected Places* (Lawrence: University of Kansas Press, 2004), 122–23. Also see Bloom, *To Show What an Indian Can Do*, 49.

42. *Chicago Tribune*, Mar. 20, 1940, 31.

43. See, for example, *Courier-Journal*, Feb. 24, 1907, sec. 4–2; Adams explains that the press also falsely portrayed the Carlisle football team as having full-Indian ancestry to build racial drama in "More than a Game," 44.

44. *Daily Capital Journal*, Apr. 30, 1898, 3. Also for "dusky maidens," see *Statesman Journal*, Jan. 25, 1903, 4; *Anaconda Standard* (Montana), Dec. 18, 1904, 9; *Los Angeles Times* (CA), Mar. 5, 1905, sec 3–2.

45. On the generally racist nature of sports journalism dealing with Native teams, also see Bloom, *To Show What an Indian Can Do*, 22–23, and Oriard, *Reading Football*, 238–47.

46. Examples include, *Lawrence Daily Gazette*, Jan. 13, 1916, 3; *Arizona Republic*, Oct. 14, 1916, 8; *Lawrence Daily Journal*, Jan. 2, 1920, 6; *Argus Leader*, Jan. 27, 1925, 9, and Mar. 12, 1932, 3; *Albuquerque Journal*, Mar. 21, 1928, 2; *Statesman Journal*, Mar. 7, 1933, 6; *Bismarck Tribune*, Feb. 7, 1935, 3.

47. Oriard similarly notes changes in the tone of reporting on Carlisle football after the novelty value "wore off," leading to what he refers to as straight reporting:

Reading Football, 243. On Lawrence residents' disinterest in Haskell basketball as a novelty, see *Lawrence Daily Gazette*, Dec. 31, 1917, 3.

48. *Albuquerque Journal*, Jan. 17, 1921, 8; *Statesman Journal*, Mar. 15, 1929, 10.

49. *Scandia Journal* (KS), Oct. 25, 1901, 4; *Great Falls Tribune*, Sept. 5, 1905, 4.

50. Philip J. Deloria, *Playing Indian* (New Haven, CT: Yale University Press, 1998), 95–127; Deloria, *Indians in Unexpected Places*, 120–25; Holm, *The Great Confusion in Indian Affairs*, 85–130; Vučković, *Voices from Haskell*, 142–43; *Sedalia Democrat*, Dec. 1, 1930, 3 ("vanishing race").

51. Stevens to Ostrem, Nov. 12, 1935, Folder 754, Box 8, DCF, Wahpeton Indian School, RG75, NARA, KC. Also see E. G. Clevenger to Peairs, Jan. 15, 1919; Peairs to Clevenger, Jan. 16, 1919; and Fuhrer to Peairs, Mar. 3, 1919, Folder "Basketball, 1919," Box 2, SCF, HI, RG75, NARA, KC. On Indian schools renaming children, see Child, *Boarding School Seasons*, 28–29.

52. Berry to Manager of DePaw University, Dec. 22, 1903, bound volume, Letters sent by the Athletic Program, Box 192, HI, RG75, NARA KC; *Evening Herald* (Ottawa, KS), Oct. 22, 1903, 2.

53. Peavy and Smith, *Full-Court Quest*, 234–35; Davies and Clow, "The St. Francis Mission Indians," 219; *Daily Capital Journal*, Mar. 13, 1929, 8.

54. *Albuquerque Journal*, Mar. 12, 1928, 2 and 4; *Moline Daily Dispatch* (IL), Apr. 9, 1928, 21; Chicago Daily News, Inc., photograph "Kee Kensol wearing traditional Native American clothing, standing outside on a train platform at a railroad station," 1928, DN-0084984, Chicago Historical Society, Explore Chicago Collections, https://explore.chicagocollections.org/image/chicagohistory/71/w951489/. On the familiarity of Great Plains American Indian imagery to general American audiences, see Moses, *Wild West Shows*, 1–4, and Lisa K. Neuman, *Indian Play* (Lincoln: University of Nebraska Press, 2013), 78 and 90–91.

55. Youpee: Peavy and Smith, *Full-Court Quest*, 120, and 157–58; and *Great Falls Tribune*, May 30, 1904, 6; Papakie: *Akron Beacon Journal* (OH), Mar 7, 1907, 5; Jordan: Adams letter to Reddy, Mar. 3, 1937, Folder 13, Box 15, NCIBT, LCU; Jordan interviewed by Thiel, Kateri Tekakwitha Oral History Project Records, 1994–1995, KTP-25, Special Collections and Archives, Marquette University; *Loyola News*, Mar. 17, 1926, 1 and 3–4.

56. McDonald quote excerpted in Schmidt, "Lords of the Prairie," *Journal of Sport History* 28 (Fall 2001): 409. On a similar dynamic at Bacone College, see Neuman, *Indian Play*, 65–69 and 90–93.

57. Hoxie, "The Curious Story of Reformers and American Indians," in *Indians in American History*, 2nd ed., Hoxie, ed. (Wheeling, IL: Harlan Davidson, 1988): 180–82; David R. M. Beck, *(Un)Fair Labor?* (Lincoln: University of Nebraska Press, 2019), 16–20; Vučković, *Voices from Haskell*, 142–43; Bloom, *To Show What an Indian Can Do*, 38–43. Schmidt suggests that Haskell's administration encouraged Native women to dance on the football field at halftime in 1919 wearing identical blankets to eliminate "any traces of specific tribal identification" and so to "nationalize" the Indian identity: "Lords of the Prairie," 406.

58. As Neuman says was the case at Bacone College after 1927, some admini-

strators and students may have condoned Native imagery in the arts and athletics to communicate that "Indians had a civilization and a culture of their own to share": *Indian Play*, 93.

59. Neuman, *Indian Play*, 226–27.

60. Barr, "Looking Backward," 28–32

61. Beane interview. Peavy and Smith similarly portray the Fort Shaw girls disdaining how inaccurate media accounts of them were and responding with a "we'll show them" attitude: *Full-Court Quest*, 155–56.

62. Powers-Beck, *The American Indian Integration of Baseball*, 4, 23–28, and 55–58; Barr, "'Looking Backward,'" 22–33; Deloria, *Indians in Unexpected Places*, 120.

63. *Statesman Journal*, Mar. 25, 1903, 3.

64. *Wichita Beacon*, Jan. 2, 1909, 7; Dec. 1908 Report, Folder "Semi-Annual Efficiency Reports, 1902–1909," Box 1, Records Relating to Personnel, CHIL, RG75, NARA, FW.

65. Peavy and Smith, *Full-Court Quest*, 279–80; *Native American*, Dec. 30, 1905, 478; *Indian Leader*, Mar. 6, 1903, 2; *Lawrence Daily World*, Feb. 5, 1901, 3.

66. *Asheville Citizen Times* (NC), Feb. 4, 1917, 9.

67. Kramer to Superintendent Jackson, Feb. 16, 1940, Folder 754, Box 26, DCF, CHEM, RG75, NARA SEA; (student file left anonymous), Box 35, Graduated Student Case Files, CHEM, RG75, NARA, SEA.

68. Picotte interview; Norbert Picotte, interview by author, Chamberlain, SD, July 17, 2016; Fasthorse, telephone interview by author, Feb. 19, 2016; Price, interview by author, Missoula, MT, Feb. 12, 2016; *Chiefs*, DVD, directed by Junge.

69. These conclusions are based on a survey of more than eight hundred newspaper articles describing Native vs. white games played between 1900 and 1940, both male and female. "Clean" meant sportsmanlike and low-fouling whereas "rough" implied an aggressive, chaotic game. The articles surveyed were drawn from newspaper databases.

70. Naismith, *Basketball*, 74–75. On early referees feeling the need to defend themselves from bodily harm, also see Basloe, *I Grew Up with Basketball*, 79–80.

71. Naismith, *Basketball*, 55, 74–75; Weyand, *The Cavalcade of Basketball*, 7–8 and 13.

72. Coaching: Johnson, *Phog*, xviii. Coaching was so undeveloped at the high school level in the early 1900s that many public schools had no athletic coaches at all: Pruter, *The Rise of American High School Sports and the Search for Control*, 53. In-house officials: Naismith, *Basketball*, 75; *Indian Leader*, Apr. 6. 1900, 2, Mar. 22, 1901, 2, Mar. 14, 1902, 2, Feb. 6, 1903, 3, Mar. 30, 1906, 5; *Lawrence Journal World*, Mar. 2, 1900, 4; *Statesman Journal*, Jan. 6, 1907, 2; *Wichita Beacon*, Jan. 2, 1909, 7; *Oregon Daily Journal*, Jan. 30, 1909, 7; *Lawrence Daily Gazette*, Feb. 25, 1915, 3. Hired officials: O. J. Farrell to A. J. Neddeau, Jan. 29, 1929, Folder 750, Box 73, Central Files, Cheyenne and Arapaho Agency, RG75, NARA, FW; *Indian Leader*, Mar. 7, 1930, 5; Stevens to Phil Canfield, Oct. 19, 1932, Folder 754, Box 8, DCF, Wahpeton Indian School, RG75, NARA, KC.

73. Jenkins, *The Real All Americans*, 135–36, 142–48, and 169–70; Powers-Beck, *The American Indian Integration of Baseball*, 59; Iverson, *Riders of the West*, 14.

74. On Chilocco publicizing the fact that student spectators and players often remained civil, see Fields, "Representations of Sport in the Indian School Journal," 251. Haskell: *Indian Leader*, Feb. 24, 1905, 3, and Mar. 5, 1909, 2. Other incidents of the *Indian Leader* alleging officiating bias against Haskell's teams include: Mar. 1, 1901, 2, Mar. 8, 1901, 2, Mar. 29, 1901, 2, Mar. 14, 1902, 2, Jan. 16, 1903, 2, and Feb. 6, 1903, 3.

75. *Lead Daily Call*, Mar. 11, 1905, 4, and *Lead Daily Pioneer-Times* (SD), Mar. 12, 1905, 6.

76. *Indian Leader*, Feb. 6, 1903, 3, and Mar. 30, 1906, 5; *Manhattan Mercury* (KS), Jan. 23, 1907, 1.

77. Allen, "Baskets and Backboards," in *Indian Leader*, Feb. 24, 1928, 6–7; Allen, *Coach "Phog" Allen's Sports Stories for You and Youth*, 147–48; Kerkhoff, *Phog Allen*, 26.

78. Means was a multisport athlete at Haskell from 1901 to 1909. He listed his height after graduation as five feet eleven, rather than the six feet two Allen cited. Frank Means File, box 79, Student Case Files, HI, RG75, NARA, KC; Frank Means to Dear Sir, Mar. 27, 1911, Folder 1911, 1 of 2, Box 3, General Corr., 1896–1922, FIS, RG75, NARA, KC.

79. Allen, "Baskets and Backboards."

80. *Indian Leader*, Dec. 28, 1906, 2. On Allen as a free throw specialist, see Johnson, *Phog*, 9.

81. Paul Fasthorse interview; Agnes and Norbert Picotte interviews; Michael Chavez, telephone interview with author, Jan. 7, 2016; Kickingwoman, personal interview, Missoula, Jan. 22, 2016; Wetzel, telephone interview with author, Feb. 5, 2016; *Reconciliation and Roundball*, Kemp and the Dakota Indian Foundation, 1990.

82. Newspapers did not commonly provide basketball box scores in the 1900s and only sporadically listed foul statistics in later decades. There are limitations to this sampling method. Certain teams are overrepresented while others are left out depending on newspaper coverage, and rules shifts mean foul statistics in 1900 are not comparable to those in 1930. The numbers of fouls were nevertheless tallied for each game and reveal that Indian school teams had more fouls per game only 45 percent of the time.

83. *Indian Leader*, Feb. 18, 1921, 6.

84. Jordan's views were expressed in interviews with Kemp and shared in correspondence with the author. On Flandreau, see Bloom, *To Show What an Indian Can Do*, 53. Churchill, Hill, and Barlow have argued, by contrast, that Indian school athletes compromised their indigenous identities and were complicit in media stereotyping of Natives: "An Historical Overview of Twentieth Century Native American Athletes," *Indian Historian* 12, no. 4 (1979): 22–32. I noted players' degrees of Native ancestry through the course of my research by consulting more than two hundred student files in various archives (which are explicit on the matter if not always accurate). I have rarely made note of this in the text, lest I misidentify or misrepresent anyone based solely on documentary records; nor was it pertinent, excepting Jordan's experiences, given how diverse players were (in terms of blood quantum)

on most Indian school teams and how rare references were to friction among them.

85. Even Bloom's aforementioned collaborator took some pride in school teams' athletic triumphs over non-Indians: *To Show What an Indian Can Do*, 54.

86. Bloom, *To Show What an Indian Can Do*, 64; Powers-Beck, *The American Indian Integration of Baseball*, 30; King, "Identities, Opportunities, Inequities, *an Introduction*," in King, ed., *Native Athletes in Sport and Society*, xiii; Laliberte, "Natives, Neighbors, and the National Game," 64; Littlefield, "The BIA Boarding School," 438; Sullivan, "Federal Indian Boarding Schools in New Mexico," 80–81; Warner, "Athletics at the Carlisle Indian School."

87. Adams, "More than a Game," 28 and 42–47; Anderson, *Carlisle vs. Army*, 4–5 and 17; Jenkins, *The Real All Americans*, 2, and 282–83.

88. Adams, "More than a Game," 46; Winnie, *Sah-Gan-De-Oh*, 53.

89. *Native American*, Feb. 6, 1904, 36 ("our basketball girls"); *Indian Leader*, Feb. 12, 1915, 1 ("determined to get"). There were also other references to "scalps," "braves," and "warriors" in Indian school publications, including: Fields, "Representations of Sport in the Indian School Journal," 252 (regarding 1907); *Indian School Journal*, 15 (1913–1914): 332; *Indian Leader*, Mar. 11, 1921, 3, Jan. 1, 1926, 118, and Feb. 5, 1926, 141. It is not always clear who authored each reference, but students and Native athletic staff members occasionally penned them under their own bylines. On the difficulty of determining authorship, see Bess, "Casting a Spell," *Wicazo Sa Review* 26 (Fall 2001): 13–38; Fields, "Representations of Sport in the Indian School Journal," 241–259; Haller, "Cultural Voices or Pure Propaganda?," *American Journalism* 19, no. 2 (2002): 65–86; Daniel F. Littlefield, Jr., and James W. Parins, *American Indian and Alaska Native Newspapers and Periodicals, 1826–1924* (Westport, CT: Greenwood, 1984), xxviii.

90. Neuman, *Indian Play*, 230–33.

91. Fortunate Eagle, *Pipestone*, 90.

92. On media references to "Braves" and "Warriors," see *Lawrence Weekly World*, Jan. 17, 1901, 7; *Indian Leader*, Feb. 22, 1907, 3, and Jan. 5, 1923, 4; *Washington Herald* (DC), Jan. 29, 1911, 16. Albuquerque and Santa Fe: Sullivan, "Federal Indian Boarding Schools in New Mexico," 70; *Albuquerque Journal*, Mar. 3, 1942, 4. Rapid City, St. Francis, and St. Stephens: Dietz to Mote, Mar. 9, 1929, Folder 754.6, "Basketball Tournament," 2 of 2, Box 26, DCF, RCIS, RG75, NARA, KC; Tournament Programs, 1935, Folder 20, Box 4, 1937, Folder 2, Box 6, 1938, Folder 9, Box 6, NCIBT, LUC; and Schiltz to Reddy, Mar. 14, 1936, Folder 13, Box 15, NCIBT, LUC.

93. Bloom discusses Santa Fe's enduring pride in their name "Braves" in *To Show What an Indian Can Do*, 128.

94. Davies, "'We Are Looking for a Splendid Tournament Here,'" 220–23; *Indian Leader*, Dec. 9, 1910, 5, and Apr. 25, 1919, 9; *Chemawa American*, Dec. 14, 1927, 2.

95. *Indian Leader*, Jan. 12, 1906, 2; *Republican News* (Hamilton, OH), Mar. 5, 1908, 7; *Chemawa American*, Feb. 16, 1927, 2; Davies, "'We Are Looking for a Splendid Tournament Here,'" 199–25; *Arizona Republic*, Mar. 3, 1935, 12.

96. In 1930, Supervisor of Indian Schools George F. Miller stated the Indian

Office's policy of permitting all-Native interscholastic competition provided it did not interfere with higher priority interracial competition: Miller to L. E. Dial, Dec. 11, 1930, Folder "Playgrounds and Athletics," Box 121, DCF, Fort Belknap Agency, RG 75, NARA, DEN.

97. *Indian Leader*, Jan. 12, 1906, 2; Wade Davies, "We are looking for a splendid tournament here," 207–10 and 213–14; Whitlock to McGregor, Oct. 10, 1927, Folder 750, Box 74, DCF, Pierre Indian School, RG75, NARA, KC; McGregor to CIA, Apr. 11, 1928, Folder 750, Box 125, CCF, General Service, RG75, NARA, DC.

98. *Indian Leader*, Jan. 12, 1906, 2, and Jan. 19, 1923, 7; *Chemawa American*, Feb. 23, 1927, 2; Kirk to Bonnin, Jan. 8, 1930.

99. Kirk to Bonnin, Jan. 8, 1930.

100. Chilocco vs. Haskell: *Indian Leader*, Jan. 12, 1906, 2. Haskell vs. Carlisle: *Journal News*, Mar. 5, 1908, 7; Tom Benjey, *Oklahoma's Carlisle Indian School Immortals* (Carlisle, PA: Tuxedo, 2010), 96–97; *Washington Post*, Feb. 16, 1908, 3.

Chapter 6. Indian Basketball

1. Phil Jackson, *Sacred Hoops* (New York: Hyperion, 1995), 55.

2. Alexander Wolff, *Big Game, Small World* (New York: Warner, 2002), 270 and 401.

3. Pete Axthelm, *The City Game* (Lincoln: University of Nebraska Press, 1999), xvi–xviii.

4. Nabokov, *Indian Running*, 18; Oxendine, *American Indian Sports Heritage*, 67–89; Gilbert, *Hopi Runners*, 21–42.

5. Gilbert, *Hopi Runners*, 8 and 67–87.

6. Wetzel, telephone interview by author, Feb. 5, 2016; DesRosier, interview by author, Missoula, MT, Feb. 11, 1916. On Native people's perception of a link between modern athleticism and running traditions, also see Stacy Sewell, "The Wind River Reservation," master's thesis of anthropology, University of Wyoming, Laramie, 2011, 51–52.

7. Beane interview. On "natural" athletes, see, for example, *Osage City Free Press* (KS), June 27, 1907, 2.

8. Beane interview. Also on sports emphasizing "the traditional value of cooperation," see Hyer, *One House, One Voice, One Heart*, 49.

9. Weyand, *The Cavalcade of Basketball*, 40; Applin, "From Muscular Christianity to the Market Place," PhD diss., University of Massachusetts, Amherst, 1982, 92; Pruter, *The Rise of American High School Sports*, 53.

10. Colglazier: "Physical Education for Boys and Girls," in *Chiloccoan, 1931*, n.p., Folder 8, Box 8, and sports rosters in *Chiloccoan, 1942*, n.p. Folder 1, Box 10, CISC, OKHS.

11. Beane interview.

12. Haskell: *Indian Leader*, Apr. 12, 1901, 2, Feb. 27, 1903, 2. Feb. 5, 1904, 2, Jan. 25, 1907, 3, and Feb. 14, 1908, 1. Chemawa: *Daily Capital Journal*, Jan. 14, 1910, 6; *Chemawa American*, Dec. 15, 1911, 3.

13. Carlisle: Jenkins, *The Real All Americans*, 173 and 197–202; Anderson, *Carlisle*

vs. Army, 66–67; Haskell: *Iola Daily Register and Evening News*, Oct. 3, 1911, 3; *Daily Gazette* (Lawrence), Oct. 16, 1911, 1; *Indian Leader*, Oct. 28, 1921, 23; *Star Tribune* (Minneapolis), Oct. 8, 1923, 9; *Miami Daily News-Record* (OK), Oct. 31, 1930, 8; *Tampa Times* (FL), Dec. 23, 1933, 7.

14. *Cincinnati Enquirer* (OH), Nov. 22, 1908, 9. On Haskell: *Indian Leader*, Dec. 25, 1908, 3; Mar. 16, 1923, 16, Nov. 30, 1923, 4, and Feb. 21, 1930, 8; *Cincinnati Enquirer*, Nov. 28, 1930, 12.

15. *Cincinnati Enquirer*, Nov. 22, 1908, 9.

16. Varsity football players frequently returned from late-season road trips and reported for basketball after practices had begun. *Indian Leader*, Jan. 5, 1923, 4.

17. Jenkins, *The Real All Americans*, 173 and 197; Anderson, *Carlisle vs. Army*, 66–67.

18. *Carlisle Evening Herald*, Mar. 26, 1897, 4; *Philadelphia Ledger* as reprinted in *Indian Helper*, Apr. 2, 1997, 1.

19. Naismith, *Basketball*, 139.

20. Haskell teams: *Indian Leader*, Apr. 12, 1901, 3, Jan. 16, 1903, 2, Feb. 15, 1907, 3, and Feb. 29, 1924, 3; *Daily Gazette*, Dec. 31, 1917, 3. Phoenix female players: *Native American*, Jan. 25, 1908, 24; Sherman male players: *Los Angeles Times*, Feb. 10, 1916, 23; Flandreau male players: *Argus Leader*, Jan. 5, 1930, 9.

21. *Native American*, Feb. 8, 1902, Card 12, microfiche; *El Paso Herald* (TX), Jan. 25, 1902, 1.

22. Rosters of selected male and female teams were used to find student files at a variety of off-reservation schools, including Albuquerque, Bismarck, Carlisle, Chemawa, Chilocco, Flandreau, Genoa, and Wahpeton, found at National Archives branches in Denver, Fort Worth, Kansas City, and Seattle, and online from the Carlisle Indian School Digital Resource Center. Only those files giving height and weight data were used. The largest number of samples concentrated between 1925 and 1935. The 147-pound average for males also matches the reported average weight of players on the Dwight Indian Training School team in 1915. This was a Presbyterian mission school in Oklahoma: *Muskogee Times-Democrat*, Dec. 17, 1915, 11. The 118-pound average for female players coincides precisely with an estimated weight the *Great Falls Tribune* (Jan. 1, 1904, 4) gave for Fort Shaw's team in 1904.

23. Naismith, "Basket Ball," 8.

24. Peterson, *Cages to Jump Shots*, 9–10 and 142; High school estimates are judged from the heights of seventeen Catholic high school teams participating in the 1937 National Catholic Invitational Basketball Tournament, *Tourney Topics*, 9 (March 1937), Folder 2, Box 6, NCIBT, LUC.

25. *Clarion-Ledger* (Jackson, MS), Mar. 22, 1928, 8.

26. Milda File, Student Case Files, Box 123, AIS, RG75, NARA, DEN; *Albuquerque Journal*, Feb. 25, 1928, 2.

27. Whether this was true for female players is uncertain given the scarcity of data. Fort Shaw's speedster Sansaver appears to have been of average height judging from her four-foot-four measurements at age nine: bound volume, Register of Pupils, 1892–1908, FSIS, RG75, NARA, DEN.

28. Edward Dominguez File, Student Case Files, CHIL, RG75, NARA, FW; *Indian Leader*, Feb. 18, 1916, 1; *Indian School Journal*, September, 1913, 338; *Wichita Daily Eagle* (KS), Jan. 28, 1914, 7; *Leavenworth Post* (KS), Feb. 3, 1916, 8.

29. 1935 official program, Folder 20, Box 4, NCIBT, LUC; *Argus Leader*, Mar. 21, 1935, 11.

30. *Reconciliation and Roundball.*

31. Deloria, "I Am of the Body," 326; Gems, "Negotiating a Native American Identity through Sport," in King, *Native Athletes in Sport and Society*, 12; Powers-Beck, *The American Indian Integration of Baseball*, 35. Guttman speaks more broadly of the satisfaction colonized groups gain from beating colonizers "at their own game" in *Games and Empires*, 179–80.

32. On the importance of kinship to Navajo Reservation independent teams during the 1970s, see Blanchard, "Basketball and the Culture-Change Process," 9–11. He argues that these teams emphasized fast-breaking speed over teamwork, which contrasts with my discussion of predominantly Native public school teams elsewhere being both speed- and teamwork-oriented (see chapter 10 and conclusion), but he cites kinship as the primary factor influencing on-court decision-making.

33. Yep, *Outside the Paint*, 1–7; Garcia, *When Mexicans Could Play Ball*, 29, 47–50, and 64–65; Gems, "Blocked Shot," 135–48.

34. *Ledger* reprint in *Indian Helper*, Apr. 2, 1997, 1. *Philadelphia Inquirer*, Mar. 26, 1897, 4.

35. *Lawrence Journal World*, Mar. 5, 1901, 4; *Wichita Beacon*, Jan. 25, 1902, 8; *Topeka Daily Capital*, Mar. 9, 1902, 9; Herbert Fallis File, Box 38, Student Case Files, HI, RG75, NARA, KC; *Indian Leader*, Feb. 6, 1903, 2.

36. *Los Angeles Times*, Apr. 3, 1904, 29; *Anaconda Standard*, Nov. 23, 1902, 14; Peavy and Smith, *Full-Court Quest*, 93, 160–61, 163, 300, and 325.

37. Albuquerque male players: *Albuquerque Journal*, Feb. 4, 1914, 3. Chemawa male players: *Daily Capital Journal*, Dec. 20, 1911, 4; *Chemawa American*, Jan. 1915, 4. Chilocco female players: *Arkansas City Daily Traveler* (KS), Jan. 11, 1908, 6. Chilocco male players: *Indian School Journal* 14 (March 1914): 332; *Wichita Beacon*, Feb. 8, 1916, 7; *Wichita Daily Eagle*, Feb. 10, 1916, 7; *Anthony Bulletin* (KS), Oct. 12, 1917, 3. Phoenix female players: *Native American*, Jan. 25, 1908, 24. Sherman male players: *Los Angeles Times*, Feb. 10, 1916, 23. Haskell and Quigley: *Lawrence Daily Journal-World*, Feb. 13, 1918, 8.

38. Chemawa: *Chemawa American*, Jan. 12, 1927, 2. Flandreau: *Argus Leader*, Jan. 27, 1925, 9. Genoa: *Nebraska State Journal* (Lincoln), Mar. 11, 1922, 3. Phoenix: *Arizona Republic*, Jan. 6, 1924, 13. Stewart: *Reno Evening Gazette* (NV), Feb. 8, 1926, 5.

39. *The Washington Herald*, Jan. 29, 1911, 16; *Arizona Republic*, Feb. 1, 1925, sec. 2–2; *Chemawa American*, Feb. 23, 1927, 2; *Indian Leader*, May 27, 1921, 17, and Jan. 10, 1930, 4.

40. Her tribal affiliation was not provided in newspaper sources (either as "Crow Feather" or "Crowfeather"), but land allotment records from 1915 list someone by that name coming from Standing Rock: "Marcella Crow-Feather, Serial

Land Patent in Corson County, South Dakota, 1915," https://thelandpatents.com/gallery/7n07wn73.

41. *Pierre Daily Capital-Journal* article reprinted in *Indian Leader*, Mar. 31, 1931, 7.

42. Haskell: *Indian Leader*, Feb. 22, 1907, 3, Mar. 39, 1907, 1, Jan. 1915, 23, and Jan. 14, 1927, 6. Wahpeton: *Willmar Tribune* (MN), Feb. 25, 1914, 1. Genoa: *Indian Leader*, Jan. 19, 1923, 7. Albuquerque and Santa Fe: *Albuquerque Journal*, Jan. 7, 1935, 2. St. Francis: *Argus Leader*, Mar. 21, 1935, 11; 1940 Tournament program, Folder 19, Box 6, NCIBT, LUC (St. Francis). Also on Fort Shaw females: Peavy and Smith, *Full-Court Quest*, 187.

43. Naismith, *Basketball*, 137–39.

44. Naismith, *Basketball*, 138–39. Although Naismith's discussion of Native players was laudatory, it was not in all ways sensitive or positive, as he also referenced coaches who said Native players were difficult to manage because they feared failure and ridicule.

45. Naismith, "Basket Ball," 8.

46. *Chicago Daily Tribune*, Mar. 2, 1907, 6; Fortunate Eagle, *Pipestone*, 90. See also: Carlisle male players: *Carlisle Evening Herald*, Mar. 26, 1897, 4. Chemawa female players: *Chemawa American*, Feb. 5, 1913, n.p. Fort Shaw female players: *Anaconda Standard*, Dec. 18, 1904, 9. Haskell male players: *Indian Leader*, Mar. 8, 1901, 2, Mar. 6, 1903, 2, and Jan. 4, 1918, 2. Sherman female players: *Los Angeles Times*, Mar. 5, 1905, sec. 3–2. St. Francis male players: *Indian Sentinel* 5 (Summer 1925): 102.

47. Beane interview.

48. *Clarion-Ledger*, Mar. 22, 1928, 8; Allen, *Coach "Phog" Allen's Sports Stories for You and Youth*, 180–81.

49. Naismith, *Basketball*, 139; Schmidt, "Louis 'Rabbit' Weller," in King, ed., *Native Americans in Sports*, 1:320–31; Oxendine, *American Indian Sports Heritage*, 254–55.

50. Bee, "Quick Break Old Story in Fancy New Clothes," *Corpus Christi Caller-Times* (TX), Jan. 6, 1912, 10; Weyand, *The Cavalcade of Basketball*, 101–02; Klein, "Keaney Invented the Fast Break and Rhode Island Made the Big Time," *Sports Illustrated Vault*, November 27, 1978, https://www.si.com/vault/1978/11/27/823193/yesterday-keaney-invented-the-fast-break-and-rhode-island-made-the-big-time; *Richmond Palladium-Item* (IN), Mar. 7, 1921, 13; *Houston Post* (TX), Dec. 14, 1924, 5; *Decatur Evening Herald* (IL), Jan. 21, 1927, 16; *Indianapolis News* (IN), Dec. 7, 1929, 13; Yep, *Outside the Paint*, 7.

51. Chemawa: *Statesman Journal*, Dec. 28, 1929, 8; *Daily Capital Journal*, Feb. 13, 1930, 11. Flandreau: *Indian Leader*, Feb. 6, 1931, n.p. Haskell: *Indian Leader*, Feb. 22, 1924, 4, Jan. 29, 1926, 134, and Jan. 30, 1931, 8. Phoenix: *Albuquerque Journal*, Jan. 15, 1933, 8.

52. Kemp, interview by author, Sioux Falls, SD, Aug. 1, 2017.

53. *Argus Leader*, Mar. 23, 1934, 3; Schunk and Brewer in *Reconciliation and Roundball*.

54. Chauncey E. Archiquette File, reproduction of Folder 5358, Box 136, CDRC; *Philadelphia Inquirer*, Mar. 26, 1897, 4; Rains, with Carpenter, *James Naismith*, 79; *Indian Leader*, June 22, 1900, 3; Kate Buford, *Native American Son* (Lincoln: University of Nebraska Press, 2012), 28–29. Buford identifies Archiquette as a quarterback in 1899, while at various other times he played running back and right end: *Topeka State Journal*, Oct. 15, 1900, 2, and Oct. 7, 1904, 2.

55. *Indian Leader*, Jan. 19, 1900, 3, Mar. 2, 1900, 2, Aug. 23, 1901, 2, and Feb. 5, 1904, 2.

56. Naismith, *Basketball*, 139–40.

57. Rains, with Carpenter, *James Naismith*, 79; *Green Bay Press-Gazette* (WI), Apr. 15, 1949, 14.

58. Weyand, *The Cavalcade of Basketball*, 59; Peterson, *Cages to Jump Shots*, 112; Naismith, *Basketball*, 78–82; Crisler, "The National Interscholastic Basketball Tournament of the University of Chicago" (Philadelphia, PA: A. J. Reach, 1924), 115; *Daily Maroon* (University of Chicago), Dec. 9, 1930, 1; Morgenstern, "The Twelfth Annual University of Chicago National Interscholastic Tournament" (New York: American Sports, 1930), 221.

59. Picotte interview; example of Haskell stalling the ball: *Indian Leader*, Jan. 22, 1926, 130.

60. *Chemawa American*, Dec. 8, 1926, 2, and Jan. 19, 1927, 2; *Daily Capital Journal*, Dec. 29, 1926, 10, Jan. 8, 1927, 2, and Feb. 13, 1930, 11.

61. *Indian Leader*, Jan. 19, 1923, 7, Jan. 29, 1926, 135, and Jan. 10, 1930, 4; Naismith, *Basketball*, 81.

62. *Albuquerque Journal*, Mar. 21, 1928, 2, Jan. 22, 1929, 2, Feb. 14, 1932, 2, Feb. 22, 1933, 3, and Feb. 6, 1937, 6.

63. *Indian Leader*, Feb. 6, 1931, n.p.; Henry Flood File, Box 40, Student Case Files, HI, RG75, NARA, KC; Flood File, reproduction of Folder 4515, Box 106, Series 1327, CDRC.

64. Collins Jordan and Vince Brewer, quoted in *Reconciliation and Roundball*.

65. *Albuquerque Journal*, Jan. 13, 1942, 4, Feb. 4, 1942, 4.

66. *Albuquerque Journal*, Mar. 14, 1936, 6, and Mar. 2, 1939, 4.

67. *Albuquerque Journal*, Mar. 9, 1938, 4, Feb. 25, 1939, 6, Feb. 26, 1939, 6, Dec. 28, 1939, 4, Mar. 15, 1940, 8, and Jan. 19, 1942, 5; *Gallup Independent* (NM), Mar. 5, 1938, 2.

68. *Albuquerque Journal*, Dec. 28, 1939, 4, and Dec. 28, 1940, 6; *Gallup Independent*, Jan. 25, 1940, 4.

69. *Albuquerque Journal*, Jan. 15, 1942, 4, Jan. 19, 1942, 5, Jan. 31, 1942, 4, Feb. 1, 1942, 4, and Feb. 4, 1942.

70. Grundman, "Jesse Barnard 'Cab' Renick," in King, *Native American in Sports*, 2:252–53; Paul Putz, "Jesse 'Cab' Renick," *Chronicles of Oklahoma* 89 (Spring 2011): 72–97.

71. Putz, "Jesse 'Cab' Renick," 80–82; Grundman, *The Golden Age of Amateur Basketball* (Lincoln: University of Nebraska Press, 2004), 2; *Albuquerque Journal*, Dec. 10, 1941, 6.

72. *Albuquerque Journal*, Feb. 5, 1942, 4; Sullivan, "Federal Indian Boarding Schools in New Mexico" (Lanham, MD: Scarecrow, 2013), 77.

Chapter 7. Champions

1. Applin, "From Muscular Christianity to the Market Place," 73–80.

2. Applin, "From Muscular Christianity to the Market Place," 138–48 and 161–71; Pruter, *The Rise of American High School Sports*, 81.

3. Their two largest victories were over the Company C soldiers from Kansas City 68–5 and the Lincoln, Nebraska YMCA 52–24. Simon Payer File, Box 91, Student Case Files, HI, RG75, NARA, KC; *Indian Leader*, Feb. 8, 1902, 1; *Lawrence Daily World*, Feb. 5, 1901, 3, Feb. 11, 1901, 3, and Apr. 6, 1901; *Lawrence Journal World*, Mar. 5, 1901, 4.

4. *Indian Leader*, Mar. 2, 1900, 2, Feb. 1, 1901, 2, Feb. 15, 1901, 2, Mar. 22, 1901, 2, Apr. 12, 1901, 2, Jun. 28, 1901, 6; *Lawrence Daily World*, Nov. 7, 1901, 3.

5. *Indian Leader*, Feb. Mar. 8, 1901, 3, and Nov. 15, 1901, 2; *Lawrence Daily World*, Dec. 10, 1901, 3; *Lawrence Weekly World*, Dec. 12, 1901, 5; Shields entries from bound ledger, Record of Students, 1890–1897, and bound ledger, Record of Employees, 1884–1919, HI, RG75, NARA, KC; Berthrong, "From Buffalo Days to Classrooms," *Kansas History* 12 (Summer 1989): 109.

6. *Topeka State Journal*, Dec. 23, 1901, 2; *Indian Leader*, Dec. 27, 1901, 3, and Jan. 17, 1902, 3; Jan. 10, 1902, 3, Jan. 17, 1902, 2, and Jan. 31, 1902, 2; *Topeka Daily Capital*, Jan. 5, 1902, 6, and Jan. 5, 1902, 2; *Lawrence Daily Journal*, Jan. 16, 1902, 4, Jan. 20, 1902, 4, and Jan. 25, 1902, 4. Nebraska victory: Caudle, *Collegiate Basketball* (Winston-Salem, NC: John F. Blair, 1960), 317; *Nebraska Basketball, 2016–2017 Media Guide* (Lincoln: Nebraska Communications Office, 2016), 158; *Nebraska State Journal*, Mar. 1, 1902, 3; *Lawrence Daily Journal*, Mar. 1, 1902, 4.

7. *Lawrence Daily World*, Feb. 3, 1902, 2; *Topeka State Journal*, Feb. 3, 1902, 2; *Lawrence Daily Journal*, Feb. 3, 1902, 4.

8. *Topeka Daily Capital*, Feb. 7, 1902, 5, Feb. 9, 1902, 9, and Feb. 19, 1902, 6; *Wichita Beacon*, Feb. 10, 1902, 8; *Indian Leader*, Feb. 14, 1902, 3.

9. N.a. "Independence Claimed the American Basketball Championship," excerpted from the *Independence Examiner*, Feb. 6, 1942, in *Missouri Historical Review* 54 (April 1960): 322; *Inter Ocean* (Chicago, IL), Jan. 25, 1901, 8, Feb. 21, 1901, 8, Mar. 9, 1901, 8; *Nebraska State Journal*, Mar. 13, 1901, 3; *Brooklyn Daily Eagle* (NY), Mar. 20, 1901, 16; *St. Louis Republic* (MO), Mar. 22, 1901, 6. Fond du Lac's rise to prominence by defeating Yale: Basloe, *I Grew Up with Basketball*, 112–13.

10. *Lawrence Daily World*, Mar. 28, 1901, 3; *Lawrence Daily Journal*, Mar. 3, 1902, 4; *Topeka State Journal*, Mar. 4, 1902, 2; *Lawrence Daily Journal*, Mar. 7, 1902, 4.

11. *Topeka Daily Capital*, Mar. 9, 1902, 2; *Lawrence Daily Journal*, Mar. 10, 1902, 4; *Indian Leader*, Mar. 14, 1902, 2.

12. *Kansas City Star* reprinted in *Indian Leader* Mar. 14, 1902, 2; *Lawrence Daily Journal*, Mar. 10, 1902, 2.

13. *Indian Leader*, Dec. 19, 1902, 3, and Jan. 16, 1903, 3; *St. Louis Post-Dispatch*

(MO), Jan. 2, 1903, 8; *The American Almanac, Year-book, Cyclopedia and Atlas* (New York American and Journal, Hearst's Chicago American, and the San Francisco Examiner, 1904), 701.

14. *Daily Gazette*, Feb. 9, 1907, 3; *Inter Ocean*, Mar. 1, 1907, 4. The championship of the West title: *Courier-Journal*, Mar. 10, 1907, 30; *Indian Leader*, Mar. 29, 1907, 1. Haskell had a 12–2 season record in 1905–06, and went 24–11 in 1907–08, but were in neither instance credited with any championships: "Haskell Indian Nations Institute Fighting Indians School History," https://www.sports-reference.com/cbb/schools/haskell-indian-nations-institute/.

15. *Albuquerque Daily Citizen* (NM), Dec. 19, 1901, 3, Dec. 28, 1901, 1, Jan. 22, 1902, 1, Jan. 23, 1902, 8, Jan. 25, 1902, 1, and Jan. 12, 1903, 5; *El Paso Herald*, Jan. 25, 1902, 1; *Indian Leader*, Feb. 14, 1902, 4; Sullivan, "Education through Sport," 84.

16. *Statesman Journal*, Jan. 14, 1903, 3, Jan. 25, 1903, 4, Feb. 17, 1903, 7, and Mar. 11, 1903, 3; *Weekly Oregon Statesman*, Feb. 20, 1903, 6; *Albany Democrat*, Feb. 27, 1903, 5; *Oregon Daily Journal* (Portland), Mar. 11, 1903, 3, and Mar. 16, 1903, 3.

17. Peavy and Smith, *Full-Court Quest*, 189–90 and 198–203; Peavy and Smith, "World Champions," 9–14; *Great Falls Tribune*, May 8, 1903, 5, and May 10, 1903, 4.

18. Moses, *Wild West Shows*, 150–67.

19. Peavy and Smith, *Full-Court Quest*, 196–97 and 219; Peavy and Smith, "World Champions," 5 and 14.

20. Peavy and Smith, "World Champions," 15–19; *Hawaiian Star* (Honolulu), May 13, 1904, 4.

21. Peavy and Smith, *Full-Court Quest*, 230–31, 299–301, and 309–10; *Indian School Journal*, July 6, 1904, 1.

22. Peavy and Smith, *Full-Court Quest*, 316–18; *Indian School Journal*, July 29, 1904, 1.

23. Peavy and Smith, *Full-Court Quest*, 324–30; *Great Falls Tribune*, Oct. 12, 1904, 4, and Oct. 14, 1904, 4; *Dillon Tribune* (MT), Oct. 14, 1904, 2.

24. Peavy and Smith, *Full-Court Quest*, 337–39; *Washington Post*, Sept. 3, 1905, 84; *Albany Democrat*, Mar. 20, 1908, 5; *Chemawa American*, Mar. 1913, 31; June 1913, 9; and Jan. 1914, 4.

25. Jason Baird Jackson, "Calling in the Members," *Anthropological Linguistics* 42 (Spring 2000): 63–64; *Checotah Enquirer* (OK), Apr. 19, 1907, 10; *Topeka State Journal*, May 28, 1907, 2.

26. *New-State Tribune* (Muskogee), June 13, 1907, 5.

27. *Osage City Free Press*, June 27, 1907, 3.

28. *New-State Tribune*, June 20, 1907, 10; *Indian's Friend* 22 (Feb. 1908): 1.

29. *Cincinnati Enquirer*, July 11, 1909, 31.

30. *Winfield Daily Free Press*, Jan. 28, 1914, 3; Fields, "Representations of Sport," 251; *Arkansas City Daily Traveler*, Dec. 2, 1908, 8, and Feb. 24, 1909, 4; *Wichita Daily Eagle*, Jan. 2, 1909, 7, and Aug. 19, 1909, 7; *Lawrence Daily World*, Jan. 6, 1909, 3; *Indian Leader*, Jan. 8, 1909, 2.

31. Albuquerque: *Albuquerque Journal*, Oct. 18, 1935, 6. Chilocco: *Indian School*

Journal 16 (Feb. 1916), 330–31; *Wichita Beacon*, Feb. 16, 1916, 11, and Feb. 21, 1916, 7; *Morning Tulsa Daily World* (OK), Mar. 12, 1916, 8.

32. Rader, *American Sports*, 183–84; Mike Douchant, *Encyclopedia of College Basketball*, 7–8; Lu David Wims, "A History of the Administration of Intercollegiate Athletics in the Ohio Athletic Conference," PhD diss., Ohio State University, Columbus, 1910, 17–40.

33. Haskell was 6–5 vs Kansas, 4–4 vs Kansas State, 1–1 vs Missouri, and 2–0 vs Nebraska: Douchant, *Encyclopedia of College Basketball*, 486; *Kansas Basketball Media Guide, 2017–18* (Lawrence: Kansas Communications Office, 2017), 190–91; After a few years' break, Haskell played Kansas State one last time during the 1918–19 season: *K-State Men's Basketball Media Guide, 2014–15* (Athletics Communications Office, K-State Athletics, Inc., 2014), 168.

34. Albuquerque: *New Mexico Men's Basketball, Media Guide, 2015–16* (Albuquerque: New Mexico Athletics Communications Office, 2015), 125. During the first decade of the twentieth century, the Albuquerque and Santa Fe Indians schools were members of the Territorial Intercollegiate Athletic Conference along with the University of New Mexico and A&M: Sullivan, "Education through Sport," 72. Chemawa: *Oregon Men's Basketball, 2014–15*, 83–84, https://issuu.com/oregonducks/docs/mbb14history; *Oregon State Men's Basketball Media Guide, 2015–2016*, 88–90, http://oregonstate_ftp.sidearmsports.com/pdf9/3920917.pdf. Phoenix: *Arizona State Basketball Media Guide, 2007–08* (Tempe: ASU Media Relations Office, 2007), 64.

35. *Morning Oregonian* (Portland), Dec. 1, 1909, 12; *Chemawa American*, Dec. 10, 1909, 2; Joshua Jerome Meisel, "Historical Demographics, Student Origins, and Recruitment at Off-Reservation Indian Boarding Schools, 1900," 45; Parkhurst, *To Win the Indian Heart*, 31. Reginald Downie was probably nineteen when he captained Chemawa's 1914 squad: Downie entries, volume 3, 42–44, Record of Employees, CHEM, RG75, NARA, SEA.

36. *Morning Oregonian*, Feb. 9, 1910, 7, and Dec. 19, 1912, 8; *Oregon Daily Journal*, Jan. 16, 1911, 16, Jan. 22, 1912, 11, and Feb. 16, 1912, 12; *Chemawa American*, March, 1913, 25, and March, 1914, 8. Clements' tribal affiliation: *Indian Leader*, Jan. 25, 1918, 12.

37. *Chemawa American*, Dec. 1915, 19; Jan. 1916, 1–3 and 25, and Feb. 2, 1927, 2. Larsen's tribal affiliation: "University Archives News, Chemawa History," posted Sept. 15, 2014, https://library.willamette.edu/wordpress/archives/2014/09/15/chemawa-history/.

38. *Sunday Oregonian* (Portland), Dec. 10, 1916, 5, and Dec. 5, 1920, sec. 2–3; *Morning Oregonian*, Jan. 27, 1917, 15, and Feb. 5, 1920, 12; *Newberg Graphic* (OR), Mar. 1, 1917, 1; George Bent to Harwood Hall, Feb. 19, 1920, Folder "Games—Mount Angel, 1920," Box 2, Corr. of the Superintendent, CHEM, RG75, NARA, SEA; *Capital Journal*, Jan. 18, 1922, 2, and Mar. 2, 1927, 6; *Chemawa American*, Feb. 23, 1927, 2.

39. Kansas Conference refusal of Chilocco: *Winfield Daily Free Press*, Jan. 9, 1923, 6. MVC refusal of Haskell: Gerald Gems, "Negotiating a Native Identity through Sport," 15; *Lawrence Daily Journal World*, Nov. 10, 1917, 2. Haskell had an

85–68–4 football record against primarily college opponents between 1900 and 1917: Schmidt, "Lords of the Prairie," 405.

40. C. M. Blair to Faculty Representatives of the MVC, May 18, 1927, Folder 750, "Amusements 1930," 3 of 3, Box 113, DCF, HI, RG75, NARA, KC; Louis Weller, "Athletics," *Chilocco Senior Class Annual, 1923*, 236, Folder 3, Box 8, CISC, OKHS.

41. Applin, "From Muscular Christianity," 134–37 and 161–81; Pruter, *The Rise of American High School Sports*, xiii, 48–49, 56–59, and 65–82; Guy Jaggard to Peairs, Mar. 17, 1921, Folder 754, "Corr. 1921–1924," Box 116, DCF, HI, RG75, NARA, KC; O.A. Farrell to Lee Anderson, Sept. 8, 1928, and Anderson to Farrell, Sept. 20, 1928, Folder 750, Box 73, Central Files, Cheyenne and Arapaho Agency, RG75, NARA, FW.

42. Other associations were established in North Dakota in 1908; Oklahoma in 1911; Wyoming in 1912; Arizona and Kansas in 1913; Oregon and California in 1914; and New Mexico and Montana in 1921: Applin, "From Muscular Christianity," 134–37 and 149–50; Pruter, *The Rise of American High School Sports*, 82 and 108; David Kemp and Tamra Zastrow ed., *A Celebration of One Hundred Years of South Dakota High School Activities and Athletics*, (Sioux Falls, SD: Mariah, 2006) 5; "History of North Dakota High School Activities Association," https://ndhsaa.com/about/history; "Oklahoma Secondary School Activities Association History," http://www.ossaa.net/docs/2017–18/OSSAAInfo/MF_2017–18_History.pdf; "History of the Arizona Interscholastic Association," http://aiaonline.org/about/; New Mexico Activities Association, "About," https://www.nmact.org/about/.

43. Spaulding to Thomas, Dec. 30, 1928, Folder "Corr. 1939–1943," Box 113, DCF, HI, NARA, KC; Oscar Lipps to A. B. Cordley, Dec. 20, 1927, Thompson File (455), Box 10, Graduated Student Case Files, CHEM, RG75, NARA, SEA; Perry to Rose, Dec. 12, 1931, and Wilferth, "Regular Meeting of the Board of Control," Mar. 9, 1933, Folder 750, Box 34, GCF, AIS, RG75, NARA, DEN; Brewster to Stevens, Nov. 17, 1933, Folder 754, Box 8, DCF, Wahpeton Indian School, RG75, NARA, KC.

44. Examples of Haskell's superintendents insisting that academics always came first, even while recruiting athletes: Haskell, 1914, Reel 59, SANSR; Peairs to Campbell, Mar. 30, 1922, Folder 750, "Amusements 1930," 3 of 3, Box 113, SCF, HI, RG75, NARA, KC.

45. Oxendine, *American Indian Sports Heritage*, 184; Bloom, *To Show What an Indian Can Do*, 17; Sculle, "The New Carlisle of the West," 196–97; Charles to Peairs, July 18, 1908, Folder "Athletics," Box 1, SCF, HI, RG75, NARA, KC (example of recruiting); Meriam, *The Problem of Indian Administration*, 398.

46. Carroll to Towner, Nov. 23, 1928, Folder 750, "Athletics, 1928–1939," Box 25, DCF, CHEM, RG75, NARA, SEA; Johnson to Director of Athletics of Madison High School, Nov. 1, 1931, Folder 754.4, and Byron J. Brophy to "Coaches, Principals, and Superintendents," Dec. 22, 1934, Folder 754, Box 124, DCF, FIS, RG75, NARA, KC; Skinner of Phoenix Indian School to Gilliam, Nov. 13, 1933, Folder 752 and Blair to Towers, July 30, 1934, Folder 750, Box 34, GCF, AIS, RG75, NARA, DEN.

47. South Dakota High School Athletic Association, *Constitution and By-Laws, 1927*, 8, Folder 750, Box 74, DCF, Pierre Indian School, RG75, NARA, KC; Blair to Towers, July 30, 1934; Skinner to Gilliam, Nov. 13, 1933.

48. Chemawa's rosters and student files in 1928 appear impeccable: Oregon High School Athletic Association, Basketball, eligibility list, Jan. 20, 1929, Folder 750, "Athletics, 1928–1939," Box, 25, DCF, cross referenced with George File (6181), Box 86 and Peratrovich File (7253), Box 103, Student Case Files, CHEM, RG75, NARA, SEA. Albuquerque: Student file left anonymous, Box 9, Student Case Files, AIS, RG75, NARA, DEN. Pierre and Flandreau: Mattson to McLean, Jan. 1, 1927, Folder 750, Box 74, DCF, Pierre Indian School, RG75, NARA, KC. Albuquerque and Phoenix: Nieman to Boys Adviser Johnson, Oct. 30, 1933; Gilliam to Nieman, Nov. 7, 1933; Skinner to Gilliam, Nov. 13, 1933; and Blair to Skinner, Nov. 18, 1933, Folder 752, Box 34, GCF, AIS, RG75, NARA, DEN.

49. Meisel, "Historical Demographics," 59; *Lincoln Star*, Mar. 3, 1921, 9; *Lincoln Journal Star*, Mar. 7, 1921, 4; Davis to Mote, Mar. 1, 1928, Folder 754.6, 1 of 2, Box 26, GCF, RCIS, RG75, NARA, KC.

50. *Lincoln Journal Star*, Dec. 28, 1922, 9, Mar. 10, 1927, 1, and Mar. 14, 1927, 4; *Nebraska State Journal*, Mar. 11, 1922, 3, and Mar. 12, 1922, 7; *Indian Leader*, Jan. 19, 1923, 7.

51. *Nebraska State Journal* Mar. 13, 1927, A7–8.

52. Adams, *Education for Extinction*, 320; Lomawaima, *They Called It Prairie Light*, 13; Vučković, *Voices from Haskell*, 37.

53. Reid to "Members," Oct. 21, 1929, Folder 750, Box 34, GCF, AIS, RG75, NARA, DEN; Baumgarten to Thompson, Feb. 11, 1927, Folder 750, (digital files courtesy of archives), DCF, Mount Pleasant Indian School, RG75, NARA, Chicago; Carroll to Goetz, Nov. 23, 1928, and Carroll to Towner, Nov. 23, 1928, Folder 750, "Athletics, 1928–1939," Box 25, DCF, CHEM, RG75, NARA, SEA.

54. Oklahoma refusing Concho and Chilocco: Anderson to Farrell, Sept. 20, 1928, Folder 750, Box 73, Central Files, Cheyenne and Arapaho Agency, RG75, NARA, FW; Blair to Wilferth, Sept. 23, 1934, Folder 752, Box 34, GCF, AIS, RG75, NARA, DEN. North Dakota's Refusals: "North Dakota State High School League Uniform Contract," Jan. 25, 1933, Folder 754, Box 8, DCF, Wahpeton Indian School, RG75, NARA, KC. South Dakota's Refusals: *Reconciliation and Roundball.* Phoenix Indian School admitted in Arizona by 1940: "Arizona Interscholastic Association Eligibility List," Jan. 17, 1940, Folder 750, "Athletics, 1939–1940," Box 129, CCF, Phoenix Indian School, RG75, NARA, LA. Sherman: Seth Van Patten to Gilliam, May 24, 1932, Folder 752, Box 33, Records of the Superintendent, CCF, 1907–1939, Sherman Institute, RG75, NARA, LA. Haskell: *Indian Leader*, Nov. 9, 1945, 1. Pipestone admitted in Minnesota by 1946: "Minnesota State High School League Official Contract," Jan. 4, 1946, Folder 754.2, Box 31, DCF, 1901–1952, Pipestone Indian School, RG75, NARA, KC.

55. Indian Office superiors knew the shift toward high school play was unpopular and would pit local superintendents against schools supporters: Willard Beatty to Warren Spaulding, Mar. 31, 1939, Folder "Corr. 1939–1943," Box 113, DCF, HI, RG75, NARA, KC. On Native alumni expressing their displeasure at the shift away from college athletic competition, see Bloom, *To Show What an Indian Can Do*, 58.

56. Carroll to Towner, Nov. 23, 1928, and Bent to Downie, "Reggie Please

explain," n.d. (likely 1929), Folder 750, "Athletics, 1928–1939," Box 25, DCF, CHEM, RG75, NARA, SEA.

57. *New Oregon Statesman*, Mar. 9, 1929, 6; *San Bernardino County Sun* (CA), Mar. 9, 1929, 2; *Daily Capital Journal*, Mar. 9, 1929, 4, and Mar. 11, 1929, 8.

58. High school representatives also apologized to the two association board members: *Daily Capital Journal*, Mar. 11, 1929, 8; *New Oregon Statesman*, Mar. 13, 1929, 4, and Mar. 14, 1929, 5.

59. *Daily Capital Journal*, Mar. 14, 1929, 11; George File (6181), Box 86 and Prettyman File (6832), Box 97, Student Case Files, CHEM, RG75, NARA, SEA; *Chemawa American*, Dec. 21, 1927, 2; *New Oregon Statesman*, Mar. 15, 1929, 10; "1929 AAA Boys Basketball," http://www.osaa.org/docs/bbx/records/1929b.pdf; "1940" http://www.osaa.org/docs/bbx/records/1940b.pdf.

60. *New Oregon Statesman*, Mar. 9, 1929, 6, and Mar. 20, 1929, 8; *Daily Capital Journal*, Mar. 13, 1929, 8.

61. "New Mexico Prep Basketball (Historical)," chuckferrissports.com; *Albuquerque Morning Journal*, Feb. 22, 1926, 2; Albuquerque Training School, 1928, pg. 12, Reel 2, SANSR; Sullivan, "Education Through Sport," 126–27.

62. Individual identities are left anonymous. The sources are drawn from boxes 9, 99, 123, 172, and 179 of Student Case Files, AIS, RG75, NARA, DEN.

63. *Albuquerque Journal*, Jan. 27, 1928, 2, Feb. 11, 1928, 2, Feb. 25, 1928, 2, and Mar. 11, 1928, 1–2.

64. Kinsel was alternatively spelled "Kensel" or "Kensol" in some sources. Legah also appears as "Hosgah" and "Oskie." On the season, they tallied 808 points to their opponents' 522: *Albuquerque Journal*, Mar. 21, 1928, 2, Mar. 28, 1928, 2, and Dec. 29, 1928, 2; *Courier-Journal*, Apr. 4, 1928, 16. Individual player files found in boxes 99, 123, 172, and 179 of Student Case Files, AIS, RG75, NARA, DEN.

65. *Albuquerque Journal*, Mar. 11, 1928, 1–2.

66. *Albuquerque Journal*, Mar. 11, 1928, 1–2; "New Mexico Prep Basketball (Historical)."

67. Pruter, *The Rise of American High School Sports*, 193–95.

68. *Albuquerque Journal*, Mar. 12, 1928, 4, Mar. 13, 1928, 2, Mar. 15, 1928, 2, Mar. 16, 1928, 1, Mar. 18, 1928, 2, Mar. 29, 1928, 2, and Apr. 2, 1928, 4.

69. *Albuquerque Journal*, Mar. 29, 1928, 2, and Apr. 1, 1928, 2; Meritt to Perry, Mar. 28, 1928, Folder 750, Box 19, CCF, NARA, DC.

70. *Courier-Journal*, Apr. 4, 1928, 16; *Chicago Tribune*, Apr. 4, 1928, 29; *Albuquerque Journal*, Apr. 4, 1928, 2. Carr Creek was eliminated in the quarter finals.

71. *Chicago Tribune*, Apr. 4, 1928, 29.

72. Wilferth, "Regular Meeting of the Board of Control," Mar. 9, 1933, and Robertson to "Member Schools," n.d., Folder 750, Box 34, GCF, AIS, RG75, NARA, DEN; Sullivan, "Education through Sport," 149–50.

73. Perry et al. to "Superintendent and Principal," Mar. 16, 1933; Perry to Faris, Mar. 18, 1933; J. L. Gill to Perry, Mar. 27, 1933; Perry to W. J. Robertson, Mar. 28, 1933; Robertson to Perry, Mar. 29, 1933; J. W. Wilferth telegram to Perry, n.d., Folder 750, Box 34, GCF, AIS, RG75, NARA, DEN.

74. Grundman, *The Golden Age of Amateur Basketball*, 6–7 and 9–11; *Indian Leader*, Mar. 16, 1923, 16; *Eau Claire Leader* (WI), Mar. 12, 1929, 8.

75. *Reliance Record* (SD), Apr. 3, 1924, 1.

76. *Lincoln State Journal*, Mar. 16, 1924, A8, Feb. 23, 1925, 3, and Feb. 4, 1926, 9; *Chadron Chronical* (NE), Mar. 1, 1928, 1; Wm. Birmingham to Edward Krupka, Feb. 27, 1928, Folder 13, Box 15, NCIBT, LUC. Holy Rosary mission also competed at Chadron on multiple occasions.

77. Davies and Clow, "The St. Francis Mission Indians and the National Interscholastic Catholic Basketball Tournament," 213–31. Catholic motives for sponsoring the tournament: "Procedures for Planning National Catholic Basketball Tournament," n.d., Folder 1, Box 1 and Carnall, "A Great Opportunity," in *National Catholic Tournament: The Catholic Classic, 1925*, official program, 4, Folder 16, Box 2, NCIBT, LUC. Winning the South Dakota Catholic tournament: *Rapid City Journal*, Mar. 8, 1937, 5. NCIBT attendance: Pruter, *The Rise of American High School Sports*, 240. St. Francis Jesuit's motives: *Indian Sentinel* 5 (Summer 1925): 103.

78. *Indian Sentinel* 5 (Summer 1925): 102–3; *Loyola News* Mar. 11, 1925, n.p.

79. LaPier and Beck, *City Indian*, 61–80; *Indian Sentinel* 5 (Summer 1925): 103; Reception Committee reports, 1925, Folder 4, Box 2, NCIBT, LUC.

80. *Loyola News*, Mar. 6, 1934, 1, and Mar. 15, 1935, 6–7; *Argus Leader*, Mar. 21, 1935, 11; NCIBT official program, 1940, 11, including excerpt from the *Chicago Tribune*, Folder 19, Box 6 Reception Committee reports, 1925 and 1926, Folder 4 and Folder 6, Box 2, NCIBT, LUC.

81. Davies, "We Are Looking for a Splendid Tournament Here," 199–225; Riney, *The Rapid City Indian School*, 127–29; "Constitution of the Northern Indian School Association," Jan. 18, 1928, Folder 750, Box 74, DCF, Pierre Indian School, RG75, NARA, KC.

82. Davies, "We Are Looking for a Splendid Tournament Here," 208–11; Birmingham to Mote, Feb. 13, 1927, Folder 754, Box 26, DCF, RCIS, RG75, NARA KC; Balmer to Mote, Jan. 27, 1928; Stevens to Mote, Feb. 11, 1928; Birmingham to Mote, Feb. 12, 1928; and Principal Allender of Rosebud School to Ziebach, Feb. 7, 1928, Folder 750, Box 26, DCF, RCIS, RG75, NARA KC.

83. *Native American*, Mar. 13, 1926, Card 130, Sept. 24, 1927, Card 135, and Nov. 3, 1928, card 139, microfiche; Riney, "Loosening the Bonds," in Trafzer et al., eds., *Boarding School Blues* (Lincoln: University of Nebraska Press, 2006), 144; McGregor to Mote, Mar. 1, 1928, Folder 754.6, Box 26, DCF, RCIS, RG75, NARA, KC.

84. *Rapid City Journal*, Mar. 18, 1927, 8; *Lead Daily Call*, Apr. 21, 1927, 1; McGregor to Mote, Mar. 1, 1928; Mote circular, Dec. 10, 1928, Folder 754, Box 26, DCF, RCIS, RG75, NARA KC. McGregor did, however, gather the South Dakota Indian schools, and Bismarck, for a track and literary meet at Pierre in May 1928: Riney, "Loosening the Bonds," 144; *Indian Leader*, Mar. 9, 1928, 4, and Mar. 16, 1928, 7.

85. McGregor to Mote, Dec. 14, 1928, and Zimmerman to Mote, Dec. 15, 1928, Folder 754, Box 26, DCF, RCIS, RG75, NARA KC; Mote to Zimmerman, Mar. 5, 1929; Frank Dietz to Mote, Mar. 9, 1929; and "Tri-State Indian School Basketball Tournament, Rapid City, South Dakota, March 15th and 16th, 1929" Folder 754.6, Box 26,

DCF, RCIS, RG75, NARA KC; Harold Hillenbrand to Dietz, Mar. 5, 1929, Folder 12, Box 15, NCIBT, LUC. Pipestone originally accepted but then backed out, rendering the use of "Tri-State" in the tournament's title a misnomer.

86. *Rapid City Daily Journal*, Mar. 13, 1929, 1, and Mar. 15, 1929, 6; Dickenson of Bismarck and Mossman of Fort Yates to Mote, Mar. 13, 1929, Folder 754.6, Box 26, DCF, RCIS, RG75, NARA KC; McLean to Whitlock, Mar. 14, 1929, Folder 754, Box 74, DCF, Pierre Indian School, RG75, NARA, KC; *Bismarck Tribune*, Mar. 16, 1929, 8.

87. I have been unable to confirm the tribal affiliations of Rapid City's players, although most appear to have been Lakota: "Inter-Indian School Tournament," team entry sheets, Folder 754.6, Box 26, DCF, RCIS, RG75, NARA KC; *Rapid City Daily Journal*, Mar. 18, 1929, 6.

88. Holy Rosary's coach in this game was listed as "Ralph" Clifford even though Bob Clifford arrived there in 1925. If a relative of his was indeed coach, Bob was nevertheless already athletic director: *Rapid City Daily Journal*, Mar. 19, 1929, 6.

89. *Bismarck Tribune*, Mar. 2, 1929, 8; *Rapid City Daily Journal*, Mar. 19, 1929, 6; "Inter-Indian School Tournament," team entry sheets; McGregor to CIA, Mar. 30, 1929, Folder 754.6, Box 26, DCF, RCIS, RG75, NARA KC. Slater: Report of Attendance, Dec. 31, 1928, Box 467, DCF, BIS, RG75, NARA, KC.

90. McGregor to CIA, Mar. 30, 1929, Folder 754.6, Box 26, DCF, RCIS, RG75, NARA KC; *Rapid City Daily Journal*, Mar. 19, 1929, 6.

91. Mote to O'Harra, Mar. 19, 1929, and McGregor to CIA, Mar. 30, 1929, Folder 754.6, Box 26, DCF, RCIS, RG75, NARA KC.

92. Riney, *The Rapid City Indian School*, 15; Mote to R. L. Spalsbury of Pierre Indian School, Feb. 23, 1931, and Mote to Stevens, Feb. 24, 1931, Folder 750, Box 465, DCF, BIS, RG75, NARA, KC. Mote to Supt. Calhoun of Pierre Indian School, Jan. 9, 1933, Folder 754, Box 465, DCF, BIS, RG75, NARA, KC.

93. Skinner, who became superintendent in 1931, had no prior employment in the Indian Service: Trennert, *The Phoenix Indian School*, 198–203. Basketball tournament and athletic play-days with Indian day schools: Skinner to Indian Junior High Schools, Feb. 19, 1934, Folder 740, "Athletics, 1937–1938,"; Skinner to Bessie Dyer et al., Mar. 8, 1934; Skinner to anonymous, Mar. 5, 1934, and Mar. 24, 1934; and Skinner to Grinnell et al., Apr. 17, 1934, all in Folder 750, "Amusements and Athletics, 1930–1932, 1934," Box 128, CCF, Phoenix Indian School, RG75, NARA, LA. Mote's oversight: *Arizona Republic*, Aug. 24, 1957 (retrospective to 1937), 6; Mote to Timothy Mackey, Feb. 15, 1938, Folder 750, "Athletics, 1937–1938," Box 129, CCF, Phoenix Indian School, RG75, NARA, LA.

94. Kemp and Zastrow, *One Hundred Years of South Dakota High School Activities and Athletics*, 44.

95. *Rapid City Daily Journal*, Jan. 10, 1936, 7, Feb. 22, 1936, 6, and Mar. 16, 1936, 6; *Deadwood Pioneer-Times*, Mar. 15, 1936, 1.

96. *Argus Leader*, Mar. 19, 1939, 11; *Rapid City Daily Journal*, Mar. 20, 1939, 5. Beane recalls Redthunder's tribal affiliation, but I am unable to determine Demarrias's: Beane interview.

97. Beane interview.

98. NCIBT official program, 1941, 25, Folder 20, Box 6, NCIBT, LUC; "Bob Clifford"; Brewer in *Reconciliation and Roundball.*

99. *Chicago Tribune*, Mar. 31, 1941, 17; Brewer in *Reconciliation and Roundball.*

Chapter 8. Collegians and Servicemen

1. Football or baseball collegians in the 1900s included Michael Balenti at Texas A&M and Eddie Rogers at Minnesota. Louis Sockalexis also played for Holy Cross College in the 1890s. For profiles, see King, ed., *Native Americans in Sports*, volumes 1 and 2. Guyon: Robert Pruter, "Joseph Napoleon 'Joe' Guyon," in King, ed., *Native Americans in Sports*, 1:137–38. On Natives using athletics as a pathway to college, see Deloria, *Indians in Unexpected Places*, 119 and 127. On the Indian schools being conducive to the rise of Native college stars in sports other than basketball, see Oxendine, *American Indian Sports Heritage*, 261–63.

2. Applin, "From Muscular Christianity to the Market Place," 136–38 and 161–67; Douglas Stark, *Wartime Basketball*" (Lincoln: University of Nebraska Press, 2016), 33.

3. Adams, *Education for Extinction*, 63, 290, and 319–22; Margaret Connell Szasz, *Education and the American Indian*, 3rd ed. (Albuquerque: University of New Mexico Press, 1999), 135–36.

4. Szasz, *Education and the American Indian*, 134–35; Cary Michael Carney, *Native American Higher Education in the United States* (New Brunswick: Transaction Publishers, 1999), 4–5 and 103–04; Bloom, *To Show What an Indian Can Do*, 92.

5. Haskell offered some junior college–level courses during the 1920s but did not formally become a junior college until 1970. Prucha has noted in *The Great Father* how Carlisle presented a false impression of its academic status by fielding college teams (698). Also see Oxendine, *American Sports Heritage*, 195–99. Beck, "American Indians Higher Education Before 1974," *The Australian Journal of Indigenous Education* 27, no. 2 (199): 18; O'Brien, "The Evolution of Haskell Indian Junior College, 1884–1974," master's thesis, University of Oklahoma, Norman, 1975, 38–43 and 67–68.

6. St. Germaine is the only Native college basketball player I have located in newspaper reports or Indian school publications reporting on their alumni, but this does not necessarily mean he was the first: *Lawrence Daily Journal*, Nov. 11, 1898, 4, and Mar. 20, 1900, 4; *Indian Leader*, Jan. 2, 1903, 3; *Des Moines Register* (IA), June 4, 1904, 2; *Minneapolis Journal* (MN), June 30, 1904, 13; *Manhattan Nationalist* (KS), Oct. 18, 1906, 9; *Salt Lake Telegram* (UT), Nov. 22, 1911, 7; *Sheboygan Press* (WI), Oct. 9, 1947, 20 (obituary); Thomas L. St. Germaine Student File, reproduction of Folder 3305, Box 65, Series 1327, RG75, NARA, CDRC, http://carlisleindian.dickinson.edu/student_files/thomas-1-st-germaine-student-file. St. Germaine later played with the Oorang Indians: Chris Willis, *Walter Lingo, Jim Thorpe, and the Oorang Indians*, 106–07. On his career as an attorney, see Satz, ""Tell Those Gray Haired Men What They Should Know,"" *Wisconsin Magazine of History* 77 (Spring 1994): 196–224.

7. *Janesville Daily Gazette* (WI), Mar. 3, 1905, 1; *Lawrence Daily World*, Dec. 17,

1906, 4; *Carlisle Evening Herald*, Feb. 12, 1910, 1; *Evening Star* (Washington, DC), Oct. 7, 1910, 17.

8. "Blair to MVC Faculty Representatives, May 18, 1927, Folder 750, "Amusements, 1930," 3 of 3, Box 113, DCF, HI, RG75, NARA, KC.

9. Cordley, Chairman, Pacific Coast Athletic Conference Board of Control to Lipps, Dec. 17, 1927, and Lipps to Cordley, Dec. 20, 1927, Coquille Thompson file (455), Box 10, Graduated Student Case Files, CHEM, RG75, NARA, SEA; *Argus Leader*, Apr. 13, 1928, 10.

10. Haskell's pleas fell short with other conferences as well. Blair to MVC Faculty Representatives, May 18, 1927; Peairs to Hare, Southern Athletic Conference, Mar. 28, 1931; and Hare to Peairs, Apr. 7, 1931, Folder 750, "Amusements, 1930," 3 of 3, Box 113, DCF, HI, RG75, NARA, KC; Larson, Border Conference Commissioner to Kelley, Nov. 4, 1938, and Kelley to Larson, Dec. 5, 1938, Folder "Correspondence, 1939–1943," Box 113, DCF, HI, RG75, NARA, KC.

11. *An Illustrated Souvenir Catalog of the Cherokee National Female Seminary, Tahlequah, Indian Territory 1850 to 1906* (Chilocco, OK: Indian Print Shop Chilocco, OK, 1906), n.p.; Mihesuah,"Out of the Graves of the 'Polluted Debauches,'" *American Indian Quarterly* 15 (Autumn 1991): 503–15; Steven Crum, "The Choctaw Nation," *History of Education Quarterly* 47 (Feb. 2007): 49–68. Dwight teams: *Spalding's Official Basketball Guide, 1916–17*, 109–13; *Spalding's Official Basketball Guide, 1917–18*, 176; *Muskogee Times-Democrat*, Dec. 17, 1915, 11; *Fort Gibson New Era* (OK), Feb. 10, 1916, 4.

12. Carney, *Native American Higher Education in the United States*, 86; Lydia Reeder, *Dust Bowl Girls*, 61–72.

13. Carney, *Native American Higher Education in the United States*, 80–82.

14. *Daily Gazette*, Dec. 30, 1912, 1, Dec. 27, 1912, 1, and May 3, 1917, 3; *Morning Tulsa Daily World*, Feb. 5, 1916, 6, and Dec. 18, 1916, 8; Barbara Osteika, "William Louis Pappan," *Inside ATF*, Nov. 2010, http://barbeo.writersresidence.com/system/attachments/files/9321/original/Pappan_InsideATF_Nov2010.pdf?1291315552.

15. Robert Pruter, "Fait Elkins," in King, ed., *Native Americans in Sports*, 1:104–5.

16. According to Clyde's daughter Cheewa James, Shacknasty, which Clark dropped from the family name, was an Anglicized pronunciation of the Modoc name Shkeitko, which meant Left-handed Man: Cheewa James, correspondence with author, Mar. 1, 2018.

17. Cheewa James, *Modoc*, 140–45, 195–99, 242 and color plate 4–5; Cheewa James, correspondence with author, Jan. 20, 2016.

18. *Springfield Leader and Press* (MO), Apr. 28, 1921, 1, and Mar. 26, 1924, 5.

19. *Springfield Leader and Press*, Sept. 27, 1921, 7, and Dec. 14, 1923, 5; *Maryville Daily Forum* (MO), Apr. 13, 1968, 2.

20. *Springfield News Leader* (MO), Jan. 16, 1924, 3, Feb. 10, 1924, 6, Feb. 14, 1924, 5, Feb. 20, 1924, 5, and Mar. 4, 1924, 5; American Indian Athletic Hall of Fame, induction program, Dec. 3, 1977, courtesy of James.

21. "Data Sheet-O.M. 'Buck' Cheadle;" "Cheadle Becomes Hall of Fame Inductee"; and "Remembering an Elder My Precious Grandmother Mary Vera

Cheadle," Folder "Biography of Buck Cheadle," Box 19, CISC, OKHS; Putz, "Jesse 'Cab' Renick," 72–74, 79–83, and 89; Grundman, "Jesse Barnard 'Cab' Renick," 252–53.

22. Putz, "Jesse 'Cab' Renick," 72–74, 79–83, and 89.

23. *Statesman Journal,* Jan. 5, 1928, 6; *Morning Register* (Eugene, OR), Jan. 7, 1928, 4, and Jan. 8, 1928, 8; *Daily Capital Journal,* Dec. 4, 1929, 10.

24. *Argus Leader,* Mar. 19, 1938, 3, and Sept. 16, 1954, 2; *Rapid City Journal*, Mar. 28, 1938, 5.

25. *Argus Leader*, Nov. 16, 1938, 9, Nov. 24, 1938, 11, Nov. 30, 1938, 9. Hare's tribal affiliation is unknown to me.

26. *Argus Leader*, Dec. 2, 1938, 9, and Dec. 11, 1938, 13.

27. *Argus Leader*, Dec. 13, 1938, 13, Dec. 14, 1938, 11, Dec. 20, 1938, 9, and Jan. 7, 1939, 8.

28. *Argus Leader*, Dec. 23, 1938, 6, Jan. 7, 1939, 3, and Feb. 23, 1939, 14.

29. *Argus Leader*, Nov. 28, 1939, 8, Dec. 6, 1939, 11, and Apr. 19, 1940, 8; *Indianapolis Star*, Jan. 2, 1941, sec. 2–1.

30. Cahn, *Coming on Strong*, 56–65 and 85–91; Grundy and Shackelford, *Shattering the Glass*, 28 and 47.

31. Reeder, *Dust Bowl Girls*, 1–7.

32. Reeder, *Dust Bowl Girls*, 1–3, 45, 53, 138–98, and 238–45; Cahn, *Coming On Strong*, 88 and 92–94.

33. Szasz, *Education and the American Indian*, 107–9; Alison R. Bernstein, *American Indians and World War II* (Norman: University of Oklahoma Press, 1991), 142 and 146; Bobby Wright and William G. Tierney, "American Indians in Higher Education," *Change: The Magazine of Higher Learning,* 1991, 17.

34. Fuller, "Stacy S. 'Bub' Howell," in King, *Native Americans in Sports* 1:151–52; Parr, "Kenneth Jerry 'Iceman' 'Casper' Adair," in King, *Native Americans in Sports* 1:4–5; "Jerry Adair," https://www.sports-reference.com/cbb/players/jerry-adair-1.html.

35. Lemons grew up in Oklahoma and was told he was Native but never which tribes he descended from: Royse Parr, "A.E. 'Abe' Lemons," in King, *Native Americans in Sports* 1:183–4; Royse Parr, "Joseph 'Bud' Sahmaunt," in King, *Native Americans in Sports* 2:269–70; "Bud Sahmaunt," https://www.sports-reference.com/cbb/players/bud-sahmaunt-1.html; "An American Indian Tribute to Abe Lemons," Mike Tosee-Bill Curtis, 2005, https://www.youtube.com/watch?v=su8MKkCti30; *Argus Leader*, Mar. 17, 1959, 14; *Daily Oklahoman*, Feb. 4, 1962, E1, and Mar. 13, 1962, 15.

36. "An American Indian Tribute to Abe Lemons"; *Daily Oklahoman*, Feb. 24, 1967, 23 and 26, and June 20, 1987, 32; *Sheboygan Press*, Sept. 13, 1968, 21; "Gary Gray," Sports Reference, College Basketball, https://www.sports-reference.com/cbb/players/gary-gray-4.html.

37. "History of Oregon Institute of Technology," https://www.oit.edu/visitors-info/about/history; *Herald and News*, Dec. 1, 1955, 12, Mar. 23, 1958, 9, Apr. 16, 1958, 11, and Dec. 12, 1958, 9.

38. John Egan "Lookin' In," *Argus Leader*, Jan. 31, 1971, 38; *Daily Plainsman* (Huron, SD), Dec. 3, 1947, 9, and Mar. 17, 1948, 9; *Daily Republic* (Mitchell, SD), Feb. 19, 1948, 12.

39. Carney, *Native American Higher Education in the United States*, 87–94; Brayboy and Barton, *Playing Before an Overflow Crowd*, 78–82 and 110–16; Stilling, "Kelvin Sampson," in King, *Native Americans in Sports* 2:270–71.

40. Brayboy and Barton, *Playing Before an Overflow Crowd*, 92–99.

41. Phillip Smith interview by Tonya Carrol, Oct. 3, 2009, Western Carolina University Oral History Collection, HIST 474/574, Western Carolina University Hunter Library, Cullowhee, NC.

42. Zah and Iverson, *We Will Secure Our Future*, 40–41; *Navajo-Hopi Observer* (Flagstaff and Winslow, AZ), Apr. 14, 2004, https://www.nhonews.com/news/2005/jun/02/april-2004/.

43. Zah and Iverson, *We Will Secure Our Future*, 39–42.

44. Zah and Iverson, *We Will Secure Our Future*, 1, 42–45, and 164.

45. Thomas A. Britten, *American Indians in World War I* (Albuquerque: University of New Mexico Press, 1997), 65–67 and 84; Peter Iverson and Wade Davies, *"We Are Still Here"* (Malden, MA: Wiley Blackwell, 2015), 53–56 and 116–17.

46. Applin, "From Muscular Christianity to the Market Place," 174–78 and 273–74; Raymond B. Fosdick, "The War and Navy Departments Commissions on Training Camp Activities," *The Annals of the American Academy of Political and Social Science* 79 (September 1918): 130–42; Douglas Stark, *Wartime Basketball*, 135–36; Naismith, *Basketball*, 140–41.

47. *Catalogue of Haskell Institute, June, 1921*, 42, in Haskell, 1921, Reel 60, SANSR.

48. *Indian School Journal* (October 1918): 66.

49. *Houston Post*, Dec. 1, 1918, 17, Dec. 2, 1918, 7, Dec. 15, 1918, 19, and Dec. 18, 1918, 10.

50. Flood to Henry Roe Cloud, Sept. 13, 1933, Folder, "Football Coaches, 1933–1939," Box 115, DCF, HI, RG75, NARA, KC; As another example, Thomas Hawk Eagle played as the only Native on an integrated AEF football team in France: Krouse, *North American Indians in the Great War*, 198.

51. Bernstein, *American Indians and World War II*, 40; Stark, *Wartime Basketball*, 137–38. For examples of wartime cutbacks on Indian school interscholastic basketball, see: Nicholson memorandum, Jan. 21, 1942, Folder 021.2, "Recreation," 3 of 3, Box 466, Education DCF, 1937–1959, Pine Ridge Indian Agency, RG75, NARA, KC; Phoenix Indian School Athletic and Recreation Committee to Mr. Morgans, Jan. 20, 1942, Folder 750, "Athletics, 1941–1942," CCF, Phoenix Indian School, RG75, NARA, LA; Arthur S. Bensell to Superintendent of Trent Public School, Jan. 4, 1946, Folder 754.2, Box 31, DCF, Pipestone Indian School, RG75, NARA, KC.

52. McGregor, "Amateur Boxing and Assimilation at the Stewart Indian School, Carson City, Nevada, 1935–1948," in Salamone, ed., *The Native American Identity in Sports*, 51–52.

53. Cheadle: "Data Sheet-O.M. 'Buck' Cheadle," Folder "Biography of Buck Cheadle," Box 19, CISC, OKHS; Renick: *Albuquerque Journal*, Dec. 10, 1941, 6, and

May 14, 1942, 4; Stark, *Wartime Basketball*, 137–46; *Carroll Daily Times Herald* (IA), Dec. 29, 1943, 4; *Stars and Stripes Weekly* (Mediterranean-Algiers), Jan. 29, 1944, 14; *Miami Daily News-Record*, Jan. 18, 1944, 4, and Dec. 21, 1945, 6, 4; Putz, "Jesse Renick," 83–84.

54. Soldier Sanders interview summary, World War II: Mountain Memories Collection, Special Collections, D.H. Ramsey Library, University of North Carolina, Asheville. http://toto.lib.unca.edu/findingaids/oralhistory/WWII/sanders_soldier.pdf.

55. Sanders interview summary; Reid Chapman and Deborah Miles, *Asheville and Western North Carolina in World War II* (Charleston: Arcadia Publishing, 2006), 75; *Asheville Citizen Times*, Mar. 6, 1991, 47, and Aug. 31, 2007, 14.

56. Roessel, *Indian Communities in Action* (Tempe: Arizona State University, 1967), 32 and 41–42.

57. Many of the Sioux Travelers discussed in the following chapter played on service teams: *News-Palladium* (Benton Harbor, MI), Dec. 11, 1946, 12; *Messenger-Inquirer* (Owensboro, KY), Jan. 22, 1947, 10. All the members of the Oklahoma Indians professional team that played in the late 1940s played on service teams: *Cumberland Evening Times*, Feb. 4, 1947, 16; *Messenger-Inquirer*, Feb. 3, 1948, 10. On service teams exposing basketball players to an ethnic and regional diversity of styles and techniques, see Stark, *Wartime Basketball*, xvi.

Chapter 9. Barnstormers

1. Peterson, *Cages to Jump Shots*, 110; Applin, "From Muscular Christianity," 98–105 and 209. The reference to the luggage is borrowed from Chinese American barnstormers, described in Yep, *Outside the Paint*, 56.

2. Moses, *Wild West Shows*, 4–5.

3. Steve Young, "American Indian Team Played with Best in '30s," *Argus Leader*, June 10, 1987, 1A–2A.

4. Yep, "Peddling Sport," 975.

5. On the struggles finding work on reservations and utility of seasonal work, see Adams, *Education for Extinction*, 28; Iverson and Davies, *"We Are Still Here,"* 74–78.

6. Andrew Hogarth, *Lakota Spirit* (Andrew Hogarth, 1992), 11.

7. On the early history of professional basketball, and conditions for players, see Peterson, *Cages to Jump Shots*.

8. Basloe, *I Grew Up with Basketball*, 190.

9. Deloria, *Indians in Unexpected Places*, 126 and 130–31; Oxendine, *American Indian Sports Heritage*, 239–55 and 217–79; Powers-Beck, *The American Indian Integration of Baseball*, 60–61.

10. Frank J. Basloe admitted to this sort of behavior in *I Grew Up with Basketball*, 46.

11. Peterson, *Cages to Jump Shots*, 64–68.

12. Peterson, *Cages to Jump Shots*, 103; Robert S. Fogarty, *The Righteous Remnant* (Kent, OH: Kent State University Press, 1981), 121–24; Hawkins and Bertolino, *The House of David Baseball Team* (Chicago: Arcadia, 2001), 7–9, 41–47, and 114;

Sanford, "African-American Baseballists and the Denver Post Tournament," *Colorado Heritage* (Spring 1995): 30.

13. Cheree Franco, "Without the All American Red Heads, There Would Be no WNBA," *Arkansas Times*, Nov. 7, 2012, https://www.arktimes.com/arkansas/without-the-all-american-red-heads-there-would-be-no-wnba/Content?oid=2522479; Grundy and Shackelford, *Shattering the Glass*, 103–7; Robert W. Ikard, *Just for Fun* (Fayetteville: University of Arkansas Press, 2005), 26; Peterson, *Cages to Jump Shots*, 104–5.

14. Peterson, *Cages to Jump Shots*, 104–5; Franco, "Without the All American Red Heads"; Grundy and Shackelford, *Shattering the Glass*, 102–4; Ikard, *Just for Fun*, 23–25.

15. Franco, "Without the All American Red Heads"; Grundy and Shackelford, *Shattering the Glass*, 103–7; Ikard, *Just for Fun*, 23–29.

16. Yep, "Peddling Sport," 971–87.

17. Peterson, *Cages to Jump Shots*, 95–107; Dave Zinkoff with Edgar Williams, *Around the World with the Harlem Globetrotters* (Philadelphia: Macrae Smith, 1953), 28; Josh Wiker, *The Harlem Globetrotters* (Philadelphia: Chelsea House, 1997), 23–43; Gems, "Blocked Shot," 148; McKissack. *Black Hoops*, 71. Barnstormers needed rest periods because they traveled with fewer players than host teams had: Edward J. Doyle, "Independent Teams Have Successful Season but Want Uniform Rules," in *The Reach Official Basket Ball Guide, 1924–25* (Philadelphia: A.J. Reach Company, 1925), 221.

18. Examples of "full-blooded" promotions: *Fort Wayne Sentinel* (IN), Jan. 5, 1920, 15; *Sheboygan Press*, Oct. 29, 1921, 3, and Jan. 9, 1931, 13; *News-Herald* (Franklin, PA), Feb. 21, 1923, 10; *Star Tribune*, Mar. 6, 1928, 13.

19. Examples of "war dances" at halftime: *Star-Gazette* (Elmira, NY), Jan. 30, 1928, 8; *Daily Republican* (Rushville, IN), Dec. 2, 1929, 5; *Sedalia Democrat*, Nov. 30, 1930, 9; *Morning Call* (Allentown, PA), Jan. 16, 1947, 18.

20. *Sheboygan Press*, Sept. 24, 1921, 3; *News-Herald*, Feb. 14, 1923, 3; *Morning Herald* (Uniontown, PA), Jan. 10, 1927, 11; *Journal and Courier* (Lafayette, IN), Jan. 13, 1932, 11. Jim Thorpe, for example, was occasionally listed as Bright Path on the World Famous Indians roster, which was the translation of the name Wa-tho-huck his mother gave him at birth: Robert W. Wheeler, *Jim Thorpe* (Norman: University of Oklahoma Press, 1981), 3. It is difficult to know which Native players were given fabricated Indian names, but the practice was made apparent by the occasional recycling of the same names for different Native players on the same teams.

21. Examples with headdresses: *Akron Beacon Journal*, Dec. 20, 1928, 27; *Messenger-Inquirer*, Feb. 3, 1948, 10. An example without: *Hancock Democrat* (Greenfield, IN), Dec. 23, 1948, 8. Rare photo of a player in full traditional attire (but shirtless with sneakers): *Marshfield News-Herald* (WI), Feb. 26, 1929, 8.

22. Nick Lassa was an inactive player serving this role. He was known as "Chief Long Time Sleep" in promotions for the World Famous Indians: *Star-Gazette* (Elmira, NY), Jan. 30, 1928, 8; Maggie Plummer, "Long Time Sleep," *Char-Koosta News*, Oct. 25, 2007, 4–5. White Feather: *Post-Crescent* (Appleton, WI), Nov. 11, 1927, 22;

Green Bay Press-Gazette, Nov. 13, 1928, 13, and Nov. 27, 1928, 11; *Rhinelander Daily News* (WI), Dec. 8, 1928, 7.

23. Powers-Beck, *The American Indian Integration of Baseball*, 51–66.

24. Pearis to Green, Sept. 1, 1903, bound volume, Letters Sent by the Athletic Program, HI, RG75, NARA, KC; C. H. Asbury of Crow Agency to George Bartholomew, Feb. 24, 1924, and Commissioner Merritt to Asbury, Mar. 3, 1924, Reel 18, Central Classified Files, 1907–1939, RG75, Series B: Indian Customs and Social Relations, University Publications of America, Bethesda, Maryland, Microfilm. Wild West shows: Moses, *Wild West Shows*, 7, 66–74, and 137–40.

25. *Chicago Tribune*, Dec. 16, 1904, 8, Jan. 15, 1905, 11, Dec. 9, 1906, 15, and Dec. 26, 1906, 10; *Des Moines Register*, Jan. 4, 1907, 7, and Jan. 6, 1907, 16.

26. *Des Moines Register*, Jan. 6, 1907, 5.

27. Peterson, *Cages to Jump Shots*, 61; also see Grundman, *The Golden Age of Amateur Basketball*, 5.

28. Basloe, *I Grew Up with Basketball*, 93–95. See also Michael A. Antonucci's discussion in the introduction to Basloe's book, xii.

29. The authenticity of these teams can be confirmed by tracing player names back to Indian school records, although it is not possible to tell by these means whether all team members were Native.

30. "The Dakota Eagles," memo, Nov. 29, 1932, Folder 754.2, Box 124, DCF, FIS, RG75, NARA, KC.

31. *Green Bay Press-Gazette*, Feb. 14, 1931, 13.

32. *Green Bay Press-Gazette*, Mar. 14, 1917, 8, Feb. 21, 1929, 13, Nov. 29, 1930, 14, and Jan. 12, 1931, 14; *Oshkosh Northwest*, Mar. 17, 1917, 12, and Mar. 10, 1939, 17; *Sheboygan Press*, Dec. 13, 1920, 5, and Jan. 14, 1932, 18; *Post-Crescent*, Feb. 1, 1928, 12; *Stevens Point Journal* (WI), Jan. 8, 1931, 4, and Jan. 23, 1931, 2.

33. According to Patty Loew, the local baseball team went by the "Braves" name, whereas off-reservation newspapers refer to the basketball team as the "Indians": Loew, "Newspapers and the Lake Superior Chippewa in the 'Unprogressive' Era," PhD diss., University of Wisconsin-Madison, 1998, 223–24.

34. Basloe, *I Grew up with Basketball*, 153–55.

35. Basloe, *I Grew up with Basketball*, 154.

36. Basloe, *I Grew up with Basketball*, 155. Odanah teams also competed later in the 1920s: *Eau Claire Leader*, Mar. 9, 1927, 7.

37. *Des Moines Register*, Dec. 16, 1916, 6, and Dec. 17, 1916, 7; *Belvidere Daily Republican* (IL), Dec. 19, 1916, 7; *Huntington Press* (IN), Jan. 8, 1920, 6.

38. Michael Sherfy, "Pete Hauser," in King, ed., *Native Americans in Sports* 1:141–42; *Huntington Press*, Jan. 8, 1920, 6.

39. *Fort Wayne Sentinel*, Jan. 5, 1920, 15; *Huntington Press*, Jan. 8, 1920, 6.

40. *Belvidere Daily Republican* (IL), Dec. 23, 1916, 4; *Huntington Press* (IN), Jan. 9, 1920, 6; *Indianapolis Star*, Jan. 12, 1920, 11.

41. *Belvidere Daily Republican*, Dec. 19, 1916, 7; *Indianapolis Star*, Jan. 17, 1920, 12, and Nov. 25, 1920, 13; *Muncie Evening Press* (IN), Jan. 26, 1920, 6; *Richmond Item* (IN), Jan. 27, 1920, 1.

42. *Palladium-Item* (Richmond, IN), Dec. 9, 1921, 15; *Journal and Courier*, Jan. 31, 1924, 11; *Times Herald* (Port Huron, MI), Jan. 30, 1924, 11.

43. CPI Inflation Calculator, https://www.bls.gov/data/inflation_calculator.htm.

44. *Buffalo Evening News*, Jan. 21, 1915, 19; *Times Herald* (Port Huron, MI), Jan. 25, 1918, 11; *Detroit Free Press* (MI), Jan. 25, 1918, 13; *Washington Herald*, Feb. 17, 1918, 10.

45. V. J. Zunigha of Okmulgee to "Dear Sir," Oct. 31, 1919, and Peairs to Zunigha, Nov. 5, 1919, Folder "Basketball, 1919," Box 2, SCF, HI, RG75, NARA, KC.

46. *Democrat and Chronicle* (Rochester, NY), Feb. 4, 1914, 17, Jan. 20, 1916, 23, and Feb. 2, 1919, 38; *Buffalo Evening News* (NY), Jan. 21, 1915, 19.

47. Chief Clinton Rickard, with Barbara Graymont, *Fighting Tuscarora* (Syracuse: Syracuse University Press, 1973), picture insert of team photo; *Democrat and Chronical*, Jan. 20, 1916, 23.

48. *Buffalo Evening News*, Feb. 28, 1918, 17; *Democrat and Chronical*, Feb. 2, 1919, 38; *Niagara Falls Gazette* (NY), Nov. 30, 1921, 14; *News-Herald*, Mar. 1, 1922, 9.

49. *News-Herald*, Feb. 28, 1922, 10; *Call Leader* (Elwood, IN), Mar. 2, 1922, 6; *Alexandria Times-Tribune* (IN), Mar. 6, 1922, 1.

50. *Buffalo Courier*, Nov. 4, 1921, 11; *Niagara Falls Gazette*, Nov. 30, 1921, 14; *Fort Wayne Journal-Gazette* (IN), Feb. 26, 1922, 13; *News Herald*, Feb. 12, 1923, 3, and Feb. 14, 1923, 3. $2.50: *Harrisburg Telegraph* (PA), Feb. 11, 1924, 15.

51. *News-Herald*, Jan. 17, 1924, 13.

52. *New Castle News* (PA), Feb. 9, 1923, 28; *Altoona Mirror* (PA), Feb. 9, 1929, 14; *Evening News* (Harrisburg, PA), Dec. 13, 1930, 17.

53. *Green Bay Press Gazette*, Apr. 20, 1920, 4; *Sheboygan Press*, Oct. 11, 1920, 3, Sept. 4, 1921, 3, and Nov. 14, 1921, 10; *Janesville Daily Gazette*, Dec. 2, 1921, 10; *Daily Tribune* (Wisconsin Rapids), Jan. 17, 1923, 6; John J. Leroy Student File, reproduction of folder 5090, box 128, Series 1327, RG75, NARA, CDRC, http://carlisleindian.dickinson.edu/sites/all/files/docs-ephemera/NARA_1327_b128_f5090.pdf.

54. *The Sheboygan Press*, Jan. 7, 1924, 3; *Eau Claire Leader*, Feb. 27, 1927, 10.

55. *Post-Crescent*, Nov. 11, 1927, 22; *Daily Tribune*, Jan. 5, 1928, 5; *Ironwood Daily Globe* (MI), Mar. 20, 1928, 7; *Green Bay Press-Gazette*, Nov. 13, 1928, 13, Nov. 27, 1928, 11, and Nov. 20, 1934, 14.

56. *Sedalia Democrat*, Nov. 30, 1930, 9; *Edinburg Daily Courier* (IN), Feb. 13, 1931, 1; *Cincinnati Enquirer*, Jan. 19, 1933, 14; *Council Grove Republican* (KS), Jan. 21, 1933, 1.

57. *Belvidere Daily Republican*, Jan. 3, 1947, 3, and Jan. 7, 1947, 6; *Standard-Sentinel* (Hazelton, PA), Feb. 4, 1947, 13.

58. *History Detectives*, episode 10, 2005, http://www-tc.pbs.org/opb/historydetectives/static/media/transcripts/2011-04-27/310_jimthorpe.pdf; Bill Pennington, "Jim Thorpe and a Ticket to Serendipity," *New York Times*, Mar. 29, 2005, online, https://www.nytimes.com/2005/03/29/sports/othersports/jim-thorpe-and-a-ticket-to-serendipity.html; William A. Cook, *Jim Thorpe* (Jefferson, NC: McFarland, 2011), 167–68.

59. Springwood, "Playing Football, Playing Indian," in King, *Native Athletes in Sport and Society*, 128–40; Buford, *Native American Son*, 233–38.

60. *Akron Beacon Journal*, Dec. 18, 1923, 23, and Jan. 1, 1924, 16; *Fremont Messenger* (OH), Dec. 26, 1923, 5.

61. *Akron Beacon Journal*, Sept. 5, 1912, 10, Jan. 27, 1913, 6, and June 16, 1920, 13; *Akron Evening Times* (OH), Dec. 8, 1919, 11, Dec. 24, 1919, 10, and June 21, 1920, 8; *Press and Sun-Bulletin* (Binghamton, NY), Mar. 18, 1920, 20.

62. *Marion Star* (OH), Feb. 12, 1923, 2, and Feb. 27, 1923, 10; *Defiance Crescent-News* (OH), Oct. 13, 1923, 6.

63. Baseball: *Lima News* (OH), Aug. 2, 1926, 10; Adrienne McGee, "Jim Thorpe's Ohio Ties," in *Lima News*, Aug. 17, 2011, D1 and D3; *Findlay Morning Republican* (OH), Aug. 8, 1926, 21. As with basketball, the football revival was initially known as the Oorang Indians and later the World Famous Indians: *Dayton Daily News* (OH), Oct. 19, 1926, 15; *Marion Star*, Oct. 26, 1926, 12, and Nov. 18, 1926, 16.

64. *Akron Beacon Journal*, Oct. 30, 1926, 21; *Coshocton Tribune* (OH), Nov. 22, 1926, 16; *Marion Star*, Dec. 17, 1926, 20.

65. *Coshocton Tribune*, Nov. 22, 1926, 3; *Richmond Item*, Dec. 22, 1926, 5, Dec. 30, 1926, 5, and Feb. 3, 1928, 11; *Star Press* (Muncie, IN), Dec. 24, 1926, 10.

66. *Times Herald*, Jan. 29, 1927, 13; *Altoona Tribune*, Mar. 8, 1927, 17, and Mar. 12, 1927, 6; *Harrisburg Telegraph*, Mar. 15, 1927, 9; *Marion Star*, Dec. 24, 1927, 16; *Evening Review* (E. Liverpool, OH), Apr. 1, 1927, 30. Parton: Haskell, 1924, Reel 60, SANSR; *Indian Leader*, June 13–20, 1924, 4; L. Wapp, *Indian Leader*, Mar. 14, 1924, 2; *Morning Herald*, Jan. 10, 1927, 11.

67. *Indian Leader*, Jan. 7, 1927, 3; *Morning Herald*, Jan. 10, 1927, 10; *Lebanon Daily News* (PA), Mar. 24, 1927, 6; *Star-Gazette*, Jan. 30, 1928, 8; *Evening Review*, Mar. 20, 1929, 13.

68. *Sentinel* (Carlisle, PA), Mar. 17, 1927, 4; *Evening News*, Mar. 6, 1929, 25; *Evening Review*, Apr. 1, 1927, 30, and Mar. 18, 1929, 13. Wapp and Jackson: Frank Waldman, *Famous American Athletes of Today* (Boston: L. C. Page, 1951), 94; Chuck Menville, *The Harlem Globetrotters* (New York: David McKay, 1978), 16.

69. *Times Herald*, Jan. 29, 1927, 13; *Lebanon Daily News*, Mar. 24, 1927, 6; *Evening Sun* (Baltimore, MD), Dec. 29, 1927, 29; *Chicago Tribune*, Mar. 8, 1928, 16; *Akron Beacon Journal*, Dec. 20, 1928, 27; *Evening Review*, Mar. 18, 1929, 13, and Mar. 22, 1929, 14.

70. *Pittsburgh Daily Post* (PA), Jan. 11, 1927, 11; *Lebanon Daily News*, Mar. 24, 1927, 6; *Evening News*, Mar. 15, 1929, 24; Buford, *Native American Son*, 254.

71. *Evening Review*, Apr. 4, 1927, 14.

72. *Harrisburg Sunday Courier* (PA), Mar. 20, 1927, 1; *Evening News*, Mar. 21, 1927, and Mar. 22, 1927, 6.

73. *Evening News*, Mar. 22, 1927, 6; *Lebanon Daily News*, Mar. 24, 1927, 6.

74. *Akron Beacon Journal*, Dec. 20, 1927, 33; *Baltimore Sun*, Dec. 31, 1927, 12; *Evening Review*, Mar. 13, 1928, 15.

75. *Marion Star*, Oct. 4, 1928, 14; *Atlanta Constitution*, Jan. 28, 1929, 8; *Bee* (Danville, VA), Mar. 1, 1929, 12; *Evening News*, Mar. 6, 1929, 25, and Mar. 15, 1929, 24. Skelley obituary: *News-Journal* (Mansfield, OH), May 2, 1969, 18.

76. Peterson, *Cages to Jump Shots*, 103–4; *Daily Republican*, Nov. 26, 1929, 5, and Dec. 2, 1929, 5; *Decatur Herald* (IL), Dec. 13, 1929, 26, and Dec. 15, 1929, 22.

77. *Muscatine Journal and News-Tribune* (IA), Jan. 4, 1933, 6, and Jan. 12, 1933, 6. Wapp with the Nebraska Indians: *News-Journal*, July 7, 1925, 9.

78. *Elyria Chronical Telegram* (OH), Dec. 28, 1933, 12; *Clarion-Ledger*, Jan. 7, 1934, 11; *Sheboygan Press*, Mar. 22, 1934, 13; *Dispatch* (Moline, IL), Nov. 21, 1934, 15; *Oshkosh Northwester*, Nov. 30, 1934, 20; *Morning Herald* (Hagerstown, MD), Jan. 1, 1938, 6; *Leaf-Chronicle* (Clarksville, TN), Dec. 15, 1937, 4; *Montgomery Advertiser* (AL), Jan. 15, 1939, 9.

79. *Akron Beacon Journal*, Dec. 9, 1927, 41; Peterson, *Cages to Jump Shots*, 116; "Porter's Window Shades vs. Diamond Oilers" scorecard, courtesy of Cheewa James.

80. Grundman, *The Golden Age of Amateur Basketball*, xvi–xvii; Putz, "Jesse 'Cab" Renick," 85; Applin, "From Muscular Christianity to the Market Place," 185–87 and 276–77; Ikard, *Just for Fun*, 16 and 18.

81. Miller to James, Nov. 25, 1927, courtesy of Cheewa James; *Albuquerque Journal*, Jan. 3, 1927, 2; *Argus Leader*, July 20, 1927, 8.

82. *Argus Leader*, July 20, 1927, 8; *Petaluma Argus-Courier* (CA), Feb. 6, 1929, 3; *Courier* (Waterloo, IA), Feb. 12, 1931, 15; "Porter's Window Shades vs. Diamond Oilers" scorecard.

83. Grundman, "Jesse Barnard "Cab" Renick," in King, ed., *Native American in Sports*, vol. 2, 253; Putz, "Jesse Renick," 84–87; Applin, "From Muscular Christianity," 276–77.

84. Later teams using Sioux Travelers name: *Knoxville Journal*, Feb. 20, 1955, 6B and *Bismarck Tribune*, Mar. 8, 1977, 17.

85. Steve Young, "American Indian Team Played with Best in '30s," *Argus Leader*, Jun. 10, 1987, 1A–2A.

86. *Galva News* (IL), Feb. 9, 1939, 6; *St. Cloud Times* (MN), Mar. 12, 1946, 8; *Rapid City Journal*, Oct. 9, 1946, 10, and June 18, 1948, 9; *Fairmount News* (IN), Jan. 9, 1947, 1; *Daily Journal* (Vineland, NJ), Jan. 21, 1948, 12; *Journal News* (White Plains, NY), Oct. 9, 1996, 6 (Jerry's obit.); *Todd County Tribune*, May 29, 2013, http://trib-news.com/obituaries/235-francis-edward-donovan (Francis's obit.).

87. Young, "American Indian Team Played with Best in '30s"; Blacksmith: *Rapid City Journal*, Mar. 5, 1946, 8, and Dec. 26, 1946, 8; *Daily Journal*, Feb. 23, 1949, 8. Cuny: *Daily Times* (Salisbury, MD), Jan. 5, 1948, 8. Little: *Rapid City Journal*, Dec. 27, 1946, 8. Valandra: *Journal News* (White Plains), Dec. 10, 1947, 10.

88. *Rapid City Journal*, Mar. 5, 1950, 25; *Daily World* (Opelousas, LA), Feb. 20, 1955, 42. Jack Little said he and four other players formed the team, but this appears to have been in 1941, a few years after Blacksmith and others were playing under the Sioux Travelers name: Hogarth, *Lakota Spirit*, 10.

89. For examples of the Globetrotters playing Native teams outside of South Dakota, see Bloom, *To Show What an Indian Can Do*, picture insert of Pipestone gymnasium (Pipestone Indian School, MN); *Kossuth County Advocate* (Algona, IA), Mar. 20, 1930, 9 (Al Seeger's Indians in Iowa); *Billings Gazette*, Feb. 13, 1939, 6 (Crow AAU team in Montana).

90. Menville, *The Harlem Globetrotters*, 19; Henry Flood to C. W. Robnett, Feb. 8, 1933, Folder 754.4, Box 124, DCF, FIS, RG75, NARA, KC; Martin Schiltz to E. C. Holton, Feb. 26, 1934, Folder 13, Box 15, NCIBT, LUC; *Argus Leader*, Mar. 14, 1938, 3.

91. Interview with Agnes and Norbert Piocotte.

92. *Argus Leader*, Dec. 16, 1938, 9, Dec. 20, 1938, 9, and Dec. 23, 1938, 6.

93. *Courier*, Mar. 14, 1941, 13; *Dispatch*, Mar. 22, 1941, 15, and Mar. 31, 1941, 17.

94. Vincent Brewer with Jerry Matthews, "Back in the Day with the St. Francis Indian School Basketball Team of 1941," *Lakota Country Times*, May, 22, 2014, http://www.lakotacountrytimes.com/news/2014–05–22/Sports/Back_in_the_Day_with_the_St_Francis_Indian_School_.html; *Rapid City Journal*, Aug. 8, 1941, 10, Mar. 16, 1948, 13, and June 9, 1948, 13; *Cumberland Evening Times* (MD), Jan. 6, 1942, 14–15; *Deadwood Pioneer Times*, Mar. 10, 1946, 1; *Lead Daily Call*, Mar. 11, 1946, 4. Travelers on service teams included Willie Blacksmith and Seth White Owl: *Owensboro Messenger* (KY), Jan. 22, 1947, 10.

95. *Owensboro Messenger*, Mar. 18, 1947, 10; *Daily Journal* (Vineland), Jan. 21, 1948, 12; *Daily Reporter* (Greenfield, IN), Mar. 9, 1948, 6; *Rapid City Journal*, Mar. 16, 1948, 13; *Rushville Republican*, Mar. 25, 1948, 4.

96. *Journal News* (White Plains), Dec. 10, 1947, 10; Young, "American Indian team."

97. *Rushville Republican*, Dec. 8, 1947, 5; *Daily Journal* (Vineland), Jan. 17, 1948, 8, and Jan. 19, 1948, 4.

98. *Rapid City Journal*, Mar. 5, 1946, 8 (Iron Wing); *Daily Sentinel* (Woodstock, IL), Jan. 4, 1940, 1; *Owensboro Messenger*, Mar. 18, 1947, 8; *Rapid City Journal*, Apr. 8, 1947, 10, and Feb. 3, 1948, 12.

99. Hogarth, *Lakota Spirit*, 10; *Freeport Journal-Standard* (IL), Jan. 18, 1939, 13; *News-Palladium*, Jan. 12, 1940, 6; *Deadwood Pioneer Times*, Mar. 10, 1946, 1; *Baltimore Sun*, Feb. 7, 1947, 17; *Rhinelander Daily News*, Dec. 5, 1947, 6; *Odessa American*, Jan. 1, 1948, 9; *Daily Journal* (Vineland), Jan. 21, 1948, 12; *Noblesville Ledger* (IN), Mar. 3, 1948, 2.

100. *Rapid City Journal*, Dec. 15, 1947, 14; *Rushville Republican*, Dec. 15, 1947, 2.

101. Peterson, *Cages to Jump Shots*, 173; Applin, "From Muscular Christianity," 241, 245, and 299.

102. On the diminishing desire of Native people to forgo their community connections to pursue professional careers later in the twentieth century, see Deloria, *Indians in Unexpected Places*, 132–33, and Oxendine, *American Indian Sports Heritage*, 265–66.

103. *Morning Herald* (Hagerstown), Feb. 24, 1949, 18; *Daily Journal* (Vineland), Mar. 1, 1949, 6; *Daily World*, Feb. 22, 1955, 24.

104. References to Lakota/Dakota people's admiration for the Travelers include Deloria, *Indians in Unexpected Places*, 129; Greg Hansen, "Current Team Continues Travelers' Heritage," *Rapid City Journal*, Jan. 7, 1983, 5; David F. Strain nomination of Martin Waukazoo to the South Dakota High School Basketball Hall of Fame, Alameda Health Consortium website, https://www.alamedahealthconsortium.org/general/martin-waukazoo-inducted-into-hall-of-fame/.

Chapter 10. Communities

1. *Indian Leader*, Mar. 9, 1900, 2–3. On student letter-writing practices and Indian Service efforts to disseminate school newspapers, see Child, *Boarding School Seasons*, 27 and 76–77; Littlefield and Parins, *American Indian and Alaska Native Newspapers and Periodicals*, xxviii–xxix.

2. Reservation boarding school attendance: Adams, *Education for Extinction*, 320; Ellis, *To Change Them Forever*, 20–21.

3. Fort Bidwell, 1920, Reel 48, SANSR; Bigman to Whiteman, Feb. 13, 1937, Folder 419.3, Box 44, DCF, Crow Indian Agency, RG75, NARA, DEN; Dial to Clark, Nov. 26, 1930, Folder 754, Box 121, Corr. Files, Fort Belknap Indian Agency, RG75, NARA, DEN.

4. Brashear to Commissioner of Indian Affairs, Apr. 16, 1937, Folder 419.3, Box 44, DCF, Crow Indian Agency, RG75, NARA, DEN; Entry for Mar. 27, 1909, Superintendent's Diary, Tulalip Indian Agency, RG75, NARA, SEA.

5. *Edgefield Advertiser* (SC), Jan. 25, 1922, 1.

6. Sneddon, "Basketball Is the Flower of Their Eye," *Reno-Gazette-Journal* (NV), Feb. 22, 1986, 9; *Nevada State Journal* (Reno), Feb. 23, 1951, 11, and Apr. 15, 1969, 12; *Reno Gazette-Journal*, Dec. 16, 1958, 16.

7. Adams, *Education for Extinction*, 275–80; Sullivan, "Education through Sport," 111–13.

8. Neilson, "The Sports of the Zunis," *Indians at Work* 2 (Jan. 1, 1935): 35; Buchner, "Shinny and 'Snakes' on Rosebud," *Indians at Work* 2 (Aug. 1, 1935): 30–31; LeSier, "Fish-Spearing at Fort Hall," *Indians at Work* 2 (Aug. 1, 1935): 39–40.

9. Baseball's popularity, see: Entry for Mar. 27, 1909, Superintendent's Diary, Tulalip Indian Agency, RG75, NARA, SEA; Superintendent of the Southern Pueblos Indian Agency to Paisano, Aug. 16, 1920, Folder 750, Box 122, GCF, 1911–1935, Southern Pueblos Indian Agency, RG75, NAARA, DEN; Peter Iverson, *Diné: A History of the Navajos* (Albuquerque: University of New Mexico Press, 2002), 125. Interaction with lacrosse and stickball: Powers-Beck, *The American Indian Integration of Baseball*, 16–18; Loew, "Newspapers and the Lake Superior Chippewa in the 'Unprogressive' Era," PhD diss., University of Wisconsin-Madison, 1998, 217–41; Blanchard, *The Mississippi Choctaws at Play*, 41–52.

10. Iverson, *Riders of the West*, 11–25.

11. Marc Rasmussen, *Six* (Pierre: South Dakota State Historical Society Press, 2011), 81–87. Native six-man teams in South Dakota: *Lead Daily Call*, Sept. 20, 1938, 1.

12. In addition to examples cited below, this paragraph is based on Tim Brayboy telephone interview by the author, Jan. 19, 2016, and the Mike Chavez interview.

13. Rickard, with Graymont, *Fighting Tuscarora*, 50–51.

14. Droulias, "Social Benefits and Cultural Consequences of Basketball in Alaska," PhD diss., University of Alaska, Fairbanks, 2013, 44–46. Metlakatla: *Statesman Journal*, Sept. 21, 1924, 6; *Ogden Standard-Examiner* (UT), Apr. 3, 1928, 9; *Fairbanks Daily News-Miner* (AK), Jan. 2, 1934, 4.

15. On the lack of facilities and high costs of basketball travel in Alaska, see

Droulias, "Social Benefits and Cultural Consequences of Basketball in Alaska," 2–4 and 50; D'Orso, *Eagle Blue*, 19 and 46.

16. *Dunkirk Evening Observer* (NY), Jun. 21, 1929, 5 (Cattaraugus); Blanchard, "Basketball and the Culture-Change Process," 9.

17. *Martin Messenger* (SD) Nov. 30, 1922, 1, Jan. 18, 1923, 3, Jan. 18, 1924, 8.

18. *Native American*, Apr. 4, 1925, 87; Martha Jane Buchner, "Shinny and Snakes on Rosebud," *Indians at Work* 2 (Aug. 1, 1935): 30–31; Voget, *They Call Me Agnes* (Norman: University of Oklahoma Press, 1995), xxi.

19. A. H. Kneale, *Indian Agent* (Caldwell, ID: Caxton Printers, 1950), 390 and 422–23; *Gallup Independent*, Feb. 17, 1936, 3.

20. Parman, "The Indian Civilian Conservation Corps," PhD diss., University of Oklahoma, Norman, 1967, 54–66 and 236.

21. Parman, "The Indian Civilian Conservation Corps," 66; N.a. *Indians at Work*, 5 (Oct. 15, 1933): 30 (Navajo CCC teams), and 10 (Jan. 1, 1936): 47–48 (Shoshone CCC leagues); Basketball scheduling letters from 1934, Folder 750, Box 73, Central Files, Cheyenne and Arapaho Indian Agency, RG75, NARA, FW; "Athletic Feet," Sept. 8, 1933, Folder "Weekly Work Reports to June 30, 1934," Box 2, Annual Work Report of Indian Conservation Work, 1934, Records of the Superintendent, Indian Emergency Conservation Work, CHIL, RG75, NARA, FW.

22. Grundman, *The Golden Age of Amateur Basketball*, 60–61; *Billings Gazette*, Feb. 13, 1939, 6, Feb. 24, 1939, 13, and Mar. 5, 1939, 8; *Great Falls Tribune*, Mar. 13, 1939, 6; *Independent-Record* (Helena, MT), Mar. 15, 1939, 7.

23. "Duties and Working Hours for Lloyd Eagle Bull," Folder 021.2, 1 of 3; "Minutes of the Agency Recreational Committee Meeting," Sept. 11, 1939, Folder 2 of 3; "Minutes Recreational Committee Meeting," Nov. 6, 1939, Folder 2 of 3; and "Minutes of the Agency Recreational Committee Meeting," Sept. 25, 1940, Folder 021.2, 1 of 3, all in Box 466, Education Decimal Files, Pine Ridge Indian Agency, RG75, NARA, KC.

24. Fort Belknap: *Indians at Work* 2 (Feb. 15, 1935): 45; *Indians at Work* 3 (Dec. 15, 1935): 51; "National Register of Historic Places Registration Form: Lodgepole Community Hall," https://npgallery.nps.gov/GetAsset/8c62c491–185b-4162-be6a-475803715ba1. Heart Butte: *Great Falls Tribune*, Apr. 28, 1931, 11, and May 6, 1931, 11; *Indians at Work* 2 (Oct. 1, 1934): 38–39.

25. Kickingwoman, interview by author, Missoula, MT, Jan. 22, 2016; *Great Falls Tribune*, Dec. 4, 1934, 3.

26. Kickingwoman interview.

27. This was not always the case, as some Natives attending public schools still traveled great distances from home for daily classes or even boarded at the school: David Wallace Adams, *Three Roads to Magdalena* (Lawrence: University Press of Kansas, 2016), 265–82.

28. Adams, *Education for Extinction*, 28; Jon Reyhner and Jeanne Eder, *American Indian Education* (Norman: University of Oklahoma Press, 2006), 224–25; Iverson, *Diné*, 173.

29. Eighth grade girls basketball at Pima Day School: Skinner to Porter, Feb. 14, 1935, Folder 750, "Amusements and Athletics, 1935," Box 129, CCF, Phoenix Indian

School, RG75, NARA, LA. Day school basketball and use of facilities on various reservations: Hackett, Principal of Little Eagle Community Day School, "A Summary of Three Years' Work," July 11, 1938, Reel 1, Series D: Education, Part 1, CCF, 1907–1939, RG75, Microfilm (Bethesda, MD, University Publications of America); McWhinnie of Wind River Indian Agency to Stone, "Day School Gymnasium," Apr. 28, 1939, and Stone to CIA, Sept. 8, 1939, Folder 414.3, Box 337, GCF, Wind River Indian Agency, RG75, NARA, DEN; Schuneman of Encinal Day School to Perry, Feb. 10, 1932, and Perry to Schuneman, Feb. 12, 1932, Folder 754, Box 34, GCF, AIS, RG75, NARA, DEN.

30. Nichols of Wanblee to "Principals of Day Schools," Jan. 25, 1941, Folder 021.2, 1 of 3; Nichols to "Principals and Teachers of Day Schools," Feb. 10, 1942, Folder 021.2, 3 of 3; and Nicholson memorandum, Jan. 21, 1942, Folder 021.2, 3 of 3, all in Box 466, Educational Decimal Files, Pine Ridge Indian Agency, RG75, NARA, KC. Day schools on the Eastern Navajo Agency were strong sponsors of the game: Hugh D. Carroll to "Day School Teachers," Nov. 12, 1936, Folder 750, Box 56.67, CCF, 1926–1939, Eastern Navajo Indian Agency, RG75, NARA, LA.

31. Szasz, *Education and the American Indian*, 89 and 128.

32. Voget, *They Call Me Agnes*, xx–xxi, 96, and 100–101.

33. On basketball's role in improving player relations but its limitations in doing so, see Linda Kay Marticke, "Racial Attitudes of Male Basketball Team Participants," master's thesis, University of Montana, Missoula, 1978.

34. Voget, *They Call Me Agnes*, 98.

35. Steven E. Dyche, *Integrated Basketball at the Little Big Horn* (Oakbrook Terrace, IL: Green Ivy, 2015), 34–37, 85–86, and 119; Adams, *Three Roads to Magdalena*, 281–97.

36. "Oklahoma: OSSAA Boys Basketball Champions (1918–2017)," http://www.iwasatthegame.com/ListOfChampions/OKStateChampionsBasketballBoys.pdf?id=19; "Oklahoma High School State Champions, Girls Basketball, since 1919," http://www.iwasatthegame.com/BKGStateChampionships.aspx.

37. "Montana High School Association State Boys' Basketball Champions of the Past, 1911–2019," https://cdn2.sportngin.com/attachments/document/14d8-1850886/Basketball_Boys.pdf?_ga=2.222815641.322863825.1564414681-1732271782 .1564414681.

38. Bouton et al., to "Dear Sir," Jan. 28, 1935; Yellowtail to Board of School Trustees, Jan. 31, 1935; Petzold to Rev. Smith, Feb. 26, 1935; and Bess Stevens to Smith, Mar. 4, 1935, all in Folder 800, "Education 1935," Box 55, DCF, Crow Indian Agency, RG75, NARA, DEN.

39. *Great Falls Tribune*, Mar. 15, 1935, 14; *Montana Standard* (Butte), Mar. 24, 1935, 10; *Salt Lake Telegram*, Mar. 14, 1935, 14.

40. *Billings Gazette*, Jan. 7, 1935, 6; *Great Falls Tribune*, Mar. 15, 1935, 14, and Mar. 16, 1935, 8.

41. *Great Falls Tribune*, Mar. 17, 1935, 9, and Apr. 12, 1935, 5; *Montana Standard*, Mar. 19, 1935, 8.

42. *Bismarck Tribune*, Mar. 19, 1956, 12.

43. Galluzzi later served as president of Haskell Junior College from 1969 to 1981. *Bismarck Tribune*, Mar. 19, 1956, 12, and Mar. 19, 1998, D1–2; *Sioux County Pioneer Arrow* (Ft. Yates, ND), Mar. 30, 1956, 1, accessed in Folder 84, Box 2, Wallace Galluzzi Papers, KSL; *Brockway Record* (PA), Apr. 5, 1956, 6.

44. *Bismarck Tribune*, Mar. 20, 1956, 1; *Sioux County Pioneer Arrow*, Mar. 30, 1956, 1.

45. *Sioux County Pioneer Arrow*, Mar. 30, 1956, 1; "New Mexico Girls State Basketball Champions," https://www.nmact.org/file/Basketball%20Girls%20Coaches%20Champions.pdf; "Wyoming state high school boys basketball champions," https://wyoming-basketball.com/boys-state-champions/.

46. Lowery, *Lumbee Indians in the Jim Crow South* (Chapel Hill: University of North Carolina Press, 2010), 20–25; Brayboy interview; Ray Oxendine, telephone interview by author, Feb. 5, 2016; Brayboy and Barton, *Playing Before an Overflow Crowd*, vi and 3.

47. Brayboy interview; Ray Oxendine interview; Brayboy and Barton, *Playing Before an Overflow Crowd*, 3.

48. Brayboy interview. Brayboy says baseball and basketball were equally popular, while other people give baseball the edge: Ronnie Chavis, telephone interview by author, Feb. 26, 2016; Rose Hill, telephone interview by author, Feb. 6, 2016; Ray Oxendine interview; Joseph Oxendine, telephone interview by author, Feb. 6, 2016.

49. Brayboy interview; Hill interview.

50. Brayboy interview; Hill interview.

51. Pruter, *The Rise of American High School Sports*, 310–11; Brayboy interview; Brayboy and Barton, *Playing Before an Overflow Crowd*, vi and 12–15.

52. Ray Oxendine interview; Chavis interview; Brayboy interview.

53. Brayboy interview.

54. Chavis interview.

55. Brayboy and Barton, *Playing Before an Overflow Crowd*, 168–69.

56. Chavis interview.

57. Brayboy and Barton, *Playing Before an Overflow Crowd*, 19; Swain, "A Recognition Long Overdue," reprinted in *Playing Before an Overflow Crowd*, 172–73; Brayboy interview; Chavis interview; Ray Oxendine interview.

58. Oxendine interview; Brayboy interview; Chavis interview.

59. Brayboy and Barton, *Playing Before an Overflow Crowd*, 177.

60. Nicolas Rosenthal, *Reimagining Indian Country* (Chapel Hill: University of North Carolina Press, 2012), 2; Iverson and Davies, *"We Are Still Here,"* 74, 143–47, and 244.

61. Works documenting Native experiences in post–World War II urban environments that have informed this discussion: Donald L. Fixico, *The Urban Indian Experience in America* (Albuquerque: University of New Mexico Press, 2000); James B. LaGrand, *Indian Metropolis* (Urbana: University of Illinois Press, 2002); Rosenthal, *Reimagining Indian Country*; Joan Weibel-Orlando, *Indian Country, L.A.* (Urbana: University of Illinois Press, 1991).

62. Mancke, "Albert Cobe: I Must Step Up," *Chicago Tribune*, May 30, 1971, sec. 5–10; *Indian Leader*, Mar. 16, 1923, 16; LaGrand, *Indian Metropolis*, 144.

63. LaGrand, *Indian Metropolis*, 66–68.

64. Pre–World War II appeal of sports to Natives in Chicago: LaPier and Beck, *City Indian*, 79.

65. Rosenthal, *Reimagining Indian Country*, 119–21; Hoikkala, "Native American Women and Community Work in Phoenix, 1965–1980," PhD diss., Arizona State University, Tempe, 1995, 133; Liebow, "A Sense of Place," PhD diss., Arizona State University, Tempe, 1986, 188 and 284–85; Charles Hoy Steele, "American Indians and Urban Life," PhD diss., University of Kansas, Lawrence, 1971, 151 and 156; Weibel-Orland, *Indian Country, L.A.*, 89 and 119.

66. Behl, "Changing Paces," PhD diss., Arizona State University, Tempe, 2001, 138; *Arizona Daily Sun* (Flagstaff), Dec. 27, 1951, 5; *Ogden Standard-Examiner*, Feb. 14, 1953, 6.

67. Churches: Rosenthal, *Reimagining Indian Country*, 119; Nicolas Rosenthal, "American Indian Athletic Association," in King, ed., *Native Americans in Sports* 1:15; William Willard, "Outing, Relocation, and Employment Assistance," *Wicazo Sa Review* 12 (Spring 1997): 41. Indian Centers: LaGrand, *Indian Metropolis*, 141; Janusz Mucha, "From Prairie to the City," *Urban Anthropology* 12 (Fall-Winter 1983): 351; Willard, "Outing, Relocation, and Employment Assistance," 41; *Sioux City Journal*, Dec. 8, 1955, 18; *Minneapolis Sunday Tribune* (MN), Mar. 18, 1962, 2; *Chicago Tribune*, Mar. 8, 1964, 51 (Gallup).

68. Rosenthal, *Reimagining Indian Country*, 119–21; Rosenthal, "American Indian Athletic Association," 15–16; Willard, "Outing, Relocation, and Employment Assistance," 41.

69. *Arizona Republic*, Nov. 21, 1953, 21, and Mar. 7, 1954, 20; Jerry Eaton, "The Glory That Has Been the Chiefs," *Arizona Republic, Arizona*, supplement, Mar. 3, 1968, 18, 20, and 22; *Arizona Republic*, Dec. 21, 1959, 64 (Zah); National Council on Indian Opportunity, *Public Forum before the Committee on Urban Indians in Phoenix, Arizona of the National Council on Indian Opportunity, April 17–18, 1969* (Washington, DC: National Council on Indian Opportunity, 1969), Dinehdeal testimony, 64–68; Russell Means and Marvin J. Wolf, *Where White Men Fear to Tread* (New York: St. Martin's Griffin, 1995), 130.

70. *Arizona Republic*, Dec. 17, 1955, 31, Jan. 24, 1958, 25, Feb. 10, 1961, 22, May 5, 1967, 68, Apr. 4, 1969, 87, and Apr. 30, 1970, 83; National Council on Indian Opportunity, *Public Forum*, 64–68.

71. *Arizona Republic*, Feb. 10, 1952, 16, Feb. 22, 1952, 4, and Mar. 5, 1961, 3; Stephen Kent Amerman, *Urban Indians in Phoenix Schools* (Lincoln: University of Nebraska Press, 2010), 94.

72. Amerman, *Urban Indians in Phoenix Schools*, 94; *Arizona Republic*, July 12, 1956, Feb. 28, 1955, 8, and Feb. 26, 1956, 28; National Council on Indian Opportunity, *Public Forum*, 73–74.

73. Haynal, "From Termination through Restoration and Beyond," PhD diss., University of Oregon, Eugene, 1994, 101–11; The Klamath Tribe, "Tribal News and

Events: Basketball," http://klamathtribes.org/news/basketball/. The Council approved $500 in tribal funds for the 1955 version of the tournament: *Herald and News*, Jan. 14, 1955, 1.

74. The Klamath Tribe, "Tribal News and Events"; *Herald and News*, Mar. 5, 1955, 13, Mar. 9, 1955, 14, and Mar. 21, 1955, 8.

75. *Arizona Republic*, Mar. 20, 1959, 74; Crow Tribal Council, "Resolution No. 125," reprinted in Committee on Interior and Insular Affairs, U.S. House of Representatives, *"Sale of Crow Indian Lands, Hearings" 85th Congress, 1st session* (Washington, DC: Government Printing Office, 1958), 209. Pretty Weasel scored twenty-one points in the final; *Herald and News*, Mar. 22, 1959, 9.

76. *Herald and News*, Mar. 15, 1956, 11.

77. *Herald and News*, Mar. 15, 1956, 8 and 11, and Mar. 15, 1961, 12.

78. *Herald and News*, Apr. 9, 1956, 9, Aug. 29, 1959, 14, Feb. 25, 1959, 14, and Feb. 28, 1963.

79. *Herald and News*, Mar. 25, 1955, 20, Feb. 14, 1957, 8, Mar. 1, 1957, 6, Mar. 17, 1957, 13, Feb. 25, 1959, 4, Mar. 23, 1959, 14, Feb. 9, 1960, 7, Feb. 28, 1960, 11, and Mar. 3, 1960, 4.

80. Haynal, "From Termination through Restoration and Beyond," 210 (Shultz quote) and 336–38; "65th Annual All-Indian Basketball Tourney" poster, http://klamathtribes.org/news/65th-annual-all-indian-basketball-tourney-march-16–18–2018/.

81. Ute: *Roosevelt Standard* (UT), Mar. 4, 1954, 1, Jan. 20, 1955, 2, and Mar. 29, 1956, 12; *Uintah Basin Standard* (Duchesne, UT), Feb. 28, 1957, 1, Mar. 28, 1957, 1. Yakama: *Port Angeles Evening News* (WA), Mar. 1, 1956, 15; *Montana Standard*, Mar. 22, 1962, 14. Okmulgee: *Miami Daily News-Record*, Jan. 29, 1958, 4. San Carlos: *Arizona Republic*, Mar. 17, 1957, 96, Feb. 26, 1960, 65. Arizona State College (NAU): *Arizona Daily Star*, Mar. 7, 1957, D3; *Gallup Independent*, Mar. 21, 1957, 5; *Arizona Republic*, Mar. 22, 1957, 48.

82. *Navajo Times* (Window Rock, AZ), Jan. 1, 1960, 9, Feb. 7, 1962, 1, Jan. 31, 1963, 12, and Mar. 7, 1963, 6; Cummins, Anderson, and Briggs, "Women's Basketball on the Navajo Nation, The Shiprock Cardinals, 1960–1980," in King, ed., *Native Athletes in Sport and Society*, 143–69.

83. Sakelaris, telephone interview by author, Feb. 26, 2016; *Idaho State Journal* (Pocatello), Mar. 16, 1965, 6, Feb. 28, 1966, 6, Feb. 24, 1967, 83, Feb. 29, 1968, 7, May 8, 1969, 26, and Feb. 11, 1970, 9.

Conclusion. An Enduring Tradition

1. On technological changes transforming life in reservation communities more generally post–World War II, see Vine Deloria, "Native Americans," *The Annals of the American Academy of Political and Social Science* 454 (March 1981): 141–42.

2. Bailey and Bailey, *A History of the Navajos* (Santa Fe, NM: School of American Research Press, 1999) 264–68 and 282–86; Snyder, Sadalla, and Stea, "Socio-cultural modifications and user needs in Navajo Housing," *Journal of Architectural Research* 5 (December 1976): 4–9; Iverson, *Diné*, 270–71.

3. Suns: *Navajo Times*, May 27, 1993, B1-B2. Dehiya interviewed by Moffett, Apr.

13, 2007, File 1, MSS 931 SC, New Mexico Sports Figures collection, 2007–2014, Center for Regional Studies, Zimmerman Library, University of New Mexico, Albuquerque. http://econtent.unm.edu/cdm/singleitem/collection/Moffet/id/2/rec/65; *Navajo Times*, Mar. 14, 2013, B-2. Williams broadcast games in Navajo for NTNN: Ed Odeven, "A Love Affair with Basketball Navajo Announcer L.A. Williams," *Arizona Daily Sun*, Mar. 4, 2005, https://edodevenreporting.wordpress.com.

4. Grundy and Shackelford, *Shattering the Glass*, 140–70 and 183–224.

5. Grundy and Shackelford, *Shattering the Glass*, 170, 183–87, and 224–30.

6. *Rocks with Wings*, VHS, directed by Rick Derby (New York: Shiprock Productions, 2002); Johnson interview by author, Farmington, NM, May 8, 2002.

7. Staurowsky, "SuAnne Big Crow," in King, ed., *Native Athletes in Sport and Society*, 189–210.

8. Division I players: Pember, "'Rez Ball' Gains NCAA Certification Thanks to Native American Basketball Invitational," *Diverse Education* 10 (April 2007), https://diverseeducation.com/article/7221/; Vickey Kalambakal, "Ryneldi Becenti," in King, ed., *Native Americans in Sports*, 1:37–38; Jourdan Bennett-Begaye, "Meet the WNBA's First Native American Basketball Player," *Fan First* (June 27, 2016), http://www.fanfirstmag.com/playmakers/meet-wnbas-first-native-american-basketball-player/.

9. Dehiya interview.

10. Peterson, *Cages to Jump Shots*, 44, 109, and 156–57; Weyand, *Cavalcade of Basketball*, 120; hooptactics™ "The Evolution of the Game," https://hooptactics.com/Basketball_Basics_History.

11. Chavez interview; Sewell, "Asserting Native American Agency in an Assimilationist Institution," 35; "Seven Generations," from *Viceland, Vice World of Sports*, Season 1, Episode 9 https://www.viceland.com; *Off the Rez*; Pember, "Rez Ball"; Abdul-Jabbar on fundamentals in Wolff, *Big Game, Small World*, 166.

12. Wetzel interview; Montana Indian Athletic Hall of Fame, "Don Wetzel Sr." http://montanaindianathletichof.org/2011.htm; Wetzel Basketball, "Ryan Wetzel Coach, Mentor, Motivator: Biograph," http://www.ryanwetzelbasketball.com.

13. Wetzel interview.

14. Wetzel interview.

15. *Indian Country Today*, Apr. 20, 2003, D1; *Native Voice* (Rapid City, SD), July 20, 2003, D1; *Arizona Republic*, July 14, 2018, C3; NABI Foundation, http://www.nabifoundation.org/.

16. Sakelaris interview.

17. Although they were often big fans of the game, a number of people shared with me their concerns that parents, schools, and whole communities sometimes overemphasize high school basketball to the detriment of other important pursuits. For example: Nancy Redhouse, interview by author, Farmington, NM, Mar. 2, 2002; Simon Tapaha, telephone interview by author, Farmington, NM, Apr. 26, 2002.

18. See, for example, Gary Smith, "Shadows of a Nation," *Sports Illustrated* (Feb. 18, 1991), http://www.si.com/vault/1991/02/18/123632/shadow-of-a-nation-the-crows-once-proud-warriors-now-seek-glory—but-often-find-tragedy—in-

basketball; Alexie, "The Only Traffic Signal on the Reservation Doesn't Flash Red Anymore," *The Lone Ranger and Tonto Fistfight in Heaven*, 43–53; Colton, *Counting Coup*; Junge, *Chiefs*.

19. Wetzel interview; Chavez interview.

20. Parr, "John Levell Starks," in King, ed., *Native Americans in Sports*, 2:291; Parr, "Cherokee Bryan Parks," in King, ed., *Native Americans in Sports*, 2:241.

21. Koenig: *Au-Authm Action News* (Scottsdale, AZ), May 4, 2017, 18; *Seminole Tribune* (Hollywood, FL), Feb. 27, 2015, A15, and Oct. 31, 2017, C2. Baker: Citizen Potawatomi Nation Public Information Office, "Drive all Day: With a Sports Resume Built on Leading High School and College Championship Games, New York Knick Ron Baker also Credits his Native Heritage for His Success," Dec. 5, 2017, https://www.potawatomi.org/drive-day-sports-resume-built-leading-high-school-college-championship-games-new-york-knick-ron-baker-also-credits-native-heritage-success/; *Indian Country Today*, Jan. 17, 2017, https://newsmaven.io/indiancountrytoday/archive/ron-baker-is-native-america-s-next-nba-star-yQtenp_7uk-m1c7SgJ1bYw/; Standig, "Ron Baker Is Heavy on Grit, but Light on Luggage since Joining Wizards," Dec. 21, 2018, NBCSports, Washington, https://www.nbcsports.com/washington/wizards/ron-baker-heavy-grit-light-luggage-joining-wizards; *Albany Democrat*, Mar. 9, 2019, B2.

22. For example: Blanchard, *The Mississippi Choctaws at Play*, 2, 44–45, and 171–72; Iverson, *Riders of the West*; Powers-Beck, *The American Indian Integration of Baseball*, 16–17. Also on basketball: Allison, "Sport, Culture and Socialization"; Blanchard, "Basketball and the Culture-Change Process"; Droulias, "Social Benefits and Cultural Consequences of Basketball in Alaska"; Iverson, *Riders of the West*, 269; Stacy Sewell, "The Wind River Reservation" and "Asserting Native American Agency in an Assimilationist Institution," 29–40; and with caveats, Anderson, "Using the Master's Tools."

23. *Indian Leader* 18, no. 29 (March 1915): 20.

24. King, "Identities, Opportunities, Inequities," xxiii; Davies, "American Indian Sports," 259–60.

25. Vennum, *American Indian Lacrosse*, 292–94; Oxendine, *American Indian Sports Heritage*, 283 and 294–99; Davies, "American Indian Sports," 259–60.

26. Blanchard, *The Mississippi Choctaws at Play*, 42–43 and 53–54.

27. Haslip and Edwards, "Arctic Winter Games," in King, ed., *Native Americans in Sports*, 1:23–24; Giles, "All-Indian Competitions," in King, ed., *Native Americans in Sports*, 1:10–13; *Games of the North*, DVD, directed by Stanton,

28. Croff interview.

29. Price interview; Michael Moore, "Vision of Grace: Cut Short, Lem Price's Life Was Defined by His Gentle Compassion," *Missoulian*, Apr. 28, 2002, E1 and E10; *Great Falls Tribune*, Mar. 9, 2004, S1.

30. DesRosier interview. On high school sports also being "the only show in town" on the Navajo reservation, see Anderson, "Using the Master's Tools," 254.

31. Chavez interview.

32. Brayboy interview; Kickingwoman interview.

33. For examples of medicine influencing basketball, see: Anderson, "Using the Master's Tools," 257; Sewell, "The Wind River Reservation," 61; Smith, "Shadows of a Nation"; Voget, *They Call Me Agnes*, 101.

34. Chavez interview; Colton, *Counting Coup*, 55; Croff interview; Junge, *Chiefs*; Kickingwoman interview; Sewell, "The Wind River Reservation," 60–62; Smith, "Shadows of a Nation"; Tapaha interview; Wetzel interview.

35. Kickingwoman interview; Chavez interview; Sakelaris interview; Bennett-Begaye, "Meet the WNBA's First Native American Basketball Player," *Fan First* (June 27, 2016), http://www.fanfirstmag.com/playmakers/meet-wnbas-first-native-american-basketball-player/.

36. DesRosier interview.

Bibliography

Archival Sources

Carlisle Indian School Digital Resource Center, Dickinson College Archives and Special Collections, Carlisle, PA

Carlisle Indian School, *United States Indian School, Carlisle, Pa.*, ca. 1895, CIS-I-0037

The Indian Industrial School, Carlisle, Pa.: 23rd Year. Carlisle, PA: The School, 1902

Student Files

Kenneth Spencer Research Library, University of Kansas, Lawrence, KS

Wallace Galluzzi Papers, 1926–1984

James Naismith Morgue Files

National Archives and Records Administration, Chicago, IL

Records of Mount Pleasant Indian School, RG75

Decimal Correspondence Files, 1926–1946

National Archives and Records Administration, Denver, CO

Records of Albuquerque Indian School, RG75

General Correspondence Files, 1917–1936

Student Case Files, 1886–1964

Records of Crow Indian Agency, RG75

Decimal Correspondence Files, 1926–1958

Records of Fort Belknap Agency, RG75

Decimal Correspondence Files, 1917–1958

Health, Education and Welfare General Correspondence, 1908–1948

Records of Fort Shaw Indian School, RG75

Letters Received, 1897–1898

Register of Pupils, 1892–1908

Roster of Employees, 1892–1910

Records of Southern Pueblos Indian Agency, RG75

General Correspondence Files, 1911–1935

Records of Wind River Indian Agency, RG75

General Correspondence Files, 1890–1960

National Archives and Records Administration, Fort Worth, TX

Records of the Cheyenne and Arapaho Agency, RG75

Central Files, 1926–1984

Records of Chilocco Indian School, RG75

Cost Ledger, 1918–1933

Records of the Pawnee Indian Agency, RG75

Subject Files (education), 1928–32

Records Relating to Personnel

Records of the Superintendent, Indian Emergency Conservation Work
Student Case Files, 1912–1980
National Archives and Records Administration, Kansas City, MO
Bismarck Indian School Series, RG75
Decimal Correspondence Files, 1915–1938
Records of Flandreau Indian School, RG75
Decimal Correspondence Files, 1916–1954
Student Case Files, 1924–1957
Records of Fort Totten Indian Agency, RG75
Subject Correspondence Files, 1884–1947
Records of Haskell Indian Nations University (Haskell Institute), RG75
Circulars Received from the Office of Indian Affairs, 1890–1911
Correspondence of the Superintendents, 1890–1942
Decimal Correspondence Files, 1917–1959
Letters Sent by the Athletic Program, 1903–1912
Record of Students, 1890–1897
Student Activities Association Ledger and Related Records, 1931–1934
Student Case Files, 1884–1980
Subject Correspondence Files, 1904–1941
Records of Pierre Indian School, RG75
Decimal Correspondence Files, 1926–1956
Superintendent's Correspondence, 1917–1926
Records of Pine Ridge Indian Agency, RG75
Education Decimal Correspondence Files, 1937–1959
Records of Pipestone Indian School, RG75
Decimal Correspondence Files, 1901–1952
Records of Rapid City Indian School, RG75
Decimal Correspondence Files, 1903–1933
Records of Standing Rock Indian Agency, RG75
Decimal Correspondence Files, 1906–1959
Records of Wahpeton Indian School, RG75
Decimal Correspondence Files, 1923–1967
National Archives and Records Administration, Los Angeles, CA
Records of Eastern Navajo Indian Agency, RG75
Central Classified Files, 1926–1939
Records of Phoenix Indian School, RG75
Central Classified Files, 1891–1951
Records of Sherman Institute, RG75
Records of the Superintendent, Central Classified Files, 1907–1939
Records of the Superintendent, Letters Sent, 1902–1948
National Archives and Records Administration, Seattle, WA
Records of Chemawa Indian School, RG75
Annual Reports, 1916–1940
Correspondence of the Superintendent, 1909–1932

Decimal Correspondence Files, 1924–1955
Graduated Student Case Files, 1900–1962
Individual Student Case Files, 1894–1957
Photographs, 1907–1971
Record of Employees, 1883–1924
Records of Klamath Indian Agency, RG75
Decimal Correspondence Files, 1916–1960
Records of Tulalip Indian Agency, RG75
Superintendent's Diary, 1909–1913
Records of Yakima Indian Agency, RG75
General Reports Relating to the Yakima Indian School, 1912–1921
National Archives and Records Administration, Washington, DC
Central Classified Files, 1907–1939, RG75
Chilocco Indian School
General Service
Hampton Institute
Oklahoma Historical Society, Oklahoma City, OK
Chilocco Indian School Collection, 1884–2005
The Gateway to Oklahoma History, https://gateway.okhistory.org/
University Archives, Loyola University of Chicago, IL
Records of the National Catholic Interscholastic Basketball Tournament

Microfilmed Archives

Bureau of Catholic Indian Missions Records, microfilm, Special Collections and Archives, Marquette University, Milwaukee, WI.

The Native American (Phoenix Indian School), microfiche, American Indian Periodicals in the Princeton University Library. New York: Clearwater Publishing Co., 1981.

Records of the Bureau of Indian Affairs, Central Classified Files, 1907–1939, RG75, Series B: Indian Customs and Social Relations, microfilm, University Publications of America, Bethesda, MD.

Records of the Bureau of Indian Affairs, Central Classified Files, 1907–1939, RG75, Series D: Education, Part 1, microfilm, University Publications of America, Bethesda, Maryland.

Superintendents' Annual Narrative and Statistical Reports from Field Jurisdictions of the Bureau of Indian Affairs, 1907–1938, M1011, microfilm. Washington, DC: National Archives and Records Services, 1975, (reports for multiple agencies on multiple reels).

Miscellaneous Archival

American Indian Athletic Hall of Fame, induction program, Dec. 3, 1977.

Mossman, Eugene to "Dear Friends in Crime," Apr. 21, 1932, Standing Rock Indian Agency, in author's possession.

"Porter's Window Shades vs. Diamond Oilers" scorecard, courtesy of Cheewa James.

Interviews

Beane, Sydney, Jr., telephone interview by author, Jan. 4, 2018.

Blue George, Elsie, interviewed by L. Whitesell, Dec. 1971, Southeastern Indian Oral History Project, Samuel Proctor Oral History Program, University of Florida, Digital Collections, http://ufdc.ufl.edu/UF00007219/00001?search=elsie+%3dblue+%3dgeorge.

Boyd, Hellen, interviewed by Kim Taylor, July 14, 1992, OH 285–4, Archives and Special Collections, Mansfield Library, The University of Montana, Missoula.

Brayboy, Tim, telephone interview by author, Jan. 19, 2016.

Chavez, Mike, telephone interview by author, Jan. 7, 2016.

Chavis, Ronnie, telephone interview by author, Feb. 26, 2016.

Croff, Iva, interview by author, Missoula, MT, Jan. 19, 2016.

Dehiya, Harrison, interviewed by Ben Moffett, Apr. 13, 2007, File 1, MSS 931 SC, New Mexico Sports Figures collection, 2007–2014, Center for Regional Studies, Zimmerman Library, University of New Mexico, Albuquerque. http://econtent.unm.edu/cdm/singleitem/collection/Moffet/id/2/rec/65.

DesRosier, Jesse, interview by author, Missoula, MT, Feb. 11, 1916.

Fasthorse, Paul, telephone interview by author, Feb. 19, 2016.

Headley, Arnold, interviewed by Sharon Kahin, Apr. 14, 1991, Warm Valley Historical Project, University of Wyoming, American Heritage Center.

Hill, Rose, telephone interview by author, Feb. 6, 2016.

James, Cheewa, correspondence with author, Jan. 20, 2016, and Mar. 1, 2018.

Johnson, Melissa, interview by author, Farmington, NM, May 8, 2002.

Jordan, Collins P., interviewed by Mark G. Thiel, Kateri Tekakwitha Oral History Project Records, 1994–1995, KTP-25, Special Collections and Archives, Marquette University, Milwaukee, WI.

Kemp, Dave, interview by author, Sioux Falls, SD, Aug. 1, 2017, and correspondence with author, numerous dates, 2009–2018.

Kickingwoman, Kevin, interview by author, Missoula, MT, Jan. 22, 2016.

Lambert, Sybil, and Barney Lambert, interviewed by Kim Taylor, July 13, 1992, OH 285–1, Archives and Special Collections, Mansfield Library, University of Montana, Missoula.

Makescry, Albert, interviewed by Leonard Maker, May 10, 1969, Doris Duke Collection, Western History Collections, University of Oklahoma Libraries, Norman, OK. https://digital.libraries.ou.edu/cdm/compoundobject/collection/dorisduke/id/15054/rec/81.

Moss, Paul, interviewed by Sharon Kahin and Sara Wiles, spring 1992, Warm Valley Historical Project, University of Wyoming, American Heritage Center.

Oxendine, Joseph, telephone interview by author, Feb. 6, 2016.

Oxendine, Ray, telephone interview by author, Feb. 5, 2016.

Picotte, Agnes, interview by author, Chamberlain, SD, July 17, 2016.

Picotte, Norbert, interview by author, Chamberlain, SD, Jul. 17, 2016.

Price, George, interview by author, Missoula, MT, Feb. 12, 2016.

Redhouse, Nancy, interview by author, Farmington, NM, Mar. 2, 2002.

Sakelaris, Mike, telephone interview by author, Feb. 26, 2016.
Sanders, Soldier, interview summary, World War II: Mountain Memories Collection, Special Collections, D. H. Ramsey Library, University of North Carolina, Asheville. http://toto.lib.unca.edu/findingaids/oralhistory/WWII/sanders_soldier.pdf.
Sattler, Richard, interview by author, Missoula, MT, May 24, 2016.
Smith, Phillip, interviewed by Tonya Carrol, Oct. 3, 2009, Western Carolina University Oral History Collection, HIST 474/574, Western Carolina University Hunter Library, Cullowhee, NC.
Sutton, William, interview, June 25, 1967, volume 8, ID T-67, Doris Duke Collection, Western History Collections, University of Oklahoma Libraries, Norman, OK. https://digital.libraries.ou.edu/cdm/compoundobject/collection/dorisduke/id/17007/show/16971/rec/1.
Tapaha, Simon, telephone interview by author, Farmington, NM, Apr. 26, 2002.
Wetzel, Ryan, telephone interview by author, Feb. 5, 2016.

Published Material, Dissertations, and Theses

Abbott, Senda Berenson, ed. *Spalding's Official Basket Ball Guide for Women, 1916–17*. New York: American Sports, 1916.
Adams, David Wallace. *Education for Extinction: American Indians and the Boarding School Experience, 1875–1928*. Lawrence: University Press of Kansas, 1995.
———. "More than a Game: The Carlisle Indians Take to the Gridiron, 1893–1917." *Western Historical Quarterly* 32 (Spring 2001): 25–53.
———. *Three Roads to Magdalena: Coming of Age in a Southwest Borderland, 1890–1990*. Lawrence: University Press of Kansas, 2016.
Alexie, Sherman. *The Lone Ranger and Tonto Fist Fight in Heaven*. New York: Harper Collins, 1994, first published in 1993.
Allen, Forrest C. *Coach "Phog" Allen's Sports Stories for You and Youth*. Lawrence, KS: Allen, 1947.
Allison, Maria. "Sport, Culture and Socialization," *International Review for the Sociology of Sport* 17, no. 4 (1982): 11–37.
Allison, Maria T., and Gunther Lueschen. "A Comparative Analysis of Navaho Indian and Anglo Basketball Sport Systems." *International Review for the Sociology of Sport* 14, nos. 3–4 (1979): 75–86.
The American Almanac, Year-book, Cyclopedia and Atlas. New York American and Journal, Hearst's Chicago American, and the San Francisco Examiner, 1904.
Amerman, Stephen Kent. *Urban Indians in Phoenix Schools: 1940–2000*. Lincoln: University of Nebraska Press, 2010.
Anderson, Eric D. "Using the Master's Tools: Resisting Colonization through Colonial Sports." *The International Journal of the History of Sport* 23 (March 2006): 247–66.
Anderson, Lars. *Carlisle vs. Army: Jim Thorpe, Dwight Eisenhower, Pop Warner, and the Forgotten Story of Football's Greatest Battle*. New York: Random House, 2007.
Andrews, K. R., N. P. Canny and P. E. H. Hair, eds. *The Westward Enterprise: English*

Activities in Ireland, the Atlantic, and America, 1480–1650. Detroit: Wayne State University Press, 1979.

Anonymous. "Basketball for Girls." *The Playground* 18 (January 1925): 646.

———. "Independence Claimed the American Basketball Championship," excerpted from the *Independence Examiner*, Feb. 6, 1942 in *Missouri Historical Review* 54 (April 1960): 322.

———. "Why the Boarding School Fails." *Indian Education* 3 (October 15, 1936): 6–8.

Antonucci, Michael A. "Introduction." In *I Grew up with Basketball: Twenty Years of Barnstorming with Cage Greats of Yesterday*, Frank J. Basloe, v–xx. Lincoln: University of Nebraska Press, 2012; first published, 1952.

Applin, Albert Gammon, II. "From Muscular Christianity to the Market Place: The History of Men's and Boy's Basketball in the United States, 1891–1957." PhD dissertation, University of Massachusetts, Amherst, 1982.

Arizona State Basketball Media Guide, 2007–08. Tempe: ASU Media Relations Office, 2007.

Axthelm, Pete. *The City Game: Basketball From the Garden to the Playgrounds*. Lincoln: University of Nebraska Press, 1999; first published 1970.

Bailey, Garrick, and Roberta Glenn Bailey. *A History of the Navajos: The Reservation Years*. Santa Fe, NM: School of American Research Press, 1999; first published 1986.

Ball, Eve, with Nora Henn and Lynda A. Sánchez. *Indeh: An Apache Odyssey, with New Maps*. Norman: University of Oklahoma Press, 1988; first published 1980.

Barr, Daniel P. "'Looking Backward': The Life and Legend of Louis Francis Sockalexis." In *Native Athletes in Sport and Society*, ed. C. Richard King, 22–39. Lincoln: University of Nebraska Press, 2005.

Basloe, Frank J. *I Grew Up with Basketball: Twenty Years of Barnstorming with Cage Greats of Yesterday*. Lincoln: University of Nebraska Press, 2012; first published 1952.

Beck, David R. M. "American Indians Higher Education before 1974: From Colonization to Self-Determination." *Australian Journal of Indigenous Education* 27, no. 2 (1999): 12–23.

———. *(Un)Fair Labor? American Indians and the 1893 World's Columbian Exposition in Chicago*. Lincoln: University of Nebraska Press, 2019.

Beers, W. G. *Lacrosse, The National Game of Canada*. Montreal: Dawson Brothers, 1869.

Behl, Carol M. "Changing Paces: Navajos in Flagstaff, 1930–1970." PhD dissertation, Arizona State University, Tempe, 2001.

Benjey, Tom. *Oklahoma's Carlisle Indian School Immortals: Native American Sports Heroes Series*. Volume 1. Carlisle, PA: Tuxedo, 2010.

Bennett-Begaye, Jourdan. "Meet the WNBA's First Native American Basketball Player." *Fan First* (June 27, 2016), http://www.fanfirstmag.com/playmakers/meet-wnbas-first-native-american-basketball-player/.

Bernstein, Alison R. *American Indians and World War II.* Norman: University of Oklahoma Press, 1991.
Berthrong, Donald J. "From Buffalo Days to Classrooms: The Southern Cheyennes and Arapahos and Kansas." *Kansas History* 12 (Summer 1989): 101–13.
Bess, Jennifer. "Casting a Spell: Acts of Cultural Continuity in Carlisle Indian Industrial School's the *Red Man and Helper.*" *Wicazo Sa Review* 26 (Fall 2001): 13–38.
Blanchard, Kendall. "Basketball and the Culture-Change Process: The Rimrock Case." *Council on Anthropology and Education Quarterly* 5 (November 1974): 8–13.
———. *The Mississippi Choctaws at Play: The Serious Side of Leisure.* Urbana: University of Illinois Press, 1981.
———. "Stick Ball and the American Southeast." In *Forms of Play of Native North Americans,* ed. Edward Norbeck and Claire R. Farrer, 189–207. St. Paul, MN: West, 1979.
Bloom, John. *To Show What an Indian Can Do: Sports at Native American Boarding Schools.* Minneapolis: University of Minnesota Press, 2000.
Brasch, R., OBE. *How Did Sports Begin? A Look at the Origins of Man at Play.* New York: David McKay, 1970.
Brayboy, Tim, and Bruce Barton. *Playing Before an Overflow Crowd: The Story of Indian Basketball in Robeson, North Carolina, and Adjoining Counties.* Chapel Hill, NC: Chapel Hill, 2003.
Brewer, Vincent, with Jerry Matthews. "Back in the Day with the St. Francis Indian School Basketball Team of 1941." *Lakota Country Times,* May, 22, 2014, http://www.lakotacountrytimes.com/news.2014–05–22/Sports/Back_in_the_Day_with_the_St_Francis_Indian_School_.html.
Britten, Thomas A. *American Indians in World War I: At Home and at War.* Albuquerque: University of New Mexico Press, 1997.
Bsumek, Erika Marie. "The Navajos as Borrowers: Stewart Culin and the Genesis of an Ethnographic Theory." *New Mexico Historical Review* 79 (Summer 2004): 319–42.
Buchner, Martha Jane. "Shinny and 'Snakes' on Rosebud." *Indians at Work* 2 (Aug. 1, 1935): 30–31.
Bucko, Raymond A., SJ. "When Does a Cactus Become and Angry Buffalo? Traditional Games of the Lakotas." *Montana: The Magazine of Western History* 57 (Spring 2007): 14–31.
Buford, Kate. *Native American Son: The Life and Sporting Legend of Jim Thorpe.* Lincoln: University of Nebraska Press, 2012; first published 2010.
Bushnell, Amy. "That Demonic Game: The Campaign to Stop Indian Pelota Playing in Spanish Florida." *Americas* 35 (July 1978): 1–19.
Bushnell, David I., Jr. *Drawing by Jacques Lemoyne de Morgues of Saturioua, A Timucua Chief in Florida, 1564.* Washington, DC: Smithsonian Institution, 1928.
Cahill, Cathleen D. *Federal Fathers and Mothers: A Social History of the United States Indian Service, 1869–1933.* Chapel Hill: University of North Carolina Press, 2011.

Cahn, Susan K. *Coming on Strong: Gender and Sexuality in Women's Sport, 2nd edition.* Urbana: University of Illinois Press, 2015.

Cajete, Gregory. *Spirit of the Game: An Indigenous Wellspring.* Skyland, NC: Kivaki, 2005.

Carlisle Indian Industrial School. *Catalogue and Synopsis of Courses, 1915.* Carlisle, PA: Carlisle Indian, 1915.

Carney, Cary Michael. *Native American Higher Education in the United States.* New Brunswick, NJ: Transaction, 1999.

Caudle, Edwin C. *Collegiate Basketball: Facts and Figures on the Cage Sport.* 1959 edition. Winston-Salem, NC: John F. Blair, 1960.

Chapman, Reid, and Deborah Miles. *Asheville and Western North Carolina in World War II.* Charleston, SC: Arcadia, 2006.

Cheska, Alyce. "Ball Game Participation of North American Indian Women." In *Her Story in Sport: A Historical Anthology of Women in Sports*, ed. Reet Howell, 19–34. West Point, NY: Leisure, 1982; first published 1974.

Child, Brenda J. *Boarding School Seasons: American Indian Families, 1900–1940.* Lincoln: University of Nebraska Press, 1998.

Churchill, Ward, Norbert S. Hill, Jr., and Mary Jo Barlow. "An Historical Overview of Twentieth Century Native American Athletes." *Indian Historian* 12, no. 4 (1979): 22–32.

Coleman, Michael C. *American Indian Children at School, 1850–1930.* Jackson: University Press of Mississippi, 1993.

Colton, Larry. *Counting Coup: A True Story of Basketball and Honor on the Little Big Horn.* New York: Warner, 2000.

Cook, William A. *Jim Thorpe: A Biography.* Jefferson, NC: McFarland, 2011.

Crisler, H. O. "The National Interscholastic Basketball Tournament of the University of Chicago." In *Reach Official Basket Ball Guide, 1924–1925*, 109–21. Philadelphia, PA: A. J. Reach, 1924.

Crow Tribal Council. "Resolution No. 125," reprinted in Committee on Interior and Insular Affairs, U.S. House of Representatives. *"Sale of Crow Indian Lands, Hearings." 85th Congress, 1st session.* Washington, DC: Government Printing Office, 1958.

Crum, Steven. "The Choctaw Nation: Changing the Appearance of American Higher Education, 1830–1907." *History of Education Quarterly* 47 (Feb. 2007): 49–68.

Culin, Stewart. *Games of the North American Indians.* New York: Dover, 1975; first published 1907.

Cummins, Ann, Cecilia Anderson, and Georgia Briggs. "Women's Basketball on the Navajo Nation, The Shiprock Cardinals, 1960–1980." In *Native Athletes in Sport and Society*, ed. C. Richard King, 143–69. Lincoln: University of Nebraska Press, 2005.

Curtis, Henry S. *Education through Play.* New York: Macmillan, 1915.

Davies, Wade. "American Indian Sports: A Historical Overview." In *American Indians and Popular Culture, Volume I, Media, Sports, and Politics*, ed. Elizabeth DeLaney Hoffman, 243–61. Santa Barbara, CA: Praeger, 2012.

———. "'We Are Looking for a Splendid Tournament Here': Sharon Mote's Quest to Promote Indian-School Basketball, 1927–1929." *South Dakota History* 41 (Summer 2001): 199–225.
Davies, Wade, and Rich Clow. "The St. Francis Mission Indians and the National Interscholastic Catholic Basketball Tournament, 1924–1941." *The International Journal of the History of Sport* 23 (Mar. 2006): 213–31.
de Borhegyi, Stephan F. "America's Ballgame." *Natural History* 69 (January 1960): 48–59.
De Bry, *Brevis Narratio Eorum Quae in Florida Americae Provincia Gallis Acciderunt...Quae Est Seconda Pars Americae.* Frankfurt: J. Wechel for T. de Bry and S. Feyrabend, 1591.
Deloria, Philip J. "I Am of the Body": Thoughts on My Grandfather, Culture, and Sports." *South Atlantic Quarterly* 95 (Spring 1996): 321–38.
———. *Playing Indian.* New Haven, CT: Yale University Press, 1998.
———. *Indians in Unexpected Places.* Lawrence: University Press of Kansas, 2004.
Deloria, Vine, Jr. "Native Americans: The American Indian Today." *Annals of the American Academy of Political and Social Science* 454 (March 1981): 139–49.
Department of the Interior. *Annual Report of the Secretary of the Interior, Volume 2, 1897.* Washington, DC: Government Printing Office, 1898.
———, Bureau of Education. *Course of Study for the Indian Schools of the United States, Industrial and Literary.* Washington, DC: Government Printing Office, 1901.
———, Office of Indian Affairs. *Annual Report of the Commissioner of Indian Affairs, Part I.* Washington, DC: Government Printing Office, 1902.
———, Office of Indian Affairs. *Annual Report of the Commissioner of Indian Affairs, Part I.* Washington, DC: Government Printing Office, 1904.
———, Office of Indian Affairs. *Annual Report of the Commissioner of Indian Affairs.* Washington, DC: Government Printing Office, 1896.
———, Office of Indian Affairs. *Annual Report of the Commissioner of Indian Affairs.* Washington, DC: Government Printing Office, 1898.
———, Office of Indian Affairs. *Annual Report of the Commissioner of Indian Affairs.* Washington, DC: Government Printing Office, 1899.
———, Office of Indian Affairs. *Annual Report of the Commissioner of Indian Affairs.* Washington, DC: Government Printing Office, 1900.
———, Office of Indian Affairs. *Annual Report of the Commissioner of Indian Affairs.* Washington, DC: Government Printing Office, 1915.
———, Office of Indian Affairs. *Rules for the Indian School Service, 1900.* Washington, DC: Government Printing Office, 1900.
———, Office of Indian Affairs. *Tentative Course of Study for United States Indian Schools.* Washington, DC: Government Printing Office, 1915.
Diaz, Natalie. "Top Ten Reasons Why Indians Are Good at Basketball." *Indian Country Today*, Jun. 7, 2013. https://newsmaven.io/indiancountrytoday/archive/top-ten-reasons-why-indians-are-good-at-basketball-a-poem-by-natalie-diaz-9efjNo_3cEOuGVHio8X2cQ/.

Donahue, Peter. "New Warriors, New Legends: Basketball in Three Native American Works of Fiction." *American Indian Culture and Research Journal* 21, no. 2 (1997): 43–60.

D'Orso, Michael. *Eagle Blue: A Team, a Tribe, and a High School Basketball Season in Arctic Alaska.* New York: Bloomsbury, 2006.

Douchant, Mike. *Encyclopedia of College Basketball.* New York: Gale Research, 1995.

Doyle, Edward J. "Independent Teams Have Successful Season but Want Uniform Rules." In *The Reach Official Basket Ball Guide, 1924–25*, 219–21. Philadelphia: A. J. Reach, 1925.

Draper, Andrew Sloan, ed. *Self Culture for Young People.* Saint Louis, MO: Twentieth Century Self Culture Association, 1906.

Droulias, Andreas. "Social Benefits and Cultural Consequences of Basketball in Alaska." PhD dissertation, University of Alaska, Fairbanks, 2013.

Dyche, Steven E. *Integrated Basketball at the Little Big Horn: A 1957 Success Story.* Oakbrook Terrace, IL: Green Ivy, 2015.

Eastman, Charles A. *Indian Boyhood.* New York: McClure, Phillips, 1902.

Eaton, Jerry. "The Glory That Has Been the Chiefs." *Arizona Republic, Arizona* supplement, Mar. 3, 1968, 18, 20, and 22.

Ellis, Clyde. *To Change Them Forever: Indian Education at the Rainy Mountain Boarding School, 1893–1920.* Norman: University of Oklahoma Press, 1996.

Fields, Sarah K. "Representations of Sport in the Indian School Journal, 1906–1913." *Journal of Sports History* 35 (Summer 2008): 241–59.

Finger, John. *Cherokee Americans: The Eastern Band of Cherokees in the Twentieth Century.* Lincoln: University of Nebraska Press, 1992; first printing 1991.

Fixico, Donald L. *The Urban Indian Experience in America.* Albuquerque: University of New Mexico Press, 2000.

Fogarty, Robert S. *The Righteous Remnant: The House of David.* Kent, OH: Kent State University Press, 1981.

Fortunate Eagle, Adam. *Pipestone: My Life in an Indian Boarding School.* Norman: University of Oklahoma Press, 2010.

Fosdick, Raymond B. "The War and Navy Departments Commissions on Training Camp Activities." *Annals of the American Academy of Political and Social Science* 79 (Sep. 1918): 130–42.

Frachtenberg, Leo. "The Value of School Athletics." *Chemawa American* (April 1916): 1–3.

Franco, Cheree. "Without the All American Red Heads, There Would Be no WNBA." *Arkansas Times*, Nov. 7, 2012, https://www.arktimes.com/arkansas/without-the-all-american-red-heads-there-would-be-no-wnba/Content?oid=2522479.

Frymir, Alice W. *Basket Ball for Women: How to Coach and Play the Game.* New York: A. S. Barnes, 1930.

Fuller, M. Todd. "Stacy S. 'Bub' Howell." In *Native Americans in Sports*, vol. 1, ed. C. Richard King, 151–52. Armonk: Sharp, 2004.

Garcia, Ignacio M. *When Mexicans Could Play Ball: Basketball, Race, and Identity in San Antonio, 1928–1945*. Austin: University of Texas Press, 2014; first published 2013.

Gems, Gerald R. "Blocked Shot: The Development of Basketball in the African-American Community of Chicago." *Journal of Sport History* 22 (Summer 1995): 135–48.

———. "Negotiating a Native American Identity through Sport: Assimilation, Adaptation, and the Role of the Trickster." In *Native Athletes in Sport and Society*, ed. C. Richard King, 1–21. Lincoln: University of Nebraska Press, 2005.

———. *The Athletic Crusade: Sport and American Cultural Imperialism*. Lincoln: University of Nebraska Press, 2006.

Gibney, Eugene C. "Basketball in Recreation Centers." In *Spalding's Official Basket Ball Guide, 1916–17*, 55. New York: American Sports, 1916.

Gilbert, Matthew Sakiestewa. *Hopi Runners: Crossing the Terrain between Indian and American*. Lawrence: University Press of Kansas, 2018.

Giles, Audrey R. "All-Indian Competitions." In *Native Americans in Sports*, vol. 1, ed. C. Richard King, 10–13. Armonk: Sharp Reference, 2004.

Grundman, Adolph H. *The Golden Age of Amateur Basketball: The AAU Tournament, 1921–1968*. Lincoln: University of Nebraska Press, 2004.

———. "Jesse Barnard 'Cab' Renick." In *Native Americans in Sports*, vol. 2, ed. C. Richard King, 252–53. Armonk: Sharp, 2004.

Grundy, Pamela, and Susan Shackelford. *Shattering the Glass: The Remarkable History of Women's Basketball*. New York: New Press, 2005.

Gulick, Luther. "Biennial Report of Luther Gulick," *Young Men's Christian Association, Year Book, 1897*, 33. New York: International Committee, 1897.

Guttmann, Allen. *Games and Empires: Modern Sports and Cultural Imperialism*. New York: Columbia University Press, 1994.

Haller, Beth A. "Cultural Voices or Pure Propaganda?: Publications of the Carlisle Indian School, 1879–1918," *American Journalism* 19, no. 2 (2002): 65–86.

Hardorff, Richard G., ed. *Washita Memories: Eyewitness Views of Custer's Attack on Black Kettle's Village*. Norman: University of Oklahoma Press, 2006.

Haslip, Susan, and Victoria Edwards. "Arctic Winter Games." In *Native Americans in Sports*, vol. 1, ed. C. Richard King, 23–25. Armonk, NY: Sharp Reference, 2004.

Hawkins, Joel, and Terry Bertolino. *The House of David Baseball Team*. Chicago: Arcadia, 2001.

Haynal, Patrick Mann. "From Termination through Restoration and Beyond: Modern Klamath Cultural Identity." PhD dissertation, University of Oregon, Eugene, 1994.

Hertzberg, Hazel W. *The Search for an American Indian Identity*. Syracuse, NY: Syracuse University Press, 1971.

Hoffman, Elizabeth DeLaney, ed. *American Indians and Popular Culture, Volume I, Media, Sports, and Politics*. Santa Barbara, CA: Praeger, 2012.

Hogarth, Andrew. *Lakota Spirit: The Life of Native American Jack Little, 1920–1985*. Andrew Hogarth, 1992.

Hoikkala, Paivi Helena. "Native American Women and Community Work in Phoenix, 1965–1980." PhD dissertation, Arizona State University, Tempe, 1995.

Holm, Tom. *The Great Confusion in Indian Affairs: Native Americans & Whites in the Progressive Era*. Austin: University of Texas Press, 2005.

Hough, Theodore. "Physiological Effects of Basket Ball." In *Spalding's Official Basket Ball Guide for Women, 1916–17*, ed. Senda Berenson Abbott, 61–65. New York: American Sports, 1916.

Howell, Reet, ed. *Her Story in Sport: A Historical Anthology of Women in Sports*. West Point: Leisure, 1982; first published 1974.

Hoxie, Frederick E. "The Curious Story of Reformers and American Indians." In *Indians in American History*, 2nd edition, ed. Frederick E. Hoxie and Peter Iverson, 177–97. Wheeling, IL: Harlan Davidson, 1998.

Hoxie, Frederick E., and Peter Iverson eds. *Indians in American History*. 2nd edition. Wheeling, IL: Harlan Davidson, 1998.

Hulton, Paul, ed. "Images of the New World: Jacques Le Moyne de Morgues and John White." In *The Westward Enterprise: English Activities in Ireland, the Atlantic, and America 1480–1650*, ed. K. R. Andrews, N. P. Canny and P. E. H. Hair, 195–214. Detroit: Wayne State University Press, 1979.

———. *The Work of Jacques Le Moyne De Morgues: A Huguenot Artist in France, Florida, and England*. London, UK: Trustees of the British Museum by British Museum Publications Limited, 1977.

Hyer, Sally. *One House, One Voice, One Heart: Native American Education at the Santa Fe Indian School*. Santa Fe: Museum of New Mexico Press, 1990.

Ikard, Robert W. *Just for Fun: The Story of AAU Women's Basketball*. Fayetteville: University of Arkansas Press, 2005.

An Illustrated Souvenir Catalog of the Cherokee National Female Seminary, Tahlequah, Indian Territory 1850 to 1906. Chilocco, OK: Indian Print Shop Chilocco, OK, 1906.

International Traditional Games Society. *Indian Education for All: Traditional Games Unit*. Helena, MT: Montana Office of Public Instruction, 2013; first published in 2009.

Israelson, Chad. "The Haskell Indians: Sports at a Native American Boarding School, 1920–1940." Master's thesis, University of Nebraska, Lincoln, 1995.

Iverson, Peter. *Diné: A History of the Navajos*. Albuquerque: University of New Mexico Press, 2002.

Iverson, Peter and Linda MacCannell. *Riders of the West: Portraits from Indian Rodeo*. Seattle: University of Washington Press, 1999.

Iverson, Peter, and Wade Davies. *"We Are Still Here": American Indians since 1890, 2nd ed.* Malden, MA: Wiley Blackwell, 2015.

Jackson, Jason Baird. "Calling in the Members: Linguistic Form and Cultural Context in a Yuchi Ritual Speech Genre." *Anthropological Linguistics* 42 (Spring 2000): 61–80.

Jackson, Phil and Hugh Delehanty. *Sacred Hoops: Spiritual Lessons of a Hardwood Warrior.* New York: Hyperion, 1995.

James, Cheewa. *Modoc: The Tribe That Wouldn't Die.* Happy Camp, CA: Naturegraph, 2008.

Jenkins, Sally. *The Real All Americans: The Team That Changed a Game, a People, a Nation.* New York: Doubleday, 2007.

Johnson, Scott Morrow. *Phog: The Most Influential Man in Basketball.* Lincoln: University of Nebraska Press, 2016.

Kachur, Curtis A. "The Freedom and Privacy of an Indian Boarding School's Sports Field and Student Athletes' Resistance to Assimilation." Master's thesis, Bowling Green State University, OH, 2017.

Kalambakal, Vickey. "Ryneldi Becenti." In *Native Americans in Sports*, vol. 1, ed. C. Richard King, 37–38. Armonk, NY: Sharp Reference, 2004.

Kansas Basketball Media Guide, 2017–18. Lawrence: Kansas Communications Office, 2017.

Kappler, Charles J., ed. United States Senate, *Indian Affairs, Laws and Treaties.* Vol. 5. Washington, DC: Government Printing Office, 1941.

Keeley, John D. "Basket Ball in Indian Schools." In *Spalding's Official Basket Ball Guide, 1916–17*, 111–13. New York: American Sports, 1916.

Kemp, David, and Tamra Zastrow, ed. *A Celebration of One Hundred Years of South Dakota High School Activities and Athletics: A History of High School Academic, Athletic and Fine Arts Activities.* Sioux Falls, SD: Mariah, 2006.

Keoke, Emory Dean, and Kay Marie Porterfield. *American Indian Contributions to the World: 15,000 Years of Inventions and Innovations.* New York: Checkmark, 2003.

Kerkhoff, Blair. *Phog Allen: The Father of Basketball Coaching.* Indianapolis: Masters, 1996.

King, C. Richard, ed. "Basketball," In *Native Americans in Sports*, vol. 1, 34–37.

———. "Identities, Opportunities, Inequities, an Introduction." In *Native Athletes in Sport and Society*, xi–xxxiii. Lincoln: University of Nebraska Press, 2005.

———. *Native Americans in Sports*. 2 vols. Armonk, NY: Sharp Reference, 2004.

———. *Native Athletes in Sport and Society.* Lincoln: University of Nebraska Press, 2005.

Klein, Maury. "Keaney Invented the Fast Break and Rhode Island Made the Big Time." *Sports Illustrated Vault*, November 27, 1978, https://www.si.com/vault/1978/11/27/823193/yesterday-keaney-invented-the-fast-break-and-rhode-island-made-the-big-time.

Kneale, A. H. *Indian Agent.* Caldwell, ID: Caxton Printers, 1950.

Krouse, Susan Applegate. *North American Indians in the Great War.* Lincoln: University of Nebraska Press, 2007.

K-State Men's Basketball Media Guide, 2014–15. Manhattan: Athletics Communications Office, K-State Athletics, 2014.

LaGrand, James B. *Indian Metropolis: Native Americans in Chicago, 1945–75.* Urbana: University of Illinois Press, 2002.

Laliberte, David J. "Natives, Neighbors, and the National Game: Baseball at the Pipestone Indian Training School." *Minnesota History* 62 (Summer 2010): 60–69.

LaPier, Rosalyn R., and David R. M. Beck. *City Indian: Native American Activism in Chicago, 1893–1934*. Lincoln: University of Nebraska Press, 2015.

LeSier, Minnie Y. "Fish-Spearing at Fort Hall." *Indians at Work* 2 (Aug. 1, 1935): 39–40.

Levine, Peter. "Basketball and the Jewish-American Community, 1920s–1930s." In *Major Problems in American Sport History*, ed. Steven A. Riess, 299–308. Boston: Houghton Mifflin Company, 1997.

Leyenaar, Ted J. J. "Ulama, The Survival of the Mesoamerican Ballgame, *Ullamaliztli*." *Kiva* 58, no. 2 (1992): 115–53.

Liebow, Edward B. "A Sense of Place: Urban Indians and the History of Pan-Tribal Institutions in Phoenix, Arizona." PhD dissertation, Arizona State University, Tempe, 1986.

Littlefield, Alice. "The BIA Boarding School: Theories and Resistance and Social Reproduction." *Humanity and Society* 13, no. 4 (1989): 428–41.

Littlefield, Daniel F., Jr., and James W. Parins. *American Indian and Alaska Native Newspapers and Periodicals, 1826–1924*. Westport, CT: Greenwood, 1984.

Loew, Patty. "Newspapers and the Lake Superior Chippewa in the 'Unprogressive' Era." PhD dissertation, University of Wisconsin-Madison, 1998

Lomawaima, K. Tsianina. *They Called It Prairie Light: The Story of Chilocco Indian School*. Lincoln: University of Nebraska Press, 1995; first published 1994.

Lowery, Malinda Maynor. *Lumbee Indians in the Jim Crow South: Race, Identity, and the Making of a Nation*. Chapel Hill: University of North Carolina Press, 2010.

Mancke, Barbara Hobbie. "Albert Cobe: I Must Step Up." *Chicago Tribune*, May 30, 1971, sec. 5–10.

Marticke, Linda Kay. "Racial Attitudes of Male Basketball Team Participants." Master's thesis, University of Montana, Missoula, 1978.

McCaskill, J. C. "Indian Sports." *Indian Leader*, July 1, 1936, 29.

McDonald, Frank W. *John Levi of Haskell*. Lawrence, KS: World, 1972.

McGee, Adrienne. "Jim Thorpe's Ohio Ties." *Lima News*, Aug. 17, 2011, D1 and D3.

McGregor, Andrew. "Amateur Boxing and Assimilation at the Stewart Indian School, Carson City, Nevada, 1935–1948." In *The Native American Identity in Sports: Creating and Preserving a Culture*, ed. Frank A. Salamone, 41–55. Lanham, MD: Scarecrow, 2013.

McKissack, Frederick, Jr. *Black Hoops: The History of African Americans in Basketball*. New York: Scholastic, 1999.

Means, Russell, and Marvin J. Wolf. *Where White Men Fear to Tread: The Autobiography of Russell Means*. New York: St. Martin's Griffin, 1995.

Meisel, Joshua Jerome. "Historical Demographics, Student Origins, and Recruitment at Off-Reservation Indian Boarding Schools, 1900." Master's thesis, University of Kansas, Lawrence, 2014.

Menville, Chuck. *The Harlem Globetrotters: Fifty Years of Fun and Games*. New York: David McKay, 1978.

Meriam, Lewis. *The Problem of Indian Administration*. Washington, DC: Brookings Institution, 1928.

Mihesuah, Devon. "Out of the 'Graves of the Polluted Debauches': The Boys of the Cherokee Male Seminary." *American Indian Quarterly* 15 (Autumn 1991): 503–21.

Milanich, Jerald T. "The Devil in the Details." *Archaeology* 58 (May/June 2005): 26–31.

Moore, Michael. "Vision of Grace: Cut Short, Lem Price's Life Was Defined by His Gentle Compassion." *Missoulian*, Apr. 28, 2002, E1 and E10.

Morgenstern, W. V. "The Twelfth Annual University of Chicago National Interscholastic Tournament." In *Spalding's Official Basketball Guide, 1930–1931*, 219–25. New York: American Sports, 1930.

Moses, L. G. *Wild West Shows and the Images of American Indians, 1883–1933*. Albuquerque: University of New Mexico Press, 1996.

Mucha, Janusz. "From Prairie to the City: Transformation of Chicago's American Indian Community." *Urban Anthropology* 12 (Fall–Winter 1983): 337–71.

Nabokov, Peter. *Indian Running: Native American History and Tradition*. Santa Fe: Ancient City, 1987; first published 1981.

Naismith, James. "Basket Ball." *American Physical Education Review* 19 (May 1914): 339–51.

———. "Basketball." In *Self Culture for Young People*, ed. Andrew Sloan Draper, 55–59. Saint Louis: Twentieth Century Self Culture Association, 1906.

———. *Basketball: Its Origin and Development*. Lincoln: University of Nebraska Press, 1996; first published 1941.

Nash, June C. *Mayan Visions: The Quest for Autonomy in an Age of Globalization*. New York: Routledge, 2001.

National Council on Indian Opportunity. *Public Forum before the Committee on Urban Indians in Phoenix, Arizona of the National Council on Indian Opportunity, April 17–18, 1969*. Washington, DC: National Council on Indian Opportunity, 1969.

Nebraska Basketball, 2016–2017 Media Guide. Lincoln: Nebraska Communications Office, 2016.

Neilson, F. Ellis. "The Sports of the Zunis." *Indians at Work* 2 (Jan. 1, 1935): 35–36.

Neuman, Lisa K. *Indian Play: Indigenous Identities at Bacone College*. Lincoln: University of Nebraska Press, 2013.

New Mexico Men's Basketball, Media Guide, 2015–16. Albuquerque: New Mexico Athletics Communications Office, 2015.

Norbeck, Edward, and Claire R. Farrer, eds. *Forms of Play of Native North Americans*. St. Paul, MN: West, 1979.

O'Brien, Charles A. "The Evolution of Haskell Indian Junior College, 1884–1974." Master's thesis, University of Oklahoma, Norman, 1975.

Odeven, Ed. "A Love Affair with Basketball Navajo Announcer L. A. Williams." *Arizona Daily Sun*, Mar. 4, 2005. https://edodevenreporting.wordpress.com/2014/04/29/a-love-affair-with-basketball-navajo-announcer-l-a-williams/.

Oriard, Michael. *Reading Football: How the Popular Press Created an American Spectacle.* Chapel Hill: University of North Carolina Press, 1993.

Osteika, Barbara. "William Louis Pappan: ATF's First Native American Investigator Killed in the Line of Duty." *Inside ATF*, Nov. 2010, 1, 5–8.

Oxendine, Joseph B. *American Indian Sports Heritage.* Lincoln: University of Nebraska Press, 1995; first published 1988.

Parkhurst, Melissa D. *To Win the Indian Heart: Music at Chemawa Indian School.* Corvallis: Oregon State University Press, 2014.

Parman, Donald Lee. "The Indian Civilian Conservation Corps." PhD dissertation, University of Oklahoma, Norman, 1967.

Parr, Royse. "A.E. 'Abe' Lemons." In *Native Americans in Sports*, vol. 1, ed. C. Richard King, 183–84. Armonk, NY: Sharp Reference, 2004.

———. "Cherokee Bryan Parks." In *Native Americans in Sports*, vol. 2, ed. C. Richard King, 241. Armonk, NY: Sharp Reference, 2004.

———. "Kenneth Jerry 'Iceman' 'Casper' Adair." In *Native Americans in Sports*, vol. 1, ed. C. Richard King, 4–5. Armonk, NY: Sharp Reference, 2004.

———. "John Levell Starks." In *Native Americans in Sports*, vol. 2, ed. C. Richard King, 291. Armonk, NY: Sharp Reference, 2004.

———. "Joseph 'Bud' Sahmaunt." In *Native Americans in Sports*, vol. 2, ed. C. Richard King, 269–70. Armonk, NY: Sharp Reference, 2004.

Peavy, Linda, and Ursula Smith. "World Champions: The 1904 Girls' Basketball Team from Fort Shaw Indian Boarding School." *Montana, The Magazine of Western History* 51 (Winter 2001): 2–25.

———. *Full-Court Quest: The Girls from Fort Shaw Indian School, Basketball Champions of the World.* Norman: University of Oklahoma Press, 2008.

Pember, Mary Annette. "'Rez Ball' Gains NCAA Certification Thanks to Native American Basketball Invitational." *Diverse Education* 10 (April 2007), https://diverseeducation.com/article/7221/.

Pennington, Bill. "Jim Thorpe and a Ticket to Serendipity." *New York Times*, Mar. 29, 2005, online, https://www.nytimes.com/2005/03/29/sports/othersports/jim-thorpe-and-a-ticket-to-serendipity.html.

Pesavento, Wilma J. "Motivations of North American Indians in Athletic Games." U.S. Department of Health Education and Welfare, National Institute of Education, *Annual Reports of the Bureau of American Ethnology*, 1974.

Peterson, Nancy J., ed. *Conversations with Sherman Alexie.* Jackson: University Press of Mississippi, 2009.

Peterson, Richard. "A Treasured Tradition, Star Quilt Giveaways Teach Generosity and Ease Racial Tensions." *Great Falls Tribune*, Feb. 23, 2014, L1 and L3.

Peterson, Robert W. *Cages to Jump Shots: Pro Basketball's Early Years.* Lincoln: University of Nebraska Press, 2002; first published in 1990.

Plummer, Maggie. "Long Time Sleep: The Stuff Legends Are Made Of." *Char-Koosta News*, Oct. 25, 2007, 4–5.

Powell, Sallie L. "'Playing Fairly and Fiercely': Paradigms of the Early Years of

Kentucky White Girls' Basketball, 1891–1919." *The Register of the Kentucky Historical Society* 109 (Spring 2011): 153–86.
Powers-Beck, Jeffrey. *The American Indian Integration of Baseball.* Lincoln: University of Nebraska Press, 2004.
———. "'Chief': The American Indian Integration of Baseball, 1897–1945." *American Indian Quarterly* 25 (Autumn 2001): 508–38.
Prucha, Francis Paul. *The Great Father: The United States Government and the American Indians*, unabridged edition. Lincoln: University of Nebraska Press, 1995; first edition 1984.
Pruter, Robert. "Fait Elkins." In *Native Americans in Sports*, vol. 1, ed. C. Richard King, 104–5. Armonk, NY: Sharp Reference, 2004.
———. "Joseph Napoleon 'Joe' Guyon." In *Native Americans in Sports*, vol. 1, ed. C. Richard King, 137–38. Armonk, NY: Sharp Reference, 2004.
———. *The Rise of American High School Sports and the Search for Control, 1880–1930.* Syracuse, NY: Syracuse University Press, 2013.
Putz, Paul. "Jesse 'Cab' Renick: In Search of an Indian Identity." *Chronicles of Oklahoma* 89 (Spring 2011): 72–97.
Rader, Benjamin G. *American Sports: From the Age of Folk Games to the Age of Televised Sports*, 6th ed. Upper Saddle River, NH: Pearson, Prentice Hall, 2009.
Rains, Rob, with Hellen Carpenter. *James Naismith: The Man Who Invented Basketball.* Philadelphia: Temple University Press, 2009.
Rasmussen, Marc. *Six: A Football Coach's Journey to a National Record.* Pierre: South Dakota Historical Society Press, 2011.
Reeder, Lydia. *Dust Bowl Girls: The Inspiring Story of the Team That Barnstormed Its Way to Basketball Glory.* Chapel Hill, NC: Algonquian, 2017.
Reyhner, Jon, and Jeanne Eder. *American Indian Education: A History.* Norman: University of Oklahoma Press, 2006; first published 2004.
Rickard, Chief Clinton, with Barbara Graymont. *Fighting Tuscarora: The Autobiography of Chief Clinton Rickard.* Syracuse: Syracuse University Press, 1973.
Riess, Steven A. *Major Problems in American Sport History.* Boston: Houghton Mifflin, 1997.
———. *Sport in Industrial America, 1850–1920.* Wheeling, IL: Harlan Davidson, 1995.
Riney, Scott. "Loosening the Bonds: The Rapid City Indian School in the 1920s." In *Boarding School Blues: Revisiting American Indian Education Experiences*, ed. Clifford E. Trafzer, Jean A. Keller, and Lorene Sisquoc, 131–54. Lincoln: University of Nebraska Press, 2006.
———. *The Rapid City Indian School, 1898–1933.* Norman: University of Oklahoma Press, 1999.
Roessel, Robert A., Jr. *Indian Communities in Action.* Tempe: Arizona State University, 1967.
Rosenthal, Nicolas. "American Indian Athletic Association." In *Native Americans in Sports*, vol. 1., ed. C. Richard King, 15–16. Armonk, NY: Sharp Reference, 2004.

———. *Reimagining Indian Country: Native American Migration and Identity in Twentieth-Century Los Angeles.* Chapel Hill: University of North Carolina Press, 2012.

Salamone, Frank A., ed. *The Native American Identity in Sports: Creating and Preserving a Culture.* Lanham, MD: Scarecrow, 2013.

Sanford, Jay. "African-American Baseballists and the Denver Post Tournament." *Colorado Heritage* (Spring 1995): 20–34.

Satz, Ronald N. "'Tell Those Gray Haired Men What They Should Know': The Hayward Indian Congress of 1934." *Wisconsin Magazine of History* 77 (Spring 1994): 196–224.

Scarborough, Vernon L., and David R. Wilcox, eds. *The Mesoamerican Ballgame.* Tucson: University of Arizona Press, 1991.

Schmidt, Raymond. "Lords of the Prairie: Haskell Indian School Football, 1919–1930." *Journal of Sport History* 28 (Fall 2001): 403–26.

___. "Louis 'Rabbit' Weller." In *Native Americans in Sports*, vol. 2., ed. C. Richard King, 320–21. Armonk, NY: Sharp Reference, 2004.

Sculle, Keith A. "'The New Carlisle of the West': Haskell Institute and Big-Time Sports, 1920–1932." *Kansas History* 17 (Autumn 1994): 192–208.

Sewell, Stacy. "Asserting Native American Agency in an Assimilationist Institution." In *The Native American Identity in Sports: Creating and Preserving a Culture*, ed. Frank A. Salamone, 29–40. Lanham, MD: Scarecrow, 2013.

———. "The Wind River Reservation: Asserting Native American Identity on the Court." Master's thesis of Anthropology, University of Wyoming, Laramie, 2011.

Sherfy, Michael, "Pete Hauser." In Native Americans in Sports, vol. 1, ed. C. Richard King, 141–42. Armonk, NY: Sharp Reference, 2004.

Smith, Gary. "Shadows of a Nation: The Crows, Once Proud Warriors, Now Seek Glory—But Often Find Tragedy—In Basketball." *Sports Illustrated* (February 18, 1991), https://www.si.com/vault/1991/02/18/123632/shadow-of-a-nation-the-crows-once-proud-warriors-now-seek-glory----but-often-find-tragedy----in-basketball.

Snyder, Peter Z., Edward K. Sadalla, and David Stea. "Socio-cultural Modifications and User Needs in Navajo Housing." *Journal of Architectural Research* 5 (December 1976): 4–9.

Spalding's Official Basketball Guide. New York, NY: American Sports Publishing Company (multiple editions).

Springwood, Charles Fruehling. "Playing Football, Playing Indian: A History of the Native Americans Who Were the NFL's Oorang Indians." In *Native Athletes in Sport and Society*, ed. C. Richard King, 123–42. Lincoln: University of Nebraska Press, 2005.

Stark, Douglas. *Wartime Basketball: The Emergence of a National Sport during World War II.* Lincoln: University of Nebraska Press, 2016.

Staurowsky, Ellen J. "SuAnne Big Crow: Her Legend and Legacy." In *Native Athletes in Sport and Society*, ed. C. Richard King, 189–210. Lincoln: University of Nebraska Press, 2005.

Steele, Charles Hoy. "American Indians and Urban Life: A Community Study." PhD dissertation, University of Kansas, Lawrence, 1971.

Stewart, Irene, edited by Doris Ostrander Dawdy. *A Voice in Her Tribe: A Navajo Woman's Own Story.* Socorro, NM: Ballena, 1980.

Stilling, Glenn Ellen Starr. "Kelvin Sampson." In *Native Americans in Sports*, vol. 2., ed. C. Richard King, 270–71. Armonk, NY: Sharp Reference, 2004.

Streep, Abe. "What the Arlee Warriors Were Playing For: On Montana's Flathead Indian Reservation, Basketball Is about Much More Than Winning." *New York Times Magazine*, April 4, 2018, https://www.nytimes.com/2018/04/04/magazine/arlee-warriors-montana-basketball-flathead-indian-reservation.html.

Sullivan, Sean Patrick. "Education through Sport: Athletics in American Indian Boarding Schools of New Mexico, 1885–1940." PhD dissertation, University of New Mexico, Albuquerque, 2004.

———. "Federal Indian Boarding Schools in New Mexico." In *The Native American Identity in Sports: Creating and Preserving a Culture*, ed. Frank A. Salamone, 57–89. Lanham, MD: Scarecrow, 2013.

Swain, Glenn. "A Recognition Long Overdue." In *Playing Before an Overflow Crowd: The Story of Indian Basketball in Robeson, North Carolina and Adjoining Counties*, ed. Tim Brayboy and Bruce Barton, 172–73. Chapel Hill, NC: Chapel Hill, 2003.

Szasz, Margaret Connell. *Education and the American Indian*. 3rd edition. Albuquerque: University of New Mexico Press, 1999; first edition published in 1974.

Taladoire, Eric, and Benoit Colsenet. "'Bois Ton Sang, Beaumanoir': The Political and Conflictual Aspects of the Ballgame in the Northern Chiapas Area." In *The Mesoamerican Ballgame*, ed. Vernon L. Scarborough and David R. Wilcox, 161–74. Tucson: University of Arizona Press, 1991.

Taylor, Kim Elise. "The Fabrication and Function of Star Quilts on Fort Peck Reservation in Northeastern Montana." Master's thesis, University of Montana, Missoula, 1994.

Thompson, Bonnie. "The Student Body: A History of the Stewart Indian School, 1890–1940." PhD dissertation, Arizona State University, Tempe, 2013.

Trafzer, Clifford E., Matthew Sakiestewa Gilbert, and Lorene Sisquoc, eds. *The Indian School on Magnolia Avenue: Voices and Images from Sherman Institute.* Corvallis: Oregon State University Press, 2012.

Trafzer, Clifford E., Jean A. Keller, and Lorene Sisquoc, eds. *Boarding School Blues: Revisiting American Indian Education Experiences.* Lincoln: University of Nebraska Press, 2006.

Trennert, Robert A., Jr. *The Phoenix Indian School: Forced Assimilation in Arizona, 1891–1935.* Norman: University of Oklahoma Press, 1988.

Troutman, John W. *Indian Blues: American Indians and the Politics of Music, 1879–1934.* Norman: University of Oklahoma Press, 2009.

United States Board of Indian Commissioners. *Twenty-Eighth Annual Report of the Board of Indian Commissioners, 1896.* Washington, DC: Government Printing Office, 1897.

Vennum, Thomas, Jr. *American Indian Lacrosse: Little Brother of War.* Washington, DC: Smithsonian Institution, 1994.

Voget, Fred W. *They Call Me Agnes: A Crow Narrative Based on the Life of Agnes Yellowtail Deernose.* Norman: University of Oklahoma Press, 1995.

Vučković, Myriam. *Voices from Haskell: Indian Students between Two Worlds, 1884–1928.* Lawrence: University Press of Kansas, 2008.

Waldman, Frank. *Famous American Athletes of Today.* Boston: L.C. Page, 1951.

Walker-McNeil, Pearl Lee. "The Carlisle Indian School: A Study of Acculturation." PhD dissertation, American University, Washington, DC, 1979.

Warner, Glenn S. "Athletics at the Carlisle Indian School." *Indian Craftsman* 1 (March 1909): 9–14.

Webb, Bernice Larson. *The Basketball Man: James Naismith.* Lawrence: University Press of Kansas, 1973.

Weibel-Orlando, Joan. *Indian Country, L.A.: Maintaining Ethnic Community in Complex Society.* Urbana: University of Illinois Press, 1991.

Weyand, Alexander M. *The Cavalcade of Basketball.* New York: Macmillan, 1960.

Wheeler, Robert W. *Jim Thorpe: World's Greatest Athlete.* Norman: University of Oklahoma Press, 1979; first published 1975.

Wiker, Josh. *The Harlem Globetrotters.* Philadelphia: Chelsea House, 1997.

Wilkerson, S. Jeffrey K. "And Then They Were Sacrificed: The Ritual Ballgame of Northeastern Mesoamerica through Time and Space." In *The Mesoamerican Ballgame,* ed. Vernon L. Scarborough and David R. Wilcox, 45–71. Tucson: University of Arizona Press, 1991.

Willard, William. "Outing, Relocation, and Employment Assistance: The Impact of Federal Indian Population Dispersal Programs in the Bay Area." *Wicazo Sa Review* 12 (Spring 1997): 29–46.

Willis, Chris. *Walter Lingo, Jim Thorpe, and the Oorang Indians: How a Dog Kennel Owner Created the NFL's Most Famous Traveling Team.* Lanham, MD: Rowman and Littlefield, 2017.

Wilson, Raymond. *Ohiyesa: Charles Eastman, Santee Sioux.* Urbana: University of Illinois Press, 1999; first published 1983.

Wims, Lu David. "A History of the Administration of Intercollegiate Athletics in the Ohio Athletic Conference," PhD dissertation, Ohio State University, Columbus, 1910.

Winnie, Lucille (Jerry). *Sah-Gan-De-Oh: The Chief's Daughter.* New York: Vantage, 1969.

Witkay, Marie Helen. "Henry Franklin Kallenberg—Pioneer Physical Educator," Master's thesis, George Williams College, Chicago, June 1958.

Wolff, Alexander. *Big Game, Small World: A Basketball Adventure.* New York: Warner, 2002.

Wright, Bobby, and William G. Tierney. "American Indians in Higher Education: A History of Cultural Conflict," *Change* 23 (Mar.–Apr. 1991): 11–18.

Yep, Kathleen S. *Outside the Paint: When Basketball Ruled at the Chinese Playground.* Philadelphia: Temple University Press, 2009.

———. "Peddling Sport: Liberal Multiculturalism and the Racial Triangulation of Blackness, Chineseness and Native American-Ness in Professional Basketball." *Ethnic and Racial Studies* 35 (June 2012): 971–87.

Young, Steve. "American Indian Team Played with Best in '30s." *Argus Leader*, Jun. 10, 1987, 1A–2A.

Zah, Peterson, and Peter Iverson. *We Will Secure Our Future: Empowering the Navajo Nation*. Tucson: University of Arizona Press, 2012.

Zinkoff, Dave, with Edgar Williams. *Around the World with the Harlem Globetrotters*. Philadelphia: Macrae Smith, 1953.

Newspapers, Newsletters, and Indian School Publications

Indian school:

Carlisle Arrow (Carlisle)
Chemawa American (Chemawa)
Indian Craftsman (Carlisle)
Indian Helper (Carlisle)
Indian Leader (Haskell)
Indian School Journal (Chilocco)
Native American (Phoenix)
Oklahoma Indian School Magazine (Concho)
Red Man (Carlisle)
Southern Workman (Hampton)

Other:

Akron Beacon Journal (OH)
Akron Evening Times (OH)
Albany Democrat (OR)
Albany Leader (MO)
Albuquerque Daily Citizen (NM)
Albuquerque Journal (NM)
Alexandria Times-Tribune (IN)
Altoona Mirror (PA)
Ames Intelligencer (IA)
Anaconda Standard (MT)
Anthony Bulletin (KS)
Argus Leader (Sioux Falls, SD)
Arizona Daily Star (Tucson)
Arizona Daily Sun (Flagstaff)
Arizona Republic (Phoenix)
Arkansas City Daily Traveler (KS)
Asheville Citizen Times (NC)
Atlanta Constitution (GA)
Au-Authm Action News (Scottsdale, AZ)

Bee (Danville, VA)
Belvidere Daily Republican (IL)
Billings Gazette (MT)
Bismarck Tribune (ND)
Brockway Record (PA)
Brooklyn Daily Eagle (NY)
Buffalo Evening News (NY)
Call Leader (Elwood, IN)
Capital Journal (Salem, OR)
Carlisle Evening Herald (PA)
Carroll Daily Times Herald (IA)
Chadron Chronical (NE)
Char-Koosta News (Pablo, MT)
Checotah Enquirer (OK)
Chicago Tribune (IL)
Cincinnati Enquirer (OH)
Clarion-Ledger (Jackson, MS)
Corpus Christi Caller-Times (TX)
Coshocton Tribune (OH)
Council Grove Republican (KS)
Courier (Waterloo, IA)
Courier-Journal (Louisville, KY)
Cumberland Evening Times (MD)
Daily Deadwood Pioneer-Times (SD)
Daily Gazette (Lawrence, KS)
Daily Journal (Vineland, NJ)
Daily Maroon (University of Chicago)
Daily Reporter (Greenfield, IN)
Daily Republic (Mitchell, SD)
Daily Republican (Rushville, IN)
Daily Plainsman (Huron, SD)
Daily Sentinel (Woodstock, IL)
Daily Times (Salisbury, MD)
Daily Tribune (Wisconsin Rapids)
Daily World (Opelousas, LA)
Dayton Daily News (OH)
Decatur Evening Herald (IL)
Decatur Herald (IL)
Defiance Crescent-News (OH)
Democrat and Chronicle (Rochester, NY)
Des Moines Register (IA)
Detroit Free Press (MI)
Dillon Tribune (MT)
Dispatch (Moline, IL)

Dunkirk Evening Observer (NY)
Eau Claire Leader (WI)
Edgefield Advertiser (SC)
Edinburg Daily Courier (IN)
El Paso Herald (TX)
Elyria Chronical Telegram (OH)
Emporia Gazette (KS)
Eugene Guard (OR)
Evening Herald (Ottawa, KS)
Evening News (Harrisburg, PA)
Evening Review (E. Liverpool, OH)
Evening Star (Washington, DC)
Evening Sun (Baltimore, MD)
Fairbanks Daily News-Miner (AK)
Fairmount News (IN)
Findlay Morning Republican (OH)
Fort Gibson New Era (OK)
Fort Wayne Journal-Gazette (IN)
Fort Wayne Sentinel (IN)
Freeport Journal-Standard (IL)
Gallup Independent (NM)
Galva News (IL)
Great Falls Tribune (MT)
Green Bay Press-Gazette (WI)
Hancock Democrat (Greenfield, IN)
Harrisburg Sunday Courier (PA)
Harrisburg Telegraph (PA)
Hawaiian Star (Honolulu)
Herald and News (Klamath Falls, OR)
Houston Post (TX)
Huntington Press (IN)
Hutchinson News (KS)
Idaho State Journal (Pocatello)
Independent-Record (Helena, MT)
Indianapolis News (IN)
Indian Country Today
Indians at Work (Bureau of Indian Affairs)
Indian Sentinel (Catholic missions)
Indian's Friend (Women's National Indian Association)
Inter Ocean (Chicago, IL)
Iola Register (KS)
Ironwood Daily Globe (MI)
Janesville Daily Gazette (WI)
Jeffersonian Gazette (Lawrence, KS)

Journal and Courier (Lafayette, IN)
Journal News (Hamilton, OH)
Journal News (White Plains, NY)
Kansan-Republican (Newton)
Kossuth County Advocate (Algona, IA)
Lakota Country Times (Martin, SD)
Lawrence Daily World (KS)
Lawrence Journal World (KS)
Lead Daily Call (SD)
Lead Daily Pioneer-Times (SD)
Leaf-Chronicle (Clarksville, TN)
Leavenworth Post (KS)
Lebanon Daily News (PA)
Lethbridge Herald (Alberta, CAN)
Lima News (OH)
Lincoln Journal Star (NE)
Lincoln Star (NE)
Los Angeles Times (CA)
Loyola News (LUC)
Manhattan Mercury (KS)
Manhattan Nationalist (KS)
Marion Star (OH)
Marshfield News-Herald (WI)
Martin Messenger (SD)
Maryville Daily Forum (MO)
Messenger-Inquirer (Owensboro, KY)
Miami Daily News-Record (OK)
Minneapolis Journal (MN)
Minneapolis Sunday Tribune (MN)
Missoulian (MT)
Moline Daily Dispatch (IL)
Montana Daily Record (Helena)
Montana Standard (Butte)
Montanian (Choteau)
Morning Call (Allentown, PA)
Morning Herald (Hagerstown, MD)
Morning Herald (Uniontown, PA)
Morning Oregonian (Portland)
Morning Register (Eugene, OR)
Muncie Evening Press (IN)
Muscatine Journal and News-Tribune (IA)
Muskogee Times-Democrat (OK)
Native Voice
Navajo-Hopi Observer (Flagstaff and Winslow, AZ)

Navajo Times (Window Rock, AZ)
Native Voice (Rapid City, SD)
Nebraska State Journal (Lincoln)
Nevada State Journal (Reno)
Newberg Graphic (OR)
New Castle News (PA)
News-Herald (Franklin, PA)
News-Journal (Mansfield, OH)
News-Palladium (Benton Harbor, MI)
New-State Tribune (Muskogee, OK)
New York Times (NY)
Niagara Falls Gazette (NY)
Noblesville Ledger (IN)
Ogden Standard-Examiner (UT)
Omaha Daily Bee (NE)
Oregon Daily Journal (Portland)
Oregon Statesman (Salem)
Osage City Free Press (KS)
Oshkosh Northwest (WI)
Owensboro Messenger (KY)
Palladium-Item (Richmond, IN)
Petaluma Argus-Courier (CA)
Philadelphia Inquirer (PA)
Pittsburgh Daily Post (PA)
Pittsburgh Press (PA)
Port Angeles Evening News (WA)
Post-Crescent (Appleton, WI)
Press and Sun-Bulletin (Binghamton, NY)
Rapid City Daily Journal (SD)
Reliance Record (SD)
Reno Evening Gazette (NV)
Reno Gazette-Journal (NV)
Republican News (Hamilton, OH)
Rhinelander Daily News (WI)
Richmond Item (IN)
Richmond Palladium-Item (IN)
Roosevelt Standard (UT)
Salina Evening Journal (KS)
Salt Lake Telegram (UT)
San Bernardino County Sun (CA)
Sandusky Star-Journal (OH)
Scandia Journal (KS)
Sedalia Democrat (MO)
Seminole Tribune (Hollywood, FL)

Sentinel (Carlisle, PA)
Sheboygan Press (WI)
Sioux County Pioneer Arrow (Ft. Yates, ND)
Springfield Leader and Press (MO)
Springfield News Leader (MO)
Standard-Sentinel (Hazelton, PA)
Star-Gazette (Elmira, NY)
Star Press (Muncie, IN)
Star Tribune (Minneapolis, MN)
Stars and Stripes Weekly (Mediterranean-Algiers)
St. Cloud Times (MN)
Stevens Point Journal (WI)
St. Louis Post-Dispatch (MO)
St. Louis Republic (MO)
Sunday Oregonian (Portland)
Times Herald (Port Huron, MI)
Todd County Tribune (Mission, SD)
Topeka Daily Capital (KS)
Topeka State Journal (KS)
Tourney Topics (NCIBT)
Tulsa Daily World (OK)
Uintah Basin Standard (Duchesne, UT)
Washington Herald (DC)
Washington Post (DC)
Wichita Beacon (KS)
Wichita Daily Eagle (KS)
Wilkes-Barre Evening Leader (PA)
Willmar Tribune (MN)
Winfield Daily Free Press (KS)
Yankton Daily Dakotan (SD)
York Daily (PA)

Films and Internet Resources

"65th Annual All-Indian Basketball Tourney" poster. http://klamathtribes.org/news/65th-annual-all-indian-basketball-tourney-march-16–18–2018/.

"1929 AAA Boys Basketball." http://www.osaa.org/docs/bbx/records/1929b.pdf; "1940" http://www.osaa.org/docs/bbx/records/1940b.pdf.

"An American Indian Tribute to Abe Lemons," Mike Tosee-Bill Curtis, 2005, https://www.youtube.com/watch?v=su8MKkCti30.

"Arlee Warriors State Dedication." https://www.facebook.com/watch/?v=963987443764499.

"Basketball in Salem." Salem Online History, www.salemhistory.net/culture/basketball.htm.

Beyond the Paint, "Arlee Warriors," parts 1 and 2. Directed by Matt Winer. NBA-TV, February 10, 2019, http://www.nba.com/video/2019/02/10/20190210-beyond-paint-arlee-warriors-part-one?collection=video/beyond-the-paint.

"Bob Clifford," South Dakota Sports Hall of Fame. http://www.sdshof.com/inductees/clifford-bob/.

"Bud Sahmaunt." https://www.sports-reference.com/cbb/players/bud-sahmaunt-1.html.

Chiefs. DVD. Directed by Daniel Junge. Denver, CO: Dewey-Obenchain Films, 2002.

Citizen Potawatomi Nation Public Information Office, "Drive all Day: With a Sports Resume Built on Leading High School and College Championship Games, New York Knick Ron Baker also Credits His Native Heritage for His Success," Dec. 5, 2017, https://www.potawatomi.org/drive-day-sports-resume-built-leading-high-school-college-championship-games-new-york-knick-ron-baker-also-credits-native-heritage-success/.

CPI Inflation Calculator, https://www.bls.gov/data/inflation_calculator.htm.

Games of the North. DVD. Directed by Jonathon Stanton. Toronto, ON: Starseed Media, 2010.

Hand Game: The Native American Game of Power and Chance. VHS. Directed by Lawrence Johnson. Portland, OR: Lawrence Johnson Productions, 2000.

"Haskell Indian Nations Institute Fighting Indians School History," https://www.sports-reference.com/cbb/schools/haskell-indian-nations-institute/.

HBO: Real Sports with Bryant Gumble. Episode 204, March 25, 2014.

"History of the Arizona Interscholastic Association." http://aiaonline.org/about/.

History Detectives. Episode 10, 2005, http://www-tc.pbs.org/opb/historydetectives/static/media/transcripts/2011–04–27/310_jimthorpe.pdf.

"History of North Dakota High School Activities Association." https://ndhsaa.com/about/history.

"History of Oregon Institute of Technology." https://www.oit.edu/visitors-info/about/history.

hooptactics™. "The Evolution of the Game," https://hooptactics.com/Basketball_Basics_History.

"Jerry Adair." https://www.sports-reference.com/cbb/players/jerry-adair-1.html.

"Kee Kensol wearing traditional Native American clothing, standing outside on a train platform at a railroad station," 1928, DN-0084984, Chicago Historical Society, Explore Chicago Collections. https://explore.chicagocollections.org/image/chicagohistory/71/w951489/.

The Klamath Tribe. "Tribal News and Events: Basketball: The 60th Annual Klamath All-Indian World Championship Basketball Tournament, Chiloquin, Oregon, March 22–24, 2013." http://klamathtribes.org/news/basketball/.

Lewis, David. "Chemawa Indian School Athletics Program." *The Oregon Encyclopedia,* https://oregonencyclopedia.org/articles/chemawa_indian_school_athletics_program/#.VzIm.

"Marcella Crow-Feather, Serial Land Patent in Corson County, South Dakota, 1915." https://thelandpatents.com/gallery/7n07wn73.

Marr, Carolyn J. "Between Two Worlds: Experiences at the Tulalip Indian Boarding School, 1905–1932." www.hibulbculturalcenter.org/assets/pdf/Between-Two-Worlds.pdf.

"Montana High School Association State Boys' Basketball Champions of the Past, 1911–2019." https://cdn2.sportngin.com/attachments/document/14d8-1850886/Basketball_Boys.pdf?_ga=2.222815641.322863825.1564414681-1732271782.1564414681.

Montana Indian Athletic Hall of Fame. "Don Wetzel Sr." http://montanaindianathletichof.org/2011.htm.

NABI Foundation. http://www.nabifoundation.org/.

"National Register of Historic Places Registration Form: Lodgepole Community Hall."https://npgallery.nps.gov/GetAsset/8c62c491-185b-4162-be6a-475803715ba1.

New Mexico Activities Association, "About." https://www.nmact.org/about/.

"New Mexico Girls State Basketball Champions." https://www.nmact.org/file/Basketball%20Girls%20Coaches%20Champions.pdf.

"New Mexico Prep Basketball (Historical)." chuckferrissports.com.

Off the Rez. DVD. Directed by Jonathan Hock. New York, NY: Cinema Guild, 2014.

"Oklahoma High School State Champions, Girls Basketball, since 1919." http://www.iwasatthegame.com/BKGStateChampionships.aspx.

"Oklahoma: OSSAA Boys Basketball Champions (1918–2017)." http://www.iwasatthegame.com/ListOfChampions/OKStateChampionsBasketballBoys.pdf?id=19.

"Oklahoma Secondary School Activities Association History." http://www.ossaa.net/docs/2017-18/OSSAAInfo/MF_2017-18_History.pdf.

Oregon Men's Basketball, 2014–15. https://isuu.com/oregonducks.

Oregon State Men's Basketball Media Guide, 2015–2016. http://oregonstate_ftp.sidearmsports.com/pdf9/3920917.pdf.

Reconciliation and Roundball. DVD. Dave Kemp and the Dakota Indian Foundation, 1990.

Rocks with Wings. VHS. Directed by Rick Derby. New York: Shiprock, 2002.

Ryan Wetzel Basketball. "Ryan Wetzel Coach, Mentor, Motivator: Biograph." http://www.ryanwetzelbasketball.com.

"Seven Generations." *Viceland, Vice World of Sports*. Season 1, Episode 9. https://www.viceland.com.

Smoke Signals. Directed by Chris Eyre (screenplay by Sherman Alexie). Miramax, 1998.

"The Sport of Life and Death: The Mesoamerican Ballgame." www.mesoballgame.org.

Standig, Ben. "Ron Baker Is Heavy on Grit, but Light on Luggage since Joining Wizards." Dec. 21, 2018, NBCSports, Washington. https://www.nbcsports.com/washington/wizards/ron-baker-heavy-grit-light-luggage-joining-wizards.

Strain, David F. Nomination of Martin Waukazoo to the South Dakota High School Basketball Hall of Fame, Alameda Health Consortium website, https://www.alamedahealthconsortium.org/general/martin-waukazoo-inducted-into-hall-of-fame/.

Index